In these racialized and polarized times, Vuyani S[indo?] model leader for the comparably polarized comm[unity?] ing from his South African context, successfully [...] must not be divorced from identity formation. In other words, we ought not talk about the leader without considering those who are the "led." Beyond that, Christians need to consider God as he stands above and behind any human community. Methodologically sound, meticulously researched, and exegetically sophisticated, Sindo has expanded our thinking about leadership and identity formation for both the West and the Majority World.

David Capes, PhD
Director,
Lanier Theological Library, Texas, USA

Vuyani Sindo has written a clear and engaging account of his research into Paul's strategy for dealing with the leadership confusion in Corinth. For anyone who wishes to appreciate the application of social scientific method to New Testament interpretation, Sindo's work is a model of accessibility. His explanation of social identity theory and its usefulness in understanding how Paul deals with a church that has "gone rogue," where his leadership is questioned, is enlightening. All the while, Sindo holds close to the text of 1 Corinthians and the historical realities of the Corinthian situation. His ability to incorporate the best careful grammatical work on the text of 1 Corinthians, social historical and social scientific disciplines, the historical critical method, and modern leadership studies makes this book invaluable.

David Seccombe, PhD
Former Principal,
George Whitfield College, South Africa

In this book, Vuyani Sindo combines aspects of social identity theory with leadership studies in order to take a fresh look at 1 Corinthians 1–4. He makes a strong case that Paul presents himself as a leader who closely identifies with the community of believers in Corinth and whose leadership is effective because they see him as one of them. Sindo's South African roots make him more attuned to collective aspects of leadership than similar studies and his approach can help the Western church rethink what biblical leadership entails at a time when it is desperately needed.

Joel White, PhD
Professor of New Testament,
Representative for International Cooperation,
Giessen School of Theology, Germany

Paul as a Prototype and Entrepreneur of Christian Identity

An Investigation into Leadership and Identity in 1 Corinthians 1–4

Vuyani Stanley Sindo

ACADEMIC

© 2024 Vuyani Stanley Sindo

Published 2024 by Langham Academic
An imprint of Langham Publishing
www.langhampublishing.org

Langham Publishing and its imprints are a ministry of Langham Partnership

Langham Partnership
PO Box 296, Carlisle, Cumbria, CA3 9WZ, UK
www.langham.org

ISBNs:
978-1-83973-969-9 Print
978-1-78641-090-0 ePub
978-1-78641-091-7 PDF

Vuyani Stanley Sindo has asserted his right under the Copyright, Designs and Patents Act, 1988 to be identified as the Author of this work.

All rights reserved. No part of this publication may be reproduced, stored in a retrieval system or transmitted, in any form or by any means, electronic, mechanical, photocopying, recording or otherwise, without the prior written permission of the publisher or the Copyright Licensing Agency.

Requests to reuse content from Langham Publishing are processed through PLSclear. Please visit www.plsclear.com to complete your request.

All Scripture quotations, unless otherwise indicated, in this work are the author's own.

Scripture quotations marked (NIVUK) are taken from the Holy Bible, New International Version®, Anglicised, NIV®. Copyright © 1979, 1984, 2011 by Biblica, Inc®. Used by permission. All rights reserved worldwide.

Scripture quotations marked (ESV) are from The Holy Bible, English Standard Version® (ESV®), copyright © 2001 by Crossway, a publishing ministry of Good News Publishers. Used by permission. All rights reserved.

British Library Cataloguing-in-Publication Data
A catalogue record for this book is available from the British Library

ISBN: 978-1-83973-969-9

Cover & Book Design: projectluz.com

Langham Partnership actively supports theological dialogue and an author's right to publish but does not necessarily endorse the views and opinions set forth here or in works referenced within this publication, nor can we guarantee technical and grammatical correctness. Langham Partnership does not accept any responsibility or liability to persons or property as a consequence of the reading, use or interpretation of its published content.

Contents

Abstract ix

Acknowledgements xi

Chapter 1 1
Introduction
   1.1 Problem Statement and Focus 1
   1.2 Preliminary Studies Already Undertaken 7
      1.2.1 Leadership in Paul in 1 Corinthians 7
      1.2.2 Paul and the Formation of Identity 14
   1.3 Problem Statement 19
   1.4 Key Research Questions 19
   1.5 Research Hypothesis 20
   1.6 Methodology 23
   1.7 Aims of the Research Project 25
   1.8 Motivation for the Study 26
   1.9 Possible Value of the Research 27
   1.10 Conclusion 27

Chapter 2 29
Methodology Outline
   2.1 What Is a Social Scientific Approach? 30
      2.1.1 Advantages of Social Scientific Approach 33
      2.1.2 The Rise of Social Scientific Approach 34
      2.1.3 Sociohistorical Approaches versus Social Scientific
            Approaches 35
   2.2 Criticism against the Use of Social Scientific Approaches
      in Biblical Studies 41
      2.2.1 The Deistic Nature of Social Scientific Approaches ... 41
      2.2.2 Social Scientific Approaches as Foreign to Biblical
            Studies 42
      2.2.3 Social Scientific Approaches and Meaning of
            Biblical Texts 44
      2.2.4 The Cultural Distance of the Ancient Text 44
      2.2.5 Social Scientific Approaches as Anachronistic –
            Bengt Holmberg as Example 45
   2.3 Social Identity Theory 50
      2.3.1 The Field of Social Psychology during the 1960s 52
      2.3.2 The Life and the Teachings of Henri Tajfel 55

2.4 The Tenets of Social Identity Theory 62
   2.4.1 Social Categorisation 63
   2.4.2 Social Identification 65
   2.4.3 Social Comparison 67
2.5 The Impact of Social Identity Theory on Leadership Studies........68
   2.5.1 The Leader as a Prototype of the In-group Identity............69
   2.5.2 The Leader as a Champion of the In-group 76
   2.5.3 The Leader as an Entrepreneur of Identity.........................78
2.6 Conclusion 80

Chapter 3 83
Historical and Literary Context of 1 Corinthians
3.1 The Social Context of Corinth and the Corinthian
   Christian Movement..84
   3.1.1 The Social Context 85
   3.1.2 The Pauline Community at Corinth 98
3.2 The Literary Integrity of 1 Corinthians 122
   3.2.1 The Argument and the Structure of 1 Corinthians...........122
   3.2.2 The Issues behind 1 Corinthians 141
3.3 The Approach of This Dissertation 149
   3.3.1 Conflicts..152
   3.3.2 Compromises...154
3.4 Conclusion 159

Chapter 4 161
Paul's Apostolic Defense: Group Prototypicality and Mimesis Tradition
4.1 Introduction 161
4.2 The Leader as a Prototype of the In-group Identity: A
   Theoretical Framework...163
4.3 The Heart of Intragroup Conflict in 1 Corinthians1–4 as a
   Quest for Belonging 168
4.4 Scholarly Treatment regarding Paul's (Re)Presentation of
   Himself as a Group Prototype..178
   4.4.1 The Traditional Approach to Paul's Apostleship and
      Mimesis Tradition 179
   4.4.2 Social-scientific Approaches: Apostleship and
      Power Dynamics..193
4.5 Theoretical Considerations for Paul's Resocialisation of the
   Corinthians 199
4.6 Conclusion 205

Chapter 5 207
   Exegesis of 1 Corinthians 1–4 (with Focus on 1:1–9)
     5.1 Introduction 207
     5.2 The Letter's Opening and Paul's Resocialization Agenda in
        1 Corinthians 1:1–9..208
     5.3 Scholarly Treatment of the "in Christ" Idiom............................214
        5.3.1 The Function of the "in Christ" Idiom in the
           Argument of 1 Corinthians 1:1–9 218
        5.3.2 The Function of the Instrumental Dative ἐν Χριστῷ
           in Paul's Social Identity Agenda..224
        5.3.3 "in Christ" idiom as Installation of Positive Identity........226
     5.4 The Transition from "in Christ" idiom to the καλέω/
        κλῆσις Terminologies in the Argument of
        1 Corinthians 1:1–9 235
        5.4.1 The Significance of καλέω/κλῆσις Terminology in
           the Argument of 1 Corinthians 241
     5.5 The Influence of the ἐν Χριστῷ and κλῆσις Terminologies
        in Paul's Apostolic Self-consciousness in Galatians and
        1 Corinthians 243
     5.6 Conclusion 250

Chapter 6 253
   Summary and Conclusion
     6.1 Summary and Findings of Chapter 1......................................253
        6.1.1 Current Trends in Leadership Studies 253
        6.1.2 Paul and the Formation of Identity.................................255
     6.2 Summary and Findings of Chapter 2......................................257
     6.3 Summary and Findings of Chapter 3......................................260
     6.4 Summary and Findings of Chapter 4......................................262
     6.5 Summary and Findings of Chapter 5......................................263
     6.6 Conclusion 265
     6.7 The Significance of the ἐν Χριστῷ Ἰησοῦ, and κλῆσις
        Terminologies for the South African Christian Context 266
     6.8 Areas for Further Research 267

Appendix 1 269
   Debate on the Translation of Ἰουδαῖοι

Appendix 2 275
   Does κλῆσις *Refer to Paul's Conversion?*

Appendix 3 279
   The Interrelationship between Paul's Apostolic Calling, His Gospel and the Identity of the Galatians

Bibliography 289

Abstract

The leadership aspect in the discourse of 1 Corinthians 1–4 has received significant attention in recent years, by scholars such as Carson, Savage, Hooker, and Clarke.[1] These scholars have demonstrated that leadership-related issues are pertinent to Paul's argument in these four chapters of 1 Corinthians. Using sociohistorical approaches, many scholars highlight the fact that Paul's presentation of leadership in these chapters contrasts sharply with the prevailing views regarding leadership in the Greco-Roman world.

There is another group of scholars, however, such as Barentsen, Tucker, and Holmberg, who incorporate social-scientific approaches in their analyses, which include social identity theory.[2] These scholars tend to focus on the power dynamic and identity-related issues in their treatment of leadership issues in 1 Corinthians 1–4. This dissertation will follow a similar line of thought to these scholars. The present task is to argue that identity discourse is an integral part of the leadership discourse in 1 Corinthians 1–4, with the aim to closely investigate the interrelationship between leadership and identity.

This interrelationship becomes apparent when Paul's use of the ἐν Χριστῷ and κλῆσις terminologies is considered. Scholarship has observed the prevalence of ἐν Χριστῷ and its associated terminologies (such as ἐν κυρίῳ, ἐν αὐτῷ, δία Χριστοῦ, σὺν Χριστῷ, σὺν αὐτῷ) in Paul's argument in 1 Corinthians 1–4, concluding that this terminology is not accidental for Paul.

Thus, for this dissertation, ἐν Χριστῷ Ἰησοῦ terminology is the key terminology on which the interrelationship between leadership and identity in

---

[1]. Carson, *Cross and Christian Ministry*; Savage, *Power through Weakness*; Hooker, "Partner in the Gospel"; Clarke, *Serve the Community*; *Secular and Christian Leadership*.

[2]. Barentsen, *Emerging Leadership*; Tucker, *You Belong to Christ*; and Holmberg, *Paul and Power*.

1 Corinthians is established. It will be argued that Paul uses this terminology to frame his discourse in 1 Corinthians 1–4. This terminology helped Paul in two key aspects: First, to get the attention and the hearing of a group of people, some of whom had rejected him as their apostle, due to their preference for one leader at the expense of the other (1 Cor 1:10–12; 3:4–5). Paul uses the ἐν Χριστῷ Ἰησοῦ terminology at the beginning of the letter to signal to the group that the subject matter about which he was writing was at the core related to in-group identity. This dissertation will argue that Paul used the ἐν Χριστῷ Ἰησοῦ terminology to help him in the consensualization process.

Second, this terminology allowed Paul to present himself as a group prototype. Again, since some members of the community had rejected him due to the Greco-Roman cultural influences on their perception of a leader, Paul counters those cultural influences by using the ἐν Χριστῷ Ἰησοῦ terminology to remind the in-group members of their salient identity "in Christ." Thus, Paul, in his use of ἐν Χριστῷ, was in fact "killing two birds with one stone." He also used the ἐν Χριστῷ and κλῆσις terminologies for his group entrepreneur strategy, by reminding the group about how their identity "in Christ" is diametrically opposed to the world's wisdom and power, the same categories that they were using to judge him. Paul, therefore, used these terminologies to shape (entrepreneur) the group identity, as he was able to demonstrate to the group what behaviour is aligned with the in-group identity.

Acknowledgements

There is an African proverb that says, "It takes a village to raise a child." There are a number of people that I am grateful to the Lord for; people who have been part of this journey in one way or the other. In no particular order, I would like to express my grateful thanks to the following people for their support and encouragement during the process of writing this dissertation:

- This book is a reworking of my PhD dissertation from Stellenbosch University, and thus, I would like to thank my supervisor, Professor Jeremy Punt, and my mentor and friend, Dr. Allan Chapple. Their careful reading and critical interaction have made this thesis a much better work than it would have been otherwise. I am grateful for their thorough insight, valuable comments, and constructive critique. Although they did not always agree with my views, they nonetheless provided ample room for my own voice to be heard. For all shortcomings in this work, I therefore take full responsibility. I would also like to extend my sincere gratitude to my PhD examiners – Prof. Roy E. Ciampa, Prof. Francis D. Tolmie, and Prof. Marius J. Nel – for their diligence in reviewing my work and for their valuable feedback. Their insights greatly enriched this book.
- My employer, George Whitefield College, for allowing me to take two years off full-time work to focus on my dissertation. I would like to particularly express my gratefulness to my colleagues, library staff Collin Majackie and Rosemary Leyte, for all their assistance in sourcing books and materials that I needed for this research.
- Trinity Theological College in Perth, Australia, for their generosity in hosting my family and me. Many thanks to Dr. Don West and

his council for the hard work that they put into making the trip possible. Their library staff, Rachel Mark and Athena West, were phenomenal in arranging books and materials that I needed for research. A special thanks to Dr. David Seccombe, together with the organization that supported us financially, for making the trip to Australia possible.

- Rev. Alan Noble, the Rector of Holy Trinity Church, Gardens, for his friendship, encouragement, understanding, and support during this research.
- Mr. Alexander James Anderson, REACH-SA, and the donor, via Bishop Desmond Inglesby, for their generous contributions towards making this research possible.
- Langham Partnership, for your support and making me part of Langham. Dr. Bill Houston, I have truly appreciated how well you have looked after us, the Langham scholars.
- My denomination REACH-SA, the Bishops, and the trustees for their generous financial and pastoral support during this research.
- Scott Grant thanks for you help with the editing of this manuscript.
- Bishop Desmond Inglesby, thank you very much for the role that you have played in my life. I give thanks to the Lord for both you and Dr. David Seccombe, for your assistance in helping me raise funds for the past two and a half years.

A special thanks to my lovely wife Ronel Sindo, and our two wonderful daughters, Sindiswa and Zandile. Thank you love, for your encouragement, patience, support, love, proof reading, and for holding the fort on the family front, and bearing with a husband who at times has been absent-minded. Thank you for your understanding during research. I give thanks to the Lord for the love and the sacrifices that you have made in order to make this possible.

Lastly, and most significantly, I would like to give thanks to the Lord Jesus Christ, for his mercy and grace. It is ultimately because of his goodness that this project came to be. As James 1:17 tells us, "Every good and perfect gift is from above, coming down from the Father of the heavenly lights, who does not change like shifting shadows."

CHAPTER 1

Introduction

1.1 Problem Statement and Focus

Leadership studies is one of the fastest growing areas of study in our time. A number of scholars link the prosperity or the decline of countries to the quality of leadership in that particular country. However, most leadership studies are very fragmented. Ayers notes that most seminal works on leadership, such as the works of Hickman, Northhouse, and Yuki do not engage with theological studies in their presentation of leadership theories.[1] Within New Testament studies, the most influential works on the books of 1 and 2 Corinthians pay little attention to the issues of leadership within the church at Corinth. For example, the collection of essays by Adam and Horrell in 2004, which are supposed to represent sections of the scholarly work that is focused on the second century, does not even contain leadership in its index.[2] The same is true for Thiselton's and Theissen's collections of essays

---

1. Ayers, "Toward a Theology"; Hickman, *Leading Organizations*; Northouse, *Leadership Theory and Practice*; Yukl, *Leadership in Organizations*.

2. Adams and Horrell, *Christianity at Corinth*. This is a big oversight on the part of the contributors to this work. The oversight is exacerbated by the fact that according to the publishers, the book is supposed to provide us with a "unique glimpse into the life of the young Christian community in a Greco-Roman environment." Even in the chapters which deal with 1 Cor 1–4, where one expects to hear about leadership, the book does not address the subject. For example, in the essay by Munck titled "The Church without Factions: Studies in 1 Corinthians 1–4," Munck does not deal with the question of leadership, which seems surprising since the plain reading of the text and other scholars suggest that, among other things, factions were a direct result of the Corinthians' squabbles over which leader they preferred. With that being said, his essay does a great job in its critique of Baur's construction of the situation in Corinth. Baur thought that the factions in Corinth were a result of two opposing "theologies";

on 1 Corinthians.[3] Scholars perusing the Corinthian correspondence seem to have overlooked this important point: in this letter Paul was dealing with a young community in its early stages of development, fraught with divisions and factionalism (based on their preferred leaders).[4] It is, therefore, an oversight not even to dedicate a chapter to an important issue such as leadership, especially if the book(s) intends to give us a "glimpse into the life of the young Christian community."[5] This research, therefore, finds itself in a neglected field of study – a study of leadership in Paul, and an African perspective on leadership in Paul.

Scholars such as Nkomo and Swart lament the fact that Africa and the African understanding of leadership are invisible in most leadership theories.[6] Nkomo further notes that even the literature that seeks to correct this has unwittingly preserved "the ideological coding of Western (primarily USA) conceptions of leadership and management."[7]

One of the difficulties associated with "Christian leadership studies" is the problem of definition, especially in the twenty-first-century setting. Take, for example, how the following Christian leadership scholars define leadership:[8]

Petrine (Jewish) Christianity and the Pauline (Gentile) Christianity. Munck, "Church without Factions," 61–64.

3. Thiselton, *1 Corinthians*; Theissen, *Social Setting*. Here again, "leader" or "leadership" is not even contained in the index. This is surprising since this commentary is also meant to address practical pastoral issues in the Corinthian correspondence. Thiselton, *1 Corinthians*, xliii. Scholars such as Clarke have adequately demonstrated that "one of Paul's chief concerns with the Corinthians in 1 Corinthians 1–6 is to deal with the issue of leadership within the Christian community," *Secular and Christian Leadership*, 109–27.

4. 1 Cor 1:10–13; 3:1–9; 3:21--22; 4:1–6. The areas of division and factionalism in the Corinthian correspondence extended beyond factionalism about which leader individuals in the community preferred, it included issues such as the failure of the community to act against the sexually immoral brother in 1 Cor 5. It can also be seen in the inability of the community to handle grievances among its members (1 Cor 6). These divisions and factionalism can also be seen when the community comes together to celebrate the Lord's Supper (1 Cor 11:17–22). The expressions of factionalism also manifest in things like "boasting, arrogance . . . and claims to be wise, spiritually gifted, theologically knowledgeable, and strong." Fotopoulos, "1 Corinthians," 420. Is it possible that part of the problem that led to all these issues, is the failure of leadership, and the failure of the Corinthians, to understand their identity in Christ?

5. Adams and Horrell, *Christianity at Corinth*, back cover.

6. Nkomo, "Postcolonial and Anti-Colonial"; Swart, "Africa Leads the Way."

7. Nkomo, 366.

8. Most of these leaders subscribe to the Christian transformational leadership approach, which is very popular in the United States of America. Scarborough provides a well-balanced critique of this approach in "Deconstructionist Critique of Christian Transformational Leadership."

Barna: "A leader is one who mobilizes; one whose focus is influencing people; a person who is goal driven; someone who has an orientation in common with those who rely upon him for leadership; and someone who has people willing to follow them."

Engstrom: "The concept of leader . . . means one who guides activities of others and who himself acts and performs to bring those activities about. He is capable of performing acts which will guide a group in achieving objectives. He takes the capacities of vision and faith, has the ability to be concerned and to comprehend, exercises action through effective and personal influence in the direction of an enterprise and the development of the potential into the practical and/or profitable means."

Sanders: "Leadership is influence, the ability of one person to influence others to follow his or her lead."

Wright: "Leadership is a relationship – a relationship in which one person seeks to influence the thoughts, behaviours, beliefs or values of another person."[9]

The above definitions tend to be anthropocentric by nature; that is, they put the leader at the centre and shine a spotlight on his or her competence to perform certain functions, particularly to influence people. These scholars could be accused of exaggerating the role of Christian leaders and diminishing the role of God.[10] This prominence of the leader's role seems to be in tension or in contrast to what Paul says in 1 Corinthians, where he clearly downplays the role of human leaders, including himself.[11] In dealing with the subject of leadership Paul tends to emphasize the role and the influence of God in his community; his theology is theocentric and he critiques secular influences

---

9. Barna, *Leaders on Leadership*, 25; Engstrom, *Making of a Christian Leader*, 2; Sanders, *Spiritual Leadership*, 27; Wright, *Relational Leadership*, 2.

10. Scarborough, "Deconstructionist Critique," 38–39. In his thesis, Scarborough has demonstrated that modern day studies on "Christian leadership" are not that different from "secular leadership studies." The only difference is that they add the tag "Christian" and do proof texting of the concepts that are found in "secular leadership" literature. Hamilton in *Wisdom in Leadership* raises similar concerns to that of Scarborough. Moreover, in their treatment of "Christian" leadership, these scholars seem to have neglected the primary message of the text. Both Winter and Clarke have demonstrated in their works that in 1 Corinthians, Paul writes to persuade the early Jesus movement to watch out for secular influences in the life of the community. Winter, *After Paul Left Corinth*; Clarke, *Secular and Christian Leadership*. Therefore, simply to take (post)modern-day secular concepts and tag them with the word "Christian" could be very misleading and can go against the spirit of the Pauline correspondence.

11. See for example, 1 Cor 1:26–31; 2:1–5; 3:5–23; 4:1–7.

on the community.¹² Thus, the challenge to this research is our twenty-first century understanding of leadership which is essentially anthropocentric (that is, it is human-centred and is anthropological and sociological by nature) which is not aligned to and is foreign to Paul's understanding of leadership, which is theocentric by nature. Clarke observes that:¹³

> The definition of Christian leadership against "worldly" leadership is a key element of Paul's discussion in the early chapters of 1 Corinthians. In chapters 1–6 of the epistle, the impact of secular society on the Corinthians' understanding of leadership may be seen. However, Paul's most direct accusation of the Corinthians for being secular in their leadership is seen in 1 Corinthians 3:3–4.

Therefore, twenty-first century foreignness to and distance from Paul's understanding of leadership present us with both a challenge and an opportunity to discover key elements of Paul's teaching on leadership.

The second challenge in Pauline leadership studies is a lexical one; that is, the absence of the Greek words that are used for "leader" or "leadership" in the New Testament, while these words were used often in the Greco-Roman world. Scholars such as Clarke, Du Plooy, Tomlin, and Button highlight the fact that many Greek words for "leadership position" or "leader" which were used in the first century context are similar to our use in the modern sense: words such as ἄρχων, ἡγούμενος, στρατήγιον, and προστάτης, together with their compounds.¹⁴ These words were used in military, civic, imperial, and other contexts in the Hellenist Greek language, but the surprising thing is that these words are seldom used for leadership functions in the New Testament, and when they are used, they are qualified. What compounds the problem

---

12. For some scholars, the use of the term "secular" in referring to people in the ancient world might be perceived as being anachronistic in that it imposes Cartesian dualistic thinking to an ancient people who may or may not have had the modern dualistic dichotomy between the sacred and the secular. The way the term "secular" is used in this study is in the same vein as found in Clarke. Clarke uses it to refer to certain aspects of the practices of the Corinthians that were representative of their identity prior to them becoming Christ's followers, practices that Paul considered inconsistent with their newly found identity in Christ. Clarke, *Secular and Christian Leadership*.

13. Clarke, 109.

14. Clarke, *Pauline Theology*, 1–3; Du Plooy, "Betekenis van Charisma"; Tomlin, *Theology of Leadership*; Button, "Leadership and Gospel."

is the fact that in the Septuagint,[15] a text with which Paul was quite familiar, the Greek words for "leadership" or "to lead" (ἄρχων and ἡγούμενος) are very common.[16] Clarke provides the following lexical appearances of the words in the Septuagint: the noun ἄρχων appears 624 times, while the composite nouns with the prefix ἀρχι-, referring to a leading official in some capacity, appear 167 times.[17] For example, in the LXX we hear of οἱ ἄρχοντες τῆς συναγωγῆς;[18] οἱ ἄρχοντες Ισραηλ;[19] οἱ ἄρχοντες τοῦ λαοῦ.[20]

According to Clarke, the frequency of ἄρχων and ἡγούμενος in the New Testament are less than a quarter of that in the Septuagint.[21] Paul uses the term ἄρχων to refer to the civil authorities in Romans 13:3, while in 1 Corinthians 2:6–8 and Ephesians 2:2, he uses the term for spiritual powers. Paul does use the verb ἄρχω in Romans 15:12, where he quotes Isaiah 11:10, "referring to the root of Jesse who will rule the Gentiles."[22] Clarke also shows that both the Gospels and Acts use terms such as ἡγεμών which was widely used to describe secular leaders, and the term στρατήγιον which was classically used for the military, to describe both Jewish religious and Greco-Roman leaders.[23] But these terms are absent in the Pauline letters, and they are seldom used to describe leaders in the Jesus movement.[24] This has led scholars such as Tomlin

---

15. The Septuagint is a translation of the Hebrew text into Greek. Even though it is difficult to establish whether or not Paul had full access to all these texts like we have them today, he nonetheless seems fairly familiar with the content of some of them. He quotes them regularly, for example, in 1 Cor 1:31 and 2 Cor 10:17 where he quotes Jer 9:22–23 (LXX). Scholars such as Donahoe have demonstrated adequately how Paul uses and appropriates the theology of Jeremiah in his letter to the Corinthians to rebuke the "Corinthians' overestimation of wisdom and eloquence," and "redirects their attention away from loyalties to specific leaders to loyalty to Christ." Donahoe, "From Self-Praise." For more scholarly treatment on Paul's use and familiarity with the Old Testament manuscripts, see Ellis, *Paul's Use of the Old Testament*, and Hays, *Echoes of Scripture*. Ellis provides a useful list of LXX citations by Paul and other New Testament writers. Ellis, *Paul's Use of the Old Testament*, Appendix II.

16. Clarke, *Pauline Theology*, 1.

17. Clarke, 1–2. In footnote 2, Clarke provides a list of the titles that were given to different leaders in the Septuagint and the passages where they can be found.

18. Exod 16:22; 34:31; Num 31:13.

19. Num 1:44; 4:34; 2 Chr 7:40.

20. Judg 10:18; Neh 10:15; Isa 28:14.

21. Clarke, *Pauline Theology*, 2. He measures the frequency of the term by looking at its appearance per one thousand words.

22. Clarke, 2.

23. Clarke, 2.

24. This dissertation will try to avoid the use of the term "Christian" to describe the early Pauline community. During Paul's day, "Christianity" was not yet a distinct religion,

to question the appropriateness of using the word "leader" for expressing leadership in the Jesus movement. In fact, towards the end of his address Tomlin says that it is only Jesus Christ who can be called a legitimate leader of his people, not human leaders.[25]

What compounds our problem regarding the definition of leadership in the Jesus movement is the fact that when Jesus uses the Greek words for leadership (ἄρχων, ἡγούμενος) in Luke 22:25–26, Mark 10:42, and Matthew 20:25, the word is phrased in the negative sense by contrasting between how the "ἄρχων," "ἡγούμενος" of the Gentiles lords it over the people, and he calls his disciples to lead through serving others. According to Luke 22:26, Jesus uses the Greek word ἡγούμενος to refer to leadership among his followers, but what is striking here is that the text is quick to qualify what that leadership looks like as opposed to how the Gentiles exercise their leadership. Jesus's followers are to lead by being servants of others, and leadership in this community does not mean that the leader has to be elevated above everyone else; instead, the leader ought to view himself/herself as the least amongst the people in the community. Thus, Button provides a helpful observation when he says, "It is important not to allow the term "leadership" and its associated concepts to prejudge a study of New Testament phenomena; the idea of leadership is sufficiently broad to provide a useful conceptual framework for studying a whole range of leadership/ministry phenomena in the early Pauline churches."[26] Therefore, this current research will include broad categories of terms that we consider today as being leadership functions, adding to the Greek words that have already been mentioned above. Other terms such as "ministry, minister [both noun and verb]" (which represents διάκονος, διακονέω) will also be used in describing the phenomenon of leadership in the early Pauline community. A word's non-use does not imply the non-existence of the concept; moreover, concepts and their enablement in

---

thus this research will use terms like "Jesus movement" or "Pauline community" to describe the New Testament phenomena. "Christianity" became a distinct entity in the second decade of the second century. For more on this, see Dunn, *Neither Jew Nor Greek*, 7; Horrell, *Pauline Churches*, 3, and; Tucker, *You Belong to Christ*, 3. This distinction does not imply that there was a theological departure in the second century from the foundations of the first century. For more on this, see Holmberg, "Understanding the First Hundred," 1–32.

25. Tomlin, *Theology of Leadership*.
26. Button, "Leadership and Gospel," 1.

language are always context-related.[27] By using interdisciplinary studies, this dissertation will later attempt to demonstrate the plausibility of this statement.

1.2 Preliminary Studies Already Undertaken

There are two pillars that form the core of this research: (1) Leadership in Paul as it is expressed in 1 Corinthians 1:1–4, and (2) Identity formation in Pauline studies (particularly in 1 Corinthians). Each of these pillars needs to be looked at in formulating our problem statement. We will now turn our attention to a consideration of these points.

1.2.1 Leadership in Paul in 1 Corinthians

There are essentially two dominant existing approaches to the subject of leadership in Paul and one more recent approach. These are the traditional approach and the socioscientific approach, and the more recent approach that is still in its infancy is an integrated approach.

1.2.1.1 The Traditional Approach

The first approach to leadership in Paul is known by three names: some scholars refer to it as the Holtzmann-Sohm hypothesis,[28] while others call it a consensus view, and still others refer to it as the traditional view. This approach tends to focus on the organisational structure of the early Pauline house churches and their subsequent development in the early Jesus movement period.[29] Scholars who adopt this approach tend to be preoccupied with the question of the relationship between charismata and office (organisational

---

27. Barr, Semantics of Biblical Language, 219.
28. Barentsen, *Emerging Leadership*, 19–23.
29. For an appraisal of the evolution of the consensus view from the Reformation period to the twentieth century, see Burtchaell, *Synagogue to Church*, 1–179. Campbell in *The Elders*, (originally 1994, the current research used a 2004 publication), did an appraisal of the consensus view from Rudolf Sohm to 1994, while Ridderbos, *Paul: An Outline*, Barentsen, *Emerging Leadership*, and Button, "Leadership and Gospel," provide a helpful summary of the "Holtzmann-Sohm hypothesis." However, for a detailed analysis of this approach, see Chapple, "Local Leadership," 3–25.

structure).[30] This approach is still popular in South Africa among a variety of scholars such as Du Plooy, Du Rand, and Vermeulen.[31]

This view holds that the early Pauline ministry was characterised as "charismatic ministry." Sohm was of the view that the church was primarily a charismatic community (that received its leadership and government from God by his spirit). Thus, leadership was first based in charismata and only later evolved into the formalised offices of bishops, elders, and deacons.[32] Holtzmann on the other hand, looking at the uncontested Pauline letters, argued that the letter to the Corinthians "portrayed a fluid manifestation of the Spirit's power, devoid of settled leadership relationships."[33] He also noticed that 1 Timothy "spoke of presbyterion as a closed college of elders."[34] Thus, according to the old consensus, "Pauline church order is charismatic church order," and charismatic church order is determined by the spirit and its gifts, and as "such church order is incompatible with formal official structures and positions."[35]

Harnack was one of the earliest critics of Sohm:[36]

> Harnack glo dat die kerk 'n sosiologiese en charismatiese gemeenskap is waar 'n charismatiese struktuur en administratiewe ordening belangrik is, maar . . . egter ondergeskik (bly) aan die geestelike en charismatiese aard van die kerk.[37]

---

30. Du Plooy, "Betekenis van Charisma."
31. Du Plooy; Du Rand, "Charisma en Amp"; Vermeulen, "Leiers Wat Dien."
32. Ridderbos, *Paul: An Outline*, 438–39.
33. Holtzmann, *Pastoralbriefe Kritisch*.
34. Barentsen, *Emerging Leadership*, 18.
35. Chapple, "Local Leadership," 8.
36. Chapple, 8. Here, he notes that the early challenge to the Holtzmann-Sohm hypothesis comes mostly from the Catholic scholars, and he highlights how the "confessional commitments (and the dogmatic presuppositions which those commitments involved)" had influenced the debate about the church order. This however, is not to say that only Catholics had a problem with the Holtzmann-Sohm hypothesis. In fact, some Catholic scholars such as Küng, Hasenhüttl, and Schürman did embrace the Holtzmann-Sohm hypothesis. See Chapple, 29. A more detailed analysis of the challenge to the consensus on the Holtzmann-Sohm hypothesis will be done below, when this dissertation considers the social-scientific approach.
37. Harnack cited in Du Plooy, "Betekenis van Charisma," 558 (see also Chapple, 24); "Harnack believed that the church is a sociological and charismatic community where a charismatic structure and administrative organization is important, but remains subordinate to the spiritual and charismatic nature of the church" (English translation).

Thus, a gradual shift starts to emerge from an emphasis on the "charismatic community" to the institutionalisation of the church, among the scholars who adhere to the traditional view of leadership in Pauline churches. The influence of Holtzmann-Sohm hypothesis among German scholarship cannot be overstated.[38] Scholars have criticised the Holtzmann-Sohm hypothesis because of its denominational biases.[39] Streeter observes that the motivations and the conclusions of this approach tended to be an apologetic for the different denominations of which the researchers were part;[40] that is, the Episcopal researchers looked for and concluded that the early house churches were Episcopalian by nature, while the Presbyterians saw Presbyterianism.[41] Due to the subjective nature of this approach, actual historical practices of the early Pauline community could not be determined definitively.[42] This research hopes to contribute towards unearthing what Paul taught regarding leadership to the Corinthian community.

---

38. Its influence is evident in scholars such as Campenhausen, *Ecclesiastical Authority and Spiritual Power*; Käsemann, *Essays on the New Testament Themes*; Schweizer, *Church Order in the New Testament*; Weber and Eisenstadt, *Max Weber on Charisma and Institution Building*; Küng, *The Church*; Boff, *Church, Charism and Power*; and Jeffers, *Conflict at Rome*. For a detailed summary of its influence on the works of the first three scholars cited in this footnote, see Chapple, "Local Leadership," 5–8.

39. Harnack is one of the earliest scholars who criticised Sohm's view of the church. Harnack, *Constitution and Law*, 220–55. Harnack was especially critical of Sohm's concept of the church as "a purely religious and spiritual entity." Harnack, 210–11. He goes on to say that "if we simply eliminate everything earthly from the nature of the church, how can the Church then be anything but a mere idea, in which each individual Christian in his isolation believes" (emphasis original). Harnack insists that the church manifests itself in society and thus "the social and corporate element cannot be sundered from the sublimest concept of the Church" (emphasis original). Harnack, 213. For more on the scholars who criticised this approach, see Chapple, "Local Leadership," 18–19. See for an example his analysis of scholars such as Brockhaus (who criticised the Holtzmann-Sohm approach on exegetical grounds and said the following): "Naiv historische Deutung Sohms, der die Aussagen des Paulus über die Charismen ohne weiteres mit der Verfassung der urchristlichen Gemeinden gleichsetzte, wirkt zwar in dem neuen Konsensus von der charismatischen Ordnung der frühen (paulinschen) Gemeinden nach, wird aber radikaler, jeder Differenzierung antbehrenden Form Sohms heute kaum noch vertreten." Further, Brockhaus "argues that there is no unified χάρισμα concept in Paul," rather he sees "χάρισμα als ein ausgesprochener paränetischer Terminus." Brockhaus, *Carisma und Amt*, 126. See also Chapple, "Local Leadership," 10.

40. Streeter, *Primitive Church*, vii; ix. See also Burtchaell, *Synagogue to Church*.

41. Burtchaell, 2.

42. Barentsen, *Emerging Leadership*, 20; Button, "Leadership and Gospel," 2.

1.2.1.2 *The Socioscientific Approach*

The second approach comes from scholars who use sociohistorical/scientific approaches.[43] Marshall said, "It has become increasingly clear that the distinction sometimes drawn between an earlier charismatic ministry and a later institutional system of 'office' is inappropriate and should be dropped from discussion."[44] The scholars pursuing sociohistorical/scientific approaches in their challenge to the traditional consensus approach focus on the social stratification of the community of the early Pauline house churches.[45] Other scholars such as Holmberg look at the relationship between the Gentile Pauline community and the Jewish community of the Jesus movement.[46] Some scholars concluded that leadership of these house churches was based on patronage relations; that is, the wealthy members of the church accommodated the church and also hosted travelling missionaries.[47]

Social-scientific scholars have criticised the Holtzmann-Sohm hypothesis from different perspectives but there is a theme that emerges in their criticism of it. First, they criticise the approach on a methodological level: here Holmberg comes across very strongly and calls it an "idealistic fallacy."[48] These scholars feel that the consensus approach "rests on defective presuppositions and methods" and that their "methods tends to be asserted rather than demonstrated."[49] Moreover, the critics of the Holtzmann-Sohm hypothesis say that it fails to pay attention to the sociohistorical context of Paul's letters in

---

43. Chapple provides a detailed analysis of the scholars who challenged the Holtzmann-Sohm hypothesis or the consensus view from 1972–84. These scholars use mostly exegetical, historical, and sociological approaches. Chapple, "Local Leadership," 9.

44. Marshall, *Critical and Exegetical Commentary*, 176.

45. Campbell, *Paul and Creation*; Gehring, *House Church and Mission*; Theissen, *Social Setting*; Meeks, "Social Context"; White, "Christianity"; Reumann, "Church Office in Paul," and Banks, *Paul's Idea of Community*. See also Meggitt and Friesen who criticise the assumptions about the social make-up of the Pauline community. They argue that early Pauline house churches consisted mostly of poor people. Meggitt, *Paul, Poverty and Survival*; Friesen, "Poverty in Pauline Studies." For a debate about the composition of the church in Corinth, see also Clarke, *Secular and Christian Leadership*, 41–57. Chapter 3 of this study will deal with this debate in detail.

46. Holmberg, *Paul and Power*.

47. Holmberg, 116–21. It is worth noting that Holmberg saw the Pauline churches as consisting of two groups of leaders; first, those who had gifts of teaching, and the second group was that of wealthy patrons. Holmberg, 116.

48. Holmberg, 205.

49. Chapple, "Local Leadership," 21.

their analysis. However, this does not mean that the socioscientific approach has got it right either, as the following paragraph demonstrates.

Button noted that some of the scholars who use socioscientific approaches tend to ignore theological interpretations.[50] In this regard, Barentsen says that studies on Pauline leadership either exclusively ignore the historical and ideological factors at the expense of social structure or vice versa.[51] Barentsen cites the striking example of the work of Andrew Clarke.[52] In his book "Serve the Community of the Church," Barentsen focuses on the historical factors, while in his book "A Pauline Theology of Church Leadership," Clarke focuses on the ideological component. Button notes that scholars such as Meeks, Campbell, and Gehring have ignored theological interpretations and have explained leadership exclusively in terms of social structures.[53] Other scholars, in their use of socioscientific approaches, imposed foreign categories on the Biblical text and the result was that they drew erroneous conclusions. An example of this can be seen in the work of Holmberg.[54] In many ways, Holmberg's work was a reaction to the denominational biases that dominated the traditional approach described in the previous section.[55] This is evident mostly towards the end of the book, where Holmberg talks about the "fallacy of idealism."[56] Here he critiques the giants of New Testament studies such as "Bultmann (1953), Von Compenhausen (1969), Hainz (1972), Käsemann (1942, 1956, 1960), Schütz (1975) and Schweizer (1959)."[57] His major contention with these giants is that they tend to interpret Paul's work as if they are purely theological works, "where the historical phenomena are often interpreted as being directly formed by underlying theological structures."[58] Holmberg correctly observes that there is a "continuous dialectic between ideas and social

---

50. Button, "Leadership and Gospel."
51. Barentsen, *Emerging Leadership*, 6.
52. Barentsen, 6.
53. Button, "Leadership and Gospel," 3; Meeks, *First Urban Christians*; Campbell, *Paul and Creation*; Gehring, *House Church and Mission*.
54. Holmberg, *Paul and Power*. A substantive review of Holmberg's book will be conducted in the next chapter.
55. Holmberg, 1.
56. Holmberg, 201.
57. Holmberg, 201.
58. Holmberg, 201.

structures."[59] Employing Max Weber's classical sociology theory, Holmberg draws questionable conclusions about the nature of the relationship between Pauline gentile mission and the Jerusalem "church"; for Holmberg, the fact that Paul collected the money for the Jerusalem "church" meant that the early Pauline community was subordinate to the Jerusalem community. He says:[60]

> The relation between actors in power relations can be described as an unbalanced exchange relation. One party gives the orders, makes demands, speaks authoritative words and the other gives in return obedience, service, personal support and money. The subordinate has to "pay" in some way.

The problem with Holmberg's assertion is that perhaps in modern times this is the case, but it is incorrect in relation to the early Pauline community. This is a danger of imposing modern-day sociological categories onto the biblical text, as warned against by scholars such as Judge and Furnish.[61] During Paul's time, it was the rich who gave to the poor. Money was "continually given by the powerful to their dependents, and this transfer of cash downwards on the social scale is the main instrument by which the status of the powerful is asserted."[62] Thus, the second approach to Pauline leadership simply replaced denominational theology with sociological models, which yielded little in terms of the actual situation confronting the early Pauline community. Hence, integrative work is still needed in the field.

1.2.1.3 *The Integrated, Group-based Approach*

There are recent studies that address the question of leadership in Paul differently, integrating the findings of both the traditional and sociohistorical/scientific approaches. This current research aligns itself closely with this group of scholars. In many ways, scholars such as Barentsen bridge the gap between the two tendencies described above.[63] Even though Barentsen uses a socioscientific approach, he integrates the findings of both the ideological/

---

59. Holmberg, 203.
60. Holmberg, 11.
61. Judge, "Social Identity"; Furnish, "Jesus-Paul Debate."
62. Judge, 211. This dissertation will deal with the issues of patronage at a later stage as they come up in the discussion.
63. Barentsen, *Emerging Leadership*.

theological (such as Clarke's works) and socioscientific approaches in his research. He examines Pauline leadership in a three-stage analysis: leadership emergence, maintenance, and succession in Ephesus and Corinth, as a means of Paul's shaping the identity of Christ-followers.[64] The integration of the social (historical) and the ideological (psychological) factors in shaping Paul's correspondence provides an analytic model in which we can get the "how" and "why" of Pauline leadership patterns as opposed to simply their content.[65]

The significance of Barentsen's book for this thesis is his main argument that leadership is a group phenomenon. He says:[66]

> A group is understood as a set of persons who all share a sense of "us," of belonging together. This sense of "us" refers to the psychological processes that are at work within individuals as they join others in a group. This sense of "us" is shared, and revolves around group beliefs and norms, which function as the group's ideology.

This understanding of group identity is very similar to that of Ubuntu philosophy, by which Africans understand their own identity. Within the African philosophical system of Ubuntu, an individual finds his or her identity and existence within the "whole interwoven structure of the immediate family, the extended family, and the entire community."[67] According to Shutte, the community is the soul of Africa.[68] Moreover, Khoza maintains that African leadership informed by Ubuntu philosophy is a group phenomenon.[69] Hence, within the African philosophical system an individual finds his or her identity in the community, and leadership is also seen as a community phenomenon. Barentsen's thesis also states that in Pauline theology leadership is a group phenomenon. This thesis seeks to investigate this assumption. This will be

---

64. Under leadership emergence, he looks at how an individual in the group becomes a group leader, while leadership maintenance looks at how an individual maintains his or her status of influence in the group. Leadership succession concerns how established leaders "empower new leaders to emerge." Barentsen, *Emerging Leadership*, 2.

65. Lowery, "Review: Jack Barentsen."

66. Barentsen, *Emerging Leadership*, 2.

67. Mzondi, "'Two Souls' Leadership," 48.

68. Shutte, *Ubuntu*, 11.

69. Khoza, *Attuned Leadership*.

done by utilising the findings of scholars such as Barentsen in leadership studies, and scholars such as Tucker and Campbell in identity studies in order to establish whether or not there is a continuation of gentile identity in the Corinthian correspondence.[70] If that can be established, the African understanding of leadership (which claims that leadership is a group phenomenon) and Pauline leadership will be compared with the aim of providing the African Christian a window into Paul, and making Pauline teaching on leadership more relevant to the South African context. In this way, Paul's correspondence to the Corinthians informs the gentile Christian identity.

Having surveyed the current state of leadership studies in Paul, and having observed the shortcomings of the two dominant approaches in the field – the traditional approach and sociohistorical/scientific approaches – this study will show that more integrated work is still required. The group-based approach becomes a potential source of better results, especially since it incorporates identity studies which are the second pillar of this research.

1.2.2 Paul and the Formation of Identity

Identity formation studies in Paul have become a fast growing discipline in recent years.[71] These studies "have brought to the fore the centrality of social identity in Paul's thoughts."[72] According to Tucker, there are two recent approaches to identity formation in Paul, namely "the universalistic approach to Christian identity" or "third race" and "(re)construction and continuation of previous social identities" in the Pauline community.[73] Most of these works are influenced by "Beyond the New Perspective" on Paul.[74]

---

70. Tucker, *Remain in Your Calling*; Campbell, *Paul and Creation*.

71. See scholars such as Tucker, *You Belong to Christ*; *Remain in Your Calling*; Campbell, *Paul and Creation*; "Rationale for Gentile"; Barentsen, *Emerging Leadership*; Esler, "Group Boundaries"; *Galatians*; *Conflict and Identity*; "Prototypes, Antitypes"; "Outline of Social Identity"; Esler and Piper, *Lazarus, Mary and Martha*; Horrell, "Becoming Christian"; "Scholarly Quest"; "Whither Social-Scientific Approaches?"

72. Tucker, *Remain in Your Calling*, 2.

73. Tucker, 2.

74. Tucker provides a fine overview of literature on identity in Paul; he first reviews scholars such as Sechrest (on pages 3–4), and Hansen (pages 4–6), whose findings on the question of social identity are different to his. Tucker then looks at scholars such as Esler and Horrell (6, mostly in the footnote). Tucker also provides an overview and the characteristic of "Beyond the New Perspective on Paul" (BNP) "which rejects universal/ethnic dichotomy in Paul," which also "finds no implicit critique of Israel or the Law." Tucker, 8–10. See also Sechrest who also provides an overview of "race and ethnicity in antiquity," Paul's relationship

Identity studies in Paul are significant for this dissertation's analysis of leadership in Paul. Scholars such as Clarke and Tucker have adequately demonstrated that leadership issues in the Corinthian correspondence were a result of previous identity influences upon the young community;[75] according to Clarke, secular influences were a direct cause of the problems and he argues that such influences have no place in this new community.[76] Tucker shows that problems with leadership resulted from the community's misunderstanding of how their previous "Roman social identity was transformed by being 'in Christ.'"[77] This dissertation sees leadership and identity as intrinsically linked in the Corinthian correspondence.

1.2.2.1 Universalistic Approach to Pauline Community Identity

This approach is built on four popular New Testament texts: Galatians 3:28, Colossians 3:11 which speak of there being "neither Jew nor Greek" in Christ, 1 Corinthians 12:13 which talks about our unity in one baptism and one Spirit, and 2 Corinthians 5:17 which says that εἴ τις , καινὴ κτίσις.[78] These verses affirm the unity of Christ's followers over social division; Hansen argues that this is the "most prominent refrain in the Pauline corpus."[79] This approach has a popular following among Pauline scholars such as Sechrest, Hansen, Esler, and Horrell, but all of them add different nuances to it.[80] For example, Sechrest follows the findings of New Perspective on Paul and argues that Paul saw those who are "in Christ," both Jews and Gentiles, as a third race whose

---

with Judaism, and, more importantly for the current section, her treatment of "Christian as the 'third race.'" Sechrest, *Former Jew*, 6–9, 9–12, 13–16. In this section, she traces the New Testament references that refer to the members of the Jesus movement as race (γένος) and she also demonstrates how the apostolic fathers saw themselves as a distinct entity which was neither Jewish nor Greek. On pages 16–18, Sechrest provides a concise review of scholarly attempts on the "third race" approach; in this section she looks at scholars like Harnack, Richardson, Bultmann, Davies, and Sanders.

75. Clarke, *Secular and Christian Leadership*; Tucker, *You Belong to Christ*.
76. Clarke, 125.
77. Tucker, *You Belong to Christ*, 7.
78. Evidence of the popularity of these scriptures (especially the first three) in this approach can be seen in the work of Hansen, "All of You Are One," where it also forms part of his title. Sechrest in *Former Jew* dedicates more than 11 pages according to the index on Gal 3:28.
79. Hansen, "All of You," 1. For more information on the influences of these verses on Paul's outlook, see Hansen, 1–3.
80. Sechrest, *Former Jew*; Hansen, "All of You"; Esler, *Conflict and Identity*; "Prototypes, Antitypes"; Horrell, "Becoming Christian."

understanding of their identity is drawn from "the Jewish understanding of race in the Second Temple Judaism."[81] Sechrest argues that "Paul thinks of himself as someone who was born a Jew but no longer considers himself one."[82] She goes on to say that Paul perceives himself as a former Jew because Paul privileged his identity of being in Christ above his previous identity as a Jew. Sechrest also notes that concerning the Gentiles; Paul refers to them as Gentile when he refers to their birth identity in Galatians 2:14, but also considers them to be former (ex-) Gentiles in relationship to their current identity and allegiances.[83] Thus, the Gentile Christ followers in Paul's thought, according to Sechrest, are members of a third distinct race. The problem with Sechrest's work has been highlighted by Tucker,[84] that is, she pays little attention to Scriptures such as 1 Corinthians 7:17–24 which seem to suggest that Paul envisages some kind of continuation of the previous social identities among those who belong to Christ. Sechrest only sees Paul's relationship with his "biological kinship" simply in terms of Paul evangelising them.[85] In fact, she goes as far as to say (after looking at 1 Corinthians 9:19–20; Galatians 1:14; 2:15) that Paul "distances himself from a Jewish self-identification." But this raises a question – what are we to make of 1 Corinthians 7:17–24 where Paul argues that those who are in Christ are not to seek a change in their ethnic identity markers?[86] Moreover, Sechrest overlooks passages such as Romans 11:13 and 15:27 where Paul clearly calls Gentiles who are in Christ, Gentiles.[87] The problem of the "third race" approach, especially as it is articulated by Sechrest, is that in practice it gives an impression of sameness. Campbell makes a helpful observation about this approach:[88] in the "contemporary world" it has landed itself as "an accessory" to an imperialistic conception of a dominating Western culture over, for example, African or Korean culture. A much more palatable and convincing argument on the "third race"

---

81. Sechrest, 5.

82. Sechrest, 159.

83. Sechrest, 161.

84. Tucker, *Remain in Your Calling*, 3.

85. Sechrest, *Former Jew*, 158.

86. "περιτετμημένος τις ἐκλήθη; μὴ ἐπισπάσθω· ἐν ἀκροβυστίᾳ κέκληταί τις; μὴ περιτεμνέσθω," 1 Cor 7:18.

87. Tucker, *Remain in Your Calling*, 3.

88. Campbell, *Paul and Creation*, 1.

approach is that of Esler[89] who sees the previous Gentile and Jewish identities being "incorporated within one new identity but not at the price of losing their subgroup identities."[90] Esler speaks of Paul as having in mind the Christ followers as one body but with differentiation in its parts (citing Romans 12:4–5).[91] The problem with the "third race" approach is that it raises more questions than answers; for example if parts of Jesus's followers' identity are subordinate to their identity "in Christ," what does that look like practically in the community?[92] How are these previous social divides overcome by being "in Christ"? Horrell, for example, asks a very pertinent question of this approach when he says:

> But what exactly does that phrase [οὐκ ἔνι Ἰουδαῖος οὐδὲ Ἕλλην] mean? To what extent does it imply a redefinition of former identities and a restructuring of former practices? That is not immediately apparent and a range of interpretations are possible.[93]

Indeed, attention to the phrase οὐκ ἔνι Ἰουδαῖος οὐδὲ Ἕλλην is not apparent in the arguments of scholars who take this approach.

1.2.2.2 (Re)Construction and Continuation of Previous Social Identities

It is worth noting, however, that it is not only Barentsen who has considered the question of identity in Paul.[94] There are other scholars such as Campbell and Tucker whose findings are also significant for the current research.[95]

---

89. Esler, *Conflict and Identity*, 307.

90. Esler believes that in Romans, Paul writes to "a movement with strongly articulated beliefs and practices . . . animosity is being expressed between its Judean and non-Judean members. A group and a group identity have clearly developed distinctive from that of the Judean communities . . . they are disturbed by the presence of subgroups and subgroup identities." Esler, 101.

91. Esler, 218. Esler sees Paul as having respect for the permanent identities of Jewish and Gentile groups, but yet calling them to live by a shared identity in Christ. Esler, 133, 218–19, 270–73.

92. Hansen, "All of You," 3.

93. Horrell, "No Longer Jew or Greek," 333.

94. Tucker provides a summary of the two recent approaches to Paul and identity formation. Tucker, *Remain in Your Calling*, 2–28.

95. Campbell, *Paul and Creation*; Tucker, *You Belong to Christ*.

William Campbell, for example, argues that the Jewish identity continued as a valid option in the early Christian movement for Jewish Christians.[96] He said:

> I wish to argue that participation in the covenant means keeping the Law and thus maintaining a Jewish identity. The Law is an identity descriptor for Jews defining how they are to live, determining every aspect of their life. In this sense it is impossible to be both Jewish and Gentile simultaneously – you are either one or the other.[97]

The question that then arises is whether the same could be said for gentile identity. Did the Gentiles continue with their gentile identity in the early Christian movement? The significant Scripture here is 1 Corinthians 7:17–24, where Paul says that the Christian community should remain in the state that they were called in. At face value, it seems that Paul argues that those who belong to Christ should not seek to change their ethnic identity markers (circumcision), especially the Jews. Horrell, looking at these verses, notes that there must have been diversity among the Corinthian community, with the Gentiles being the majority.[98] The question arising then is, since the Gentiles were the majority, did Paul expect them to keep their gentile identity markers, and what is the interplay between being "in Christ" and their gentile identity? Moreover, Paul is generally "accredited as being the architect of the gentile inclusion in Christ," also, it was he "who fought continuously for the inclusion of Gentiles on equal terms with the Jews and resisted all attempts to treat them as proselytes or potential Jews," and scholars also see "the Antioch incident" as "Paul's triumph over Jewish influence in the church" (emphasis original).[99] This research seeks to investigate how the interplay between the gentile identity and being "in Christ" may be supportive of the formation of the African Christian identity.

---

96. Campbell, "Rationale for Gentile Inclusion," 23.
97. Campbell, 23.
98. Horrell, Pauline Churches, 9.
99. Campbell, *Paul and Creation*, 87.

1.3 Problem Statement

In leadership studies thus far, there have been two dominant approaches but both have been problematic in the sense that they have been subjective by nature and the actual historical realities of what Paul taught regarding leadership still need further attention. The preferred approach to leadership studies for this research is the integrated group-based approach, as it incorporates both the findings of the traditional approach and the socioscientific approach. With the exception of Barentsen,[100] most New Testament scholars who investigate leadership in Paul tend to neglect identity formation. Even scholars such as Clarke, whose thesis is that in 1 Corinthians Paul was arguing against secular influences on the church in Corinth, and that Paul reshapes the Corinthian ἐκκλησία understanding of church leadership, comes short of demonstrating that Paul, by critiquing secular leadership influence upon the Corinthians, was in fact fostering Christian identity formation.[101] Identity studies, on the other hand, have paid little attention to the subject of the continuation of gentile identity, even though scholars such as Campbell have written extensively about the continuation of the Jewish identity in the Jesus movement.[102]

Thus, the problem statement of my research is to explore Paul's teachings on leadership in relationship to his exercise of leadership in 1 Corinthians 1–4 and to investigate its significance for the formation of gentile identity in Christ.

1.4 Key Research Questions

In order to effectively address the problem statement of the relationship between Paul's sense of leadership and the formation of an identity in Christ, as portrayed in 1 Corinthians 4, the following five questions will be considered:

1. What is the relationship between identity "in Christ" and leadership?

---

100. Barentsen, *Emerging Leadership*.
101. Clarke, *Secular and Christian Leadership*.
102. Campbell, *Paul and Creation*.

2. In what ways does Paul's use of the ἐν Χριστῷ and κλῆσις terminologies for his apostolic defence help him to prove to the Corinthians that he is indeed an in-group prototype?
3. In what ways does Paul's use the ἐν Χριστῷ and κλῆσις terminologies to critique the Corinthian secular understanding of leadership?
4. How does Paul's use of these terminologies help him to (re)shape the Corinthians' own understanding of their identity "in Christ"?

1.5 Research Hypothesis

Thiselton and Gadamer have noted that there is a tendency among New Testament scholars in their use of "historical criticism" and "historical reconstruction" methods in reconstructing the world and teaching of the New Testament to distance the text from modern readers.[103] Even though this is helpful in placing the text of 1 Corinthians firmly within its original context, and has helped us not to impose our twenty-first-century vision on Paul, it has nonetheless made Paul foreign to the (post)modern African context. However, as Ricoeur says, the aim of all hermeneutics is "to 'make one's own' what was previously 'foreign.'"[104] Thiselton provides a useful insight when he says:

> research on Paul's Corinth brings to light features that appear to offer some unexpectedly close parallels with issues that belong also to the early twenty-first century. To apply such terms as consumerism, local theology or a postmodern mood either to Corinth or to the church in Corinth may seem initially to suggest uncritical and premature hermeneutical assimilation and foreclosure. Yet patient exegesis and closer attention to several themes in recent research may lead us to reconsider such assumptions.[105]

---

103. Thiselton, "Significance of Recent Research," 320–52; *Two Horizons*, 51–84; *1 Corinthians*, 607–12; Gadamer, *Truth and Method*, 290–98.

104. Ricoeur, *Interpretation Theory*, 91; See also Thiselton, "Significance of Recent Research," 321.

105. Thiselton, 321.

Indeed, the current research seeks to pay careful attention to the themes of leadership and identity formation in Paul and, as recent scholarship has shown, Pauline theology of leadership is a communal phenomenon. Paul was a contextual theologian; he developed his teachings on leadership in the midst of conflict. In 1 Corinthians he dealt with factionalism; that is, the Corinthians were divided according to the leaders they preferred to follow. This meant that the community life that developed after Paul had left Corinth did not correspond to Paul's ideas for a Christian community. It seems that the root cause of this was that "some in Corinth were continuing to identify primarily with key aspects of their Roman social identity rather than their identity 'in Christ.'"[106] Thus, confusion around identity seems to have been the cause of the problems in Corinth. Paul, in his rebuke of the Corinthians, showed them that they were using incorrect criteria to judge him, and he also corrects them in how they are to view their leaders – that is, all Christian leaders are actually for the benefit of the church and they belong to the church (1 Cor 3:21–23). Also, in this letter, Paul shows the Corinthians what true leadership looks like and explains the role of the Christian leaders. The central argument of this research is captured well by the words of Philip Esler: "Leaders must be 'entrepreneurs of identity, capable of turning 'me' and 'you' into 'us,'" they need to bestow "shared social identity, meaning, purpose, and values."[107]

This research will focus on the broader section of 1 Corinthians 1–4. It will however, pay careful attention to 1 Corinthians 1:1–9, as this dissertation is of the view that these nine verses are representative of the themes that Paul fleshes out throughout the letter. Scholars such as Tite, Tolmie, and Snyman have argued for the significance of the epistolary prescript in Paul's letter.[108] They argue that epistolary prescripts have a much bigger role to play for Paul than just following the traditional ancient letter writing patterns. Tite argues that Paul used the epistolary prescript with a rhetorical purpose in mind, in that it plays a role of a "discursive positioning" between the "sender(s) and the recipient(s)."[109] Further, Tolmie argues that Paul never "uses a static pattern for the opening salutation of his letters, but instead

---

106. Tucker, *You Belong to Christ*, 2.
107. Esler, *Conflict and Identity*, 38.
108. Tite, "How to Begin?", 57–99; Tolmie, *Persuading Galatians*, 31–47; Snyman, "Persuasion in 1 Corinthians 1:1–9," 2.
109. Tite, 59.

adapts" them in order to address a particular situation.[110] Similarly, Snyman contends that Paul presented his best arguments in the epistolary prescript of 1 Corinthians.[111] Thus, for this dissertation 1 Corinthians 1:1–9 sets the tone for the entire letter, and this becomes obvious when one incorporates social identity theory in analysing it. Scholars such as Clarke see 1 Corinthians 1–4 as Paul dealing with the question of leadership.[112] Clarke sees Paul in these chapters critiquing the secular categories of leadership and their application by the Corinthians, and concludes that there is no place for them in the "Jesus movement." As already stated above, Tucker sees the issues in 1 Corinthians 1–4 to be about the Corinthians' misunderstanding of how their previous Roman identity relates to them now that they are "in Christ."[113] If one follows Clarke's thesis on what Paul is doing in 1 Corinthians 1–4, one might wrongly conclude that there is no place for previous identity and previous leadership practices in the "Jesus movement community."[114] Because this dissertation is concerned about the identity-related issues in 1 Corinthians, it will from time to time engage with scholarly discussions regarding Paul's teachings in 1 Corinthians 7:17–24, even though this is not the main focus of this dissertation. In 1 Corinthians 7:17–24, Paul urges the Corinthians not to seek to change their former identity now that they are in Christ. This Scripture seems to envisage some sort of continuity of the previous identity prior to being "in Christ." The question then becomes, what previous aspects of "secular" or "Gentile" identity were allowed to continue in this community, and how do those previous identities, if they are allowed in the community, impact on their understanding of leadership practises? This Scripture is significant for gentile identity formation, and as already established in this thesis, it has been neglected by the scholars who use the universalistic approach to Pauline identity formation.

My hypothesis is that Paul's discourse in 1 Corinthians 1–4 demonstrates the interrelationship between leadership and identity. This becomes apparent when one considers Paul's use of the ἐν Χριστῷ and κλῆσις terminologies.

---

110. Tolmie, *Persuading Galatians*, 31.
111. Snyman, "Persuasion in 1 Corinthians 1:1–9," 2.
112. Clarke, *Secular and Christian Leadership*.
113. Tucker, *You Belong to Christ*.
114. Clarke, *Secular and Christian Leadership*, 97; 113.

For this dissertation, Ἰησοῦ terminology is the key terminology on which the interrelationship between leadership and identity in 1 Corinthians is established. It will be argued that Paul uses this terminology to frame his discourse in 1 Corinthians 1–4. This terminology helped Paul in two key aspects:

First, to get the attention and the hearing of a group of people, some of whom had rejected him as their apostle due to their preference for one leader at the expense of the other.[115] Paul uses the Ἰησοῦ terminology at the beginning of the letter to signal to the group that the subject matter about which he was writing was at the core related to in-group identity. This dissertation will argue that Paul used the Ἰησοῦ terminology to help him in the consensualisation process.

Second, this terminology allowed Paul to present himself as a group prototype.[116] Again, since some members of the community had rejected him due to the Greco-Roman cultural influences on their perceptions of a leader, Paul counters those cultural influences by using the Ἰησοῦ terminology to remind the in-group members of their salient identity "in Christ." Thus, Paul in his use of ἐν Χριστῷ was in fact "killing two birds with one stone." Paul also used the ἐν Χριστῷ and κλῆσις terminologies for his group entrepreneur strategy by reminding the group about how their identity "in Christ" is diametrically opposed to the world's wisdom and power, the same categories that they were using to judge him. Thus, Paul critiques elements of that identity that are inconsistent with their identity in Christ, but at the same time he shapes how their previous identities continue under the lordship of Christ.[117] Paul wanted them to remain Gentiles (who believe in Christ), not become quasi-Jews.

1.6 Methodology[118]

Earlier in this proposal, two dominant approaches to Pauline leadership studies were dealt with – the traditional approach and the socioscientific

---

115. 1 Cor 1:10–2; 3:4–5.

116. See chapter 2 regarding the meaning of "group prototype" and "group entrepreneur."

117. The matter of the composition of the Corinthian community will be fleshed out in chapter 3.

118. This section will not provide an in-depth analysis of social identity theory; instead, it will simply provide a brief overview of the theory – an in-depth analysis will be done in a separate chapter.

approach. We saw that the traditional approach tended to foster denominational biases and that the actual historical situation in Pauline churches was not fully ascertained, while the socioscientific approach simply replaced the old denominational approach with sociological models. Thus, a more integrative approach is still needed; a methodological approach that can use the insight of the traditional approach (without denominational biases) and the insight from the socioscientific approach, which has contributed immensely to our understanding of the social and cultural make-up of the early Pauline communities.

This dissertation will incorporate both social scientific and historical-critical grammatical approaches.[119] There will not be a text-by-text analysis in the sense of a running commentary on the book to the Corinthians, nor will it deal with all possible grammatical issues of the selected texts or documents. Rather, starting with the text, this dissertation will pay careful attention to the argument of 1 Corinthians 1:1–9 in light of the broader argument of 1 Corinthians 1–4 as it relates to the subject of leadership and identity. The grammatical issues that will be considered are those that have a direct bearing on the argument as it relates to leadership and identity.

The current research thus seeks to study Paul's theology of leadership in 1 Corinthians 1–4, paying particular attention to 1 Corinthians 1:1–9 (as this section is viewed as setting the agenda for the whole letter). This will be done through the lens of social identity theory, which integrates both these old approaches and also adds, for example, psychological, intergroup relations, and self-identification processes. It hopes to discern Pauline leadership patterns in 1 Corinthians 1–4, with the view that its findings could aid further research in the application of Paul's views on leadership in the African Christian leadership context.[120] Identity formation is one of the central themes

---

119. According to Tucker, "social historians focus on Jewish, Greek, or Roman texts and artefacts to establish the context for understanding the setting of the Christ-movement," while the "Social theorists rely on resources from various social-scientific theories to provide insight into the significance of the evidence that is uncovered form both texts and material remains." Tucker, *You Belong to Christ*, 5. More on the differences between these two approaches and whether it is possible to incorporate both of them will be the subject of our enquiry in the following chapter.

120. It is worth noting that the application of Pauline leadership to the African context will be very limited in this study, as this work is primarily a New Testament work, and not a practical theology study. Thus, in chapter 6, this work will, to a very limited extent, try to apply Paul's "in Christ" teachings to the South African context.

of both the Old and the New Testament.[121] The Old Testament was preoccupied with how Israel, the covenant community, was to be separate and different from the nations around them. The same could be said of the New Testament, which calls on Christians to be different from the world in which they live.[122] We can thus say that in both the Old and the New Testaments, identity formation is an important aspect of the biblical faith.

Due to the fact that social identity theory originated in the field of psychological studies, its appropriateness for the field of New Testament studies has been questioned by scholars such as Holmberg who view its application to the New Testament as being secular, reductionist, and imposing foreign categories to the biblical text.[123] These objections will be dealt with and answered in chapter 2 of this research. Due to the objections that have been levelled against the use of methodologies developed from fields other than New Testament studies, and also, due to the historical distance of the Pauline correspondence from our (post)modern context, this research will incorporate a social historical approach in its exegesis of the Greek New Testament text.[124] Careful attention will be paid to "epigraphic, numismatic and literary source material." This will be done with the view that it will place the Pauline correspondence firmly in its historical context.[125] Once the text has been analysed in its historical context, and the historical data established, the second stage of the process will be to interpret that historical evidence via identity theory.

1.7 Aims of the Research Project

This research primarily falls within the field of New Testament studies, and it seeks to integrate Pauline leadership in 1 Corinthians 1–4 with identity

---

121. Baker, "Social Identity," 129.
122. Rom 12:2.
123. Holmberg, *Sociology and New Testament*, 134–9.
124. More differences between the social historical approach and social-scientific approach will be provided in chapter 2. Suffice to say for now that scholars such as Clark and Tucker have argued convincingly about the usefulness of incorporating social historical studies and social theories. Clarke and Tucker, "Social History," 41–56. Social historians provide the evidences that can be used to prove or disprove social theorists' claims.
125. Clarke, *Secular and Christian Leadership*, 6.

formation. The end goal is a blueprint for formation of leaders and their Christian identity in Africa that rests on a solid biblical foundation.

1.8 Motivation for the Study

Four things motivated me to embark on this study. First, my interest was piqued by literature, specifically the article by Antony C. Thiselton, "The Significance of Recent Research on 1 Corinthians for Hermeneutical Appropriation of This Epistle Today," and the book by Robert Jewett, "Paul the Apostle to America: Cultural Trends & Pauline Scholarship." Both these scholars show in their works how we can respect the historical distance of the text but in the same vein appropriate it for the issues facing the twenty-first-century church.

Second, Mangu says that most African scholars "have shied away from the debate on leadership on their continent,"[126] while Nkomo says that most material on leadership is by Western, predominantly American scholars.[127] This research will contribute to leadership studies in terms of African experience of leadership.[128]

Third, I am hoping that this research will help REACH-SA in terms of growing its understanding of contextual leadership.[129]

Fourth, I am currently lecturing on leadership at George Whitefield College. Research of this nature will benefit the students, and it is my hope

---

126. Mangu, "State Reconstruction," 7.

127. Nkomo, "In Search."

128. There are some misconceptions regarding what makes a particular work "African" or an "African contribution." At times, these terms conjure up exotic meanings, in that people expect one to write about things like ancestral worship or life in deep dark villages. This work approaches "African contribution" in an implicit manner. That is, since the author of this study is African with an African worldview, some of these influences might impact how he views certain things. With that being said, a reference in chapter 6 will be made in terms of how the ἐν Χριστῷ terminologies might be a useful tool for the church in South Africa to counter the toxic enviroment of populist political rhetoric, which tends to accentuate people's differences based on the colour of their skin.

129. REACH-SA is traditionally known as the Church of England in South Africa. As a member of this denomination, I am hoping that this dissertation could be used by the denomination as it tries to navigate what it means to be a church of God in the African context. I hope that the insight that this dissertation will offer regarding the significance of Paul's use of the ἐν Χριστῷ terminology will aid REACH-SA's discourse regarding its own identity.

to convey to these students how to be better-informed leaders of the church in South Africa.

1.9 Possible Value of the Research

This research hopes to contribute to the field of New Testament studies in the following ways:

1. To expand social identity theory in the New Testament (as this methodology is still in its infancy stage).
2. To understand leadership in the Corinthian correspondence as it interplays with identity formation.
3. To understand the place and the role of the previous Gentile identities in the Christian faith.
4. To improve the quality of Christian leadership in South Africa.

1.10 Conclusion

A detailed summary and conclusion to this chapter is provided in chapter 6 of this dissertation. For now, it suffices to say that this dissertation will argue that there is an interrelationship between leadership and identity in 1 Corinthians 1–4. In order to argue for that hypothesis, the focus of this chapter was to provide the rationale for the current study, and it sought to place this dissertation within the context of the current studies that have been done on the subject of leadership and identity in Paul. In terms of its approach, this dissertation will argue for a mediating position between two extremes with regard to methodological approach on the subject of leadership and identity. Under leadership approaches, this chapter has observed that there are three approaches that are utilised by scholars, and their strengths and weaknesses were highlighted. These approaches are: (a) the traditional approach, which is also known as the Holtzmann-Sohm hypothesis; (b) the socioscientific approach; and (c) the integrated, group-based approach, which incorporates the findings of both the traditional approach and socioscientific approach. In its methodology, this dissertation follows the integrated group-based approach, with an emphasis on the socioscientific approach, which also incorporates social identity theory. However, this presents a problem for this dissertation as it is in danger of incorporating the same weaknesses that have been observed regarding the socioscientific approach, particularly the fact that it can be anachronistic in nature. In order to avoid the anachronistic tendencies of socioscientific approaches, chapter 2 will now spell out the methodology of this dissertation in greater detail.

CHAPTER 2

Methodology Outline

In the preceding chapter, it was argued that this study would employ a variety of methodological approaches (that is, social scientific, social identity, and historical-critical grammatical approaches) in its analysis of the interrelationship between leadership and identity formation in the Corinthian correspondence. In its use of these different methodologies, the best efforts will be made to avoid fragmentation. The primary aims of this chapter are to outline the key aspects of these methodologies and address the objections that have been made regarding the use of social scientific approach and social identity theory in New Testament studies. This is done with the view of contributing or adding nuance to how social identity theory could be applied to the reading of leadership and identity in the Pauline correspondence of 1 Corinthians 1–4. While a social scientific approach to the biblical text "should always be closely related to the ancient setting,"[1] contextual questions such as the destination, time of composition, and the problems that Paul was dealing with in 1 Corinthians will only be dealt with in the next chapter.

Of the two dominant approaches to leadership in Paul that were mentioned in chapter 1, this chapter will revisit the social scientific approach with the view of identifying where it went wrong, so that those mistakes will be avoided in our use of social identity theory, which is a subcategory of the social scientific approach. This chapter comprises two parts: first, it will broadly consider the social scientific approach, and then it will look at social identity theory and how it could be used in the analysis of the interrelationship between leadership and identity formation in the Corinthian correspondence.

---

1. Esler, *Galatians*, 29.

2.1 What Is a Social Scientific Approach?

There has been a growing interest in the social world of the early Pauline community,[2] as well as the social relations of the apostle Paul.[3] Since the time of the Tübingen school, particularly Baur, scholarship has been interested in Paul's relationship with the other apostles and his co-workers.[4] While there are not many scholars who still follow the same line as Baur, whose focus was on the conflict between the so-called "Pauline Christianity" and "Petrine Christianity,"[5] many scholars are nonetheless interested in Paul's relationships with other apostles and his co-workers.[6] Recent works that focus on these aspects include Malina, who pays careful attention to the relationship between Paul and Timothy.[7] Additionally, there has been research into Paul's relationships with his congregations. Porter and Land state that the catalyst for this has been the "contemporary concerns about power and the use (and

---

2. Still and Horrell provide the most detailed description of this field since the work of Meeks. Still and Horrell, *After the First Urban Christians*; Meeks, *First Urban Christians*.

3. Porter and Land, "Paul and His Social," 1–2.

4. For the influence of the Tübingen school on Pauline scholarship, see Dietrich and Himes, *Legacy of the Tübingen School*. The most relevant essay in this series for the current dissertation is by Himes in his treatment of Möhler's theological development. Himes, "Divinizing the Church," 95–110. Möhler, while a Catholic scholar, was critical of the Roman Catholic ecclesiology. Unlike the Roman Catholic Church, which during his time focused on the church as an institution, and scholars in their treatment of leadership were more interested in institutional apologetics, Möhler emphasised the church as a community of the Holy Spirit, and suggested that the possession of the spiritual gifts took priority over ordination in equipping candidates for priesthood.

5. Porter and Land note that only Goulder follows Baur's reconstruction closely in his analysis of missions in Corinth. Porter and Land, "Paul and His Social," 1; Goulder, *St. Paul versus St. Peter*. However, both Hodge and Horrell demonstrate that Baur's influence still persists among the New Testament scholars to this day. Hodge, *If Sons, Then Heirs*, 6–9; Horrell, "Ethnicisation, Marriage," 440–42. Even though current scholarship may not be using a narrow contrast between the so-called "legalistic Judaism and a universalistic Christianity, where the spirit brings true freedom to all who believe," Horrell and particularly Hodge demonstrate how from the works of E. P. Sanders till recently, not much has changed. Horrell, 440; Hodge, 7–8. Take for example the work of Sanders and the New Perspective on Paul. Even though Sanders argues against the misrepresentation of the first century Judaism, he remains nonetheless guilty of perpetuating the dichotomy that is witnessed in the works of Baur. Similarly, scholars such as Dunn and Wright, even though their terminology is different to that of Baur, nonetheless "continue to replicate" the Hegelian framework category of "universal/ethnic dichotomy." Dunn, *New Perspective on Paul*, 99–120; Wright, *Climax of Covenant Christ*, 13–4; Horrell, 442. See Hodge for more on this. Hodge, *If Sons Then Heirs*, 8.

6. Campbell, *Paul and Creation*, 38–42; Nanos, "What Was at Stake?", 282–320; and "Inter- and Intra-Jewish," 396–407.

7. Malina, *Timothy*. See also Batluck's helpful critical analysis of Malina. Batluck, "Paul, Timothy, and Pauline," 35–56.

abuse) of power";[8] here, scholars are interested in seeing how Paul sought to influence and control his converts.[9] All this interest in Paul and his social relationships, both with his fellow apostles and his congregations, helps us to see that Paul was a "social creature," and it also helps us to "understand better the social dynamics involved in his mission work."[10]

One catalyst of this interest in Paul and his social relationships without a doubt has been a social scientific approach to the Bible,[11] an approach of which social identity theory is a subdiscipline. Thus, before this dissertation defines social identity theory, we will first attempt to provide a broad definition of social scientific approach.[12]

According to Elliott:[13]

> Social scientific criticism of the Bible is that phase of the exegetical task which analyses the social and cultural dimensions of the text and of its environmental context through the utilization of the perspectives, theory, models, and research of the social sciences.

Social scientific scholars of the Bible have the conviction that the:[14]

> New Testament writings manifest a complex interpenetration of society and Gospel, of context and kerygma ("the proclamation

---

8. Porter and Land, "Paul and His Social," 2.

9. Four scholars worth mentioning here are Holmberg, Castelli, Schütz, and Ehrensperger, and all of them are important for this dissertation, since they focus on the Corinthian correspondence, which is also the focus of this dissertation. Holmberg, *Paul and Power*; Castelli, *Imitating Paul*; Schütz, *Paul*; Ehrensperger, *Paul and Dynamics*.

10. Porter and Land, "Paul and His Social," 2.

11. While this approach is not new in biblical scholarship, there remains unresolved issues regarding what constitutes a real social scientific work. For more on this debate, see Horrell who introduces the debate and tries to resolve it by proposing that social scientific approaches need to incorporate literary ethnography, where New Testament studies "immerse themselves into the world constructed and presented by a particular text." Horrell, "Whither Social-Scientific Approaches?", 6–20; 17–18. In part, this is what this study seeks to achieve in chapter 3, in its emphasis on both the literary and historical context of the letter of 1 Corinthians.

12. This dissertation will consider topics such as the advantages of the social scientific approach, differentiation between social scientific approach and sociohistorical approach, and objections against the use of social scientific approach in biblical studies.

13. Elliott, *What Is Social-Scientific Criticism?*, 7.

14. Esler, *First Christians*, 2.

of faith"), and that we cannot hope to understand either without an appropriate methodology for dealing with the social side.

The social scientific approach is viewed as a "component" or "sub-discipline" of the "historical-critical method which investigates biblical texts as meaningful configurations of language intended to communicate between composer and audiences."[15] Three things are studied in this process: (1) "the conditioning factors and intended consequences of the communication process"; (2) "the correlation of the text's linguistic, literary, theological (ideological), and social dimensions"; and (3) "the manner in which this textual communication was both a reflection of and a response to a specific social and cultural context."[16]

Thus, scholars who use the social scientific method are not advocating for a complete disbanding of literary and historical approaches to the Bible.[17] Rather, they find these approaches inadequate in explaining the world of the biblical text. Moreover, some of the scholars who employ literary and historical approaches have shown little awareness of their own biases (since they are left unexplained), and they have been accused of naiveté.[18] The criticism of the old literary and historical approaches is well articulated by Scroggs:[19]

> To some it has seemed that too often the discipline of theology of the New Testament (the history of ideas) operates out of a methodological Docetism, as if believers had minds and spirit unconnected with their individual and corporate bodies. Interest in the sociology of the early Christianity is no attempt to limit reductionistically the reality of Christianity to social dynamics;

---

15. Elliott, *What Is Social-Scientific Criticism?*, 7.
16. Elliott, 7.
17. Esler, *First Christians*, 2; Horrell, "Introduction," 6–7.
18. May, *Body for the Lord*, 12. May makes an excellent point that "one cannot simply interpret historical data in an empirical manner without the use of some form of theory – all data is theory-laden. Those who refuse the use of explicit sociological models are perhaps doomed to use implicit models, for instance, from their own experience of twentieth-century society as a framework for analysis." For more on this, see Horrell's criticism of scholars such as Clarke, Morgan and Barton, and Giddens, who are sceptical about the use of social theories in biblical studies. Horrell, *Social Ethos*, 27–28; Clarke, *Secular and Christian Leadership*; Morgan and Barton, *Biblical Interpretation*; Giddens, *Central Problems*.
19. Scroggs, "Sociological Interpretation," 165–66. See also: Horrell, "Introduction," 6; Barton, "Social-Scientific Criticism," 279.

rather it should be seen as an effort to guard against a reductionism from the other extreme, a limitation of the reality of Christianity to an inner spiritual, or objective-cognitive system. In short, sociology of early Christianity wants to put body and soul together again (emphasis original).

Thus, the social scientific approach seeks to do away with the dichotomy that was previously prevalent in biblical studies that divided soul and body, where the biblical text was removed from its context. Social scientific scholars came to the realisation that "understanding of the New Testament on theological grounds alone is very inadequate."[20] It is a "method of understanding that takes seriously the continuous dialect between ideas and social structures."[21]

2.1.1 Advantages of Social Scientific Approach

There are some advantages associated with the social scientific approach in biblical studies, and two in particular can be mentioned here. First, it helps biblical scholars to ground the ideas of the biblical text in their social world, "remembering that ideas (and perhaps particularly those of a community-builder like Paul) produce, and are (at least to some degree) produced by, a society."[22] Biblical texts, like all other ancient texts, are culturally and socially embedded; thus, in order for one to fully understand these texts, one should not only look at the genre, content, structure and meaning of these texts but careful attention also needs to be paid to the social-cultural aspects of the text. Second, it helps scholars to describe or explicate social relationships that are implicit in the text,[23] making them explicit to us (because the original or intended audience was familiar with them, there was no need for the author to make them explicit). Thus, the social scientific approach helps the (post) modern reader to be sensitive to the "different 'social and cultural locations' separating" us "from ancient authors and their communities."[24]

---

20. Sircar, "Contribution of Sociological Research," 31.

21. Holmberg, *Sociology and New Testament*, 3.

22. May, *Body for the Lord*, 9.

23. Examples at times implicit in the text could include things like "kinship and fictive kinship; patronage and clients; differing modes of economic and social exchange," etc. Elliott, "Social-Scientific Criticism."

24. Elliott, "Social-Scientific Criticism."

2.1.2 The Rise of Social Scientific Approach

There has been a growth and revival[25] of interest among biblical scholars for the use of social scientific approaches.[26] Barton attributes the rise of interest in the social scientific approach to the following factors:[27] (1) The rise of interdisciplinary studies in the late nineteenth century. (2) The influence of scholars such as Nietzsche, Durkheim, Marx, and Freud on other disciplines of studies, particularly their influence regarding the hermeneutics of suspicion. (3) The new insights that have been uncovered through newly-discovered

---

25. According to Horrell, the social scientific approach to the Bible is not a new phenomenon. Horrell, "Introduction," 4–7. See also Elliott, "Social-Scientific Criticism"; the interest in the social world of the Bible is sometimes dated back to the nineteenth century work of Deissmann, Light from the Ancient East. Deissmann was convinced that the early Pauline communities primarily comprised people from the "lower classes" and that there was "the fact of the close inward connection between the gospel and the lower classes." Deismann, *Light from Ancient East*, 403; see also Deismann and Wilson, *St. Paul*. Another early pioneer of this approach is attributed to Judge – "The Social Pattern of the Christian Groups in the First Century"; "Early Christians as a Scholastic Community" – both 1960. Unfortunately, both of Judge's 1960 works went mostly unnoticed by the New Testament scholars. Judge lists three reasons why his 1960 works went unnoticed by the New Testament scholars: (1) The title of the earlier essay "The early Christians as a scholastic community" failed to "indicate some of the main preoccupations of the article – the question of what categories of social description were appropriate to a movement occurring in the Roman world, and the prosopography of the Pauline mission." In this article, Judge questioned the prevailing status quo of the time, that the early Pauline community was composed of the "people who lacked any great stake in society." He demonstrated that the early Pauline community was made up of the mixture of people from different social stratifications, a "socially well-backed movement." These conclusions are clearer in his 1960 essay, "The Social Pattern of the Christian Groups in the First Century," where he draws the conclusion that Christ's early followers were broadly drawn from diverse constituencies, which were representative of household structures of the day, and which were dependent on the leading members. (2) Judge states that the other reason why his 1960 works went unnoticed was because he used a methodology that at that time was foreign to the New Testament scholarship. (3) Some of the classic historians questioned his findings, since they did not perceive the book of Acts as a credible source, as the author of Acts, they thought, sought to present Christianity as a "non-revolutionary" movement. "Social Identity," 201–3. Thus, Judge's work has not received the attention it deserves. His work, however, remains one of the best scholarly works that has done a historical investigation on the social status of Christ's followers. It is this thorough investigation by Judge that has attracted a new crop of scholars who have shown interest in his work; among these are Porter, "How Do We Define?", and Button, "Leadership and Gospel," 8–11.

26. For a survey of biblical scholars' use of social sciences, see Horrell and Elliott. Horrell, "Introduction"; Elliott, "Social-Scientific Criticism." See also Barentsen for a statistical analysis on identity research in social science. Barentsen, *Emerging Leadership*, 37–38. For a defence of the use of the social scientific approach in biblical studies, see Esler who follows along the similar contours of Holmberg, both of whom argue against what they call the ideological fallacy of the literary and historical approaches to the Bible. Esler, *First Christians*, 1–17; Holmberg, *Paul and Power*.

27. Barton, "Social-Scientific Criticism"; Horrell, "Becoming Christian," 278.

manuscripts such as the Qumran texts, which, according to Barton, provided us with "new comparative data for social history and sociological analysis."[28] (4) A change in historiography methodologies in which scholars are not only concerned about the views of the elite but there have been an interest on the views of the masses (history from below).

It is best to understand the social scientific approach in the New Testament as a further "development of historical criticism,"[29] as it also seeks to study the New Testament text in the light of its own first-century Mediterranean context.[30] There is, however, a debate among the New Testament scholars concerning the correlation between the sociohistorical approaches and social scientific approaches. It is important to first distinguish these two approaches before we proceed.

2.1.3 Sociohistorical Approaches versus Social Scientific Approaches

The sociohistorical approaches tend to focus on the descriptive task of the New Testament world,[31] it tends to be diachronic in its emphasis,[32] and it focuses on the questions of dating, "authorship, language, genre, historical backgrounds" of the given text.[33] While the social scientific approach asks similar but different questions, it seeks to interpret the text synchronically,[34] where it looks at the typical patterns of institutions and cultural conditions that would have characterised the early Jesus followers.[35] A social scientific approach mostly incorporates the models of social (or cultural) anthropology,

---

28. Barton, 278.

29. There has been a debate among the New Testament scholars concerning what makes a particular study sociohistorical and what makes other works social scientific. This debate is seen mostly among the scholars who review the work of Meeks. This study will focus on this debate later when it considers the work of Meeks. Meeks, *First Urban Christians*.

30. Barton, Cambridge Companion, 69–70; "Social-Scientific Criticism," 277.

31. For a summary of the differences between sociohistorical studies and social scientific studies, see a helpful table summary by Neyrey, "Social-Scientific Criticism," 180.

32. In short, a diachronic approach considers cause and effect over time. Barton, *Cambridge Companion*, 69; "Social-Scientific Criticism," 277.

33. Barton, "Social-Scientific Criticism," 277.

34. A synchronic approach is cognisant of the fact that "meaning is generated by social actors related to one another by a complex web of culturally-determined social systems and patterns of communication." Barton, 277.

35. Neyrey, "Social-Scientific Criticism," 180; Barton, 277.

sociology, and (to a lesser extent) psychology.[36] Many scholars who use the social scientific approach attempt to incorporate anthropological and sociological academic giants such as Alexis de Tocqueville, Emile Durkheim, Max Weber, Ernst Troeltsch, Mary Douglas, Edward Evans-Pritchard, Clifford Geertz, and Peter Berger as models in their analysis of the Bible.[37] Their "theories regarding social motivations, organization, and consciousness, including the relationship of society to the individual and the individual to the society" provide fertile ground for (post)modern biblical scholars who seek to apply (post)modern sociological categories to the ancient biblical text.[38]

It is, however, worth noting that not all scholars agree about the difference between sociohistorical and social scientific approaches. While scholars such as Neyrey see these approaches as fundamentally different,[39] others such as Horrell and Garret, though acknowledging the differences between the two approaches, maintain that they are mutually inclusive.[40] Horrell states that he follows the scholars who maintain that "there is no sustainable methodological distinction between historical and social science and therefore maintains that the distinction between historical sociology and social history is, or should become, meaningless."[41] The difference among the scholars concerning what makes one's work properly social scientific can be clearly seen when scholars review Meeks's work. Thus, to add clarity, we will now review Meeks's work.

---

36. Barton, *Cambridge Companion*, 67.

37. Esler, *First Christians*, 3. See Esler and Piper where they provide much more information about the contribution of these scholars to the social scientific approach. Esler and Piper, *Lazarus, Mary and Martha*, 15–24.

38. Porter, "How Do We Define?", 9.

39. Neyrey, "Social-Scientific Criticism," 177.

40. Horrell, "Introduction," 17; Garrett, "Sociology of Early Christianity," 90.

41. Horrell, 17. Garrett shares Horrell's sentiments in that both of them do not see how social historians can ignore the insights of the social scientific approach. Garettt, 90. See also Meeks who states this as his approach. Meeks, *First Urban Christians*, 6. Meanwhile, Clarke and Tucker argue that in order for social scientific theories to avoid being accused of anachronism, proper historical work needs to be done in order to ascertain historical data. Only once historical data have been established using historical tools can we use social scientific models to interpret it. Thus, proper social scientific theories also cannot afford to ignore insights from the sociohistorical approach. Clarke and Tucker, "Social History," 41–52.

2.1.3.1 Meeks's Contribution to Social Scientific Approach

As already noted above, the social scientific approach is not a new phenomenon in New Testament exegesis; its popularity for being used in biblical studies is traced to the work of Meeks.[42] One might be surprised, however, to see Meeks's work, The First Urban Christians, described as being social scientific; since throughout the book Meeks describes his task as that of a social historian.[43] In light of this, what justification do we have for categorising 'First Urban Chrsitians' as a social scientific approach text, and is this not a conflation of social historical approach and social scientific approach?[44] First, even though Meeks describes his endeavours as that of a social historian, he nonetheless uses what many would probably describe as a social scientific

---

42. Meeks, First Urban Christians. This work of Meeks is important for this dissertation, because as we analyse it, it will help us to see further what constitutes one's work as social scientific or sociohistorical. It is worth noting that Esler and Piper trace the use of the social scientific approaches in the New Testament to Meeks's ground-breaking work on the gospel of John, "The Man from Heaven in Johannine Sectarianism," which according to Esler "sought to explain a dominant theme in the Fourth Gospel" by using "insights drawn from a sociological work" of Peter Berger and Thomas Luckman. Esler, *Lazarus, Mary and Martha*, 10. There were other works before Meeks's *First Urban Christians*, which are viewed as classic works, which sought to study the social world of Jesus's followers, works by scholars such as Theissen's pioneering work on the Palestinian social setting of the Jesus movement (his 1974 work, which was translated into English in 1978 as: *The First Followers of Jesus*), and Gager's *Kingdom and Community*. Due to the fact that there are other works that precede Meeks's work, it is best to view Meeks as popularising the use of social scientific approach to Pauline studies. Meeks, *First Urban Christians*. Popularising in this instance should not be viewed as watering down the previous studies. In the words of Horrell, Meeks's 1983 *First Urban Christians* is a "landmark study," that represents "a mature flourishing" of the innovative studies of the initial period. Horrell, "Whither Social-Scientific Approaches?", 6.

43. Meeks, *First Urban Christians*, 2.

44. As stated, these approaches are sometimes paired against each other. For example, Malina, while seeing similarity between these two approaches, nonetheless sees them as fundamentally different (sentiments that are also shared by Neyrey). Malina, "Review," 346; Neyrey, "Social-Scientific Criticism," 177. Quoting Barraclough, Malina says that there are two differences between social historical approach and social scientific approach. The first is that the social historical approach's "conceptualization tends to be implicit, arbitrary, and unsystematic," whereas social scientific approach is "explicit and systematic." Barraclough, *Main Trends in History*; Malina, 346. In his later works, Malina sees the other difference being to use models-based approaches that are accepted by the scholars in the field of social science studies. Malina, *Social World of Jesus*, 3. While social historians are less concerned with models-based approaches, they tend to focus more on the "social and historical background and practices of the early" Jesus followers. Mbevi, "Paul and Ethnicity," 12. It is worth noting that Malina sees Meeks's *First Urban Christians* as social historical rather than social scientific; he sees Meeks's conceptualization as "implicit, arbitrary, and unsystematic." Malina, "Review," 347.

approach.[45] He writes "In writing social history ... we cannot afford to ignore the theories that guide social scientists."[46] Meeks goes on to say that his use of a social scientific approach is "suggestive, rather than generative in the manner of experimental science."[47] By this statement, he rejects the notion that an investigation into the life of the early followers of Jesus will undertake "to discover or validate laws about human behaviour in general."[48] He sees his undertaking as "analogous to Clifford Geertz's description of social anthropologist's task as an ethnographer, a describer of culture."[49] He goes on to say: "the description is interpretative ... For that purpose, theory is necessary both to construct interpretation and to criticize construction, but it must 'stay rather closer to the ground than tends to be the case in sciences more able to give themselves over to imaginative abstraction.'"[50] Thus, Meeks uses a social scientific approach in an "eclectic" way.[51] He takes the "theory piecemeal, as needed, where it fits."

The impact of Meeks's work must not be underestimated. In fact, scholars such as Horrell, Oakes, Longenecker, Adams, Still, Lawrence, and Martin have come out in defence of Meeks,[52] with each taking a chapter from Meeks and developing it, adding further nuances to Meeks's contribution in the light of the recent scholarship developments since 1983. Ultimately, these scholars contend that Meeks's work has "stood the test of time." It is, however, important to note that since Meeks uses social scientific approach in an "eclectic and piece-meal" fashion that does open him up to criticism.[53]

---

45. A defence of Meeks's work as social scientific study, is provided by Horrell, where he defends Meeks's use of social scientific approach in the light of the criticism of Malina. Horrell, "Whither Social-Scientific Approaches?," 6–20; Malina, *Social World of Jesus*.

46. Meeks, *First Urban Christians*, 5.

47. Meeks, 5–6.

48. Meeks, 6.

49. Meeks – by comparing his work to that of a social anthropologist – has moved beyond the scope of a social historian to the field of social sciences. Meeks, *First Urban Christians*, 6.

50. Meeks, 6.

51. Meeks, 6.

52. Horrell, "Whither Social-Scientific Approaches?"; Oakes, "Constructing Poverty Scales"; Longenecker, "Exposing Economic Middle"; Adams, "First-Century Models"; Still, "Organizational Structures"; Lawrence, "Ritual and First Urban"; Martin, "Patterns of Belief."

53. Meeks, *First Urban Christians*.

The people who have been very critical of Meeks's work have been the members of the "context group";[54] Elliott, Malina, and Pilch are the main proponents of the "context group,"[55] with Elliott and Malina coming out particularly strongly against Meeks. Elliott's major criticism of Meeks's work is that it suffers from the lack of "methodological clarity," due to its incorporation of various methodologies.[56] Elliott is of the view that nothing can be "gained by such methodological obfuscation other than the possible appeasement of those naive about their own social premises and unwilling to acknowledge the role theory plays in any authentic scientific undertaking."[57]

This criticism highlights the growing schism that continues among the scholars who employ social scientific approaches. Neyrey has observed that two tendencies emerged since the 1970s in the use of the social scientific approach to the Bible.[58] On the one hand, a group of scholars such as Malina, Elliott, and himself who, in their use of social scientific approaches, focus on formally applying model-based social scientific theories in their interpretation, testing, and (re)constructing of the biblical text.[59] On the other hand, one finds a group of scholars who are considered to be sociohistorical since they do not clarify their underlying theory and method sufficiently for them to be understood, evaluated, and emulated.[60]

---

54. See Pilch and Dvorak about the history of the context group. Pilch, "Honoree," 1–4; Dvorak, "John H. Elliott's Social-Scientific," 252–53.

55. Elliott, "Review"; Malina, "Review"; Pilch, "Rezension von: Meeks."

56. Elliot, 332.

57. Elliott, 332.

58. Neyrey, "Social-Scientific Criticism," 177–78. See also Garret and Harland who make a similar point. Garret, "Sociology of Early Christianity," 90–92; Harland, *Dynamics of Identity*, 3–5.

59. Malina, "Early Christian Groups"; Social *World of Jesus*; Elliott, "Review"; *What Is Social-Scientific Criticism?*; "Social-Scientific Criticism;" Neyrey, "Social-Scientific Criticism."

60. Elliott, "Review," 330. This ongoing debate about the difference between these two methodological approaches in New Testament scholarship can be clearly seen in recent exchanges between Esler and Horrell, and also Esler where he responds to Horrell. Esler, *Galatians*, 253–60; Horrell, "No Longer Jew or Greek," 83–105; Esler, "Jesus and Reduction." While this study will not offer a full review of their debate, it will highlight the major area of differences. The issue began when Esler reviewed Horrell's work, *Social Ethos*. Esler, *Galatians*, 253–60. In his review, Esler focused his attention "on the theoretical issues" which form Part I of Horrell's book, where he discusses the methodological issues. Esler, 255. Esler first takes issue with how some of the New Testament scholars use the term "models" loosely. He says: "Many practitioners of social scientific interpretation use the word 'model' as a fairly general expression for the various ideas and perspectives they employ in their exegesis." Esler, 254. While he is aware that "modelling is unavoidable," he prefers that scholars should make explicit

Meeks's work, however, helps us to see the varying degrees in which scholars incorporate other models in their analysis of the biblical text. Holmberg views Meeks's work as a "mediating position" of those who incorporate the combination of sociohistorical and social scientific approach in their work. This is the direction that this dissertation will take.[61] Horrell, commenting on Meeks's work, says that this is a work of a "moderate functionalism,"[62] where the emphasis of the question to be asked is how the early Jesus movement worked, as compared to scholars who are preoccupied with which model one should use to analyse the New Testament data. This dissertation does not simply follow the "context group" because it seems fraught with problems and it could invite accusations of anachronism. Pilch says that the "context group" "adopts models from the social sciences and uses them both as tools for gathering data sets and interpreting data sets."[63] While agreeing with Pilch on this point, this dissertation does not agree entirely with what he says next, that is, that "they draw on Mediterranean 'informants' (e.g. Seneca) to provide information that might fill in gaps in biblical materials" (emphasis added). This researcher is of the view that there is a serious danger in overreliance on models, especially when they are used to fill in the gaps that exist in the data that cannot be verified using historical method.[64] This is considered one of the problems with the position of the scholars who belong to the context group. Filling in the gaps has proven costly for scholars such as Holmberg,[65] whose work has been judged by scholars such as Furnish and Judge as being anachronistic.[66]

This dissertation, in dealing with the accusation that the social scientific approach to the Bible is anachronistic, will look at the work of Holmberg as

---

use of models in their approach rather than use "implicit modelling." Esler, 255. Thus, Esler's concern about a social scientific approach is on the explicit models that scholars employ. On the other hand, Horrell is "unsympathetic to the use of models" in the interpretation of the biblical text. Even though he is interested in the social realities behind the text, he nonetheless thinks that the models could be distortive. Horrell, *Social Ethos*.

61. Holmberg, "Methods of Historical Reconstruction," 267–68.

62. Horrell, "Whither Social-Scientific Approaches?", 7.

63. Pilch, "Honoree," 1.

64. For more on this, see Horrell's detailed appraisal of the "context group." Horrell, "Introduction," 12–15.

65. Holmberg, *Paul and Power*. It is worth noting though that his work predates the formation of the context group. His views, however, are representative of this group.

66. Furnish, "Jesus-Paul Debate"; Judge, "Social Identity."

a case study and evaluate where he went wrong, and see how those mistakes can be avoided in this research. This is done with the view that we can gain valuable insights from his methodological approach.

2.2 Criticism against the Use of Social Scientific Approaches in Biblical Studies

A number of criticisms have been levelled against the use of social scientific approaches in the biblical studies.

2.2.1 The Deistic Nature of Social Scientific Approaches

The first criticism against the use of social scientific approaches to biblical studies is that it has a tendency of being, at best, deistic by nature, in its approach everything is interpreted as "social phenomena" and divine interference in human affairs is muted.[67] This seems to go against what the Bible authors believed about their own writings; they believed that the biblical texts that they were writing were the very words of God, and that in the writing process they were carried along by the Holy Spirit.[68] Moreover, they believed that the words they wrote had the power to change humanity, and they also believed that "God had supernaturally changed" them.[69] Therefore, any model which seeks to eliminate God's interferences in the biblical texts seems to be an imposition upon the reference frame of these texts, and goes against the authorial intent. However, the trend is changing, and recently scholars show awareness of the dangers of imposing foreign worldviews onto the biblical text. There is also a growing strand of scholars who acknowledge authors' notions regarding divine interference in the biblical world.[70]

---

67. Barentsen, *Emerging Leadership*, 42; Berding, "Hermeneutical Framework," 13. Berding's article, which assesses whether evangelical scholarship should use social scientific approach, has raised this as one of the major issues related to the use of this approach, especially by the New Testament scholars with evangelical convictions, such as myself. As a reformed evangelical Anglican and African I believe that ultimately "all scripture is God-breathed," and has transcultural applications. I have difficulty with any model which "eliminates the supernatural work of God." 2 Tim 3:16–17; cf. Berding, 13. However, I also believe that in order to understand the meaning of any given text properly, it needs to be looked at in the light of its social context.

68. 2 Tim 3:16–17; cf. 2 Pet 1:20–21.

69. Berding, "Hermeneutical Framework," 14; cf. Heb 4:12–13.

70. Barentsen, *Emerging Leadership*, 42.

2.2.2 Social Scientific Approaches as Foreign to Biblical Studies

The second criticism or challenge facing social scientific approach is the nature of the approach itself, which is essentially foreign to the Bible as a historical text. Barentsen notes that:

> Modern social science methods have been developed through the collection of data through quantitative and statistical research, which cannot be directly applied to historical texts. NT historical data often are fragmented, presented from one perspective only, and with very limited resources to carry out a cross-check with other locations or times.[71]

This difficulty is also well-articulated by Tidball in the following observation about the impact of social scientific models on the biblical text:

> Historical sociology is a branch of the discipline that has special difficulties all of its own. Sociologists can usually support their theories by devising some way of testing them such as through surveys, interviews or participant observation. But for obvious reasons the members of a bygone age are not available to be investigated in this way! The researcher therefore will inevitably be less assured than they would be in contemporary sociology.[72]

This problem is compounded even more when it comes to social identity theory which was developed in the field of behavioural psychology that often gains insights through the "direct interrogation of the subjects."[73] As Tidball has observed, the problem with this is that scholars do not have access to the original audience to whom Paul was writing, nor do they have "direct personal contact" with Paul himself, where we can observe him in terms of his speech, behaviour, and body language.[74] These are ingredients that

---

71. Barentsen, 42. See the example of this below under the minimal studies section, where scholars such as Tajfel et al. carried out laboratory tests to verify their theories. This is difficult to reproduce for the biblical text as we do not have direct access to the apostle Paul and his community; we have only a text written by Paul from his own perspective to work with. Tajfel et al., "Social Categorization."

72. Tidball, *Introduction to Sociology*, 21.

73. Clarke and Tucker, "Social History," 42.

74. Tidball, Introduction *to Sociology*, 21.

are necessarily to be investigated in order to conduct a proper behavioural physiological analysis. It thus seems that, in order to avoid reductionism and anachronism, a social historical analysis is important. Hence, this dissertation argues that social identity theory needs a social historical approach.[75] Clarke and Tucker contend that these theories are useful when they are merged together:[76] "Social theory provides a framework for interpreting the evidence that the historian finds, while social historians provide the evidence needed to substantiate purported theoretical claims."[77] This argument is further articulated by Africa who argues strongly for the combination of historical research and psychological process when he says:

> History is both made and written by men, and in either case, no explanation is adequate which does not include psychology ... Much about antiquity will remain unknowable to any historical approach, and psychohistory must admit the fragile nature of the source for ancient history. Whether or not Freudian concepts are employed, historians will continue to make psychological judgments about the Greeks and Romans.[78]

Thus, it seems paramount that a social historical approach needs to be incorporated in any social identity approach to the ancient text. This idea also finds support from social psychologist Henri Tajfel, whose methodology (social identity theory) this dissertation will use, when he says: "Attempts at

---

75. This approach to social identity theory is not new. For example, even though Finney does not identify his methodology as a combination of social identity theory and social historical analysis, he nonetheless incorporates social historical approach in his analysis. The result is that he comes to a similar conclusion as Winter. Finney, *Honour and Conflict*, 276–87; Winter, *After Paul Left Corinth*. Finney uses social identity theory to examine the role of honour in identity formation of the Corinthian ἐκκλησία. Finney, *Honour and Conflict*. He pays careful attention to the conflict surrounding the Lord's Table in 1 Cor 11:17–34. He concludes that the conflict was a result of different people trying to pursue honour by "outdoing each other in quantity and quality of the food and drink they were bringing." Finney, "Conflict in Corinth," 280; cf. Tucker and Baker, "Introduction," 5. According to Finney, Paul's solution to this problem was to emphasise the cross of Christ as the basis on which the Corinthians could derive their identity. Finney, 284–87. Interestingly, Finney draws this conclusion by relying mostly on the epigraphical, linguistic, and historical evidences. This is essentially the same thing that Winter does, whose work is described as social historical approach, as he relies more on the archaeological epigraphical, historical, and linguistic analysis of the text. Winter, After *Paul Left Corinth*, xi–viv.

76. Clarke and Tucker, "Social History," 41–58.

77. Tucker and Baker, "Introduction," 2.

78. Africa, "Psychohistory, Ancient History, and Freud" 26.

applications of social psychological generalizations to any concrete social context are bound to fail unless they are made against the background of a detailed social, cultural, economic and historical analysis."[79]

2.2.3 Social Scientific Approaches and Meaning of Biblical Texts

One of the strongest points of contention regarding the use of social scientific approaches in biblical studies is the location of the meaning of the given text. Scholars such as Malina and Elliott have contended that meaning is located purely in the social context of the given text, and they do not focus on the translation and grammatical analysis.[80] Linked with this, Malina rejects the "propositional model of language which deals with texts at the word and sentence level."[81] Malina says that, "meanings, past and present, that are realized in language, are in fact ultimately rooted in a social system."[82] Elsewhere he says that, "again, where do the meanings come from? The answer is the social system."[83] Some aspects need to be observed in these statements. First, Malina refers to "meanings" of the text rather than "meaning." This suggests that the meaning of a text is what an interpreter makes it to be. Second, it assumes that meaning is grounded purely on social constructs, but this tends to overlook religious aspects regarding meaning. This study is of the view that meaning cannot be based solely on social context, even though a social context helps us understand the text better. This researcher is of the view that exegesis is necessary in order to understand the meaning of a particular text, contrary to what Malina believes when he says: "people within the same system do not need interpretation: they can usually understand quite directly, if not intuitively."[84]

2.2.4 The Cultural Distance of the Ancient Text

The fourth criticism against the social-sciences has been the tendency to be reductionist, and treat the ancient Mediterranean as a homogeneous entity

---

79. Tajfel, *Differentiation between Social Groups*, 2.
80. Elliott, *What Is Social-Scientific Criticism?*, 49.
81. Berding, "Hermeneutical Framework," 10.
82. Malina, *New Testament World*, 172.
83. Malina, *Christian Origins*, 1.
84. Malina, 176.

without discerning the differences between village life and city life.[85] The ancient Mediterranean context was not a cultural monochrome, it "involved itself in sophisticated conventions and highly complex relationships."[86]

Social scientific approaches have also been criticised for their tendency to assume that the cultural setting of the (post)modern Mediterranean world is similar to that of the first century context; this comes up very strongly in the work of Malina and also Holmberg.[87] But the defenders of the social scientific approach have hit back against this criticism, and pointed out that it claims too much. Keay says that "if societies are incomprehensible to each other, then nothing could be known of ancient society, for the ancient world would be wholly other."[88] This researcher however, is of the view that it is possible to bridge the gap between the (post)modern world and an ancient text, as long as one places more emphasis on the epigraphic evidence that supports any given model about life in the Mediterranean context.[89] This dissertation will be the first one to admit that cross-cultural applicability of the social scientific approach has been indeed problematic, and has caused serious problems for scholars such as Holmberg.[90] It is to his work that we now turn.

2.2.5 Social Scientific Approaches as Anachronistic – Bengt Holmberg as Example

Holmberg's 1978 book, Paul and Power: The Structure of Authority in the Primitive Church as Reflected in the Pauline Epistles, has been used by scholars such as Judge, Clarke, and Esler as an example of the social scientific approach as being anachronistic and reductionist.[91] In Holmberg's work, based on his PhD dissertation at Lund University, Sweden, he limits his investigation

---

85. Berding, "Hermeneutical Framework," 15.
86. Winter, *After Paul Left Corinth*, xii.
87. Malina, *New Testament World*; Holmberg, *Paul and Power*. Bruce highlights this point in his review of Malina's 1983 work. Bruce, "Review of New Testament," 112. Similar sentiments are also shared by Berding. Berding, "Hermeneutical Framework," 15.
88. Keay, "Paul the Spiritual Guide," 119.
89. Bruce, "Review of New Testament," 112; cf. Berding, "Hermeneutical Framework," 15.
90. Holmberg, *Paul and Power*.
91. Judge, "Social Identity"; Clarke, *Secular and Christian Leadership*; Esler, "Socio-Redaction Criticism," 138–39.

to "the genuine Pauline epistles" such as Romans, 1 and 2 Corinthians, Galatians, Philippians, 1 Thessalonians and Philemon.[92]

In many ways, Holmberg's work is a reaction to the denominational biases that dominated the traditional approach, which we have already considered in the previous chapter.[93] This is mostly evident toward the end of the book, where Holmberg refers to the "fallacy of idealism."[94] Here Holmberg critiques the giants of New Testament studies, and his major contention is that they have a tendency of interpreting Paul's works as if they are purely theological works, "where the historical phenomena are often interpreted as being directly formed by underlying theological structures."[95] His work is not primarily a theological study; rather he is interested in the distribution of power and exercise of authority[96] in the early Pauline primitive church.[97] In his interpretation or analysis of the historical data, Holmberg employs Max Weber's classical sociology theory.[98]

Holmberg's book consists of two parts; in the first part (pages 9–121), he uses historical criticism methods to look at the "distribution of power in the Primitive church."[99] This is the noncontroversial part of the book since in many ways it repeats historical data accepted by most scholars. In this section, the author focuses on the relationship between the leaders of the "Jewish Christian church in Jerusalem and the leaders of the Gentile Christian church (especially Paul)." He also focuses on the relationship that existed in the Pauline region of the church; the relationship between Paul and his co-worker and between the churches themselves.[100] The questionable findings of

---

92. Holmberg, *Paul and Power*, 3–4.

93. Holmberg, 1.

94. Holmberg, 201. Section 1.2.1.2 has mentioned and dealt with the scholars who have been on the receiving end of Holmberg's criticism, when he deals with what he calls fallacy of idealism. This dissertation in this section will now continue with highlighting further reasons why Holmberg is critical of their views.

95. Holmberg, 201.

96. By "authority," Holmberg means "social relations of asymmetric power distribution considered legitimate by participating actors." Holmberg, *Paul and Power*, 3.

97. Holmberg, 3.

98. Holmberg focuses on the following works of Weber: "Wirtschaft und Gesellschaft," and the English translation "Economy and Society" edited by Roth and Wittich in his analysis concerning the dynamics of power in Paul. Holmberg, 125–36.

99. Holmberg, 4.

100. Holmberg, 6.

the first part of the book include some of his conclusions about the priority of the Jerusalem church. For example, on page 50, he states that "Paul saw the 'Word of God' as proceeding from the Jerusalem church to him." He goes on to say that the Jerusalem church was "the divinely chosen centre for doctrinal decision." He also concludes in his exegesis of 1 Corinthians 15:3–11 that Paul saw himself as an inferior apostle. But this seems to fly in the face of what Paul says in Galatians 1:11, where Paul insists that the gospel he preached is not of human origin. While it is true that Paul saw himself as "the least of the apostles, unworthy to be called an apostle," the question needs to be asked: how much of this statement functions as a rhetorical device? Did Paul actually see himself as inferior to the other apostles in the literal sense of the word? In the light of 1 Corinthians 3:5, it would seem that 1 Corinthians 15:9 should be viewed as a rhetorical device, and not as Paul actually saying that he is inferior to the other apostles.

In the second part of the book (pages 123–204), Holmberg employs a sociological methodology to the New Testament to interpret the historical data gathered in the first part, in an attempt to unlock or reveal "aspects of the Primitive Church which would otherwise have remained unknown."[101] But his conclusions have received major criticism from most scholars, with Judge being the main detractor. Judge in his criticism of Holmberg does a word play, where he takes Holmberg's phrase "idealistic fallacy" (where one interprets historical phenomena as if they were just pure theological ideas) and turns it against Holmberg and calls his "enterprise 'sociological fallacy'"[102] Judge questions the usefulness of a social scientific approach in its entirety and he thinks that the cons outweigh the pros. Judge is of the view that unless scholars do painstaking field work of the "social facts of life characteristic of the world to which the New Testament belongs . . . the importation of social models that have been defined in terms of other cultures is methodologically no improvement on the 'idealistic fallacy' [which was coined by Holmberg, in *Paul and Power*]. We may fairly call it the 'sociological fallacy.'"[103]

---

101. Holmberg, 6.
102. Judge, "Social Identity," 209.
103. Judge, 210. Esler observes that Judge makes three assumptions in this criticism: (1) that "sociological models must be historically tested or 'verified' before they can be applied"; (2) that "sociological models are 'defined' with respect to particular cultures" and, therefore cannot be "applied to first-century society"; and (3) that it is possible to carry out "historical field work"

The reason that Judge is so harsh on Holmberg is that in his opinion Holmberg misunderstood the meaning of receiving and giving money in the Greco-Roman world. Holmberg interpreted the parts about giving in 1 Corinthians in terms of a "dependents and followers," instead of the "patronage" system.[104] He failed to do "painstaking field work," which would have shown him that during Paul's day, a patronage system prevailed. Holmberg admits that indeed this was a mistake on his part.[105] He says: "Judge was right about the lack of 'fieldwork' on my part. At that time, I knew almost nothing about patronage in ancient Mediterranean cultures, nor its financial implications."[106] However, as Holmberg correctly points out, this is not a "sociological fallacy," as Judge supposes.[107] Rather, it was him imposing a European-North American worldview onto the biblical text. But, this does not mean that we now have to throw out the baby with the bath water. Further refining is necessary, and Holmberg's mistake should serve as a warning to all. Holmberg in his later work has done the painstaking fieldwork that Judge lambasted him about and demonstrated that indeed in the early Pauline community, there were instances where the money moved from the "lower" to the "greater" (a service of προπέμπεσθαι "to be equipped for travel").[108] This is a service where the local Pauline community would support travelling missionaries, and for Holmberg this is the evidence that "apostolic authority is manifested also by the flow of money and support from the believers."[109]

Holmberg's work highlights the real danger of the social scientific approach. It is important that whatever model one uses, one is also aware of the cultural difference between the (post)modern and Ancient Mediterranean

---

as purely objective enterprise without influence from one's own worldview and preconceived implicit models. Esler, "Socio-Redaction," 139. Esler notes that the first two assumptions by Judge actually shows that he completely misunderstood social sciences, especially models, as he treats them as "something akin to social laws," while they are just "mental constructs" and "research tools." Esler, 140. The third assumption reveals how Judge is blind to his preconceived historical presupposition in his analysis of the historical data. All researchers look at historical data through their own worldviews. Social scientific models are just one of the ways that scholars have used to account for their biases.

104. Judge, "Social Identity," 210.
105. Holmberg, "Methods of Historical Reconstruction," 256.
106. Holmberg, 256.
107. Holmberg, 256.
108. Holmberg, 256–59.
109. Holmberg, 257.

world. In the West in particular, the dominant culture is individualism, while epigraphic evidence shows that in the Ancient Mediterranean world, the dominant culture was collectivism.[110]

It thus seems that sociohistorical information needs to play a more prominent role than usual in the social scientific interpretation of the Bible if one is to avoid the mistake that Holmberg made in 1978. Even though this study will employ social identity theory as a model of analysis, it will nonetheless place more emphasis on sociohistorical analysis, and careful attention will be paid to Pauline leadership and identity in the light of other available ancient materials.[111]

---

110. Barentsen, *Emerging Leadership*, 42–43. In the individualistic society, "Individuals decide for themselves, and will compete and sacrifice for personal goals" while in the collectivist society, individuals "automatically obey ingroup authority, and are willing to sacrifice (themselves) to maintain ingroup integrity even at personal costs." Barentsen, 43. This, however, needs to be put in balance so that we do not place too much emphasis on the collective to the point where the individual is completely lost. This point of criticism has been levelled against Malina by Batluck. Batluck, "Paul, Timothy, and Pauline"; Malina, *Timothy*. Malina throughout the book describes Paul and Timothy as collectivist people who lived in a collectivist society, and he describes collectivists as an "opposite pole of individualism . . . First-century persons like Timothy and Paul and Jesus were collectivistic personalities. . . . A collectivistic personality is one who needs other persons to know who he or she is. Every person is embedded in another, in a chain of embeddedness [sic], in which the test of interrelatedness is crucial to self-understanding. A person's focus is not on himself . . ., but on the demands and expectations of others, who can grant or withhold acceptance and reputation. In other words, individuals do not act independently. In a collectivistic world, to act independently would make no sense." Malina, *Timothy*, 3–4. Malina's book *Timothy* correctly challenges the imposing of our (post) modern-day individual worldview onto the text. The problem with Malina's book, however, is that it is too extremist in its presentation of individualism and collectivism, to the point where the individual is completely lost in the community. Collectivism does not cater for all that Paul has to say in his letters. Batluck correctly argues for the "continuum of corporeality," where the individual is continuously influenced by the complex mixture of the individualistic thinking and collectivists thinking; Paul himself embodied this in his leadership. Batluck, "Paul, Timothy, and Pauline," 56. At one point in 1 Cor 3, Paul addressing the issue of factionalism in the congregation, asks a question, "what then is Apollos? What is Paul? Servants through whom you believed, as the Lord assigned to each." This verse supports the collectivism understanding, but in the same chapter Paul also says: "According to the grace of God given to me, like a skilled master builder I laid a foundation" (1 Cor 3:10, see also verses 6, 12–15). Here Paul elevates what he did as an individual, which seems to support individualistic thinking. Moreover, when Paul talks about judgment in verses 12–15, people will account as individuals. Thus, it is important when analysing Paul, that one is careful not to do a blanket contrast between individualism and collectivism, without sensitivity to the nuance of his argument.

111. This is one of the advantages of social-identity theory, for it helps a scholar "to analyse the collective group identity of the ancient Mediterranean world, but also assists (particularly) the Western scholar in properly accounting for his own individualistic perspective." Barentsen, *Emerging Leadership*, 43.

Up until this point, this study has been engaging the debate regarding the appropriateness of using social-scientific approaches in New Testament study. It has highlighted the anachronistic tendencies by some scholar who have engaged the topic of leadership in 1 Corinthians using these methodologies. While the danger of anachronism is real, this researcher is of the view that if one incorporates sociohistorical studies, one might circumvent that danger. However, before outlining how that will be done in relation to social identity theory, social identity theory warrants discussion.

2.3 Social Identity Theory[112]

The phrase "social identity" is often used in everyday English, but in the field of social sciences, it also functions as technical jargon.[113] It has been pointed out above that in considering a social-scientific approach, this study has given more attention to disciplines such as anthropology and sociology. Social identity theory represents a branch within the broader social-scientific field. This sub-discipline was largely brought to prominence by Henri Tajfel – a social psychologist – and is in its infancy with regard to application to biblical studies.

The social identity approach is a psychological meta-theory that incorporates the "principles and assumptions articulated within social identity and self-categorisation theories."[114] In New Testament studies, social identity theory represents an interpretative tool that belongs under the umbrella of

---

112. The following section of this study is indebted mostly to three scholars who have used social identity theory in their research, Esler, Barentsen, and Tucker. Esler, *Conflict and Identity*; Barentsen, *Emerging Leadership*; Tucker, *You Belong to Christ*; *Remain in Your Calling*. All three have demonstrated how social identity theory could be beneficial for the study of the New Testament. Barentsen's work is particularly helpful for this study as his book deals with the same subject matter of leadership and identity in the Pauline corpus. There are, however, areas where his study falls short, particularly around the exegesis of the Pauline text (there is scant exegesis in Barentsen's work). It is also worth noting here that this section of the dissertation will not consider the objection or the criticism that has been made against the use of social identity theory in the biblical studies, as most of the criticism that has been levelled against the social-scientific approach also applies here and has been dealt with above. Rather, this section will try to provide a condensed analysis of social identity theory and state how it will be used in this dissertation.

113. Esler, "Jesus and Reduction," 327.

114. Haslam, *Psychology in Organizations*, 281. Social identity and social categorisation theories will be explained below.

social-scientific approaches, where it is related to rhetorical, narrative, and literary approaches. Barentsen notes that social identity theorists study the "broad range of social, historical, and literary features of the biblical text."[115] Baker notes that social identity theory study of the biblical text is not a new phenomenon;[116] application of the basic principles of social identity theory can be seen in the work of Judge in 1980.[117] Most scholars, however, consider Philip Esler to be the pioneer of social identity theory in biblical studies. Esler popularised social identity theory in his work titled *Community and Gospel in Luke-Acts: The Social and Political Motivations of Lucan Theology,*"[118] as well as in his works on Galatians, Romans, and John.[119] Other scholars who have employed social identity theory are: Hakola, Roitto, Shkul, Tucker, Backer, and Barentsen, to name just a few.[120]

In outlining the development of social identity theory, we will first briefly look at the field of social psychology in the 1960s before the arrival of Tajfel, in order to demonstrate the impact of Henri Tajfel's work in this field. This dissertation will also look at the life and the works of Henri Tajfel himself, the father of social identity theory. The life of Tajfel is significant in our analysis of social identity theory, as it will give us the context in which his interest developed and how his life shaped his observations - partciuclarly with regard to how he perceived inter-group relationships.[121]

---

115. Barentsen, *Emerging Leadership*, 41.

116. Baker, "Social Identity," 129.

117. Judge, however, did not use the term "social identity theory," since his interest was rather in the social setting of the early Pauline community. Baker might perhaps be conflating social-scientific approaches with social identity theory. Judge, "Social Identity." While the two are similar and in biblical studies social identity theory can be categorised with the former, there is nonetheless a clear distinction between the two.

118. Esler, *Community and Gospel*.

119. Galatians ("Group Boundaries and Intergroup Conflict in Galatians" and *Galatians*), Romans (*Conflict*), and John (*Lazarus, Mary and Martha*), co-authored by Piper.

120. Hakola, "Burden of Ambiguity"; "Friendly Pharisees"; "Social Identity"; Roitto, *Behaving as Christ-Believers*; Shkul, *Reading Ephesians*; Tucker, *You Belong to Christ*; and *Remain in Your Calling*; and Tucker and Baker's edited work, *T&T Clark Handbook*; Baker, "Identity, Memory"; "Early Christian Identity Formation"; and Barentsen, *Emerging Leadership*.

121. Baker, "Social Identity," 130; Turner, "Henri Tajfel," 2–3; and Esler, "Outline of Social Identity", 13.

2.3.1 The Field of Social Psychology during the 1960s

At the turn of the twentieth century, two disciplines, experimental psychology, and sociology, were combined to create a new discipline called "social psychology." This new discipline sought to explain the "individual-group dynamic in the psychology of human social interaction."[122] This, however, proved to be more difficult to achieve than it was originally thought. Farr illustrated the failure of the merger of these two disciplines. He observed that two major textbooks that were written during this period continued with their previous disciplines without taking into consideration the merger of the two fields of study.[123] Farr used as an example the textbook by McDougall,[124] showing that this textbook was essentially a psychological textbook, while on the other hand, Ross wrote what "was essentially a sociology textbook."[125] Moreover, as Barentsen notes, during this time the field of social psychology was also facing major criticism for its lack of "methodological adequacy, testing procedures, and the societal applicability of social psychology."[126]

The main issue here was that the field, in its study of groups, could not agree on the dynamics of the group. This became evident in the debate between William McDougall and Floyd Allport. McDougall "argued for the existence of a 'group mind,'" since he believed that "society has a mental life which is more than the mere sum of the mental lives of its units; and a complete knowledge of the units, if and in so far as they could be known as isolated units, would not enable us to deduce the nature of the life of the whole."[127] This view was completely opposite to the views of other scholars, particularly Allport, who treated groups as a "collection of individuals."[128] It seemed, however, that Allport won the debate as his views became the dominant approach during the 1960s and early 1970s. The work of Floyd Allport was still influential in academic institutions during the time of Henri Tajfel.[129]

---

122. Keay, "Paul the Spiritual Guide," 87.
123. Farr, "Theoretical Cohesion," 193–95.
124. McDougall, *Introduction to Social Psychology*.
125. Cf. Keay, "Paul the Spiritual Guide," 87.
126. Barentsen, *Emerging Leadership*, 33.
127. McDougall, *Group Mind*, 7. See also Keay, "Paul the Spiritual Guide," 87.
128. Barentsen, *Emerging Leadership*, 33.
129. Allport was considered a founder of experimental social psychology. Katz, *Social Psychology of Organizations*, 351–53.

Allport was of the view that "there is no psychology of groups which is not essentially and entirely a psychology of individuals."[130] Allport's approach was highly individualistic, which reflected more than anything the culture of the United States of America. For him, groups dissolved into individuals that they represented, thus group psychology was reduced to be the psychology of individuals.[131]

The result was that there was a general lack of testing on the impact that group membership had on the actions of an individual who was a member of a particular group. Scholars mostly answered questions regarding why people joined or stayed in groups in individualistic terms. The researchers argued that people joined and stayed in groups because they were serving their own best interests. "People join groups when they find other group members attractive and, in particular when they consider the benefits to outweigh the potential costs."[132] Haslam et al. use as an example the work of Napier and Gershenfeld to show the dominance of the individualistic approach to group dynamics.[133] They note that Napier and Gershenfeld provide three major reasons why people join groups: "(1) They like the task or the activity of the group . . . (2) They like people in the group . . . (3) Although the group does not satisfy the person's needs directly, it is a means of satisfying his or her needs" (emphasis original).[134] The bottom line in this view is that people join groups for selfish reasons; people join the groups to satisfy their personal interest and their mutual needs.[135] The problem with this view, however, is

---

130. Allport, 9. See also Esler, "Outline of Social Identity," 16, and Keay, "Paul the Spiritual Guide," 87.

131. For more information about America representing an individualistic society, as opposed to the ancient and current Mediterranean which are collectivistic societies, see Malina, *New Testament World*, 1–47. In the collectivistic society, people share the belief that the groups of which they are members are an end in itself, not a means to an end. People sought to uphold and embody group goals, self was viewed in the light of collective self, something similar to the African philosophy of Ubuntu, that states that "I am because we are." Malina, 12–13. The focus of the collectivistic society is on the common good of the ingroup, what benefits the community and one's family. This community tends to be more concerned about bringing honour to the community and one's family. This is completely different to the individualistic society, "where freedom from others and self-reliance are important values"; where an individual's goals have priority over the group goals. Malina, 9.

132. Haslam, Reicher, and Platow, *New Psychology of Leadership*, 46.

133. Haslam, Reicher, and Platow, 47.

134. Napier and Gershenfeld, *Groups: Theory and Experience*, 53–79 (emphasis original). See also Haslam, Reicher, and Platow, 47.

135. Haslam, Reicher, and Platow, 47.

that it does not answer why at times individuals join groups where there are no clear benefits for them individually. For example, why does a young man choose to become a soldier, where the prospect of death is high? Surely there is no immediate benefit for him for such an action.[136] Thus, the individualistic approach which was represented by Allport failed to answer adequately why people joined groups; second, it failed to comprehend the impact group membership had on the individual and vice versa.

An individualistic approach is not limited to the field of social psychology; its influence and impact can also be seen in the field of leadership studies. For far too long, leadership studies have concerned the "personal traits and qualities that make out a great leader. And even where research has acknowledged that leadership is not about leaders alone, the emphasis has remained very much on the characteristics of an individual leader."[137] The emphasis tends to be on the individual psychology of the leader; how they were raised, what their intellectual and social developments are that could or can make them great leaders.[138] All these questions and the answers that have been provided in addressing them tend to be individualistic, and centres on the person of the leader, and no attention is given to his or her social environment, the impact it has on him or her and vice versa. Also, the people he or she is leading tend to be relegated to the background. This is evident in most of the leading leadership theories, be it, the "great man theory" or "transformational leadership theory." This of course does not mean that a focus on the personal traits and character of the leader are necessarily a bad thing in and of itself; for example, Paul in 1 Timothy 3 emphasizes the personal traits of the leader. However, a sole focus on the person of a leader to the neglect of the greater context and group(s) involved is an imbalanced view, especially when it comes to the Corinthian correspondence in which Paul constantly fights factionalism around the personalities of the preferred leaders. He advocates more for the shared identity in Christ. He refers to leaders as mere servants (1 Corinthians 3:4–9).

Barentsen notes that the impact of the individualistic approach to the field of social psychology meant that there was a "loss of interest in group

---

136. Haslam, Reicher, and Platow, 48.
137. Haslam, Reicher, and Platow, *New Psychology of Leadership*, xxi.
138. Haslam, Reicher, and Platow, 1.

dynamics."[139] The dominance of Allport's individualist approach was challenged only later by scholars such as Muzafer Sherif (in the 1960s, especially his study on minimal groups), and Solomon Asch.[140]

Henri Tajfel, thus, arrived in the field of social psychology that was facing a "crisis of confidence."[141] Esler notes that scholars such as Tajfel and Serge Moscovici, who represented the European scholars who founded *The European Journal of Social Psychology*, challenge the status quo, which was at the time represented by the Allport's school regarding group dynamics.[142] The European scholars were more interested in addressing the question of "how, that is, through what psychological processes, society at large or a group in particular managed to install itself in the mind of individuals and to affect their behaviour."[143] What the European social psychology sought to achieve is very important for our study, especially as this dissertation looks at Paul's interest in the Corinthian correspondence in advocating a certain group-orientation among the members of his community. Throughout the letter of 1 Corinthians, Paul repeatedly uses the language of "us" versus "them," believers versus those who perish, folly versus wisdom, and "world" versus "us." Every time he uses this language, Paul sought to change the behaviour of the community, the in-group. In order to appreciate the significance of this "ingroup" and "outgroup" language, it is important first to consider who Henri Tajfel was, and what he taught on social identity theory.

2.3.2 The Life and the Teachings of Henri Tajfel

There is widespread agreement among scholars[144] that social identity theory has its origins in the work of Henri Tajfel on social factors in perception,[145]

---

139. Barentsen, *Emerging Leadership*, 33.

140. The minimal group study sought to establish the minimal conditions required in order for discrimination to take place.

141. Hogg and Grieve, "Social Identity Theory," 79–80. See also Barentsen, *Emerging Leadership*, 33.

142. Esler, Galatians, 41.

143. Esler, 41.

144. Scholars such as Baker, "Social Identity," 130; Hogg, Terry, and White, "Tale of Two Theories," 258; Barentsen, *Emerging Leadership*, 33; Esler, *Conflict and Identity*, 19; Esler, "Outline of Social Identity," 13; Clarke and Tucker, "Social History," 45.

145. Tajfel, "Quantitative Judgment in Social Perception"; "Social and Cultural Factors in Perception."

and in his studies on discrimination.[146] But the theory was fully developed when he worked in collaboration with his PhD student John Turner in the mid- to late 1970s at the University of Bristol.[147]

Scholars such as Horrell, Barentsen, and Esler all agree that Tajfel's interest in social identity was a result of his life experiences.[148] Turner says of Henri Tajfel,[149] "much more than most, his social psychology, the problems he studied, the theories proposed and the approaches he saw as necessary and significant, remained closely bound up with the tragedies and experience of his earlier life."[150] This study will now consider aspects of his personal experiences that kindled his interest in social identity theory. But this also has to be seen in the light of what was happening in the discipline of social psychology during the 1960s and early 1970s.

2.3.2.1 *The Life of Henri Tajfel*

Henri Tajfel was born to a Jewish family in 1919 in Wloclawek, Poland.[151] When the Second World War broke out, he was studying chemistry at the Sorbonne University. He was then called to serve in the French army, but was captured by the Germans and became a prisoner of war, and was sent to "various prisoner of war camps."[152] He survived the German prisoner of war camps, because the Germans thought that he was French, and never discovered his Polish Jewish identity. Upon his release in May 1945 he discovered, to his horror and astonishment, that none of his family or friends had survived the war.[153] After the war he worked with different organisations, including the UN Refugee Organisation, in various European countries that tried to help,

---

146. Tajfel, "Stereotypes"; "Cognitive Aspects of Prejudice"; "Experiments in Intergroup Discrimination."

147. Tajfel and Turner, "Integrative Theory." For a collection of his works, see Tajfel, *Human Groups*.

148. Horrell, "Becoming Christian," 312; Barentsen, *Emerging Leadership*, 33; Esler, "Outline of Social Identity," 13–22.

149. Turner worked with Tajfel for a period of just over ten years, and they wrote numerous articles together.

150. Turner, "Henri Tajfel," 4.

151. For brief biographical information about Henri Tajfel and how his life experiences influenced and informed his understanding about prejudice and intergroup relations, see Esler, "Outline of Social Identity," 13–39; "Jesus and Reduction," 325–57.

152. Esler, "Outline of Social Identity," 13.

153. Tajfel, *Human Groups*, 1–2.

rehabilitate, and rebuild the lives of orphans and adults who survived the concentration camps. He notes that his interest in psychology was born out of these experiences.[154] He studied psychology at Birkbeck College in London and recalls that in his final year of undergraduate study, he was awarded a scholarship by the Ministry of Education for an essay titled "Prejudice." He jokingly mentions that he thinks the "interviewers must have decided that" he was "exceptionally well-qualified to know what [he] was talking about"; he thinks that this was the reason why he was awarded the scholarship.[155] Tajfel's prisoner-of-war experience left an indelible mark. His biographer Steve Reicher reveals how his experiences impacted on him:

> These experiences shaped his subsequent career in three ways. First, he developed an abiding interest in prejudice; second, he recognised that his fate was tied entirely to his group identity; third, he understood that the Holocaust was not a product of psychology but of the way in which psychological processes operate within a given social and political context.[156]

Turner, one of his students and a close confidant, also attests to how Tajfel's early life experiences impacted on him. He says: "Much more than for most, his social psychology, the problems he studied, the theories he proposed and the approaches he saw as necessary and significant, remained closely bound up with the tragedies and experience of his earlier life."[157]

The key idea of social identity theory – from Tajfel's earlier exposition of the theory[158] – was a concern "with the social psychology of human groups in conflicts."[159] Tajfel hoped that social identity theory would give "social psychologists a reasonable chance of having something meaningful to say about the wider social realities."[160] Thus, social identity theory is a pragmatic approach that seeks to understand the persisting problem in our world, the

---

154. Tajfel, 1–2.
155. Tajfel, 2.
156. Reicher, "Tajfel, Henri".
157. Turner, "Henri Tajfel," 4.
158. Tajfel described the task of this particular book as representing "the first few years ... of the development of theory and research adopting a new perspective in an area which is crucial to social psychology." Tajfel, *Differentiation between Social Groups*, 1.
159. Tajfel, 1.
160. Tajfel, 1.

"'differentiation' between social groups."[161] He was interested in why conflict and discrimination persisted in a world that was fast becoming a global village, where there is large-scale communication between nations and different groups of people, where it seems like there is increasing inter-dependency, yet people seek to preserve their "distinctiveness," their special characteristics, and identity.[162] Tajfel made key findings regarding social identity theory in his minimal group studies.

2.3.2.2 Tajfel and the Minimal Group Studies[163]

Tajfel benefited much from an experiment carried out by Muzafer Sherif in the 1960s. Sherif was working from the "interactionist perspective," and his experiment, also known as the "Robbers cave experiment,"[164] added a new nuance in the understanding of intergroup relations and prejudice.[165] Basically, the experiment revealed that a mere categorization of people (in this experiment 24 boys of age 12 in a summer camp) into one group and not the other, produced a social comparison within the groups which, in turn, led to a noticeable difference in how the in-group behaved. Friendships and bonds were forming, but at the same time there was an increase in discrimination against the members of the outgroup.[166] Sherif interpreted these findings and concluded that discrimination was a result of the conflict of interests. However, "the conflict of interest theory" was later challenged by scholars such as Robbie and Horowitz, and also Ferguson and Kelly.[167] These scholars demonstrated that discrimination happens without the conflict of interest. Tajfel, noticing the criticism against Sherif, sought to answer the question; if conflict was not necessarily a precursor to discrimination, then what is the

---

161. Tajfel, 2.

162. Tajfel, 2; cf. Esler, "Outline of Social Identity," 16.

163. For more information on the minimal group studies, see Tajfel where he elaborates further on the experiments he conducted. Tajfel, 77–98. See also Haslam who provides an excellent summary of the experiments and their impact on social identity theory. Haslam, *Psychology in Organizations*, 18–22.

164. Keay, "Paul the Spiritual Guide," 90.

165. A brief summary of the "Robbers cave experiment" can be found at: http://www.age-of-the-sage.org/psychology/social/sherif_robbers_cave_experiment.html

166. Tajfel, *Differentiation between Social Groups*, 27–28; Esler, *Galatians*, 42; "Outline of Social Identity," 17; Horrell, "Becoming Christian," 313.

167. Keay, "Paul the Spiritual Guide," 91.

minimal cause of discrimination?[168] Sherif's experiment revealed to Tajfel that a mere sense of belonging to an ingroup as opposed to being outsider to the group produced "two major principles. These are 'accentuation and assimilation: people tend to exaggerate the differences between categories (i.e., with the outer group) and simultaneously minimise the differences within categories (i.e., with the in-group).'"[169]

It is worth noting that Tajfel, in line with scientific practises, did not just take Sherif's findings for granted; he twice conducted a similar experiment to that of Sherif's. The goal of these studies was "to establish the minimal of conditions in which an individual will, in his behaviour, distinguish between an ingroup and an outgroup."[170] In both experiments, Tajfel et al. eliminated from the experiment any conditions that normally lead to ingroup favouritism. These include things like, "face-to-face interaction; conflict of interest; (and) any possibility of previous hostility between the groups."[171] In the first study, he wanted to investigate the minimum of conditions that it took for people to show discrimination. Here, Tajfel used schoolboys who were divided into two groups randomly, but the schoolboys were told that the division was on the basis of "fairly trivial criteria – either their estimation of the number of dots on a screen or their preferences for abstract painters."[172] This random selection was done purposefully to exclude those factors that were previously considered to play a role in intergroup discrimination, such as the "history of conflict, personal animosity, or interdependence" as already noted above.[173] This first experiment revealed to Tajfel and his colleagues that even under these minimal conditions, the participants tended to favour their in-group by giving it more points and thus discriminate against the members of the other group.[174] The first study revealed that mere "cognitive perceptions were necessary to motivate intergroup discrimination" and in-group favouritism.[175] Interestingly, these were groups without any social context; hence they were

---

168. Keay, 91.
169. Brown, cited in: Horrell, "Becoming Christian," 313.
170. Tajfel, *Differentiation between Social Groups*, 77.
171. Tajfel, 77.
172. Tajfel, 77–78; cf. Haslam, Psychology in Organizations, 18.
173. Haslam, 18.
174. Haslam, 18.
175. Keay, "Paul the Spiritual Guide," 91.

"minimal." These findings were contrary to the expectations of Tajfel et al., who did not expect discrimination to happen under these minimal conditions. Keay says that these "minimal groups were expected to function as control or base groups, revealing conditions where no discrimination or bias occurs."[176]

The second experiment changed the conditions of the experiment slightly,[177] and sought to find out the necessary preconditions for the emergence of discrimination.[178] Basically, the second experiment produced a new dimension where, if participants from both groups could practice fairness and stick to the given strategy, both groups could make more money out of the experiment. In this experiment, the participants were given money to allocate to different participants. What was discovered was that the participants allocated more money to those individuals who were classified the same as them. The findings revealed that the participants tended to devise strategies that favoured the in-group dominance over the other group. At the end of the second experiment, Tajfel et al. concluded that:

> In a situation devoid of the usual trappings of ingroup membership and all the vagaries of interacting with an outgroup the subjects still act in terms of their ingroup membership and an intergroup categorization. Their actions are unambiguously directed at favouring the members of their ingroup as against the members of the outgroup. This happened despite the fact that an alternative strategy – acting in terms of the greatest common good – is clearly open to them at a relatively small cost.[179]

This experiment revealed several things to Tajfel et al. First, it challenged the theories that were established about intergroup conflicts that were the status quo during Tajfel's time.[180] The experiment confirmed what the first experiment had revealed, that the "mere act of individuals categorizing

---

176. Keay, 91.

177. See Haslam for more information about the matrix of this experiment. Haslam, *Psychology in Organizations*, 18–19.

178. Keay, "Paul the Spiritual Guide," 91.

179. Tajfel et al., "Social Categorization," 172.

180. These theories considered intergroup discrimination "solely in terms of 'objective' conflict of interest or in terms of deep-seated motives that it may serve." Tajfel et al., "Social Categorization," 176.

themselves as group members was sufficient to lead them to display ingroup favouritism" (emphasis original).[181] Second, the minimal studies revealed that the categorization of the participants into groups impacts their behaviour and thus it gives them distinct meaning. Tajfel says:

> This meaning was found by them in the adoption of a strategy for action based on the establishment, through action, of distinctiveness between their own "group" and the other, between the two social categories in a truly minimal "social system." Distinction from the "other" category provided . . . an identity for their own group, and thus some kind of meaning to an otherwise empty situation.[182]

Thus, Tajfel observed that our sense of "belonging to a group has three [interrelated] dimensions":

1. "the cognitive dimension": the sense of knowledge that one belongs to a particular group, which involves social categorization;

2. "the evaluation dimension": this dimension is about the value significance, which covers the positive or the negative connotations of belonging to a particular group;

3. "the emotional dimension" (i.e., love or hatred, like or dislikes): this refers to the attitudes members hold towards insiders and outsiders.[183]

Chapters 4 and 5 of this dissertation will consider in what ways Paul's use of "in Christ" and the "calling" terminologies correspond to Tajfel's three dimensions that make people feel positive about their group membership.[184] Esler notes that there is one dimension that is missing in Tajfel's three dimensions, and that it "contributes greatly to the cognitive dimension of belonging

---

181. Haslam, *Psychology in Organizations*, 19.

182. Tajfel, "Criticism of a Social Science," 39–40. See also Haslam, Psychology in Organizations, 19–20.

183. Tajfel, *Differentiation between Social Groups*, 28; cf. Esler, *Galatians*, 42.

184. Tajfel, 28.

to the group and also helps foster the evaluative and emotional dimension in a positive way"; that dimension is a "future orientation."[185]

Thus far, we have considered the historical developments of social identity theory, particularly as it was originally expressed by Henri Tajfel. The following section will now consider the tenets of this theory, as we have them today.

2.4 The Tenets of Social Identity Theory

In its current form, social identity theory encompasses two social psychological theories: social identity theory (as originally expounded by Tajfel[186]) and self-categorization theory (which was later expounded by Turner;[187] Turner built on the findings of his predecessor Tajfel in developing self-categorization as a stand-alone theory). According to Steffens, the starting point of social identity theory is that people perceive and think of themselves as individuals, that is, "I" (personal identity), as well as members of a particular group that they belong to, that is, "we" (social identity).[188] But "as social identity becomes more salient, people undergo a process of depersonalization in which they become less aware of themselves as individuals with idiosyncratic characteristics and more aware of themselves as members of a group who are interchangeable with other group members," that is, "we students," or "we theologians."[189] There are multiple levels of social identity in each one of us at any given time and, depending on the context, we can emphasise one aspect of our identity over the others, that is, in a rugby match between South Africa and New Zealand, we can emphasise "we South Africans" versus "they New Zealanders" but within the South African social group identity, there are also other layers of identification that are context-dependent. For example, when South Africans talk about social injustices, they divide themselves based on the colour of their skins, "white" versus "black" South Africans, while among the same group of "black" South Africans there are also different levels of identifications, that is, "Xhosa" versus "Zulu." Thus, in social identity there

---

185. Esler, *Galatians*, 42.
186. Tajfel, Differentiation *between Social Groups*; Tajfel and Turner, "Social Identity Theory."
187. Turner, *Rediscovering Social Group*.
188. Steffens, "Leaders' Personal Performance," 41.
189. Steffens, 41.

are various levels "of abstractiveness – from less inclusive lower-level (Xhosa or Zulu) identities to more inclusive high-level identities (South African)."[190]

Social identity is defined as:

> that part of an individual's self-concept which derives from his (sic) knowledge of his membership of a social group (or groups) together with the value and emotional significance attached to that membership ... however rich and complex may be the individuals' view of themselves in relation to the surrounding world, social and physical, some aspects of that view are contributed by the membership of certain social groups or categories. Some of these memberships are more salient than others; and some may vary in salience in time and as a function of a variety of social situations (emphasis original).[191]

This definition gives us the three interrelated dimensions of social identity that have already been looked at above; the cognitive dimension, an evaluation dimension, and an emotional dimension. Thus, social identity theory encompasses three facets (some of which have already been alluded to above) in its psychological sequence; these are social categorisation, social identification, and social comparison.

2.4.1 Social Categorisation

Social categorisation is the cognitive process relevant to a person's perception of being part of an ingroup, or of an outgroup.[192] This, however, should not be

---

190. Steffens, 41.

191. Tajfel, *Human Groups*, 255. Interestingly, Esler uses part of this definition, but he does not attribute it to Tajfel. Esler, *Conflict and Identity*, 20. Tajfel is aware that "this definition is a limited definition of 'identity' or 'social identity.'" It does, however, help us to avoid endless discussions about self, and thus helps us to concentrate on the "limited aspects of the concept of self which are ... relevant to certain limited aspects of social behaviour." Tajfel, 255.

192. Baker, "Social Identity," 130; Esler, *Conflict and Identity*, 20. Tajfel describes social categorization as "a process of bringing together social objects or events in groups which are equivalent with regard to an individual's actions, intentions and system of beliefs," hence, here the emphasis is on the cognitive process. Tajfel, *Human Groups*, 254. For more nuanced information about self-categorization processes, see Haslam, *Psychology in Organizations*, 30–34. Self-categorization can happen at different levels, Haslam gives three levels as examples: (1) Superordinate level (human beings in contrast to other species), (2) Intermediate social level (as an ingroup in contrast to other groups), and (3) Subordinate personal level (as an individual different from other relevant in-group members). Haslam, *Psychology in Organizations*, 30. This dissertation is concerned with self-categorization at the intermediate social level. Haslam notes

confused with identity theory which "focuses on the self as comprised of the various roles an individual occupies (e.g., mother, friend, employee)."[193] Social identity theory emphasises group processes and intergroup relations rather than role behaviour. According to Hogg et al., at its core is the idea that social categorisation "(e.g., nationality, political affiliation, sports team) into which one falls, and to which one feels one belongs, provides a definition of who one is in terms of the defining characteristics of the category – a self-definition that is a part of the self-concept."[194] Turner notes that "social categorization is a 'means of systematizing and ordering the social environment particularly with regard to its role as a guide for action, and as a reflection of social values.'"[195] It also provides a "system of orientation which creates and defines the individual's own place in society" (emphasis original).[196]

Tajfel proposed that the groups to which people belonged were an important source of pride and self-esteem.[197] In order for the in-group to develop such a sense of superiority, the in-group discriminates against the out-group. For example, for fans of the Western Province rugby team who think that theirs is the best team, in order to bolster the self-identity of their team they need to discriminate or hold prejudices against other teams such as the Bulls or Sharks. Thus "categorisation of self and others into in-group and out-group defines people's social identity and accentuates their perceived similarity to people's cognitive representation of the defining features of the group (i.e., their group prototypicality, or normative-ness)."[198] Under social categorisa-

---

that more than one self-categorization is available for an individual at any given time, and it is up to them to choose which self-categorization is important for what context. Haslam, *Psychology in Organizations*, 30. This is a meta-contrast principle that is developed by Turner et al. which states that "categorization is inherently comparative and hence is intrinsically variable, fluid and relative to a frame of reference." Thus self-categorisation is context-dependent, it does not "represent fixed, absolute properties of the perceiver, but relative, varying, context-dependent properties." For example, people of the same ingroup might accentuate their differences within the ingroup, if the discussion within the group centres around gender issues, and the same applies to intragroup comparisons, "us" versus "them." Turner et al., "Self and Collective," 458.

193. Desrochers et al., "Identity Theory," 2. For an extended discussion on the difference between social categorisation as part of social identity theory and as part of identity theory, see Hogg, Terry, and White, "Tale of Two Theories," 262; Burke and Jan, "Identity Theory."
194. Hogg, Terry, and White, 259.
195. Turner, "Social Comparison and Social Identity," 7.
196. Turner, 7.
197. Tajfel, *Differentiation between Social Groups*.
198. Hogg, Terry, and White, "Tale of Two Theories," 261.

tion, people are essentially "depersonalised," and we divide them according to "us" versus "them." People are stereotyped according to the group that they belong to rather than as unique individuals (for e.g., guys are messy and unclean).[199] Tajfel and Turner here note that this is "the major characteristic of social behaviour" related to this theory, that in "relevant intergroup situations, individuals will not interact as individuals, on the basis of their individual characteristics or interpersonal relations, but as the members of their groups standing in certain defined relationships to members of other groups."[200] Thus, part of social categorisation involves discrimination against other groups and involves a great deal of ingroup favouritism.

2.4.2 Social Identification

According to Tajfel and Turner, social identification is the process by which an individual identifies with the in-group more openly.[201] This can be viewed as the intra-group relationship. This occurs when the individual identifies with the values and norms of the in-group and takes them as his/her own values and norms. The shared social identification transforms the way the group members see and treat each other; the members of the group are not seen as "the other." It helps the group members to act in a harmonious manner. Reicher, Spears, and Haslam note the benefits that are brought by social identification, that the "increased social support amongst group members makes them more able to cope with actual and anticipated difficulties and hence decreases stress and anxiety while increasing optimism and the sense of self-efficacy."[202]

There are three basic assumptions that Tajfel and Turner specify as necessary to establish this theory. These are:

1. The individual strives to maintain his/her self-esteem: strives for a positive self-concept.
2. Social groups or categories and the membership of them are associated with positive or negative value connotations. Hence, social identity may be positive or negative according to the

---

199. Hogg, Terry, and White, 261.
200. Tajfel and Turner, "Integrative Theory," 35.
201. Tajfel and Turner, "Social Identity Theory," 40.
202. Reicher, Spears, and Haslam, "Social Identity Approach," 28.

evaluations (which tend to be socially consensual, either within or across groups) of those groups that contribute to an individual's social identity.

3. The evaluation of one's own group is determined with reference to specific other groups through social comparisons in terms of value-laden attributes and characteristics. Positively discrepant comparisons between the in-group and out-group produce high prestige; negative discrepant comparisons between the in-group and out-group result in low prestige.[203]

Thus, the theory postulates three things:

1. Individuals strive for self-esteem;
2. Positive social identity happens when the individual perceives the in-group that they are part of to be superior to the out-group, and thence their membership of the group boosts their self-esteem;
3. If their social identity is not satisfactory, there are two things the individual can do; first, they might strive to leave their group and join some more distinct and positive group, or second, the individual will stay and try to improve the group.

The third point is significant for the current research. Scholars such as Reicher, Spears, and Haslam, and Van Knippenberg and Hogg, have noted that leadership is easier where there is a positive social identification by the group members,[204] while "where people do not share a common social identity, leadership over them is impossible – for where there are no agreed collective norms, values, and priorities that characterise the group, no-one can be entrusted to represent the group."[205] This, however, does not mean that leadership cannot be achieved; it can happen when an individual person is seen by the group "to be prototypical of the group" – the more the group notices this in that particular individual, the more likely that person will be seen as a leader and that person in return will "be able to influence other group members."[206] Reicher, Spears, and Haslam also note that "group prototype

---

203. Tajfel and Turner, "Social Identity Theory," 16.
204. Reicher, Spears, and Haslam, "Social Identity Approach," 29; Van Knippenberg and Hogg, *Leadership and Power*.
205. Reicher, Spears, and Haslam, 29.
206. Reicher, Spears, and Haslam, 29.

varies from one comparative context to another, so different people will come to be seen as suitable leaders."[207] It is worth noting that these scholars are of the view that where there is a strong common social identity within the group, the need for leaders might be very minimal and people will be able to help one another and influence each other as they share common goals. Thus, leadership becomes a group phenomenon. In the event that the group does not share a strong social identification, the job of the leader is to actively "construe the nature of the shared identity and of their own selves in order to claim prototypicality – and hence the right to speak for the group. In short, successful leaders have to be skilled *entrepreneurs of identity*" (emphasis original).[208]

2.4.3 Social Comparison

Turner analysing the work of Tajfel, notes that according to Tajfel, "mere classification of subjects into in and out groups is a sufficient as well as necessary condition to induce forms of ingroup favouritism and discrimination against the outgroup."[209] But there is more to this than meets the eye. The value ascribed to the group to which one belongs will be measured by how that group compares with other groups. Basically, in social comparison people's self-esteem rises or falls in relation to how they feel in terms of measuring up to other people; the same is true when it comes to group membership. Tajfel observes that "'positive aspects of social identity' . . . the reinterpretation of attributes and the engagement in social action . . . only acquire meaning in relation to, or in comparison with, other groups."[210] Thus, "the characteristics of one's group as a whole (such as its status, its richness or poverty, its skin colour or its ability to reach its aims) achieve most of their significance in relation to perceived differences from other groups and the value connotations of these differences . . . A group becomes a group in the sense of being perceived as having common characteristics or common fate only because other groups are present in the environment."[211]

---

207. Reicher, Spears, and Haslam, 29.
208. Reicher, Spears, and Haslam, 30.
209. Turner, "Social Comparison and Social Identity," 1; Tajfel et al., "Social Categorization."
210. Tajfel, *Human Groups*, 258.
211. Tajfel, 258. See also Turner, "Social Comparison and Social Identity," 7.

Now that we have briefly outlined social identity theory, this research will turn to its use in leadership studies.

2.5 The Impact of Social Identity Theory on Leadership Studies[212]

Having shown how social identity theory was developed, focusing particularly on the insight it provides into group dynamics, we will now consider the impact of social identity theory on leadership studies, particularly in the field of social psychology. Social identity theory has been applied in this field to various organizational studies, especially by scholars such as Haslam; Haslam, Van Knippenberg, Platow, and Ellemers; Van Knippenberg and Sleebos; and Van Knippenberg.[213] There has been a growing use of social identity theory in leadership studies as well. Among the scholars who employ this theory in leadership studies we have scholars such as: Ellemers, De Gilder, and Haslam; Haslam et al.; Hogg; Hogg and Van Knippenberg; Turner and Haslam; Van Knippenberg and Hogg; and Steffens.[214]

So, how is social identity theory relevant for looking at the interrelationship between identity and leadership in the Corinthian correspondence? Social identity approach argues that there are three things that are necessary for a leader to manage the social identity of their group, which also make a leader successful in exerting influence upon the group; viz. (1) the leader needs to be a prototype of the group, (2) the leader needs to be a group champion, and (3) a leader needs to be an entrepreneur of group

---

212. Most of the findings in this section are based on the quantitative research that has been conducted by social identity theory scholars in the field of social psychology. See, as an example, the experiment conducted in 2007 by Haslam and Reicher titled: "Identity Entrepreneurship and the Consequences of Identity Failure: The Dynamics of Leadership in the BBC Prison Study" which is the basis of these findings.

213. Haslam, *Psychology in Organizations*; Haslam, Van Knippenberg, Platow, and Ellemers, "Social Identity at Work"; Van Knippenberg and Sleebos, "Organizational Identification"; Van Knippenberg, "Work Motivation and Performance."

214. Ellemers, De Gilder, and Haslam, "Motivating Individuals and Groups"; Haslam, Reicher, and Platow, *New Psychology of Leadership*; Hogg, Van Knippenberg, and Rast III, "Social Identity Theory"; Hogg and Van Knippenberg, "Social Identity and Leadership Processes"; Turner and Haslam, "Social Identity, Organizations"; Van Knippenberg and Hogg, "Social Identity Model"; Steffens, "Leaders' Personal Performance."

social identity.[215] This study will now consider each of these three findings and investigate how they might help in providing insight in the analysis of the Corinthian correspondence.

2.5.1 The Leader as a Prototype of the In-group Identity

Leadership prototypicality can be defined as a leader's ability in "representing the unique qualities that define the group and what it means to be a member of this group. *Embodying* those core attributes of the group that make this group special as well as distinct from other groups. Being an exemplary and model member of the group" (emphasis original).[216] The following section will now unpack this definition.

In using social identity theory to look at the question of leadership and identity in the Pauline Corinthian correspondence, the emphasis (particularly around identity) is on the social aspect of identity "as opposed to personal identity"; that is, identity defined in terms of belonging to a particular group.[217] Social identity theory approaches leadership as a group phenomenon, as opposed to the prevailing views of leadership studies where the emphasis tends to be on the persona, and the charisma of the leader. Both Hogg, and Lord et al., explain that abstract leadership category types are insufficient in explaining what makes leaders more effective in their communities, as they tend not to consider group dynamics.[218] Even those perspectives that are cognisant of relational properties of leadership, do not pay enough attention to the cognitive processes involved in forming group identity. This comes

---

215. It is worth noting that not all these three aspects apply equally to our analysis of 1 Cor 1–4. In chapters 4 and 5, this dissertation will focus mostly on Paul's group prototypicality and to a limited extent on Paul as a group entrepreneur. The aspect regarding group championship falls beyond the scope of this dissertation in that the texts that deal with this aspect in 1 Corinthians are mostly found in 1 Cor 8–11:1. However, one might venture to argue that the fact that Paul upon receiving a disturbing report from Chloe's household (1 Cor 1:11) wrote the letter to the Corinthians already demonstrates that Paul is a group champion in that he is not indifferent to the plight that has befallen the community. He wants them to live a life that is consistent with their identity in Christ.

216. Steffens et al., "Leadership as Social Identity," 1002.

217. Horrell, "Becoming Christian," 311. A group is defined as: "a collection of individuals who perceive themselves to be members of the same social category, share some emotional involvement in this common definition of themselves, and achieve some degree of social consensus about the evaluation of their group and of their membership in it." Horrell, 312.

218. Hogg, Van Knippenberg, and Rast III, "Social Identity Theory," 189; Lord et al., "Contextual Constraints."

through strongly in the work of Turner, and Haslam.[219] In particular, Turner has been very critical of the view that "particular personal characteristics" of a leader determine their success. Social identity theory, especially under self-categorization theory, shows that different types of leaders will be better suited for different tasks, and that personal characteristics need to align with the values and the identity of a given group, and this identity and values of what is required in a leader will also be influenced by the context that the group faces. Under social categorization, the social identity theory asserts that people or groups "generally want to have a clear sense that their ingroup is different from, and superior to, outgroups."[220]

What this means is that the members of the group who better capture the in-group identity (prototypicality), (especially in comparison with the outgroup) are more likely to exert more influence on the group, and thus lead the group (leadership emergence) than those who do not embody the values of the group. Steffens states that the person's "ability to influence other group members is argued to follow a *gradient* that is contingent on the degree with which he or she is perceived as *relative ingroup prototypical* of a social category" (emphasis original).[221] Haslam says that the person who is an ingroup prototype is that one who is most likely to influence the group; "as the (most) prototypical group member, the leader best epitomizes (in the dual sense both of defining and being *defined* by) the social category of which he or she is a member" (emphasis original).[222] Once the leader is viewed as "one of us," the in-group members will be more loyal to that person, as compared to someone who is viewed as "one of them."

An example of this is given by Haslam et al. in their analysis of the US presidential elections of 2000.[223] CBS News conducted a poll about the two candidates George W. Bush and Al Gore, and asked who was the more intelligent of the two candidates. The majority of the respondents (59%) agreed that Al Gore was highly intelligent, while 55% of the respondents thought

---

219. Turner, *Rediscovering Social Group*; Haslam, *Psychology in Organizations*; Haslam, Reicher, and Platow, *New Psychology of Leadership*.

220. Steffens, "Leaders' Personal Performance," 49; cf. Tajfel and Turner, "Integrative Theory."

221. Steffens, 49–50.

222. Haslam, *Psychology in Organizations*, 45.

223. Haslam, Reicher, and Platow, *New Psychology of Leadership*, 83–84.

that Bush was of average intelligence. Even some of Bush's own supporters were of the opinion that Al Gore was more intelligent than Bush.[224] Al Gore's intelligence did not guarantee success for him. But, why was this the case? Given that most literature on leadership considered intelligence an important characteristic of a leader,[225] why did intelligence not guarantee success for Al Gore? Social categorization theory showed that Bush's group (that is, in-group), when confronted by the more intelligent outgroup (Al Gore supporters), devalued intelligence as a necessary quality for a strong leader. Statistics revealed that whereas 72 percent of Al Gore supporters wanted a president who is of above average intelligence, this was true for only 56 percent of Bush's supporters.[226] There is growing empirical evidence that shows that group prototypicality trumps other qualities that traditionally have been deemed necessary for leadership success. The following table, taken from Van Dick and Kerschreiter, provides scholarly empirical findings that show the importance of a leader's prototypicality on the shared ingroup identity:[227]

Criteria	Main Finding with Respect to Prototypicality
Perceived leader(ship) Effectiveness	Prototypical leaders are perceived as effective, especially if followers identify with the group.[228]

---

224. Haslam, Reicher, and Platow, 84.

225. Judge and Piccolo, "Transformational and Transactional Leadership"; Lord, de Vader, and Alliger, "Meta-Analysis."

226. Haslam, Reicher, and Platow, *New Psychology of Leadership*, 84.

227. Van Dick and Kerschreiter, "Social Identity Approach," 370–72. Similar findings are also available in the work of Hogg, Van Knippenberg, and Rast III where they state that: "The main tenet is that group prototypical leaders are better supported and more trusted, and are perceived as more effective by members than are less prototypical leaders; particularly when group membership is a central and salient aspect of members' identity and members identify strongly with the group." Hogg, Van Knippenberg, and Rast III, "Social Identity Theory," 258. Steffens provides the same empirical data, and argues that group prototypicality is an important feature in the leader in order for him/her to influence the group, but Steffens adds that prototypicality is not sufficient on its own, it also needs group championship; that is, a leader needs to be viewed as doing it "for us." Steffens, "Leaders' Personal Performance," 49–55; 73–109. Citing Haslam, *Psychology in Organizations*, 2001 original edition, Steffens says that the evidence supports the claims that are married with "recent theorizing that suggest that leaders have to be perceived not only to embody a shared identity but also to champion group interest (as well as to craft and embed a shared identity)." Steffens, 105.

228. Cicero, Bonaiuto, Pierro, and Van Knippenberg, "Employees' Work Effort"; Fielding and Hogg, "Social Identity, Self-Categorization"; Hains, Hogg, and Duck, "Self-Categorization and Leadership."

Criteria	Main Finding with Respect to Prototypicality
Perceived leader(ship) effectiveness after failure	Prototypical leaders are perceived as more effective after a failure than non-prototypical leaders; after a success, there is no such difference.[229]
Perceived leader(ship) effectiveness after failure depending on the type of goal	Prototypical leaders are perceived as more effective after failing to achieve a maximal goal than non-prototypical leaders; after failing to achieve a minimal goal there is no such difference.[230]
Perceived leadership effectiveness, job-satisfaction, and turnover intentions of followers	The effect of the leader's prototypicality on outcome variables is moderated by followers' perceived role ambiguity, such that perceived leadership effectiveness, as well as followers' job satisfaction and turnover intentions are influenced more strongly by prototypicality if followers experience more role ambiguity.[231]
Perceived leadership effectiveness	The leader's prototypicality reduces the influence of interactional fairness on perceived leader(ship) effectiveness.[232]
Perceived performance and perceived prototypicality of the leader	The leader's prototypicality (manipulated experimentally) has a positive influence on the perception of their performance. Conversely, the leader's performance (manipulated experimentally) has a positive influence on the perception of their prototypicality.[233]

---

229. Giessner, Van Knippenberg, and Sleebos, "'License to Fail?'"
230. Giessner and Van Knippenberg, "License to Fail."
231. Cicero, Pierro, and Van Knippenberg, "Leadership and Uncertainty."
232. Janson, Levy, Sitkin, and Lind, "Fairness and Other Leadership."
233. Steffens, Haslam, Ryan, and Kessler, "Leader Performance and Prototypicality."

Criteria	Main Finding with Respect to Prototypicality
Follower performance	Leader self-sacrificing behaviour has little influence on follower performance if the leader is prototypical for the group. Leader self-sacrificing behaviour has a larger influence on follower performance when the leader is non-prototypical.[234]
Leader endorsement	The influence of voice provided by the leader on leader endorsement is substantially reduced when the leader is perceived to be prototypical for the group, especially when followers are highly identified with their group.[235]
Perceived procedural fairness of the leader	Group members highly identified with the organization view prototypical leaders as more procedurally fair. The perceived procedural fairness in turn mediates the effect of prototypicality (among the highly identified group members) on group members' self-perceived status in the organization.[236]
Perceived charisma	Prototypical leaders are attributed greater levels of charisma than non-prototypical leaders, regardless of their group-oriented versus exchange rhetoric. Non-prototypical leaders are only attributed high levels of charisma when they employ group-oriented rhetoric.[237]

---

234. Van Knippenberg and Van Knippenberg, "Leader Self-sacrifice."
235. Ullrich, Christ, and Van Dick, "Substitutes for Procedural Fairness."
236. Van Dijke and De Cremer, "How Leader Prototypicality."
237. Platow et al., "Special Gift We Bestow."

Criteria	Main Finding with Respect to Prototypicality
Perceived charisma; follower identification with the leader	Leader prototypicality and leader identification with the group interact with respect to perceived leader charisma and the follower's identification with the leader, such that highly identified leaders are able to inspire followership even when they are not very prototypical. Results are more pronounced for highly identified followers.[238]
Follower trust in their co-workers	Leader prototypicality moderates the effect of perceived leader fairness on follower trust in their co-workers, such that unfairness of the prototypical leader had a negative effect on trust in co-workers; this effect was not apparent for non-prototypical leaders.[239]
Team-oriented leadership	Leader accountability (through transparency) relates less to team-oriented behaviour for prototypical leaders than for non-prototypical leaders. This effect is more pronounced for leaders who identify more strongly with their team.[240]

Thus, empirical evidence suggests that being "one of us," or a leader being perceived as a prototype of the in-group, is more important than any individual characteristic of a leader, and thus prototypicality to the in-group identity can either make or break a leader.

Haslam, Reicher, and Platow put it thus, "In-group prototypicality is not a set characteristic of 'us' but rather a function of how 'we' relate to 'them'; as the nature of 'them' changes, so does the in-group prototype and hence the qualities that mark out a person as a leader."[241] In the case of Bush and Gore (above), people were more loyal to the in-group prototype, "he is one of us." Being one of "us" was thus elevated above intelligence and other features that are deemed important for leadership. Older literature on leadership,

---

238. Steffens et al., "Of the Group."
239. Seppälä, Lipponen, and Pirtillä-Backman, "Leader Fairness."
240. Giessner et al., "Team-Oriented Leadership."
241. Haslam, Reicher, and Platow, *New Psychology of Leadership*, 84.

by neglecting the psychological processes that are used when people prefer certain leaders, fail to account for these results, especially when intergroup comparison takes place. Within the intragroup comparison, personal characteristics of a leader are important, as the leader needs to be the prototype of the group. He or she needs to exemplify all the characteristics that identify members of the group. When the leader is seen as the embodiment of the values of the in-group, this gives him/her legitimacy to lead the group, for not only is the leader perceived as "one of us" but he or she is also an exemplary "one of us," and thus prototypical. Group members are easily influenced by the leaders who embody group prototypes.[242] In-group prototypicality can also account for leadership emergence. This is a social attraction process whereby the more a particular group member embodies the in-group identity, the more other members are likely to be drawn to that particular member, and the easier it will be for him/her to influence other group members.[243] They become the prototype of what that group membership is all about, or what each member should be, or could be. Thus, by implication the leader's prototypicality also presents what membership of the group is not about. Hence, the more the leaders reflect the group prototype, the more they will have influence on the group identity, and thus become identity managers. The more a leader is seen by the group as a representation of one of "us," the more likely the leader is to succeed in leading that particular group. It is, however, important to note that this is context-driven and that the group identity might change as group circumstances change, for e.g., during a time of war and a time of peace.[244] In its treatment of the Corinthian correspondence, this dissertation will investigate how Paul portrays himself as a group prototype. Linked with this is how Paul used his teaching about leadership acts as a basis for identity management. In 1 Corinthians 1–4, Paul uses many descriptors to present himself as a group prototype. First, he describes himself as "κλητὸς ἀπόστολος Χριστοῦ Ἰησοῦ διὰ θελήματος θεοῦ" (1 Cor 1:1), Second, he compares the message of the cross to the wisdom of the world, and states that the message of the cross is folly to those who are perishing (outgroup) but it is the power of God and the wisdom of God to those who are being

---

242. Hogg, Van Knippenberg, and Rast III, "Social Identity Theory," 189.
243. Hogg, Van Knippenberg, and Rast III, 189.
244. Haslam, Reicher, and Platow, *New Psychology of Leadership*, 77–108.

saved (ingroup) (1 Cor 1:18–31).[245] Thus, he makes a contrast between the in-group and the outgroup. But linked with this, he describes his approach when he came to the Corinthians: "Κἀγὼ ἐλθὼν πρὸς ὑμᾶς, ἀδελφοί, ἦλθον οὐ καθ' ὑπεροχὴν λόγου ἢ σοφίας καταγγέλλων ὑμῖν τὸ μαρτύριον τοῦ θεοῦ."[246] Is it therefore possible that in 1 Corinthians 1–2, Paul is portraying himself as a group prototype? This question will be dealt with in chapter 4 under the exegesis section. Suffice to say for now under this section on group prototypicality in leadership: an important question that needs to be dealt with, is how does Paul's self-representation and his teachings about the foolishness of the cross and his coming to the Corinthians without lofty speech or wisdom, present him as the group prototype?

2.5.2 The Leader as a Champion of the In-group[247]

A leader as a prototype of the group dominated social identity theory for over two decades, and other qualities that made one a great leader were generally neglected.[248] The tide has since changed, and now social identity theory scholars also argue that in order for a leader to exert influence upon the group identity, he or she needs to be not just prototypical of the group (that is, embodying group values and identity), he or she also needs to be perceived as championing the group goals and identity (that is, identity advancement), "doing it for us."[249] Particularly, it states that leaders need to be perceived by

---

245. Clarke, in *Secular and Christian Leadership*, calls this secular versus Christian leadership.

246. 1 Cor 2:1–4; see particularly 1 Cor 2:6–10 where Paul aligns the wisdom he imparts with God's wisdom.

247. Even though group championship will not be developed further in this study because some aspects of it, in applying them to Paul, fall beyond the scope of this work (i.e. 1 Cor 9), theoretical findings regarding group championship are still worth considering as they help us to understand different aspects of what is involved in making a leader successful.

248. Steffens et al., "Leadership as Social Identity," 1001.

249. Haslam, Reicher, and Platow, New Psychology of Leadership, 109–36; Steffens, "Leaders' Personal Performance," 56–71; 73–109; Haslam and Platow, "Link between Leadership," 1469–79. There is growing empirical data within social identity theory studies which supports the importance of group championship; however, it has not reached the proportions of group prototypicality. For more empirical findings of group championship, see Haslam, Reicher, and Platow, Van Dick and Kerschreiter; De Cremer and Van Knippenberg; Haslam and Platow, and particularly Steffens who argues for an interplay between group prototypicality and group championship. Haslam, Reicher, and Platow, *New Psychology of Leadership*, 109–35; Van Dick and Kerschreiter, "Social Identity Approach," 373–75; De Cremer and Van Knippenberg, "Cooperation as a Function"; Haslam and Platow, "Link between Leadership"; Steffens, "Leaders'

the followers as having the group interest (promotion of the collective) at heart rather than their personal interest; they "need to be seen to 'do it for us' rather than 'for them' (a competing group) or 'for themselves.'"[250] Thus, a leader's effectiveness will to a large extent be dependent on being perceived "as acting as ingroup champions."[251] These findings can prove fruitful for our analysis of Paul, particularly when we deal with the issues of dispute between Paul and his young community in 1 and 2 Corinthians.[252]

Unlike with group prototypicality, where the leader's ability and achievements are mute, with the leader as a champion of the group, the leader's personal performance comes to the fore. The leader's ability to exert influence upon a group will be based on his or her capacity to lead the group; leadership is not just about being prototypical, "it is also about doing."[253] Thus, performance is also an essential quality of a good leader. Group championship has also been demonstrated to trump other personal traits that are traditionally deemed important for a good leader. For example, fairness, within the intergroup context, is regarded as an important quality for a leader to have, but studies have also shown that within intergroup comparison fairness becomes less significant for the followers, than group championship.[254] This, however, should not be construed as saying that advancing shared group identity means that one has to "derogate outgroups" or treat them unfairly.[255] Rather, it means that followers who perceive the leader as a prototype of the group and see him or her as acting for the best interests of the in-group (which are in line with in-group values and norms), would be more supportive of that leader, even

---

Personal Performance," 73–108. For identity leadership inventory that has been used to assess and validate leadership championship as a necessary requirement for good leadership, see Steffens et al., "Leadership as Social Identity," 1005–19.

250. Steffens, "Leaders' Personal Performance," 56.

251. Steffens et al., "Leadership as Social Identity," 1004.

252. For an extended discussion regarding the problems between Paul and his young community, see Sindo, "Socio-Rhetorical Approach," 103–10, and Ashley, "Paul's Paradigm for Ministry," 41–44. This aspect of social identity theory could be used to argue that Paul all along wanted to demonstrate to the community that everything he did was to their benefit.

253. Haslam, Reicher, and Platow, New Psychology of Leadership, 109.

254. Platow, Reid, and Andrew, "Leadership Endorsement."

255. Steffens et al., "Leadership as Social Identity," 1004.

if he or she acts unfairly towards the outgroup.[256] Thus, identity advancement or group championship could be defined as:

> Advancing and promoting core interests of the group. Standing up for, and if threatened defending, group interests (and not personal interests or those of other groups). Championing concerns and ambitions that are key to the group as a whole. Contributing to the realization of group goals. Acting to prevent group failures and to overcome obstacles to the achievement of group objectives.[257]

2.5.3 The Leader as an Entrepreneur of Identity

When one looks at the findings of social identity in leadership, particularly its emphasis on group prototypicality, one might easily think that leadership success or emergence depends entirely on the whim of the group being led, and that the leader is passive in the whole process. With leaders as entrepreneurs of identity, "the leader is an active constituent of the group, who is simultaneously involved in the defining of and defined by the group" (emphasis original).[258] Haslam argues that in order for a leader to be successful and to exact influence on the group, the leader needs to have the ability to "craft a sense of us," and thus he/she needs to be an "entrepreneur of the social identity of the group."[259] Leaders do this by arguing for the "appropriateness of particular categorizations" – those that distinguish between the in-group ("us") and the outgroup ("them"), "in a manner that defines the leader and in-group positively and as distinct from outgroup."[260] Steffens et al. describe leaders' identity entrepreneurship as involving:

> Bringing people together by creating a shared sense of "we" and "us" within the group. Making different people all feel that they are part of the same group and increasing cohesion and inclusiveness within the group. Clarifying people's understanding of

---

256. Platow et al., "Endorsement of Distributively"; cf. Steffens, "Leaders' Personal Performance," 57.
257. Steffens et al., "Leadership as Social Identity," 1004.
258. Haslam, Psychology in Organizations, 47.
259. Haslam, 47.
260. Haslam, 47.

what the group stands for (and what it does not stand for) by defining core values, norms, and ideals.²⁶¹

This description has a huge significance for our analysis of leadership and identity in the Pauline correspondence of 1 Corinthians. Barentsen notes that in 1 Corinthians, Paul was not dealing with the initial phase of identity formation.²⁶² Rather, he was dealing with the next phase of identity formation; what Malina in his application of group formation theory calls the "storming" phase.²⁶³ The intragroup comparison and "cultural patterns created uncertainty" in the Pauline community at Corinth "about their social identification, which resulted in internal conflict and poor identity performance."²⁶⁴ The fact that the community was made up of smaller "house churches" resulted in each of these small communities valuing one leader over the other, hence Paul heard from the oral report of Chloe's people that there was division and strife (1 Cor 1:10–11). This expressed itself in the assertion, "I belong to Paul" or "I belong to Apollos," etc. Barentsen notes that this indicates that subgroups were forming around preferred leaders by the people in the community (1 Cor 1:12).²⁶⁵ Paul, in addressing these issues, first reminds the Corinthian community of their identity which, interestingly, he links with a broader identity of all those who call on the name of Jesus Christ. In addressing them Paul says: "τῇ ἐκκλησίᾳ τοῦ θεοῦ, ἡγιασμένοις Ἰησοῦ, τῇ οὔσῃ ἐν Κορίνθῳ, κλητοῖς ἁγίοις, σὺν πᾶσιν τοῖς ἐπικαλουμένοις τὸ ὄνομα τοῦ κυρίου ἡμῶν Ἰησοῦ Χριστοῦ ἐν παντὶ τόπῳ αὐτῶν καὶ ἡμῶν" (emphasis added). Moreover, throughout the first four chapters Paul does not align himself with any group, nor does he bring about division, contrast, or competitiveness between himself, Apollos, and Peter. Rather, he portrays all three of them as part of the same team, instead of being competitors.²⁶⁶

In trying to shape the identity of the community, Paul is also quick to show how their behaviour is not consistent with their new identity in Christ. He characterises their thinking as being worldly (σαρκίνοις) and immature, and

---

261. Steffens et al., "Leadership as Social Identity," 1004.
262. Barentsen, *Emerging Leadership*, 78.
263. Malina, "Early Christian Groups," 104.
264. Barentsen, *Emerging Leadership*, 78.
265. Barentsen, 78.
266. 1 Cor 3:5–9.

not consistent with the ingroup identity which lives by the Spirit (1 Cor 3:1). It will be argued later on in this dissertation that what Paul is doing here is identity entrepreneurship, that is, he is crafting a sense of what it means to be people who live in the light of the divine wisdom (1 Cor 1:18–21), people whose foundations rest solidly on the power of the God and the Holy Spirit through the gospel message that Paul preached (1 Cor 2:1–5).

2.6 Conclusion

This chapter has looked at the pros and cons of using social-scientific methodologies for the analysis of the biblical texts. It argued that, while there is a danger that scholars who used social-scientific approaches can be anachronistic, that danger can be circumvented if scholars incorporate historical-critical methods in their analysis, as the historical-critical methods help one to gather the data that can be interpreted using social-scientific approaches.

This dissertation also argues that it aims to use social identity theory as a heuristic model in the interpretation of the Corinthian correspondence, to demonstrate the interrelationship between identity and leadership. Under social identity theory, leadership is defined as a process whereby one or more members of the group influence other members in a way that motivates them to contribute to the achievement of group goals.[267] Three things flow from this: (1) Leadership can never be just about the personality of the leader, it is always also about followers, the people who are being influenced and who ultimately are the ones who do the work of translating the leader's vision into outcomes. (2) Leadership is not just about having power over people, it is about having power through the people. This is achieved by the leader's being the prototype of the group, so that the leader makes people do things because they want to do them, not because they feel that they have to do them. It is "about shaping beliefs, desires, and priorities. It is about achieving influence, not securing compliance."[268] (3) Leadership is never about the individual, that is, "me." It is always about the group, "us." Thus, leadership

---

267. Haslam, Reicher, and Platow, *New Psychology of Leadership: From Theory to Practice*. Part of this work was also presented at BPS Division of Occupational Psychology Conference Brighton, January 8—10, 2014. See: https://www.youtube.com/watch?v=nwcf_E9pUUA.

268. Haslam, Reicher, and Platow, xix.

is a group process which details the relationship between the leaders and the followers. In essence, it could be argued that in terms of social identity theory, leadership needs to be dedicated to the task of constantly bringing about a sense of group identity, where a leader constantly reminds the group members of their salient identities, and how the group members ought to act in the light of their core identity values.

The main concern of this chapter was to outline the key aspects of the methodologies that are to be employed by this dissertation and address the objections that have been made regarding the use of social scientific approach and social identity theory in New Testament studies. Due to the inherent danger of this approach being anachronistic, the next chapter will pay careful attention to both the historical and literary context in order to avoid such anachronistic tendencies that are inherent in the methodological approaches of this dissertation.

CHAPTER 3

Historical and Literary Context of 1 Corinthians

The aim of this chapter is threefold: First, it seeks to describe the social context of Corinth and the Corinthian Christian-movement; second, it seeks to argue for the literary integrity of 1 Corinthians; and third, it seeks to identify the underlying cause of the problems in 1 Corinthians. The reason for the concern regarding both the literary and sociohistorical context of 1 Corinthians is because of the dangers that were observed in the previous chapter regarding the anachronistic tendencies among scholars who employ social-scientific approaches. In chapter 2, this study dealt with the objection by scholars such as Judge regarding the appropriateness of using social scientific theories, which includes social identity theory. To avoid the danger of anachronism, the author argued in chapter 2 that this study will incorporate sociohistorical methods in its use of social identity theory. This was argued in line with the suggestion of Clarke and Tucker,[1] who advised that it was necessary for the social scientific theories to engage with social historians, as the latter provide the evidence needed to substantiate social scientific theoretical claims. Hence, this dissertation will now consider the social context of Corinth and, in so doing, it will also engage with the social-historical scholars.

---

1. Clarke and Tucker, "Social History."

3.1 The Social Context of Corinth and the Corinthian Christian Movement

This section comprises two parts. First, it will consider the social context of Corinth, and the second part of this section will deal with the Pauline community at Corinth. We have already stated that while it will be using a variety of methodologies, it nonetheless stresses the importance of the social-historical context of the original audience. Thus, the first part of this section seeks to understand the social world of the Pauline community at Corinth, with the purpose of reconstructing the configuration and the identities of this community, while the second section seeks to deal with historical issues surrounding the Pauline community at Corinth. Issues to be considered include the dating, the purpose, and the composition of the book of 1 Corinthians. This will be done by "using perspectives from the social sciences to understand the texture of early Christian life in all of its particularity."[2] The task of this section is well articulated by Keay in his critique of the historical-critical approaches to the Bible.[3] Historical-critical methods tend to approach Pauline studies "as an abstract world of conflicting ideas rather than a social world of flesh and bone persons relating to one another in real-world settings."[4] Thus, this chapter seeks to establish the social context of the Corinthian correspondence.

---

2. Meeks, "Social Context," 266.

3. Keay, "Paul the Spiritual Guide," 2.

4. Keay, "Paul the Spiritual Guide," 2. Keay's comment is given in the context of advocating for social-scientific approaches to the Bible. While the researcher agrees that there are shortcomings to the historical-critical method, it is also cognisant of the shortcomings of the social-scientific approaches. As Judge has correctly pointed out, at times the social-scientific approaches tend to tell us more about the modern sociological theories, than actually offering us a better description of the early Pauline community at Corinth. Judge, "Social Identity," 209–12. This danger is also well-articulated by Savage: "The danger of this approach is that social history is reduced to modern sociological theory and consequently we learn more about contemporary social scientific theories than the actual situation in antiquity," *Power through Weakness*, 14. Thus, this study will prioritise the gathering of social facts and will give more weight to those social facts to help us in our interpretative process. This study, however, does not follow Judge and Savage's qualms about anachronism drafted into the conversation by social identity theory. The reason being that it incorporates both historical-critical methods and social-scientific approaches in its analysis, in order to mitigate against the threat of anachronism in the application of social identity theory to the ancient texts. Historical-critical methods are incorporated in our social identity approach with the hope that this will help us to shed light on the text in its own ancient context. Once the text is located in historical context, this study will proceed to interpret the meaning of the text using social identity theory. For more on this, see section 2.1.3 of this study, where the researcher argued using the proposal by Clarke and Tucker, that social identity theory needs to incorporate historical-critical methods in order for it not to be accused of being anachronistic. Clarke and Tucker, "Social History," 42.

Winter, commenting on the hermeneutics of the New Testament, says the following: "One of the critical first steps in interpretation [should be] to seek to locate an ancient text such as 1 Corinthians in the first-century horizons of its religious, cultural, and social contexts. Only then does it seem appropriate to proceed with further questions of interpretation."[5] Thus, before proceeding with any social scientific or social identity analysis, one needs "to assemble all the relevant extant data,"[6] which is precisely what this chapter seeks to achieve.

The major sources of this information will be the New Testament text itself, and epigraphical evidence that sheds light on what was happening in the Corinthian congregation.[7] Since the New Testament text forms a major part of our investigation, we will first consider the social context of Corinth (our main focus here will be the city of Corinth). It will then proceed to consider the Pauline community at Corinth (our main focus here will be on Paul's contact with the Corinthian community and how this community at Corinth came to be). All of this is done with the hope that once all relevant data is collected, our task in addressing the other two remaining issues mentioned above will be more accountable.

3.1.1 The Social Context

The aim of this section is to draw an accurate picture of the city of Roman Corinth, and the Corinthian congregation. This is done with the view that it will shed more light on the dynamics that were present in the Pauline community at Corinth.[8] Scholars such as Engels say, "The problems that Paul

---

5. Winter, *After Paul Left Corinth*, xiii.

6. Winter, xiii.

7. Fortunately for this dissertation, there have been numerous studies that explore Corinth during the time of Paul. Among these studies are the works of scholars such as: Theissen's Social Setting, Meeks's "Social Context," 266–77; *First Urban Christians*, 9–110; *Moral World*, 11–39; Gallagher, "Social World of Saint Paul", 91–99, and Engels, *Roman Corinth*. There is also a collection of primary sources and archaeological essays by scholars such as Murphy-O'Connor, as well as a collection of essays that describe the urban context of Corinth by Schowalter and Friesen, and monograph series by scholars such as Winter and Clarke, to name just a few. Murphy-O'Connor, *St. Paul's Corinth*; Schowalter and Friesen, "Prospects for a Demography"; Winter, *After Paul Left Corinth*; *Philo and Paul*; Clarke, *Secular and Christian Leadership*; *Serve the Community*.

8. A reconstruction of Roman Corinth is not without its fair share of difficulties. As De Vos notes, the problem for reconstructing Roman Corinth is the "poor quality of material remains," and also "most of the inscriptions" regarding Corinth are "fragmentary" and also many of them are late. De Vos notes that "little is known of the city apart from the central forum area" (emphasis original). De Vos, *Church and Community Conflicts*, 179. This, however,

encountered at Corinth were a reflection of the nature of the city's people,"[9] while De Silva writes that "many of the specific problems which Paul must address in both [Corinthians] letters radiate from the more basic issue of the believers' continued allegiance to their primary socialization."[10] Keay on the other hand says, "The social conditions prevailing provide insight into the Corinthians' attitudes toward Paul and the source of his problems there."[11] Based on what these scholars say, it thus seems important first to address the issue of the social description of the city of Corinth. This will be done with the aid of social historians, epigraphical evidence, and ancient writers.

Located roughly halfway between Athens and Sparta, Corinth occupied the strip of land that connects the Peloponnese with the Greek mainland.[12] Corinth was important for controlling trade between Asia and Rome. Its two harbours, Lechaeum on the Corinthian Gulf and Cenchreae on the Saronic Gulf, made the city an essential link between the east and the west, enabling traders to negotiate the dangerous oceans around the southern tip of the Peloponnese (Cape Malea).[13] Cicero,[14] describing Corinth's ideal location for navigational purposes, says, "It was situated on the straits and in the very jaws of Greece, in such a way that by land it held the keys of many countries, and . . . it almost connected two seas, equally desirable for purposes of navigation, which were separated by the smallest possible distance."[15] Corinth

---

should not deter us as the fragments can still be of immense value, especially when they are taken in conjunction with evidence gathered from the Greco-Roman world at large. Savage, *Power through Weakness*, 15.

9. Engels, *Roman Corinth*, 110.
10. De Silva, "Let the One," 73.
11. Keay, "Paul the Spiritual Guide," 266.
12. For the history of the origins of the name of Corinth and the general description of the city, see Pausanias (*Descr.* 2.1–14); and Strabo (*Geog.* 8.6.23). See also Murphy-O'Connor's work, *St. Paul's Corinth*, where he has conveniently assembled all the ancient texts referring to Corinth.
13. Strabo, *Geog.* 8.6.20.
14. Cicero, *Agr.* 2.87.
15. Strabo describes Corinth and its advantage for trade as follows: "[Corinth] is situated on the Isthmus and is master of two harbours, of which the one leads straight to Asia, and the other to Italy; and it makes easy the exchange of merchandise from both countries that are so far distant from each other. And just as in early times the Strait of Sicily was not easy to navigate, so also the high seas, and particularly the sea beyond Maleae, were not, on account of the contrary winds; and hence the proverb, 'But when you double Maleae, forget your home.' At any rate, it was a welcome alternative, for the merchants both from Italy and from Asia, to avoid the voyage to Maleae and to land their cargoes here." Strabo, *Geog.* 8.6.20. Due to the dangerous voyage around the Peloponnese, people preferred to walk across the Isthmus.

became very wealthy due to its advantageous location.[16] It was not great only because of its geographical location; it was also wealthy because of the quality of its soil. According to Cicero, Corinth had the "most excellent and productive land,"[17] and, apparently, the "wealth of Corinth was legendary."[18] The location of Corinth is perhaps one of the reasons why Paul chose this city as the strategic location for one of his church plants; it was ideally located to make sure that his gospel could influence people from many different areas. Murphy-O'Connor notes that "the intense traffic in all directions assured him of superb communications.[19] He could not have chosen a more suitable base for his move into Europe." According to Favorinus, the list of the people who visited Corinth were "the traders or pilgrims or envoys or passing travellers."[20]

Corinth, however, endured a devastating tragedy in 146 BCE after the city, together with the Achaean League, proclaimed war on Rome's ally, Sparta. Lucius Mummius destroyed Corinth for its role in the war.[21] Most of the ancient reports suggest that many of the men of the first Corinth were killed, while the women and children were sold into slavery.[22] After the Romans'

---

16. Strabo, *Geog.* 8.6.19–20; Homer, *Iliad*, 2.570. See also Donahoe who points to the ancient works such as that of "Apuleius, *Metam.* 10.18, 35; Plutarch, *Mor.* 831A; *Tim.* 14.2; Pliny the Elder, *Nat.* 34.6, 48." Donahoe, "From Self-Praise," xv.

17. Cicero (*Leg. Agr.* 1.5.) from main text. It is not clear though whether this was the state of the land before or after the destruction, for in his analysis of the land of Corinth after the destruction, Strabo says that the land was not very fertile and he described Corinth as "both beetle-browed and full of hollows." Strabo, *Geog.* 8.6.23.

18. Strabo, *Geog.* 8.6.19–23. cf. Murphy-O'Connor, *St. Paul's Corinth*, 4. See Strabo's (8.6.20) description of the wealth of Corinth.

19. Murphy-O'Connor, "Corinth That Saint Paul Saw," 148. Strabo says that the advantageous geographic location of Corinth played a significant role even to the Corinth of the later time (i.e. the new Corinth). Strabo, *Geog.* 8.6.20.

20. Favorinus, Dio Chrys. *Disc.* 37.8. This of course refers to the new Corinth that was built by Julius Caesar, the Corinth in which Paul established his congregation.

21. Cic. Agr. 1.5.; Pausanias, *Descr.* 2. 1.2.; Strabo, *Geog.* 8.6.23; Dioddorus Siculus, *Hist.* 27.1; 32.4.5.

22. Pausanias, *Descr.* 7.15.1–16.9; cf. Strabo, *Geog.* 8.6.23; Diodorus Siculus, *Hist.* 32.27; Livy, *Perioch.* 52. It is worth noting though that the destruction of Corinth was not total, as reported by Pausanias 2.1.2. and Diod. Sic. 27.1; 32.4.5., who seem to suggest that it lay in a state of complete abandonment until the time it was rebuilt by Julius Caesar. In Tuscluan disputation 3.53, Cicero speaks of witnessing the natives of Corinth as slaves. He also mentions that when he visited the region in 63 BCE, there were people in the region of Corinth, some of whom were farming the land. De Vos notes that even though some people were left in Corinth after its destruction, they might have stayed there as squatters or tenants. He contends that there is nothing that "suggests there was any semblance of the normal city." Thus, for all practical

destruction, the city laid desolate for many years.[23] It was only rebuilt in 44 BCE by Julius Caesar as a Roman colony, shortly before his death.[24] Some scholars claim that the new Corinth became the capital of the Roman province of Achaia.[25] The new rebuilt Corinth was named *Colonia Laus Julia Corinthiensis* in honour of Julius Caesar. De Vos notes that upon colonization the city was rebuilt extensively, old surviving buildings were refurbished, and it was made to be a thoroughly Roman city; with South Stoa measuring 500 feet, it was one of the "longest buildings in Greece,"[26] while its agora was among the largest in the Roman empire.[27] The beauty of the city and its buildings was a matter of pride in antiquity; loyal citizens would sacrifice large sums of money to support elaborate building schemes,[28] and "their sole reward was the proud boast of a finer agora, a grander temple."[29] This was reward enough for both the rich and the poor alike, as "boasting in one's city

---

purposes, in 146 BCE the city ceased to function, and it was deprived of its civic and political identity. De Vos, *Church and Community Conflicts*, 181.

23. In his letter to Cicero, Servius Sulpicius describes the desolate state of Corinth and other cities. He says: "I began to survey the localities that were on every side of me. Behind me was Aegina, in front Megara, on my right Piraeus, on my left Corinth: towns which at one time were most flourishing, but now lay before my eyes in ruin and decay." Cicero, *Fam.* 4.5.4. For a graphic and poetic description of the destruction of Corinth, see also Antipater's *Greek Anthology*, 7.493; 9.151.; and 7.297. As noted in the previous footnote, this does not mean that the city became a ghost town with not even a single soul living in it, but rather that there was no formal political life at Corinth. Horrell and Adams say that there is in fact archaeological evidence that suggests that the destruction was not total, and that there were people who resided in Corinth between 146 and 44 BCE, and archaeological evidence also shows that there were buildings that "survived fairly intact." Horrell and Adams, "Scholarly Quest," 3.

24. Strabo, *Geog.* 8.6.23. There is a debate among the scholars about exactly when Corinth was re-founded and by whom. While Strabo 8.6.23 says that it was re-founded by Julius Caesar, some scholars maintain that Caesar planned to re-find it as a colony, but the actual foundation took place after his death. Tucker notes that scholars mostly credit the rebuilding to Octavian, but Walbank maintains that it was Marc Antony, the administrator of Caesar's will, who carried out the rebuilding. According to Tucker, "after Actium, Antony's name was erased from memory and his achievements were accredited to Augustus." Tucker, *You Belong to Christ*, 94. This dissertation will credit the rebuilding to Julius Caesar as it was his idea to initiate the whole process.

25. Nguyen, *Christian Identity in Corinth*, 122; Finney, *Honour and Conflict*, 54. Finney says that the "inscriptions show that the colonial elite took full advantage of the fact that Corinth was the seat of the provincial procurator and closely associated with the proconsuls to cultivate personal ties with Roman officialdom." Finney, 54.

26. De Vos, *Church and Community Conflicts*, 182.

27. Savage, *Power through Weakness*, 36.

28. Dio Chrys. *Or.*, 46.2–4.

29. Savage, *Power through Weakness*, 25.

was a matter of personal standing."[30] Donahoe notes further that boasting and honour were part and parcel of the culture of the times, and that the "people of Corinth frequently expressed their honor and civic pride through benefactions, abilities, and positions of leadership."[31] She also observes that "honor is the public recognition of one's social standing that comes in two ways: ascribed honor (inherited from one's family descent, gender, or order of birth) and acquired honor (derives from one's virtuous deeds and benefactions, civic roles and offices, military prowess, success at athletic games, verbal challenge-riposte competitions, or other such activities). Acquired honor may be gained or lost as one seeks to receive public recognition." Boasting and chasing honour were so pervasive in the Greco-Roman world and Corinth in particular that people "erected inscriptions praising their own accomplishments, contributions to building projects, and social status."[32] The evidence of chasing honour in Corinth could be seen through a "plethora of temples, statues, buildings, monuments, theatres, and baths."[33] Clarke notes that "to have one's name inscribed above the door of some important, new, public building, or to erect a statue to oneself with a fulsome inscription was a powerful status symbol."[34] Thus, "the beauty, prominence, and stature of Corinth no doubt incited pride in its residents."[35] Hence, it comes as no surprise that the Pauline congregation at Corinth had a tendency towards boasting,[36] because this was a key feature of the society that they lived in.

---

30. Savage, 25. cf. Dio Chrys. *Or.* 44.9, 46.3. Dio Chrys. (*Or.* 44.9) writes about the rivalry that existed between ancient cities, and also the pride of citizens about the splendour of their cities.

31. Donahoe, "From Self-Praise," xvii.

32. Pausanias, *Descr.* 2.2.8; 2.7.2–5; 2.10.1, 3, 5, 7; cf. Donahoe, "From Self-Praise," xviii.

33. Donahoe, xviii.

34. Clarke, *Secular and Christian Leadership*, 31. For more on this, see Plutarch, *Mor.* 820D, who says: "But if it is not easy to reject some favour or some kindly sentiment of the people, when it is so inclined, for men engaged in a political struggle for which the prize is not money or gifts, but which is a truly sacred contest worthy of a crown, a mere inscription suffices, a tablet, a decree, or a green branch."

35. Donahoe, "From Self-Praise," xviii; cf. Dio Chrysostom, *Or.* 9.8, 21. For archaeological evidence and inscriptions that show how prevalent the search for honour and social status was in Corinth, see the work of "The American School of Classical Studies at Athens" in Meritt, *Greek Inscriptions*.

36. See, 1 Cor 1:31; 3:21; 4:7; 5:6; 13:3 versus Paul's ironic boasting: 1 Cor 1:28; 9:15–16; 15:31. Kwon notes that Paul used the Greek verb καυχάομαι six times, while he used the other καύχημα three times, and καύχης once. Kwon, *1 Corinthians 1–4*, 142–43. For a detailed use of καυχάομαι and words related to it in the ancient society (such as ἀλαζονεί/α, ἀλαζώ/ν, αὐξέ/w,

The new Corinth became distinctly Roman and had a strong resemblance to Rome, in terms of ethos, cultural identity, and laws. This was also evident in its architecture which resembled Italian cities (that is, Pompeii).[37] Both De Vos and Nguyen note that the new colonizers made a deliberate effort to make sure that Corinth resembled Rome and not the surrounding Greek cities.[38] Even its new name, *Colonia Laus Julia Corinthiensis*, was a clear attempt by the Romans to distinguish Corinth from its erstwhile Greek format. Winter, observing the Roman influence on the culture of Corinth, says the following: "Whether rich or poor, bond or free, the cultural milieu which impacted life in the city of Corinth was *Romanitas*. This does not mean that there were no ethnic minorities, but it does mean that the dominant and transforming cultural influence was Roman."[39] In contrast to other Roman colonies, the newly rebuilt Corinth was inhabited mostly by poor Romans and freed slaves, whose socioeconomic status was only marginally better than that of

---

ἐπαινέ/w, κομπέ/w, μεγαλαυξέ/w, μεγαλhγορέ/w, περιαυτολογέ/w, περιπερεύ/omai, φιλοτιμέ/omai), see Donahoe, "From Self-Praise," 35–45. In chapter 1 of her work, Donahoe shows that anthropocentric boasting was a dominant idea in the Greco-Roman literature.

37. Nguyen, *Christian Identity in Corinth*, 122; Finney, *Honour and Conflict*, 54. For more on this, see "The Corinth Computer Project" (on http://corinth.sas.upenn.edu/), which was led by scholars from the University of Pennsylvania. This project investigates "the nature of city planning during the Roman period to create an accurate computer generated map of Corinth's overall dimensions and roadway system." Donahoe, "From Self-Praise," xvi. Also, most of the inscriptions that have been recovered regarding Corinth attest to the Roman character of Corinth as they are written in Latin instead of Greek, which supports the claims that Corinth was indeed a Roman Colony. Engels, *Roman Corinth*, 71. See also De Vos for more on the Roman character of Corinth. De Vos, *Church and Community Conflicts*, 182–83.

38. De Vos, 182; Nguyen, 122. While the epigraphical evidence demonstrates that Corinth became a Roman city, since the inscriptions from 44 BCE till pre-Hadrian were all in Latin instead of Greek, this should not make us think that the break between the old and new Corinth was total. As Murphy-O'Connor notes, there was a continuation of some of the religions of the old Corinth into the new Corinth. Murphy-O'Connor, *St. Paul's Corinth*, 43. Also, as Cicero (Tusc. 3.22.53) indicated, when he visited Corinth in his youth in about 79–77 BCE there were people dwelling in the ruins of Corinth, while in Agr. 2.87, Cicero indicates that there were people who were farming the land in Corinth.

39. Winter, *After Paul Left Corinth*, 22.

the slaves;[40] Pausanias and Philo also speak of this.[41] Walters says that the new "Corinth was settled by 12,000–16,000 colonists."[42] Finney suggests that this was one of the clever ways that Rome used to get rid of some of its undesirables, since Rome was overpopulated by both freed persons and the urban poor.[43] This move offered incredible opportunities to the freed persons

---

40. Carson, Moo, and Morris, *Introduction to New Testament*, 263. Strabo (*Geog.* 8.6.23c) says: "Now after Corinth had remained deserted for a long time, it was restored again, because of its favourable position, by the deified Caesar, who colonised it with people that belonged for the most part to the freedmen class." Elsewhere, Strabo (*Geog.* 17.3.15) notes that there were also "some soldiers" who were among the early colonialists. cf. Plutarch, vita Caes. 47.8. Most of the inscriptions, however, tend to focus more on the freedmen than the veterans. Spawforth writes the following regarding the absence of epigraphical evidence in support of the veterans being among the first colonizers of Corinth: "The under-representation of the veteran element reflects both its relative unimportance in the original foundation, as well as the failure of descendants of ordinary veteran soldiers to break into the upper ranks of the ordo." Spawforth, "Roman Corinth," 174. The issue regarding whether the veterans were part of the first colonizers or not is mostly about the interpretation of Plutarch, vita Caes. 47.8. (which at face value seems to contradict Strabo, *Geog.* 8.6.23c). See, Murphy-O'Connor at this point for a proper interpretation of vita Caes. 47.8. Murphy-O'Connor, *St. Paul's Corinth*, 112. This dissertation, however, is of the opinion that while Corinth was colonised mostly with people who were freedmen and freedwomen, there most probably were veterans in their midst for security's sake.

41. Pausanias (2.1.2.) notes that the new "Corinth is [was] no longer inhabited by any of the old Corinthians, but by colonists sent out by the Romans." Horrell and Adams make an interesting point though. They say that the new residents of Corinth must have included both the Romans and the Greek, particularly the Greeks who were "already living in and around Corinth prior to its refounding." Horrell and Adams, "Scholarly Quest," 3. This point is consistent with what this dissertation has already established in this section. Savage also notes that the people who were sent to Corinth also included the "Romanized Greeks." To support his claim, he cites SEG 18.143, which describes a Greek named Junia Theodora as a "Roman living in Corinth." Savage, *Power through Weakness*, 37. Thus, it would be wrong to assume that the bulk of the colonists were only Romans. Finney notes that "the bulk of the available *liberti* in 44 BCE were Judeans, Syrians, Egyptians, Gauls, and many from Asia minor." Finney, *Honour and Conflict*, 55. If this is true, then we can see that the new Corinth was colonised by a diverse group of people. This then would suggest that questions about identity might have been something that was very important for the Corinthians as a whole. It was a young cosmopolitan city that comprised diverse ethnic groups, which included people from various parts of the globe visiting it for trade, and to top it all it was a Roman city in the middle of the Greek territories. Dio Chrsy. *Or.* 37.8. Keay notes that "Corinth's unique identity as both Greek and Roman created a certain tension for the city and its inhabitants. Keay, "Paul the Spiritual Guide," 271. Although modern scholars sometimes speak of an ancient "Greco-Roman" culture, it would be wrong to think that this suggests a homogenized blend of the two cultures. Certainly there was mutual influence, but the two remained distinct and not entirely complementary." Thus, for this dissertation, especially due to its focus on identity, it is important to debunk this all too common and misleading doublet.

42. Walters, "Civic Identity in Roman," 402.

43. Finney, *Honour and Conflict*, 54. Romano, "Post-146 B.C. Land Use," 13; Also Donahoe, commenting on the Roman re-founding of Corinth, says the following regarding the colonialization of Corinth by freed slaves: "It should be emphasized that Corinth was not

for socioeconomic advancement. Appian suggests that the people who were sent to Corinth by Julius Caesar were ἄποροί which is sometimes translated as "poor."[44] But Murphy-O'Connor notes that the basic "meaning of this adjective is 'having no way in, out, or through.'" He says, though, that when ἄποροί is applied to a person it means "hard to deal with, unmanageable."[45] Whichever way one interprets it, the picture that emerges is that the new colonisers of Corinth were people who "felt themselves locked into a certain social level through lack of opportunity."[46] Appian links Caesar's foundation of Corinth with these ἄποροί demanding land.[47] The new Corinth offered an amazing opportunity for social-economic advancement, with new wealth to be gained by these ἄποροί of the freedman stock. Spawforth notes that the colony provided opportunities for freed persons and their families to rise to high status and hold important magisterial positions, and he says: "Although freedmen were not normally eligible for magistracies in Roman colonies, in

---

refounded for the purpose of settling ex-soldiers: rather, Corinth was populated mainly by ex-slaves. This type of resettlement programme obviously suited the policies of the aristocratic families in the Roman Senate who . . . could not themselves operate the business of the new East-West trade route that Colonia Laus Julia Corinthiensis would service. The freedmen-agents were an important part of the population sent to Corinth, serving the wealthy families who foresaw the colony as a potentially strong commercial center. These freedmen were sent out to ensure Roman control of the markets at this point on the east-west trade route and to secure positions for interested Roman families in this new distribution center in the eastern Peloponnesos." Donahoe, "From Self-Praise," xvi–xvii.

44. Appian, *Pun.* 8.136. Murphy-O'Connor questions the credibility of Appian's information as his work exhibits contradictions at times. Murphy-O'Connor, *St. Paul's Corinth*, 120–21. Spawforth notes that the numismatic evidence suggests that a significant number of the freedmen (19% to be precise) were "wealthy and politically successful." Spawforth, "Roman Corinth," 169. Thus, Spawforth draws the conclusion regarding the new colonizers of Corinth: "The picture which emerges [from his investigation of both epigraphic and numismatic remains of Corinth] from this study is of a colony which in its early years was dominated socially and politically by wealthy men of freedman stock and by Roman families with business interests in the east, some no doubt of freedman stock themselves." Spawforth, 174. This work is more inclined to agree with Appian than Spawforth, the reason being the extent to which the new settlers went in order to acquire wealth. According to Strabo (*Geog.* 8.6.23), one of the ways in which freedmen at Corinth became rich was by robbing the graves of Corinth. This seems to suggest that these people discovered new wealth at Corinth, not that they already had wealth by the time they went there. This of course does not deny that there were some wealthy freedmen in the Roman Empire, but they were the exception to the rule. The following ancient text suggests that it was possible to be wealthy as freedmen; Trimalchio, for example, in Petron. *Sat.* 75–76 tells us that he became wealthy by inheriting his master's estate. See Juvenal 1.338–39, for similar sentiments.

45. Murphy-O'Connor, *St. Paul's Corinth*, 120.
46. Murphy-O'Connor, 120.
47. Appian, *Pun.* 8.136.

Caesar's colonies an exception was made."[48] Spawforth argues further that "it is fair to surmise that colonial Corinth's reputation for being 'freedman-friendly' continued to attract freedmen in the years after the foundation."[49] Spawforth makes an example of two people who came to Corinth as freedmen and found success at Corinth.[50] He says Philinus was among the people who came to Corinth and "achieved wealth and political and social success." He also suggests that Babbius was probably one of the original colonists, who "climbed into the provincial 'aristocracy.'" His descendants became men of high standing. His son, Babbius Magnus, and grandson, Babbius Maximus, both held important positions in Delphi.

By the time Paul first made contact with the Corinthians, Corinth "may well have had a strong claim as the third city of the empire, after Rome and Alexandria," writes Finney.[51] Paul must however have also found a city "with shallow roots."[52] Savage notes that "there were few traditions, a changing aristocracy and a relatively open society," by the time Paul reached Corinth.[53] Walters notes that "the civic identity of Roman Corinth was changing rapidly during the first century CE, and these changes resulted in a growing ambiguity in the population's civic religious identity, producing decurions and magistrates who were less likely to police private religious associations in the city."[54] Scholars such as Murphy-O'Connor think that this is one of the several factors that might have convinced Paul to leave Athens for Corinth.[55] In Corinth, Paul could get a better hearing as the Corinthians were open to new ideas, as opposed to the people of Athens who had well-established roots and who treated new ideas with suspicion. Corinth "was a wide-open boomtown" where everything was possible, and people were sure to listen to

---

48. Spawforth, "Roman Corinth," 169.
49. Spawforth, 170.
50. Spawforth, 168–69.
51. Finney, *Honour and Conflict*, 55. This might be an exaggeration on Finney's part. While no one can deny the importance of Corinth for trade, and how the city grew at an accelerated pace, it is doubtful that by the time that Paul arrived at Corinth the city was bigger than Smyrna, Ephesus, and Carthage. Fee, *First Epistle to Corinthians*, 2–3.
52. Savage, *Power through Weakness*, 35.
53. Savage, 35.
54. Walters, "Civic Identity in Roman," 410.
55. Murphy-O'Connor, "Corinth That Saint Paul Saw," 147.

new ideas in the hope of making a profit.[56] The freedom of the Corinthians to choose any religion they wanted meant that in Corinth, individuals and groups would have had more freedom to define their own religious identities; the result being a climate where groups like the Christians could assemble in their households without the same level of hostility or suspicion of other cities.[57] This, however, might have had an unintended consequence for Paul's community at Corinth, as Walters makes the following observations, which are worth quoting at length here:

> Paradoxically, the lack of conflict with outsiders resulted in more internal conflicts, because potential converts faced fewer of the social pressures that would have deterred persons of status from converting. Corinth – and the Corinthian Christian community – permitted persons of varying social strata, varying levels of commitment, and varying sorts of allegiances to identify in some measure with the church. Conflict was inevitable.[58]

The new Corinth was growing at an accelerated pace; "most of the inscriptions which testify to building activity fall within the short period between Augustus and Nero."[59] It had become a flourishing manufacturing,[60] trade, banking and financial centre.[61] The new city featured "three theatres (including the only Roman amphitheatre in Greece)."[62] Archaeological evidence reveals that even homes were extravagantly built with "mosaics, frescos and marble statues."[63] However, this material splendour may have been a con-

---

56. Murphy-O'Connor, 147.
57. Walters, "Civic Identity in Roman," 416.
58. Walters, 416.
59. *Paus.* 2.2.6; cf. Savage, *Power through Weakness*, 35–36.
60. Finney notes that a significant part of Corinth's wealth seemed to have come from its manufacturing industries, such as "Corinthian bronze, terra-cotta, dyeing, marble-carving, and pottery." Finney, *Honour and Conflict*, 56. Josephus (War. 5.201) bears witness to the quality of the Corinthian Brass, while Murphy-O'Connor says that "in the first century C.E. Corinthian bronzes were considered collector's items." cf. Pliny, Let. 3.1.9.; 3.6; see also Plut. De Pyth. 12.399; Murphy-O'Connor, *St. Paul's Corinth*, 109.
61. Corinth seems to be one of the three major banking sectors of the ancient world, together with Athens and Patrae (modern day Patras). For more on this, see Murphy-O'Connor, 109–10.
62. Savage, *Power through Weakness*, 36.
63. For a visual representation that shows both the beauty and the massive scale of Roman Corinth, see the work of "The American School of Classical Studies at Athens" at http://www.

tributing factor to some of the issues that arose in the Pauline community at Corinth, particularly within the context of an honour/shame society, where people were preoccupied with chasing personal status. Savage shows that there is a link between the prosperity and beauty of the city and how people felt about their standing in the world.[64] In fact, the Corinthians were known for boasting about their Corinthian citizenship.[65] This seems to be an attitude that Paul wanted corrected throughout 1 Corinthians, in the light of the cross of Christ.[66]

According to Murphy-O'Connor, Corinth became a hub of tourist activities following the recommencement of the Isthmian Games, which were the second most significant games after the Olympics in the Greco Roman world.[67] The Isthmian Games were held every two years, in spring. Murphy-O'Connor notes that it is highly likely that these games occurred in 51 CE during the time of the proconsul Gallio (cf. Acts 18:12).[68] He further observes that these games "drew crowds [and contestants] not only from Greece but from all the free Greek cities of the east."[69] It is possible that Paul witnessed these games or the preparations for, or the aftermath of, them as he stayed in Corinth for about eighteen months (cf. Acts 18:11). Horrell and Adams also note that "in addition to the biennial Isthmian games, there were also the quadrennial Caesarean games and the Imperial contests."[70] Scholars postulate that in 1 Corinthians 9:24–25, Paul derived his athletic imagery from having

---

ascsa.edu.gr/index.php/News/newsDetails/3d-animation-brings-new-life-to-roman-era-corinth, accessed on 22 March 2017.

64. Savage, *Power through Weakness*, 24–25.

65. Mart. Ep. 10.65.

66. Donahoe adequately demonstrates that throughout 1 Corinthians (i.e. 1 Cor 1:10–14:21; 5:1–13; 9:1–27; 13:1–13; and 15:30–32), Paul addresses "the Corinthians' overestimation of wisdom and eloquence, redirects the Corinthians' attention away from loyalties to specific leaders to loyalty to Christ, redefines the standards by which the Corinthians should view themselves and their leaders, counters the Corinthians' tendency to engage in anthropocentric 'boasting.'" Donahoe, "From Self-Praise." She further notes that in 1 Corinthians Paul was grappling with the Corinthians' "inability to grasp the application of theocentric 'boasting' which leads Paul to address certain aspects and values of secular Corinth that have penetrated the Corinthian community." Donahoe, "From Self-Praise," ii.

67. Murphy-O'Connor, Theology of Second Letter, 6.

68. Murphy-O'Connor, 6.

69. Murphy-O'Connor, "Corinth That Saint Paul Saw," 148.

70. Horrell and Adams, "Scholarly Quest," 5.

witnessed these games.[71] The games provided business opportunities for people like Paul, Priscilla, and Aquila, as their expertise in tent making was in high demand (cf. Acts 18:1–3). Most participants and spectators required tents for housing, and the shopkeepers required tents to display their products, as they created temporary markets nearer to the games.[72] The games might also have provided someone like Paul with the opportunity to proselytise, as he would have had the opportunity to interact with an array of people from different parts of the world, with the potential for his message to reach a broader audience. This, together with the fact that Corinth was at the crossroads of the ancient world, made the city a strategic location for Paul and his message to be heard by many people. Aelius Aristides describes the centrality of Corinth for the ancient world as follows:[73]

> It [Corinth] receives all cities and sends them off again and is a common refuge for all, like a kind of route or passage for all mankind, no matter where one would travel, and it is a common city for all Greeks, indeed, as it were, a kind of metropolis and mother in this respect.

As already seen above, due to its location, Corinth became a cosmopolitan city and this gave rise to religious pluralism (cf. 1 Cor 8:5). Murphy-O'Connor and Furnish observe that archaeological excavations in the city of Corinth have revealed a number of temples and shrines that corroborate the claim that religious pluralism was prevalent in Corinth (cf. Pausanias 2.2.4–3.10 who provides a vivid description of the gods and goddesses that the Corinthians worshipped, and their temples).[74] Archaeologists have unearthed a range of gods, from the Egyptian gods and goddesses (i.e., Isis and Serapis) to the Greek gods. They have also found evidence that attests to emperor worship. However, evidence suggests that the worship of Greek gods dominated the worship life of the city of Corinth.[75] Furnish noted that even though the

---

71. Murphy-O'Connor, St. Paul's Corinth, 15; Horrell and Adams, 5.
72. Murphy-O'Connor, Theology of Second Letter, 7.
73. Ael. Ar. Orat. 46.24.
74. Murphy-O'Connor, Theology of Second Letter, 5; Furnish, "Corinth in Paul's Time," 15–18. See also Bookidis who argues that there was a continued influence of the Old Greek Corinth on the new Roman Corinth, particularly when it came to religion. Bookidis, "Religion in Corinth," 141–64.
75. Furnish, 15–18; Ashley, "Paul's Paradigm for Ministry," 27.

city was destroyed in 146 BCE, a number of the temples and shrines were damaged, but not completely ruined.[76] This resulted in some of the old Greek cults remaining active and, by the time of the rebuilding of Corinth, many of the temples were repaired or rebuilt by the colonists. The majority of these Greek gods and goddesses were associated with fertility; this is perhaps the reason that Paul had to repeatedly address issues concerning sexual immorality among the Corinthians (cf. 1 Corinthians 5, 6, and 7).

What is absent from the archaeological data is material concerning the Jewish presence in Corinth. However, we know from the historical data that there was a large and vibrant Jewish community at Corinth in the first century CE.[77] Sindo notes that "one does not know how much can be made from the fact that at Corinth emphasis was placed on the harmony of all religions and their compatibility with other religions."[78] Finney thinks that the Judeans were "held in contempt by the wider community or were targets of ethnic prejudice."[79] He thinks that this better explains why, for example, when the Corinthian Judeans brought the case before the proconsul Gallio regarding Paul, Gallio refused even to hear the case. In Acts 18, the reason given for Gallio's dismissal of the case is that he refused to be drawn into a controversy within the Judean sect. Finney notes that it is possible that "Gallio's dismissal of the case may have been due not only to its nature but also to the weak Judean influence in Corinth."[80] He further notes that this "highlight(s) negative civic attitudes towards Judeans."[81] Thus, for example, when Sosthenes the synagogue-ruler was severely beaten, Gallio was unconcerned.

Sindo notes, "Religion in Roman-Corinth was an integral part of life and impacted heavily on the cultural, social, political and commercial realities of everyday life."[82] It is worth noting though that people were less concerned with the specific proclivities of different religious formations, and were more

---

76. Furnish, 15.

77. Philo, *Gaius* 281–82. cf. Murphy-O'Connor, St. Paul's Corinth, 78. Finney notes that "the fact that Priscilla and Aquila settled there [Corinth] after their expulsion from Rome by Claudius (Acts 18:2) may imply that the city had a reputation for being tolerant towards Judeans." Finney, *Honour and Conflict*, 56.

78. Sindo, "Socio-Rhetorical Approach," 82; cf. Ashley, "Paul's Paradigm for Ministry," 28.

79. Finney, *Honour and Conflict*, 57.

80. Finney, 56.

81. Finney, 56.

82. Sindo, "Socio-Rhetorical Approach," 82.

concerned with the favour of the gods. This resulted in an unwelcome consequence for the Jewish community, as their religion emphasised purity and a separation of oneself from pollution by Gentile "idolatrous worship."

This section presented a historically viable portrait of Roman-Corinth and also alluded to why Paul might have been attracted to establish a community at Corinth. We saw that Corinth was a strategic location, which made it possible for Paul's message to reach the known world. We also noted that the Corinth that Paul saw was still a young city that had shallow roots, which meant that he had a better chance of getting a hearing there. But, this section also showed that while Corinth was a land of opportunity, some of its cultural practices were on a collision course with Paul's message. We will now consider Paul's contact with the Corinthians in the following section.

3.1.2 The Pauline Community at Corinth

In trying to understand Paul's relationship with the Corinthian community, we will employ sociohistorical methods in trying to construct Paul's association with the Corinthians. The book of Acts will be utilised in trying to formulate the logical and chronological sequence of Paul's movements.[83] Particular attention will be given to Paul's second missionary journey as it was during this period that he made contact with Corinth.[84] Understanding Paul's association with the Corinthians is significant for this study, as it has a

---

83. For a chronology of Paul's missionary journeys and their dating, see Porter and Murphy-O'Connor. Porter, *Apostle Paul*, 50–60; Murphy-O'Connor, *Paul*, 1–31. This study will only focus on the second missionary journey, particularly Acts 18, which provides an account of Paul's association with the Corinthians. Also, for a geographic description of the route that Paul might have taken in his journey from Athens to Corinth, see Murphy-O' Connor, "Corinth That Paul Saw," 148–49.

84. There is a debate among scholars about the historical accuracy of the book of Acts, with scholars such as Doughty calling Acts 18 a fictional history. Doughty, "Luke's Story of Paul." For a brief historical outline concerning this debate, see Porter and Keener. Porter, Apostle *Paul*, 48–50; Keener, Acts 15:1–23:35, 2681–84. The historical accuracy of the book of Acts was first questioned by Ferdinand Christian Baur, who viewed the book of Acts as "second-century apologetic argument to show the unity of early Christianity." Porter, 48. Goulder is among the recent scholars who have sought to revive Baur's theory of the origins of Christianity. Goulder, *St. Paul versus St. Peter*. This dissertation considered Acts to be historical, however, more as an "apologetic history in the form of a historical monograph with a narrow focus on the expansion of the gospel message from Jerusalem to Rome." Keener, Acts: Introduction and 1:1–2:47, 115. See Keener and Schnabel, who both argue for the historical reliability of Acts, in the form of an ancient historical monograph. Keener, *Acts 1:1–2:47*, 166–220; Schnabel, *Acts*, 28–33. In his analysis of Paul's mission and ministry, Porter takes Acts to be an historically reliable document that can be used to map out the chronology of Paul's missionary journeys. Porter, *Apostle Paul*.

bearing on our comprehension of the letter of 1 Corinthians. It helps us deal with a number of questions that affect the exegesis of 1 Corinthians: (1) Did Paul, during his stay at Corinth, leave behind a well-established community in terms of their understanding of their new religious ethos? Linked to this, what was the social makeup of the community when Paul established this community? (2) Based on the initial number of the adherents to his message when he planted this community, what previous identities might have been at play in this community, that is, was the community mostly Gentile, Jewish or a combination of both? Or was there a change in the ethnic makeup after Paul left, and thus the community was struggling with how the message received from Paul related to their current circumstances. (3) What is the chronology of events in the letter of 1 Corinthians? (4) What was Paul's relationship with the community and what might have resulted in his leadership being rejected by some in the community?

Paul's relationship with the Corinthians was a multifaceted affair that lasted approximately seven years, around 50–57 CE,[85] and encompassed several visits, letters, and reports. When one reads 1 and 2 Corinthians, one can see that there was constant interaction between Paul and this community. Paul sent letters to them and they also wrote to him.[86] In 1 Corinthians 5:9–11, Paul mentions a previous letter, where he taught the Corinthians not to associate with immoral members who claim to be a brother or sister. Similarly, in 2 Corinthians 2:4, he refers to another letter which he wrote out of great distress and anguish of heart. If one takes these two letters together with the two surviving letters we have, it is fair to estimate that Paul, at the very least, penned four letters to the Corinthian ἐκκλησία.[87] There also seems to be evidence that Paul returned to Corinth at least once after his initial

---

Other scholars who follow a similar approach to this are: Hemer, "Observation on Pauline Chronology," 3–18, and Carson, Moo, and Morris, *Introduction to New Testament*, 223–31.

85. This is of course dependent entirely on the date one chooses as the date that Paul first made contact with the Corinthians. For scholars who chose an earlier or a later date, the years will shift slightly.

86. 1 Cor 5:9; 1 Cor 7:1.

87. Scholars debate whether these two letters are incorporated in 1 and 2 Corinthians, for a discussion of this, see Hurd, *Origin of 1 Corinthians*, 235–37; Taylor, "Composition and Chronology," 71; 75–79; Thiselton, *First Epistle to Corinthians*, 36–40; and Horrell, *Social Ethos*, 89–91. On the possibility that portions of the previous letter that is mentioned 1 Cor 5:9 as being preserved in 2 Cor 6:14–7:1, see Watson, "2 Cor. X–XIII."

visit of one and a half year stay.[88] Donahoe thinks that Paul probably made three visits,[89] while Keay thinks that Paul made one visit after his initial stay.[90] This dissertation agrees with Donahoe; the first visit of Paul to Corinth is the one mentioned in Acts 18:1–10, the second visit is normally described as the painful visit (1 Cor 16:5–8; cf. 2 Cor 2:1), and the inference made by Paul in 2 Corinthians 12:14, 20–21, and 13:1–2, together with Acts 20:2–3, suggests that Paul made a third visit to Corinth. Members of the ἐκκλησία visited Paul and reported activity within the ἐκκλησία to him (1 Cor 1:11; 16:17). Lastly, Paul sent Timothy to Corinth.[91] All of these show that there was a good amount of communication between the Corinthian congregation and Paul, this of course notwithstanding the fact that scholars differ on the exact number of visits Paul made to the Corinthians and on how many letters he wrote to them. But when did Paul come to Corinth?

According to Acts 18:1–17, Paul first came to Corinth near the end of his second missionary journey in 50 CE, after his arrival from Athens (a journey that would have taken him three days on foot as it was about 85 km).[92] Acts 18:1–2 states that upon Paul's arrival at Corinth, he stayed with Aquila and Priscilla,[93] working with them as a leatherworker[94] during the week and preaching in the synagogue on the Sabbath days.[95] Acts 18:2 states that Aquila and Priscilla had recently come to Corinth as the result of Claudius's

---

88. 1 Cor 16:3; 2 Cor 1:15—2:1; cf. Acts 18:11.

89. Donahoe, "From Self-Praise," 7.

90. Keay, "Paul the Spiritual Guide," 268.

91. 1 Cor 4:17; 16:10; 2 Cor 1:1.

92. See 2 Cor 1:19. It is not clear why Paul left Athens to go to Corinth. But most scholars believe that it was because of the various opportunities that Corinth offered.

93. As Bruce suggests, nowhere does the text suggest that Aquila and Priscilla became followers of Jesus Christ through the ministry of Paul. We can thus assume that they were already "Christians" by the time they arrived at Corinth. Bruce, "Christianity under Claudius," 316.

94. Traditionally the term σκηνοποιός is translated as tentmaker, but recent scholars such as Keener have pointed out that the etymology of the term suggests that a better translation for it is leatherworker, rather than tentmaker. For more on the etymological significance of this term, see Keener, *Acts:* 15:1–23:35, 2732–33.

95. Acts 18:3, 11; cf. 1 Cor 4:12. Hock notes that Paul in "his subsequent trip(s) to Corinth (cf. 1 Cor 16:5; 2 Cor 1:15–16; see also 2 Cor 12:13; 13:1)" probably worked again as a tentmaker, "since he was proud that he had never been a burden on the Church (2 Cor 11:9)." Hock, *Social Context of Paul's Ministry*, 50.

edict.[96] Only upon the arrival of Silas and Timothy from Macedonia does Paul devote himself to preaching and teaching for most of the time (Acts 18:5). Perhaps Silas and Timothy brought him financial support from the churches in Macedonia, and this enabled him to free up more time to do evangelism.[97]

This, however, was not a smooth period of ministry. Opposition arose from among the Jews and Paul moved his preaching to the house of Titus Justus, a God-fearer (Acts 18:6, 12–18). He lived next door to the synagogue. Due to Paul's ministry, Crispus, the ruler of the synagogue, was converted, along with many of the Corinthians and thus the Corinthian church (ἐκκλησία) was established. In all, Paul stayed in Corinth about a year and a half (Acts 18:11).

There is, however, a debate among scholars about the exact year of Paul's arrival at Corinth and his composition of the letter to the Corinthians. This centres around two things: when was the edict issued, and during which years was Gallio[98] proconsul of Achaia? These two dates have been used in trying to provide a fixed date for Paul's ministry at Corinth. The dating of 1 Corinthians is very important for our analysis, especially since it is also the aim of this study to understand the attitudes of the Pauline community at Corinth, particularly in relation to their identity and their choice of leaders. Savage notes that "the time when Paul ministered in Corinth was one of rapid change. Style of speech, in particular, underwent profound revision."[99]

3.1.2.1 Claudius's Edict

The edict of Claudius has extensive ramifications for our understanding of the social context and the dating of the Pauline community at Corinth. Murphy-O'Connor notes that Luke, by mentioning the edict of Claudius, is showing his intention "to date Paul's arrival in Corinth."[100] Unfortunately,

---

96. This point will be revisited below, when this dissertation considers the year Paul founded the church at Corinth.

97. See 2 Cor 11:8–9; Phil 4:15. Hock correctly points out that he should not see this support as amounting to a salary, "nor as large enough or frequent enough to permit to put down his tools." Hock, *Social Context of Paul's Ministry*, 50. Hock points out that the Macedonian aid should be seen as "something that filled Paul's needs in addition to his own work. In other words, this aid filled up 'what was wanting, after Paul had plied his trade.'" Hock, 93.

98. Scholars believe that Gallio "secured the office of proconsul through the influence of his brother, Seneca, the philosopher, following the latter's restoration from an exile lasting from A.D. 42–49." Winter, "Gallio's Ruling," 213.

99. Savage, *Power through Weakness*, 14.

100. Murphy-O'Connor, *Paul*, 9.

while this event might have been clear and fixed for Luke's audience, it is not so for us today. Second, the edict has a huge significance for our study of 1 Corinthians, especially when we consider the makeup of the Pauline community at Corinth, since it meant that there was an influx of Jews to Corinth as a result of it. Scholars argue about whether the edict was issued in 41 or 49 CE,[101] and whether it was directed against all Jews or just Jewish Christians.[102] Jewett argues that the edict only affected Christians and thus for him only the Jewish Christians were banned from Rome,[103] while the book of Acts (18:2) states that the edict was directed at πάντας τοὺς Ἰουδαίους. Jewett argues that even though Acts 18:2 uses πας referring to all Jews, we should see this as a hyperbolic use of πας.[104] He goes on to say that it was not all 50,000 Jews that were expelled, rather it was the "Christian" agitators.[105] Jewett builds his case

---

101. For more on this, see Lüdemann, *Paul, Apostle to Gentiles*, 164–70; Jewett, *Dating Paul's Life*, 36–38; Murphy-O'Connor, *Paul*, 8–15; and a well-detailed treatment of it by Bruce, "Christianity under Claudius," 309–26. This dissertation follows scholars such as Bruce, Porter, and Jewett who take the 49 CE date. Bruce, "Christianity under Claudius"; Porter, *Apostle Paul*, 55; Jewett, *Dating Paul's Life*, 37.

102. For a well detailed and technical analysis of this debate regarding the edict of Claudius and its impact on the early followers of Jesus Christ in Rome, see Spence, *Parting of Ways*, 65–117. To distinguish between those who believed in Jesus and those who did not within the Jewish community, this study will use terms like "Jewish believers in Jesus" or "Jewish Christ followers," in speaking about the Jews who believed in Jesus. The researcher will use the term "Jews" without qualification in referring to the Jews who did not believe in Jesus. By "Jewish believers" or "Jewish Christ's followers," this study means "Jews by birth or conversion who in one way or the other believe Jesus was their saviour." Skarsaune, "Jewish Believers in Jesus," 3. For early use of the term "Jewish believers," see John 8:31; Origen, *Cels.* 2.1.; Eusebius, *Hist. eccl.* 6.25.4; 4.5.2; 3.3.25.5; and Jerome, *Epist.* 112.3. For more on the justification of the use of the terms "Jewish believers" or "Jewish Christ followers," see Skarsaune and Paget, who provide both the definition and the history of the research concerning the use of the terms Jewish Christians and Jewish Christianity. Skarsaune, 3–21; Paget, "Definition of Terms," 22–54. This study is also aware of the debate surrounding the translation of the word Ἰουδαῖοι. For more on this debate, see Appendix 1.

103. Jewett, Dating *Paul's Life*, 36.

104. Jewett, 37.

105. This is based on the ambiguous Latin text by the Roman historian Suetonius who mentions the Jewish expulsion by Claudius and states: "Since the Jews constantly made disturbances at the instigation of Chrestus, he [the Emperor Claudius] expelled them from Rome." However, scholars debate the identity of Chrestus. Scholars such as Bruce, Jewett, and Lane interpret Chrestus to be Christ and the reference impulsore Chresto to be referring to Christians, while scholars such as Slinger vehemently oppose such an interpretation. See Spence, *Parting of Ways*, 68–70 for more on this; Jewett, *Dating Paul's Life*; Bruce, "Christianity under Claudius"; Lane, "Social Perspectives," 204–05. For more on the grammatical analysis of Suetonius' Latin and its impact on our understanding of Claudius's edict, see Spence, 65–81.

on the evidence that is provided by the Roman historian Dio Cassius,[106] who refers to a large number of Jews in Rome, which made their expulsion impossible.[107] But it is possible that Jewett is mixing up two dates here, 41 CE and 49 CE. Both Bruce and Murphy-O'Connor agree that the events described by Dio Cassius took place at the beginning of Claudius's reign, which was around 41 CE.[108] This dissertation agrees with Bruce that it is unlikely that Dio is referring to the same occasion as the one which some writers see as having taken place in 49 CE.[109] Both Acts 18:2 and Suetonius refer to Claudius's expulsion of the Jews from Rome, while "Dio says that he did not expel them, but put restrictions on their assembling together."[110] Therefore, it is highly probable that Claudius first restricted the Jewish freedom in order to control them but "when these measures proved inadequate to deal with the trouble, he took more drastic steps later," and expelled them.[111] Also, the fifth century church historian Orosius says that Claudius gave his edict on the ninth year of his reign.[112] Therefore, this dissertation is of the view that Acts 18:2 refers to Claudius's edict of late 49 CE or early 50 CE.

The question, however, remains: at whom was the edict directed – Christians or Jews? The simple answer to this question is both, as during Paul's days, early Christ followers were viewed as a sect within the Jewish religion, and as such they would have suffered the same fate as the rest of the Jewish people throughout the empire under the reign of Claudius.[113] This of course does not mean that the early followers of Jesus and the Jews were not aware of the differences between the two religions, but the incidence that is reported in Acts 18:12–17 suggests that those differences were not known at

---

106. Dio Cassius, *Hist.* ix.6.6.
107. Jewett, *Dating Paul's Life*, 37.
108. Bruce, "Christianity under Claudius," 315; Murphy-O'Connor, Paul, 11.
109. Bruce, 315. See Witherington, Conflict and Community in Corinth, 71.
110. Bruce, 315.
111. Bruce, 315.
112. This researcher is aware that there are issues surrounding Orosius's credibility since he "erroneously attributes this datum to Josephus," while there is no such reference in Josephus. Jewett, Dating *Paul's Life*, 38. Scholars such as Harnack have nonetheless come out in support of the date of the edict being issued in the ninth year of Claudius's reign. Harnack, *Constitution and Law*; See also Jewett, 38.
113. Bruce, "Christianity under Claudius," 310.

this time by the people outside these communities.[114] Scholars such as Dunn note that it is only in the second century that there was a clear distinction between the Christians and the Jews.[115] The reason why some scholars think that this edict was directed at Christians was because of the witness of fifth century Christian historian Paul Orosius who wrote:[116]

> In the ninth year of the same reign, Josephus reports that the Jews were expelled from the city by Claudius. But Suetonius convinces me more who speaks in the following manner: "Claudius expelled the Jews from Rome, who were constantly stirring up revolutions because of their ill-feeling toward Christ." But it is by no means discernible whether he ordered the Jews to be checked and repressed because they were stirring up revolutions against Christ, or because he wished the Christians also to be expelled at the same time as those of a related religion.

This dissertation is of the view that the edict affected both Jews and Christians, but particularly those Jews who believed in Jesus Christ. This view is also supported by the Roman historian Suetonius who makes mention of it when he says the following in reference to Claudius's edict: "because the Jews of Rome were indulging in constant riots at the instigation of Chrestus (impulsore Chresto) he expelled them from the city."[117] However, the Latin of this text is ambiguous, as Lane demonstrates.[118] Lane explains that there are two ways in which this text can be interpreted. It could mean: (1) "He expelled from Rome the Jews constantly making disturbances at the instigation of Chrestus," or (2) "Since the Jews constantly make disturbances at the instigation of Chrestus, he expelled them from Rome." Lane observes that the first interpretation allows that Claudius expelled only those Jews who

---

114. Bruce, 310.

115. Dunn, *New Perspective on Paul*, 4–17. This point is still a subject to debate however, as the Emperor Nero, in his persecution of Christians, was able to single out Christians from the Jews as early as the first century. In fact, Tacitus (Ann. 15.44) makes it clear that the populace hated the Christians. Yet, it might still be argued that in the first century Christianity was affiliated to the Jewish religion, as Christians still went to the Jewish synagogues during this time. A clear parting of ways occurred in the second century.

116. *Historiae adversus paganos* 7.6: 15–16. Translation by Deferrari, "Seven Books of History," 297.

117. Suet. *Claud.* 25.4.

118. Lane, "Social Perspectives," 204.

were causing disturbances (which will be the leaders of the Jesus movement and the Jews), while the second interpretation suggests that he expelled all the Jews, a task that we saw was impossible from the inception of Claudius's reign. Thus, it was mostly the Christian Jews who were expelled from Rome as the result of this edict.

What Suetonius's text shows is that, even though during the time of Claudius the Jesus-following community was not distinguishable from the Jewish faith by outsiders, by 120 CE the division was clear.[119] This dissertation is of the view that the edict was decreed in 49 CE as a result of the tension within the Jewish community; between those who believed in Jesus Christ and those who did not. But, when the edict was passed it affected mostly the "ring leaders" within what was now to become two communities. This will explain the special mention of Aquila and Priscilla by Luke since they played a huge role in supporting the Jesus movement.[120] Claudius's edict must have had a huge impact both socially and religiously for the early Jesus movement. As Lane has stated:[121]

> it [the expulsion of the Jewish Christians] must have created a crisis of leadership and mission. In the absence of centralized leadership within the Jewish community of Rome, Jewish Christians appear initially to have had a measure of success in propagating their message in individual synagogues, without encountering concerted resistance. After 49 C.E., however, it is likely that they would not have been welcome at many, perhaps all, of the Roman synagogues.

---

119. This argument is of course contradictory to the argument of Spence in *Parting of Ways*, who contends that the parting of ways between the Jewish believers in Jesus and the orthodox Jews occurred earlier on. While this might be the case because of the tension that existed earlier on within these communities, this dissertation is not convinced that the division was visible to the people outside these communities. Of course, by the time of Nero this was not the case, as Nero was able to single out those who believed in Jesus, and persecute them.

120. Cf. Acts 18:24–26; Rom 16:3–5; 1 Cor 16:19; 2 Tim 4:19. There is a great deal of "evidence from antiquity that patronage and leadership went hand in hand, especially when a member's generosity extended to the gift of his home for communal use." Lane, "Social Perspectives," 210. Thus, we can deduce that Aquila and Priscilla played a leadership role within the early Jesus movement, which is supported by the fact that in Acts 18:24–26, they played a role in correcting Apollos's theology, and thus were involved indirectly in his discipleship.

121. Lane, "Social Perspectives," 206.

This does seem feasible, and it also explains why in Acts 18:12 the Jews rose in one accord against Paul and took him to Gallio.

The implication of Claudius's edict is thus as follows: (1) It helps us to a certain degree to know that Paul arrived at Corinth in late 49 or early 50 CE. But this will only be clearer when we consider the second date that is provided in Acts 18:12; the time that Gallio was proconsul of Achaia. (2) It helps us to have a better understanding of the social context in which Paul's ministry in Corinth took place. That is, there was an influx of Jewish-Christians into the city as the result of the Jewish expulsion. Perhaps these Jewish Christians came to know Christ through the ministry of the apostle Peter, thus there was a faction in the Corinthian community that claimed to follow Peter.[122] Among these Jewish Christians would have been influential people like Aquila and Priscilla and the ἀρχισυνάγωγος Crispus of Acts 18:8 who has been identified as Crispus whom Paul baptised in 1 Corinthians 1:14.[123] The internal evidence of 1 Corinthians 12:2 also suggests that the congregation comprised mostly Gentiles but with an important contingent of Jews (cf. 1 Cor 1:14).

The mention of the households of Aquila and Priscilla (cf. 1 Cor 16:19), and Crispus (1 Cor 1:14) by Paul in 1 Corinthians, together with that of Stephanas (cf. 1 Cor 1:16) and Gaius (cf. 1 Cor 1:14) suggests that there were not only influential Jewish people in the congregation but also wealthy patrons who were able to offer their homes for the church to meet.[124] If we read this together with 1 Corinthians 1:26–28, we get a picture that suggests that the congregation comprised people from different social and economic backgrounds.[125]

---

122. There is not much in terms of source that indicates that Peter was ever in Corinth, besides an allusion by Paul that Peter was accompanied by his wife in his travels, in 1 Cor 9:5. It thus seems probable that the faction that claimed to have been following him, somehow benefited from his ministry during their time in Rome (this will be considered in more detail in the exegesis section of this dissertation).

123. Edsall, *Paul's Witness*, 57.

124. For more on this, see section 1.2.3 which discusses the socioeconomic status of the Pauline community at Corinth.

125. This statement is a simplification of the debate. There is an abundance of discussion concerning the social status of the Pauline community at Corinth. Further engagement with it here will be superfluous. However, for a summary treatment of this discussion, see below the section; "The Socio-economic Status of the Pauline Community at Corinth." See also the following scholars who have adequately dealt with the issue, though they reach different conclusions: Friesen, "Poverty in Pauline Studies"; Horrell, *Social Ethos*, 91–101; Judge, *Social Patterns*; "Paul's Boasting," 1–56, 117–36; Theissen, "Social Structure," 65–84; "Social Conflicts,"

3.1.2.2 The Proconsul Gallio

Establishing the date of Gallio's time in office is very important for us in estimating the time that Paul founded the church in Corinth, as Acts 18:12 makes it clear that it was during the time of Gallio that the Jews staged an insurrection against Paul. Much of the debate regarding the time that Gallio was the proconsul revolved around the discoveries of the Delphic inscription of Claudius which mentions Lucius Junius Gallio who is specifically named in Acts 18:12 as the proconsul of Achaea.[126] In the inscription of Delphi, Claudius refers to Gallio as "my friend and proconsul" (ὁ φ[ίλος] μου κα[ὶ ἀνθύ]πατος).[127] This inscription has not only been used to try to determine the exact date of Paul's contact with the Corinthians but also to map out the chronology of events in his ministry.[128] Jewett notes that some scholars think that the Jews approached Gallio as soon as he came into office, and states that if indeed this was the case, that would give us a precise date for when Paul came to Corinth and the inception of his ministry there.[129] However, as Haacker has correctly observed, there is nothing in the text of Acts 18:12 that indicates the precise time during Gallio's reign; the text does not say "that Gallio had just taken up office" when the Jews approached him.[130] However, since the proconsul only served for a year in office, there is still value in establishing the period of Gallio's time in office as this will give us a reference point for Paul's ministry in Corinth.[131] Scholars such as Haacker, Winter, and Jewett believe that Gallio secured the office of proconsul through the influence of his brother, Seneca, the philosopher, following the latter's restoration from an exile which was imposed on him between 42–49 CE.[132] Therefore, we know two things thus far: (1) Gallio was a proconsul of Achaia for one year; (2) this must have taken place after 49 CE when his brother returned from exile. This is now where the inscription of Delphi becomes useful. According to

---

371–91; Meeks, *First Urban Christians*, 51–73; "Social Context," 266–77; and Donahoe, "From Self-Praise," xix–xxvi.

    126. Thiselton, *First Epistle to Corinthians*," 29; Winter, "Gallio's Ruling," 213.
    127. Winter, 213.
    128. Winter, 213; Thiselton, *First Epistle to Corinthians*, 29.
    129. Jewett, *Dating Paul's Life*, 38.
    130. Haacker, "Gallio," 902.
    131. Jewett, Dating *Paul's Life*, 38–39.
    132. Haacker, "Gallio," 901; Winter, "Gallio's Ruling," 213; Jewett, Dating *Paul's Life*, 38.

Jewett, the inscription records a case where the "Emperor Claudius decided in Delphi's favour during the period that Gallio was in Corinth."[133] Also, this inscription provides us with the date that Claudius's letter, "was written during the period of his 26th acclamation as Imperator." Scholars note that the 26th acclamation of the Caesar would have occurred in the first half of the year 52 CE. Since the proconsul normally served only a year and began his term in the spring, the debate is whether the inscription refers to a Gallio who had only recently left the proconsul-ship or who has been proconsul for a few months. Again, thus far we know that Gallio was a proconsul after 49 CE, when his brother returned from exile, possibly the spring of 50 CE or the spring of 51 CE. If one takes the view that Claudius wrote the letter while Gallio was a proconsul, then Gallio began his reign in the spring of 51–52 CE and Claudius's letter was written towards the end of his proconsul-ship. This will mean that Paul was in Corinth from late 51 CE or early 52 CE. But if one takes the inscription to have been written shortly after the reign of Gallio, as this dissertation does, and takes this together with the evidence about the expulsion of the Jews by Claudius in 49 CE from Rome, we can with high probability assume that Paul was in Corinth between the autumn months of 50 CE to early months of 52 CE, and that the Pauline community at Corinth was established during this time. Now that we have established that Paul was in Corinth between late 50 to early 52 CE, we will now consider the socioeconomic status of this community at Corinth.

3.1.2.3 *The Socioeconomic Status of the Pauline Community at Corinth*

In recent times, there has been a growing interest regarding the social status of the Pauline community at Corinth. As seen in the previous chapters, this interest coincided with the use of social scientific approaches to the Bible. There is no consensus among New Testament scholars regarding the socioeconomic status of the Pauline community at Corinth; rather, there are two camps regarding this issue. (1) Some are of the view that the Pauline community at Corinth was "mostly comprised of people from lower social strata," and (2) others hold to the view that "the socio-economic level of the Corinthian

---

133. Jewett, 39.

community varied from quite poor to relatively well-off."[134] Scholars such as Friesen and Martin call the first group the "old consensus," while the second group is referred to as the "new consensus."[135] Scholars such as Donahoe and Meeks generally credit Adolf Deissmann as being the first person to propagate the views of the first group,[136] a historical interpretation that has since been challenged by Friesen.[137] Deissmann argues that the early Jesus movement included mostly people from the lower social classes.[138] Friesen says that Deissmann was then followed by Kautsky, who analysed the early Pauline community in the light of Marxist ideology.[139] The old consensus views are summarised by Meeks as follows:[140]

> The notion of early Christianity as a proletarian movement was equally congenial, though for quite different reasons, to Marxist historians and to those bourgeois writers who tended to romanticize poverty. Of particular importance in shaping this century's common view of Paul and his congregations was the opinion of Adolf Deissmann, professor of New Testament at Heidelberg, then at Berlin . . . Until recently most scholars who troubled to ask Deissmann's question [about the social setting of Paul's assemblies] at all ignored the ambiguities of the evidence that Deissmann had at least mentioned. The prevailing viewpoint has been that the constituency of early Christianity, the Pauline congregations included, came from the poor and dispossessed of the Roman provinces.

Scholars such as Judge, Malherbe, and Meeks are part of the second group, that challenged the findings of the old consensus, and argued that the Pauline community consisted of people of varied social status; from poor

---

134. Donahoe, "From Self-Praise," xx.
135. Friesen, "Poverty in Pauline Studies," 324; Martin, "Review," 57.
136. Donahoe, "From Self-Praise," xx; Meeks, *First Urban Christians*, 51–52.
137. Friesen, "Poverty in Pauline Studies," 325.
138. Deissmann and Wilson, *St. Paul*, 144.
139. Friesen, "Poverty in Pauline Studies," 324.
140. Meeks, *First Urban Christians*, 51–52.

to individuals who were well off.[141] Theissen builds upon the works of these scholars and challenged the notion that the Pauline community was made up only of poor people.[142] He argues that the Pauline community were people from varied social strata, with the majority coming from lower classes but nonetheless with the minority of people from the upper classes. He says:[143]

> Early Christianity was located in the plebs urbana, but attracted also a small minority of people at the periphery of the local upper class. These were above all people with dissonance of status, caused by lower birth, by gender or by the fact that they were aliens (peregrini) or well-to-do people outside the privileged circle of the decurions. Within these limitations early Christianity comprised all social levels and groups, which we discover on and below the level of the local power elite. In particular cases Christianity also penetrated the elite.

The views of scholars such as Judge, Malherbe, Meeks, and Theissen became known as "the new consensus." It is worth noting though, that Theissen questions the appropriateness of using the term "the new consensus."[144] He says that "The 'new consensus' is neither new nor is it a consensus." He sees the "new consensus" as a renewed sociohistorical interest by scholars that yielded different results. His issue with the term "new consensus" is that it gives the impression that scholars agree about the social description of the early Pauline community while this was far from being the case. This dissertation, while agreeing with Theissen's observation that there is no real consensus among the scholars who hold this view, will nonetheless retain the term "new consensus" as a way of generalizing about the scholars who adhere to the view that the Pauline community included both the rich and the poor. There are two reasons why the term is kept here: first, there is a widespread acceptance among New Testament scholars that the Pauline community included people of varied socioeconomic status. Second, as Friesen has correctly pointed out,

---

141. Judge, *Social Patterns*; Malherbe, *Social Aspects*; and Meeks, *First Urban Christians*. For Judge's views regarding the makeup of the Pauline community at Corinth, see chapter 2 under the section, "The Rise of Social Scientific Approach."

142. Theissen, *Social Setting*, 69–119.

143. Theissen, "Social Structure," 73.

144. Theissen, 66.

both Malherbe and Meeks are in harmony in perceiving their enterprise to be part of the new consensus.[145] Malherbe actually says: "it appears from the recent concern of scholars with the social level of early Christianity, that a new consensus may be emerging."[146]

The new consensus has since been challenged by scholars such as Meggitt and Friesen.[147] Meggitt has been one of the strong critics of the new consensus. He argues that people from the poor class comprised the early Christian community.[148] To make his point, Meggitt divides the ancient Roman community into two groups; the small superwealthy elite (which were only 1% of the populace) and the non-elite (which comprised the other 99% of the populace), who lived in destitution.[149] For Meggitt, "Paul and his followers should be located amongst the 'poor' of the first century, . . . they faced the same anxieties over subsistence that beset all but the privileged few in that society."[150] Meggitt incorporates the definition of Garnsey and Woolf and defines the poor as "those living at or near the subsistence level, whose prime concern is to obtain the minimum food, shelter and clothing necessary to sustain life, whose lives are dominated by the struggle for physical survival."[151] For him, there were no elite among the Pauline community.[152] With regard to the elite, the 1 percent of the population, Meggitt concludes that the "distribution of what little income was available in the Mediterranean world was entirely dependent upon political power: those devoid of political power, the non-élite, over 99% of the Empire's population, could expect little more from life than abject poverty."[153] After analysing the various arguments offered by the "new consensus" regarding the social makeup of the Pauline communities,[154] he postulates that the early Christ followers "shared fully in

---

145. Friesen, "Poverty in Pauline Studies," 324–26; Malherbe, *Social Aspects*, 31; Meeks, *First Urban Christians*, 73.

146. Malherbe, 31.

147. Meggitt, *Paul, Poverty and Survival*; Friesen, "Poverty in Pauline Studies"; "Prospects for a Demography."

148. Meggitt, *Paul, Poverty and Survival*.

149. Meggitt, 1–7.

150. Meggitt, 179.

151. Meggitt, 5; Garnsey and Woolf, "Patronage of Rural Poor," 153.

152. Meggitt, 4.

153. Meggitt, 50.

154. Meggitt, 75–154.

the bleak material existence that was the lot of the non-élite inhabitants of the Empire" (emphasis original).[155] While scholars like Theissen and Martin generally commend Meggitt for his handling of the primary sources, the major criticism against him has been how he divides the Roman society.[156] His simplistic rigid categorization of people as simply rich and poor, without being cognisant of the range of economic statuses among the ordinary 99 percent of the empire's populace, has been seen as a major weakness of his work. Scholars such as Donahoe have correctly observed that Meggitt's presentation of the "non-elite group as a socially homogeneous group" overlooked the differences that existed within this group, for example, between a slave and a slave-owner.[157] While scholars agree with him that owning a slave(s) did not automatically make one a member of the elite group, there is nonetheless a difference between the slave and a slave-owner,[158] something for which Meggitt fails to account. Meggitt glosses over these differences that existed within this group and says that slave-ownership has no bearing on the social status of the slave-owner.[159] He says that, "a Christian having a 'household' cannot serve as a probable indicator of elevated social status at all" (emphasis original).[160] But this statement fails to take into account the difference in economic hardships that existed between the slave and a slave-owner. The fact that a person was a slave-owner meant that they had a disposable income and were not as destitute as Meggitt suggests in his definition of "poor." A slave-owner could trade or lend out his or her slave if he or she needed financial assistance, while that option was not available for the slave, who owned nothing.[161] It thus seems that Meggitt's analysis fails to explain the social status of the early Pauline community properly or the conflict that existed within the Pauline community at Corinth that was seen to be a result of the different social status(es) that existed within the community.[162]

---

155. Meggitt, 153.
156. Theissen, "Social Structure"; Martin, "Review," 53.
157. Donahoe, "From Self-Praise," xxii.
158. Donahoe, xxii; Martin, "Review," 55.
159. Meggitt, *Paul, Poverty and Survival*, 131–32.
160. Meggitt, 132.
161. See Martin, "Review," 55–56, for more on this.
162. For more on this, see Martin, "Review"; Theissen, "Social Structure"; "Social Conflicts," 371–91; Donahoe, "From Self-Praise," xxi–xxvi.

As already noted above, Friesen has also been one of the scholars who are critical of the "new consensus" and modified the work of Meggitt slightly.[163] While Meggitt only saw the Roman society through the binary lenses of the elite and non-elite (with the elite being rich and non-elite being poor and destitute), Friesen expanded that model by including among the non elite varying degrees of poverty. He writes: "Rather than using the vague binary categories of rich/poor, a poverty scale is proposed with seven categories ranging from 'below subsistence level' to 'imperial elites.'"[164] Utilizing this scale to analyse the socioeconomic status of the Pauline communities that are referred to in the authentic Pauline letters, Friesen concludes, "Paul's congregations were probably composed mostly of individuals living near, at, or below subsistence level. Leadership within the congregation seems to have come mostly from the families of those living near subsistence level and those with moderate surplus resources."[165] The following table demonstrates Friesen's seven level poverty scale, that shows the breakdown of the various socioeconomic levels of the Roman society.[166] The percentages that are given here are taken from his second table where he measures the actual percentage of people in each category based on a city of 10,000 people or more.[167] The asterisk (*) represents figures where Friesen admits that they are speculative.[168]

---

163. Friesen, *Urban Religion*.
164. Friesen, "Poverty in Pauline Studies," 323.
165. Friesen, "Prospects for a Demography," 370.
166. Friesen, "Prospects for a Demography," 365; "Poverty in Pauline Studies," 340–47.
167. Friesen, "Prospects for a Demography," 366; "Poverty in Pauline Studies," 340, 346–47.
168. Friesen, "Poverty in Pauline Studies," 346–47. See also White, who also does a review of Friesen's work, for more on this. White, *Where Is the Wise Man?*, 79–80.

PS 1: Imperial Elite	Imperial dynasty, Roman senatorial families, some retainers, local royalty, some freed-persons	0.04%*
PS 2: Regional or Provincial Elites	Equestrian families, provincial officials, some retainers, some decurial families, some freed-persons, some retired military officers	1%*
PS 3: Municipal Elites	Most decurial families, wealthy men and women who did not hold office, some freed persons, some retainers, some veterans, some merchants	1.76%*
PS 4: Moderate Surplus Resources	Some merchants, some traders, some freed-persons, some artisans (especially those who employ others), military veterans	7%
PS 5: Near Subsistence[169] Level	Many merchants and traders, regular wage earners, artisans, large shop owners, freed-persons, some farm families	22%
PS 6: At Subsistence Level	Small farm families, labourers (skilled and unskilled), artisans (especially those employed by others), wage earners, most merchants and traders, small shop/tavern owners	40%*
PS 7: Below Subsistence Level	Some farm families, unattached widows, orphans, beggars, disabled persons, unskilled day labourers, prisoners	28%*

Based on his seven-level poverty scale, Friesen draws the following conclusions regarding the socioeconomic status of the Pauline communities (based on the undisputed letters of St. Paul):[170]

1. He says that most of the people in the Pauline community were poor, with the majority of people from PS 5–7, and that these people were mostly living near or below the subsistence level. He says that "some of the leaders in the Pauline community were [also] poor as was Paul himself."

---

169. Friesen defines "subsistence level" "as the resources needed to procure enough calories in food to maintain the human body." Friesen, "Poverty in Pauline Studies," 343.

170. Friesen, "Prospects for a Demography," 367–69.

2. According to Friesen, there was only a handful of people in the Pauline congregations who lived above the poverty line PS 4–5.[171] These are Chloe (PS 4), Gaius (PS 4), Erastus (PS 4–5), Philemon (PS 4–5), Phoebe (PS 4–5), Aquila (PS 4–5), and Prisca (PS 4–5). Thus for Friesen, of the individuals mentioned in Pauline letters, only seven can be classified as having moderate surplus resources.[172]
3. Paul's letters do not provide any clear evidence that some members of the assembly were super-wealthy (PS 1–3). He notes that there might be two exceptions to this, Phoebe and Erastus, but he says that "from what we know of the general economy, however, the odds are greatly against this."[173]

The seven levels of poverty provide a useful heuristic tool that can be used to stabilize academic discourse in its analysis of the ancient discourse on poverty.[174] There are, however, clear shortcomings in Friesen's work. First, by his own admission, some of the percentages that he offers are speculative, particularly those of PS 4–5.[175] So, how are we to know with certainty that the number of people who occupied this sector of the population was as many as Friesen claims them to be?[176] For example, Longenecker has shown that a more probable figure for PS 4 should be around 17 percent, while for PS 5 it should be around 25 percent.[177] That is a big shift towards people who had a surplus of income. Also, how are we to know with certainty that the

---

171. Friesen, 367–68.
172. Friesen, 368.
173. Friesen, 368.
174. Longenecker, "Exposing Economic Middle," 249.
175. Friesen, "Poverty in Pauline Studies," 347.
176. In his poverty scales (particularly PS 6–7), Friesen relies on the work of Whittaker, but as Longenecker has observed, Friesen takes only the lower limit in his consideration of this group, while Whittaker allows for a variable of 14% between PS 6–7. Friesen, "Poverty in Pauline Studies," 343; Longenecker, *Remember the Poor*, 317–18. Thus if one were to take the upper limit, a different picture of the Greco-Roman economic stratification would emerge. For example, if one takes the upper end of Whittaker's scale the following can be seen: PS 4 changes from 7% to 17%, PS 5 changes from 22% to 25%, while PS 6 becomes 30% instead of the 40% of Friesen, and PS 7 becomes 25% instead of 28%. For more on this, see Longenecker, 317–32. It is worth noting though, that Longenecker agrees with Friesen about the absences of the PS 1–3 group in the Pauline communities. Longenecker, "Exposing Economic Middle," 270.
177. Longenecker, 318.

percentage of wealthy in the early Pauline community is a reflection of Roman society in general?

Friesen's picture of the Pauline community being made up almost exclusively of impoverished people is derived from his general understanding of the Roman economy.[178] Friesen describes the people in the Roman economy as follows:[179]

> Almost everyone lives near the level of subsistence, but there is a very small wealthy elite that controls commerce and politics. In between the masses and the elite there is no economic middle class, because a preindustrial society has so few economic mechanisms for gaining significant wealth. Some people do, however, manage to achieve moderate surplus income for various reasons, and these people occupy the large gap between the elite and the masses.

There is a problem with this statement by Friesen. First, he treats all the Roman cities the same and fails to account for the fact that "'the Roman economy was not a homogeneous entity,' but rather 'a series of interlocking regional ones.'"[180] By generalising about Roman society, Friesen fails to consider the uniqueness of Corinth as a new Roman colony and the opportunities that existed there (as seen above).[181] There were unique opportunities in Corinth for people to earn an income owing to Corinth's position of eminence, and Corinth also offered great opportunities for upward mobility that might not have existed in the larger Roman Empire. Thus, this dissertation is of the view that the "new consensus" still offers a better explanation of the makeup of the Pauline community at Corinth. It was a community that consisted of people with varied wealth, from the poor to the super-rich. This study is of the view that it is difficult to know with certainty the percentages in terms of the social stratification of this community, and so this will be pure speculation.

---

178. White, *Where Is the Wise Man?*, 78.
179. Friesen, "Prospects for Demography," 364.
180. Longenecker, "Exposing Economic Middle," 250.
181. For more about the general assumptions that Friesen makes in his work, see Oakes, "Constructing Poverty Scales," 367–71.

What is clear though from Scripture is the following picture regarding this community. It was a mixed community of ethnically diverse people (who came from different religious backgrounds), it had both Jews and Gentiles,[182] with Gentiles being the majority of members.[183]

This study agrees with proponents of the new consensus such as Winter, Clarke, and Theissen that there were individuals in the Corinthian community who were wealthy.[184] It cannot, however, state with the same confidence as these scholars that some of the individuals were members of the elite in the Greco-Roman society. Scholars of the new consensus have argued that the individuals mentioned by Paul such as Sosthenes (Acts 18:17; 1 Cor 1:1), Stephanas (1 Cor 1:16; 16:15, 17), Crispus (Acts 18:8; 1 Cor 1:14), Gaius (Acts 19:29; 20:4; Rom 16:23; 1 Cor 1:14), Priscilla and Aquila (Acts 18:2–3; 1 Cor 16:19), Erastus (Acts 19:22; Rom 16:23; 2 Tim 4:20), Titius Justus (Acts 18:7), and Phoebe (Rom 16:1), were all wealthy. For example, in Romans 16:23 Paul makes mention of the whole Corinthian congregation meeting at Gaius's house, which suggests that Gaius had a large house which could accommodate the entire Pauline community.[185] This on its own suggests that Gaius

---

182. Acts 18:4–8. cf. 1 Cor 7:18; 1 Cor 1:22–24; 9:20; 10:32; 12:13; Philo, *Legat.* 281

183. 1 Cor 6:9; 8:7–10; 12:2; cf. De Vos, Church and Community Conflicts, 195; Fee, *First Epistle to Corinthians*, 3–4; Witherington, Conflict and Community in Corinth, 24.

184. Winter, *Philo and Paul*, 192–95; Clarke, *Secular and Christian Leadership*, 44–49; Theissen, *Social Setting*, 73–99. Theissen raises an important point, that litigation within the Pauline community is a sign that there were wealthy individuals within the community. He writes "it must be kept in mind that members of the upper classes generally have greater confidence in receiving justice from a court or prevailing in their interpretation of the law, especially since they can pay for good attorneys." Theissen, *Social Setting*, 97. Generally, poor people and people of the lower status avoided the courts as they could not afford them, and also did not have a good grasp of complicated legal jargon.

185. Moo notes that "Gaius was a common name; and at least three different men in the NT bore it: Gaius 'of Derbe' (Acts 20:4; cf. 19:29); a Gaius from Corinth (1 Cor 1:14); and a Gaius who was a church leader in Asia Minor (3 John 1)." Moo, *Epistle to Romans*, 935. Moo, Dunn, and Middendorf all agree that the Gaius of Romans 16:23 is almost certainly the same Gaius "whom Paul mentions as having baptised" in 1 Cor 1:14. Moo, 935; Dunn, *Romans 9–16*, 910; Middendorf, *Romans 9–16*, 1592. While Last doubts that it was the same Gaius, it is worth noting that this is a minority view among New Testament scholars. Last, *Pauline Church*, 63. Last even concedes that many scholars regard Gaius of Rom 16 to be the same Gaius who was baptised by Paul in 1 Cor 1:14. Last, 62. The major point of contention among New Testament scholars regarding Gaius is whether he hosted the whole Corinthian congregation in his home or whether he hosted travelling missionaries. Dunn contends that "Gaius' house could hardly have accommodated all the Christians in Corinth" (a position that is also held by Moo. Dunn, *Romans*, 910–11; Moo, 935. He says that at best his house could accommodate 50 Christians. But as Middendorf has correctly observed, Dunn's argument "stems from unwarranted contention" that "nowhere else in the undisputed letters does Paul use ἐκκλησία of the universal church, only

was wealthy. The new consensus scholars have correctly observed that the inclusion of terms like οὐ πολλοὶ (not many) among them were σοφοί (wise), δυνατοί, (powerful), and εὐγενεῖς (of noble birth) in 1 Corinthians 1:26 suggests that some of the "members do fit the characteristics associated with high social status."[186] It is also important that, when one considers the meaning of the terms that are used in 1 Corinthians 1:26 (that is, σοφοί, δυνατοί, εὐγενεῖς), one must also consider the meaning of these terms in the light of the unique context of Roman-Corinth, not in the light of the empire as a whole. As this dissertation has sought to demonstrate, Roman-Corinth was unique in terms of its social context, compared to the larger Greco-Roman empire as a whole. Corinth offered unique opportunities that were not necessarily available to the other parts of the empire. Hence, scholars such as Winter propose that the terms referred to in 1 Corinthians 1:26 "refer to the ruling class from which sophists and rhetors came,"[187] while Clarke says that there is no doubt that there were some in the congregation who came from the ruling class of society.[188] While this dissertation agrees that there were wealthy individuals in the Pauline community at Corinth, it is, however, less inclined to think that there

---

of the church in a particular area or region." Middendorf, *Romans*, 1593. His reasoning, however, is not supported by the text of Rom 16:23. The text clearly suggests that Gaius hosted the whole congregation of Corinth and also hosted visitors from the ἐκκλησία at large, with Paul being an example of the latter, thus Dunn's assertion seems to "pose a false alternative." Middendorf, 1593. In a recent work by Last, the meaning of Rom 16:23 has been turned on its head. Last, 65–71. Instead of debating whether Rom 16:23 means Gaius hosted the whole Corinthian congregation or hosted Paul, Last suggests that the debate should be whether Gaius was a guest of Paul or a guest of the whole congregation. Last proposes that the language that Paul uses to describe Gaius as a ξένος suggests that Gaius was a guest, not a host. Last, 63. He supports his interpretation of ξένος as guest instead of host on the basis that there is no corresponding description in the cultic group association for a host being described as a ξένος. But this brings more questions than answers. First, did the early Christ followers see their community modelled around the cult associations of their times? Second, what are we to make of the argument by Paul where he calls the Pauline community to be countercultural? Third, Last agrees that the term ξένος does occasionally mean host. Last, 65. Therefore, the fact that he cannot find a corresponding use of it as host in the literature of the cult associations does not mean that it stops meaning host. Moreover, the argument that Gaius was a guest of Paul and the guest of the Corinthian congregation seems to be misplaced in the larger argument of Rom 16. Why does Paul mention Gaius as his guest and that of the congregation in Corinth? Last does not answer that question, nor does he demonstrate how his interpretation of ξένος helps us to understand Rom 16. Hence, this study will still view ξένος as meaning "host" instead of "the guest."

186. Donahoe, "From Self-Praise," xxiv.

187. Winter, *Philo and Paul*, 200.

188. Clarke, *Secular and Christian Leadership*, 45. For more on the debate regarding the identity of Erastus, see: Goodrich, "Erastus of Corinth," 583–93; Clarke, "Another Corinthian Erastus Inscription," 146–51; *Secular and Christian Leadership*, 46–57; Friesen, "Poverty in

were individuals from the PS 1 (imperial elite) and PS 2 (regional or provincial elites) group, with Erastus and Gaius being the only representatives of that group. Scholars debate the actual meaning of the words of Paul in Romans 16:23 where he refers to Erastus as a city treasurer ("Ερaστος ὁ οἰκονόμος τῆς πόλεως). There are two major issues regarding the identity of Erastus: (1) Is he the same Erastus as the one who, as aedile of Corinth, paid for a large paving project, that is referred to in the inscription of a paving that was uncovered by archaeologists? The inscription reads: "Erastus laid the pavement at his own expense in return for his aedileship"; (2) What is the meaning of the phrase "ὁ οἰκονόμος τῆς πόλεως"?

With regard to the first point, if the identity of the Erastus of Romans 16:23 is the same as that of the inscription, then we will have a clear example of a member of the elite among the members of the Pauline community, and that will have a clear "link with secular leadership of Roman Corinth."[189] While some scholars from the new consensus maintain that the Erastus of the inscription is the same as the one mentioned by Paul in Romans 16:23, scholars such as Meggitt, Cadbury, and Friesen argue against that view.[190] Meggitt argues that "it is . . . improbable that the Erastus of Rom 16:23 is identifiable with the figure mentioned in the Corinthian inscription."[191] She goes on to argue that Erastus's socioeconomic situation was most likely the same as the

---

Pauline Studies," 354–55; Meggitt, "Social Status of Erastus," 218–23; Cadbury, "Erastus of Corinth," 42–58.

189. Clarke, *Secular and Christian Leadership*, 46.

190. Meggitt, "Social Status of Erastus," 223; Cadbury, "Erastus of Corinth," 42–58; Friesen, "Poverty in Pauline Studies," 354–55. The following scholars consider the Erastus of Romans 16:23 to be the same Erastus who laid the pavement at Corinth in return for election as an aedilis: Engels, Roman *Corinth*, 108; Furnish, "Corinth in Paul's Time," 20; Clarke, "Another Corinthian Erastus Inscription," 151; *Secular and Christian Leadership*, 54–56; Witherington, *Conflict and Community in Corinth*, 33; Yeo, *Rhetorical Interaction*, 87; Savage, *Power through Weakness*, 40; and De Vos, Church and Community Conflicts, 199–200. Scholars such as Moo, Fee, and Thiselton note that there is a problem with this view, in that it cannot be proven absolutely, but they nonetheless think that it is probable that the Erastus of Rom 16:23 is the same one who laid the pavement at Corinth. Moo, *Epistle to Romans*, 935–36; Fee, *First Epistle to Corinthians*, 3; Thiselton, *First Epistle to Corinthians*, 9. This is the position that is taken in this study. As seen above, this view has been rejected by other scholars, with Friesen saying that this is a case of mistaken identity. Friesen, "Wrong Erastus," 231–56. Friesen recently has gone as far as saying that the Erastus of Rom 16:23 was not even a believer in Jesus Christ (meaning he was not a member of the Pauline community at Corinth). Friesen, 249–56. Friesen says that Erastus "was someone with whom Paul and other believers had ongoing positive contact but who was not a participant in their assemblies." Friesen, 256.

191. Meggitt, "Social Status of Erastus," 223.

status of his fellow believers, and thus, we cannot present him as proof that there were people who were socially powerful in Corinth.[192] Similar sentiments are also shared by Cadbury who writes that it is improbable to conclude for sure that the Erastus of the inscription is the same Erastus of Corinth due to "difficulty of supposing that any man's cursus honorum included both arcarius (rei publicae) and aedilis."[193]

Friesen, on the other hand, follows Cadbury's assertion that the title ὁ οἰκονόμος τῆς πόλεως denotes a slave and thus he locates Erastus on the PS 4 or PS 5 scale.[194] The problem with these scholars though, is that they fail to show why Paul in Romans mentions the secular position of Erastus. Winter (who holds to the view that Erastus of Romans 16:23 is the same as the one of the inscription), has offered a better explanation for why Paul mentions Erastus. He says:[195]

> Paul does not normally mention the present, secular occupation of the other Christians who are mentioned in his letters. In doing so in the case of Erastus, he was able to provide an example for his readers of the role that the well-to-do Christian could undertake in seeking the welfare of the city. The filling of this public office by Erastus was an outworking of the role of the Christian as a civic benefactor referred to in Romans 13:3–4 and 1 Peter 2:14–15.

If this is indeed the case, as this researcher is inclined to believe, it seems probable that Erastus was someone of high status and familiar to the Romans, contrary to Friesen who puts him at PS 4 or PS 5. Also, while οἰκονόμος in some contexts refers to a domestic slave (that is, 1 Cor 4:1),[196] there is a high probability that it could also refer to the Corinthian office of aedile; as Clarke notes that in the first century context, οἰκονόμος τῆς πόλεως was a "Greek equivalent for aedile."[197] Even if οἰκονόμος is not equivalent to aedile, and is

---

192. Meggitt, 223.
193. Cadbury, "Erastus of Corinth," 58.
194. Friesen, "Poverty in Pauline Studies," 354–55.
195. Winter, *Seek the Welfare*, 195.
196. Interestingly, BDAG defines ὁ οἰκονόμος τῆς πόλεως of Rom 16:23 as a lofty position of a city treasurer.
197. Clarke, *Secular and Christian Leadership*, 56. For more on this, see Clarke, Witherington, and Theissen. Clarke, 56; Witherington, *Conflict and Community in Corinth*,

equivalent to the "much humbler role" of a clerk,[198] there is "no reason why we should not think that our Erastus was the city treasurer [or clerk] at the time Paul wrote and that he was later honoured with the office of aedile."[199] This dissertation thus concurs with Donahoe that, although it is disputed, the "likelihood that Paul's Erastus is the same Erastus named in the inscription as one holding the honoured position of aedile nevertheless is high since it would seem unlikely that Paul would mention the secular status of a member of the community for no apparent reason."[200] Savage, on the other hand, views Erastus as a wealthy freedman who was able through hard work and ambition to become part of the elite group.[201] He says that Erastus was able to "illustrate something dear to all Corinthians – that with little ambition and application one could rise from level zero to social respectability and a measure of power" (emphasis original).[202] Witherington correctly observes that the fact that Erastus was a freedman should not make us minimise his status, particularly in a city like Roman Corinth.[203] He notes that "freedmen could ... be extremely wealthy, hold high public office and become important benefactors" (citing Gill).[204]

Thus far, this study has argued that the Pauline community in Corinth comprised both Jews and Gentiles, some wealthy and many poor (cf. 1 Cor 1:26). First Corinthians 1:26–28, though, also reveals that most of the members in the Corinthian congregation were of a low social status. This is evident from the literal translation of 1 Corinthians 1:26: "οὐ πολλοὶ σοφοὶ κατὰ σάρκα, οὐ πολλοὶ δυνατοί, οὐ πολλοὶ εὐγενεῖς." οὐ πολλοὶ clearly indicates that many of the members did not belong to the group that was considered wealthy and elite. Thus, the Corinthian correspondence addresses people who are ethnically diverse, religiously diverse, and of different socioeconomic status. Our

---

32–35; Theissen, *Social Setting*, 80. For a position contrary to these scholars, see Hultgren, who contends that the equivalent Latin for the Greek οἰκονόμος is quaestor, not aedile, and that the appropriate Greek equivalent for the Latin aedile is ἀγορανόμος. Hultgren, *Paul's Letter to Romans*, 599.

198. Bruce, *Romans*, 266.
199. Morris, *Epistle to Romans*, 544. See also Bruce, *Romans*, 266, for similar sentiments.
200. Donahoe, "From Self-Praise," xxv.
201. Savage, *Power through Weakness*, 40.
202. Savage, 40.
203. Witherington, *Conflict and Community in Corinth*, 34.
204. Witherington, 34.

main concern with this group is how Paul shapes the identity of such people and we will address this question in chapters 4 and 5.

3.2 The Literary Integrity of 1 Corinthians

In the previous two chapters, this study sought to address a number of points concerned with leadership and identity in 1 Corinthians. This section will consider the text of 1 Corinthians which will be the subject of our analysis regarding the interrelationship between leadership and identity in 1 Corinthians 1–4. In such analysis, this study will rely mostly on the significance of the "in Christ" and the κλῆσις terminologies in making its case.[205] These terminologies, it will be argued in chapters 4 and 5, permeate the whole of 1 Corinthians. Thus, it will be anachronistic to assume that Paul uses them the same way throughout the book, unless we can first establish the unity of the book, particularly in the light of scholarly debate regarding the literary integrity of the book. Moreover, due to the methodological choice of this study, of which it was argued in chapter 2 that it will incorporate sociohistorical analysis using social identity theory, it is necessary to engage scholars' discussions concerning the flow and the logic of 1 Corinthians correspondence; is it a single letter or a collection of letters? Thus, the current chapter will deal with the literary concerns of 1 Corinthians in order to address the important question about the integrity of the text that will be used for our social identity theoretical analysis in the following chapter.

3.2.1 The Argument and the Structure of 1 Corinthians

The purpose of this section is to investigate whether the letter of 1 Corinthians is one literary unit. One might wonder about the rationale for the inclusion of a discussion on the literary unity of 1 Corinthians, particularly for a dissertation that is mostly dealing with the uncontested literary unit of 1 Corinthians 1–4. It is worth noting that the discussion regarding the literary unity of 1 Corinthians goes beyond just structure – it also deals with the question regarding the heart of Paul's argument in the entire book. Rosner poses the following questions in this regard: "Does 1 Corinthians have an argument and

---

205. See chapters 4 and 5 of this study regarding the significance of these and other terms for Paul's social identity endeavours.

structure? Or is the letter simply Paul's response to various problems in the Corinthian church in no particular order"?[206] This is significant for this work, which will be employing social identity theory in its analysis. It is important that one does not impose a model without first properly understanding the argument and the structure of the document that one is dealing with, within its own social context – because if the key passages of our analysis were originally intended for a different context from that which are present in the letter in its current form, that may lead to their meaning assuming a somewhat different significance from that which they now have.[207]

Establishing the unity of 1 Corinthians is very significant for two reasons in the discussion of the subject of leadership and identity in 1 Corinthians 1–4. First, it allows us to consider the broader framework of the letter; particularly, it helps us to see whether later on within the letter Paul further elaborates on some of his earlier teachings. A good example of this is the mimesis tradition, which will be the subject of our investigation in chapter 4. First Corinthians 4:16 reads: παρακαλῶ οὖν ὑμᾶς, μιμηταί μου γίνεσθε. Looking at this on its own without paying careful attention to how this imitation language is used in the entire letter, one might be tempted or be persuaded to agree with Castille that Paul uses imitation language in order to consolidate all power to himself.[208] This reading tends to present Paul as an egomaniac who was power hungry. If, however, in considering the imitation language of 1 Corinthians 4:16, one pays careful attention to the argument of the broader letter, one would see that this language is further qualified in 1 Corinthians 11:1, where we read μιμηταί μου γίνεσθε, καθὼς κἀγὼ Χριστοῦ. Thus, it will be argued in chapter 4 of this study that in light of 1 Corinthians 11:1, Paul's call to the Corinthians to follow his example is in the same vein as the teachings of Seneca, where a student is to follow the example of the teacher, as the teacher provides a paradigm for the moral life.[209] A similar point could be made regarding the use of the κλῆσις terminologies, which is a component of the investigation of this dissertation. As seen in chapter 1 of this study,

---

206. Rosner, "Logic and Arrangement," 16. This particular view comes up very strongly in Garland, 1 Corinthians.

207. Chapple, "Local Leadership," 297.

208. Castelli, Imitating Paul, 120.

209. Seneca (Ben. 4.25.1; 7.31.5). For more on this see, chapter 4 of this dissertation where it will explore the different roles that the mimesis tradition played in the ancient world.

some scholars, particularly those who espouse the universalistic approach to Christian identity, tend to treat the κλῆσις terminologies theologically in that they mostly focus on what God has done in setting the in-group apart from the world. While this dissertation will be arguing along the similar vein, an awareness of how this terminology is used in 1 Corinthians 7:17–24 helps us to be cognizant of the fact that the term does not only have a theological function in Paul. Paul does use it at times to refer to the social aspect of our identity and demonstrate how some of these aspects continue to have a role in our newly found identity in Christ. Thus, even though this dissertation only focuses on 1 Corinthians 1–4, the unity of the letter has a bearing on how one understands and interprets these chapters.

Second, engaging the discussion concerning the literary unity of 1 Corinthians also helps us to participate in wider scholarly discourse on 1 Corinthians. There is currently no consensus regarding the unity and the central themes of 1 Corinthians.[210] Most scholars today generally believe that Paul wrote the letter of 1 Corinthians,[211] with the exception of a few who believe that 1 Corinthians 11:2–16 and 14:34b–36 are an interpolation by a post-Pauline scholar.[212] Scholars such as Robertson and Plummer, testifying to the authenticity of 1 Corinthians, say the following: "Both the external and the internal evidence for the Pauline authorship are so strong that those who attempt to show that the apostle was not the writer succeed chiefly in proving their own incompetence as critics."[213] The issues surrounding 1 Corinthians, though, tend to be around the question of unity and the overall argument of the epistle.[214]

---

210. Malcolm, "Structure and Theme," 256.

211. Even the partition theorists believe that the raw material that is in 1 Corinthians is undoubtedly Paul's, they just don't believe that the final product as we have it is how Paul wrote and arranged the material originally, arguing that 1 Corinthians as we have it today exhibits marks of an editor. Chapple, "Local Leadership," 297.

212. Witherington, Conflict *and Community in Corinth*, 71.

213. Robertson and Plummer, Critical and Exegetical Commentary, xvi.

214. It is worth noting though that 1 Corinthians is not really the first but the second letter that Paul wrote to the Corinthians (1 Cor 5:9).

3.2.1.1 Traditional Approach regarding the Argument of 1 Corinthians

Traditionally, scholars viewed chapters 1–6 as Paul dealing with the oral report from Chloe's people regarding quarrel among the Corinthians,[215] while in chapters 7–16 he deals with the matters raised by the Corinthians in the letter to him (this section is marked by the Περὶ δὲ ὧν ἐγράψατε formula that is found in 1 Cor 7:1 and repeated in 7:25; 8:1; 12:1; 16:1,12, as Περὶ δὲ).[216] However, scholars struggle to see a relationship between these units; even those who favour the unity of the letter.[217] Conzelmann for example, while holding to the unity of the letter, nonetheless observes that the letter exhibits "loose construction" and "breaks and joints."[218] The same is true for Murphy-O'Connor who also, while holding on to 1 Corinthians as a single letter, states that "the salient feature of 1 Corinthians is the absence of any detectable logic in the arrangement of its contents."[219] Still other scholars such as Garland suggest that "1 Corinthians may be summed up as a warning against various perils."[220] The problem of an undiscernible argument of 1 Corinthians is a feature that also seems to be present in the work of scholars

---

215. Cf. 1 Cor 1:10–11. This is of course broadly speaking, as some scholars' view 1 Cor 1–4 as a single unit. See Thiselton, *First Epistle to Corinthians*, v–vii, who treats 1 Cor 5–6 as separate from 1 Cor. 1–5; see also Witherington, *Conflict and Community in Corinth*, vi–vii, who does the same.

216. See Mitchell for the list of scholars who have used this formula as key in understanding the structure of 1 Corinthians. Mitchell, "Concerning περὶ δὲ", 229. Interestingly, this formula has been used by both the scholars who argue for the unity of 1 Corinthians and the partition theorists alike (see Mitchell for more on these scholars). Mitchell, "Concerning περὶ δὲ", 230–32. Welborn is among the scholars who use this formula to argue for his partition theory of 1 Corinthians. Welborn, "Corinthian Correspondence," 214. Mitchell, after analysing the use of περὶ δὲ in the light of the ancient Greek literary and epistolary texts, disputes the assumption that when περὶ δὲ is used in 1 Corinthians, it always signals a reference to the letter that Paul received from them. Mitchell, 254–56. She also disputes the assumptions of the partition theorist that περὶ δὲ constitutes a separate unit.

217. Garland, in trying to unify the letter to the Corinthians, combines these two literary features that are found in 1 Corinthians. Garland, *1 Corinthians*, 20–21. He argues that the letter has been prompted by a series of the oral reports – both from Chloe's people, Stephanas, and possibly Apollos himself (even though Paul does not name all of them) (1 Cor 1:11; 5:1; 11:18; and 15:12) – and the responses to the questions that the Corinthians sent to him via Stephanas. Garland concludes that Paul in his response "alternates between reaction to the oral reports and answers to the Corinthian letter." Garland, 21.

218. Conzelmann, 1 Corinthians, 2. See also Bailey who deals with the issues surrounding the composition of 1 Corinthians. Bailey, *Poet & Peasant*.

219. Murphy-O'Connor, *Paul*, 253.

220. Garland, 1 Corinthians, 21.

such as Witherington, who argues that in 1 Corinthians Paul deals with social rather than theological issues and for him the letter should be seen as "either a problem-oriented letter or a progress-oriented letter."[221] He takes the former category – the problem-oriented approach. Similarly, Winter thinks that the major issue that Paul was dealing with was the secular or cultural influences upon the community.[222] While these scholars might agree that 1 Corinthians deals mostly with social issues instead of theological ones, they nonetheless do not portray the unity of the letter in their writings, besides simply grouping the various themes that can be found in the letter. Other scholars, however, do not merely struggle to see the relationship between different parts of 1 Corinthians, but rather think that 1 Corinthians, as we have it, is a composite document.

---

221. Witherington, *Conflict and Community in Corinth*, 73. This position is contrary to Baur's thesis. Baur reduced the issues surrounding 1 Corinthians to between two existing theological parties; the Jewish Christians (Cephas-Christ party that is mentioned in 1 Cor 1:12) and the Hellenistic Christian (Paul-Apollos) party (cf. 1 Cor 1:12). However, as scholars such as May and Fee have demonstrated, Baur's thesis falls on two grounds: (1) Nowhere in 1 Corinthians does Paul deal with the issues surrounding the observance of the Jewish law, an issue that was a characteristic of the debate that he had with the Jerusalem church. May, *Body for the Lord*, 45; Fee, *First Epistle to Corinthians*, 25. Moreover, the presence of Peter in Corinth is less certain, besides mention of Peter and his wife in 1 Cor 9:5, where we might infer that perhaps Peter once visited Corinth with his wife. So, there is no way to be sure that the "Cephas party" had any direct link to him. (2) It is also interesting to note that nowhere in the letter does Paul denounce or attack Peter's ministry, which would have seemed to suggest that there was a conflict between him and Peter. Moreover, the letter does not explicitly identify any theological statements by Peter or Apollos. Thus, Baur's thesis regarding the cause of the problems in Corinth does not hold any water. We are, therefore, left with two theories regarding the nature of the problems in the Corinthian correspondence: (1) the internal division in the church and Paul's attempt to reconcile the different groups, and (2) the dispute between Paul and the church over the relationship with the social environment of the Corinthian congregation.

222. Winter, *After Paul Left Corinth*, x. Winter thinks that the continuing influence of previous cultural identities (and the change in circumstances after Paul left Corinth) upon the young community has been ignored by scholars in general. Winter, x, 1, 4. He goes on to say that the Pauline community at Corinth "after becoming followers of Christ . . . did not automatically abandon the culturally accepted ways of doing things in Corinth." Winter, x. He also feels that New Testament scholarship has failed to take into account primary sources that have been made available by historians and archaeologists that can shed more light on what was happening at Roman Corinth. Winter, xi. This study will later argue along similar lines to Winter.

3.2.1.2 1 Corinthians as a Compilation of Various Pauline Letters

An extreme view on the literary structure of 1 Corinthians is that it is a "redacted compilation of Pauline letters."[223] Welborn, in his defence of why he chooses to focus on 1 Corinthians 1–4 in his book, says the following regarding the unity of 1 Corinthians:[224]

> I do not regard canonical 1 Corinthians as a unified text. Almost one hundred years ago, Johannes Weiss, whose commentary on 1 Corinthians remains unsurpassed, expressed doubts about the integrity of canonical 1 Corinthians, noting breaks in the train of thought, discrepancies in reports of events, sudden changes of tone, and differences in outlook and judgment. In my view, the questions raised by Weiss have not been answered by recent attempts to defend the integrity of 1 Corinthians on the basis of rhetorical analysis. Hence, I follow Weiss in the hypothesis that 1 Cor. 1.1–6.11 was originally an independent letter, the last of three substantial fragments preserved in canonical 1 Corinthians.

Welborn's statement in many ways highlights the issues that the partition theorists have regarding the unity of 1 Corinthians; the purported "breaks in the train of thought, discrepancies in reports of events, sudden changes of tone, and differences in outlook and judgment." Welborn partitions 1 Corinthians as follows: Letter A: deals with association with the immoral and idolaters (10:1–22; 6:12–20; 10:23–11:32), Letter B: Paul responds to the Corinthians' questions (7–9; 12–16), and Letter C: counsel of concord (1:1–6:11).[225]

The so-called "break in the train of thought" and supposed "contradictions in Paul's argument" in 1 Corinthians also comes through strongly in Martin's

---

223. Malcolm, "Structure and Theme," 257. See Chapple for an extended treatment of the scholars who represent this view. Chapple, "Local Leadership," 296–301. See Thiselton and Collins for a survey of historical developments of the partition theories. Thiselton, *First Epistle to Corinthians*, 36–39; Collins, *First Corinthians*, 10–14. Ho notes that whenever scholars argue about the inconsistency of Paul's writing, they normally look at 1 Cor 5–11:1 as a case in point. Ho, "Cleanse Out Old Leaven," 9.

224. Welborn, *Paul, the Fool of Christ*, 13.

225. Welborn, "Corinthian Correspondence," 214.

interpretation of the book.[226] Martin thinks that these contradictions may have been a contributing factor to why Paul did not win the argument with the Corinthians. He says:[227]

> I am not so convinced. I believe it quite possible, indeed, probable that with respect to several of the issues discussed in this book, Paul did not win the day. In some cases, after all, he was arguing a rather weak case. For example, it is hard to see how Paul can insist that sexual intercourse between a Christian man and a prostitute pollutes the pneuma of Christ (Chapter 7 above) and simultaneously argue that the holiness of Christ's body works the other way in the case of mixed marriages: that the unbelieving spouse, rather than polluting the Christian partner, experiences a sort of "reverse contagion," being made holy by contact with the sanctified body of the believing spouse (Chapter 8). It would not surprise me at all if Paul's disputants at Corinth found his arguments here unpersuasive.

Most of the scholars who hold this view are redaction theorists, who ultimately believe that 1 Corinthians as we have it portrays marks of an editor, who sought to "thematically repackage Paul's letters of Corinthian advice for a more ecumenical audience."[228] According to Thiselton, the following scholars also argue that 1 Corinthians is a composite document; Weiss argued that 1 Corinthians is constituted of two or three letters, Schmithals said that there were three, while Jewett said there were five, and Yeo maintained that there were four letters in 1 Corinthians.[229] Using mostly redaction criticism, the scholars who propose different partition theories have two main objections against the unity of 1 Corinthians: "*a lack of unified literary coherence*; and *evidence of an editor.*"[230]

---

226. Martin, *Corinthian Body*, 251.
227. Martin, 251.
228. Malcolm, "Structure and Theme," 257.
229. Thiselton, *First Epistle to Corinthians*, 36–37.
230. Malcolm, "Paul and Rhetoric," 66 (emphasis original). See Malcolm's second chapter, where he compares his thesis of the macro-rhetoric of 1 Corinthians in relation to other scholars. Malcolm, 65–126. Here he deals with scholars such as Welborn who do not see 1 Corinthians as a unit, and others such as Héring and Schmithals, who also do not see a unified literary coherence in 1 Corinthians. He also deals with scholars such as Gamble, Sellin, and Jewett,

The problem though with partition theories is well articulated by Thiselton when he says that partition theorists "seldom agree where the partitions exist."[231] Chapple says that, "the lack of agreement between the many hypotheses concerning 1 Corinthians as to both the number and contents of the putative originals tells against the probability that any of them is correct."[232] A similar point to this is also stated by Fee, who says that the "fact that there is little agreement in the theories suggest that the various reconstructions are not as viable as their proponents would lead one to believe."[233] Fee goes on to say that the "alleged contradictions [that are highlighted by the partition theorist in the 1 Corinthian correspondence] are invariably resolvable exegetically."[234] Perhaps, one of the reasons why it is difficult for redaction theorists to accept that there is a single unifying theme in 1 Corinthians is that they truly believe that the Pauline editor had an ulterior motive, as he sought to represent a conservative push toward a particular Pauline party.[235] However, this raises a "crucial question: why did the final editor put them together in such an 'inconsistent' way"?[236] In addition, if the issue of the inconsistency of the letter does not rest solely on Paul but on its editor in pursuit of his own agenda, then why did the editor juxtapose the pieces in such a self-contradictory way? These are some of the questions that the partition theorists still have to answer.

One of the strongest arguments against the partition theory is that there are no surviving manuscripts that question the unity of 1 Corinthians. The

---

who believe that there is evidence of an editor within the final composition of 1 Corinthians. In his rebuff of their arguments, Malcolm convincingly appeals to 1 Clement, a letter that uses ideas from 1 Corinthians as a way of establishing the unity of 1 Corinthians. He then proceeds to consider the scholars who see 1 Corinthians as a single unit; these scholars draw on the perspectives of Greco-Roman letter forms, rhetorical criticism, and pastoral rhetoric in arguing that 1 Corinthians is a literary unit.

231. Thiselton, *First Epistle to Corinthians*, 37.

232. Chapple, "Local Leadership," 301.

233. Fee, *First Epistle to Corinthians*, 15.

234. Fee, 15. See Chapple, who resolves exegetically Schmithals's and Weiss's objections about the inconsistency and alleged contradictions in 1 Corinthians. Chapple, "Local Leadership," 298–300.

235. Malcolm, "Structure and Theme," 257. See Malcolm for a critique against this particular reading of 1 Corinthians. Malcolm, 275. For an effective response against the partition theories, see Mitchell and Malcolm, who both argue for the unity of 1 Corinthians. Mitchell, *Paul and Rhetoric*, 65–183; Malcolm, 75–96.

236. Ho, "Cleanse Out Old Leaven," 10.

earliest Greek manuscripts, Papyrus Chester Beatty II (P 46), which is dated to be around 200 CE, contains most of 1 Corinthians as we have it today, with the exception of three verses – 1 Corinthians 9:3, 14:15, and 15:16 – which are missing.[237] It thus seems questionable whether the partition theories offer us much in terms of understanding 1 Corinthians.

3.2.1.3 The Unity of 1 Corinthians

Scholars have proposed different ways to argue for the unity of 1 Corinthians: these range from rhetorical analysis of the letter to theological analysis.

3.2.1.3.1 Rhetorical Analysis of the Unity of 1 Corinthians

Most scholars who use rhetorical analysis in providing a unifying theme for the letter, tend to classify the 1 Corinthians correspondence as a call to unity.[238] This emerges strongly in the work of Mitchell.[239] She employs rhetorical interpretation to demonstrate that 1 Corinthians is an example of a unified and coherent deliberative rhetorical strategy, where Paul argues for unity over division in his Corinthian community.[240] Mitchell's thesis regarding the unity and the argument of 1 Corinthians is that "1 Corinthians is a series of arguments ultimately based on the subject of factionalism and concord." For her, the call to unity in 1 Corinthians 1:10 serves as "the πρόθεσις (the thesis statement)" of the whole epistle and that "the entire letter of 1 Corinthians is indeed consonant with this thesis statement, the appeal to the church at Corinth to be unified and end its factionalism."[241] Both Mitchell and Kennedy, in their use of deliberative rhetorical analysis, come to the conclusion that

---

237. Thiselton, *First Epistle to Corinthians*, 36; cf. Collins, First Corinthians, 10–11.
238. Rosner, "Logic and Arrangement," 17.
239. Mitchell, *Paul and Rhetoric*.
240. Mitchell, 183. See pages 68–80, 180–81 of *Paul and Rhetoric* where Mitchell demonstrates that certain terms and phrases that are found throughout 1 Corinthians were used in ancient times for discussions about factionalism and concord, and since these terms are not limited to the first four chapters of 1 Corinthians but are found throughout the book, she argues that 1 Corinthians should be seen as a call to unity.
241. Mitchell, 66. Among the scholars who argue along the same lines as Mitchell, who thinks that 1 Cor 1:10 is a theme sentence for the entire letter, is Kennedy (New Testament Interpretation). Kennedy also comes to the following conclusion regarding 1 Cor 1:10: "Paul begins with a poem (1:4–9) revealing none of his anxiety about the Corinthians... He follows this in verse 10 with the proposition of the entire letter, summarized in a single sentence. Then comes a brief narration (11–12) explaining the background event which prompted him to write." Kennedy, *New Testament Interpretation*, 24.

1 Corinthians 1:10 is the thesis of the entire epistle.[242] The same sentiments are shared by Hays.[243] Even though he does not think Paul is using deliberative rhetoric, he nonetheless concludes that 1 Corinthians 1:10 sums up what the letter is about. He says: "the fundamental theme of the letter is sounded in 1:10," and goes on to say that everything that follows is the elaboration of this theme. For Mitchell, the main body of 1 Corinthians is 1 Corinthians 1:10–15:58.[244] She says that this epistle body can be divided into four sections that prove her thesis statement (of 1 Cor 1:10): 1 Corinthians 1:18–4:21 is censure of factions; 1 Corinthians 5:1–11:1 appeals to the integrity of the Corinthian community against outside defilement; 11:2–14:40 shows the manifestations of Corinth factionalism when coming together; 15:1–57 deals the resurrection as the final goal; outside the main body we have the epistolary prescript 1:1–3; while 1:4–9 is the rhetorical προοίμιον, and at the end in 16:1–24 we have an epistolary closing. Most scholars agree that Mitchell's work is to be applauded for its application of the Greco-Roman rhetorical model, but others are not convinced about her thesis statement being applicable to the whole of 1 Corinthians. They see it rather as fitting well with the content of 1 Corinthians 1–4.[245]

One of the strongest critics of Mitchell's thesis has been Yeo, who while agreeing with some aspects of Mitchell's main argument that Paul used deliberative rhetoric in order to bring about concord within the ἐκκλησία, is not convinced that this applies to the rest of the letter.[246] He uses 1 Corinthians 6:12–20 which deals with sexual immorality and 1 Corinthians 15 which deals with the resurrection as an example of how it could not be argued that 1 Corinthians 1:10 serves as the theme for the whole book.[247] Yeo is not the only scholar who has noticed the shortcomings of Mitchell's thesis;

---

242. Mitchell, *Paul and Rhetoric*; Kennedy, *New Testament Interpretation*.
243. Hays, *First Corinthians*, 21.
244. Mitchell, *Paul and Rhetoric*, x–xi.
245. Porter, "Understanding Pauline Studies," 19–20; Ciampa and Rosner, *First Letter to Corinthians*, 20–21; Welborn, "Corinthian Correspondence," 215. Welborn questions Mitchell's argument that all of 1 Corinthians is a deliberative rhetoric. He points to 1 Cor 9 as an example where Paul himself characterizes this chapter as an "apology." Welborn, "Corinthian Correspondence," 215.
246. Yeo, *Rhetorical Interaction*, 76. Yeo's main focus in 1 Corinthians is on the unity of chapters 8, 9, and 10. He rejects the unity of 1 Corinthians as a whole and these chapters in particular. Mitchell's thesis seems to be a catalyst for Yeo's rejection of the unity of the letter.
247. Yeo, 76.

other scholars are Porter, Porter and Olbricht, Fitzmyer, and Malcolm.[248] These scholars do not think that Mitchell has properly demonstrated that 1 Corinthians is indeed a deliberative rhetorical document, and also Mitchell's thesis that 1 Corinthians is a call to unity has been questioned. Porter, for example in his critique of Mitchell, does not think that the "use of similar wording in the rhetorical and epistolary handbooks" presented by Mitchell is strong enough.[249] He says: "The fact that similar words are used in these handbooks does not prove that one should use the categories of ancient rhetoric to analyse letters."[250]

Similarly, Ciampa and Rosner, while agreeing that disunity or a call to unity is the important topic of 1 Corinthians 1–4, do not agree that this is the dominant theme of the whole letter.[251] They are of the view that disunity is one of several issues that plagued the Corinthian community, but not the sole issue. They are of the view that a theological analysis will yield better results in terms of arguing for the unity of the epistle of 1 Corinthians. It is to this analysis that we now turn.

---

248. Porter, "Understanding Pauline Studies," 19–20; Porter and Olbricht, Rhetoric and New Testament, 90; Fitzmyer, First Corinthians, 55; Malcolm, "Paul and Rhetoric," 78–84.

249. Porter, "Understanding Pauline Studies," 20.

250. Porter, 20. Further, in his recent work, "When It Was Clear," Porter has questioned the whole enterprise of applying a classical rhetorical approach to Paul. This comes through clearly in his critique of Ben Witherington who argues that Paul was a master of Greco-Roman rhetoric and applied common categories for oral speech to his letters. Porter says that the scholars who use rhetorical approach to the Bible tend to assume that rhetoric was used widely in the ancient world by almost everyone. Porter, "When It Was Clear," 534. He calls this the "rhetoric in the air hypothesis." He demonstrates that this hypothesis has serious weaknesses since Paul was not an accomplished and trained rhetorician. Porter, 542–43. He also argues that rhetoric was not as prevalent as scholars suggest. He says that "ancient rhetoric was not a driving force behind the writing of the NT," and did "not provide a guide to its earliest interpretation." Porter, 544. Porter's thesis is that Paul was a letter writer and, therefore, his letters are to be understood as such. Porter states that interpretive tools that we use to interpret Paul's letters ought to help us enhance our understanding of the meaning of the text, and he argues that linguistic criticism will yield better results for us in this endeavour. Porter, 543. Interestingly, Winter is also cautious against the use of rhetorical analysis in our interpretation of 1 Corinthians. Winter, "'Underlays' of Conflict," 154. Winter cautions against the approaches of scholars such as Witherington, Bünker, Mitchell, and Eriksson. Winter, 154; Witherington, Conflict and Community in Corinth; Bünker, Briefformular und Rhetorische; Mitchell, Paul and Rhetoric; Eriksson, Traditions as Rhetorical Proof. In his analysis, he says there is no need to "divide the letter into an exordium, narration, probationes and peroratio (which are the hallmarks of rhetorical analysis)." He further goes on to say that there is no need for "using deliberative or other forms of rhetorical classification." He argues that the letter of 1 Corinthians "is a personal" letter compared to other ancient rhetoric classicism.

251. Ciampa and Rosner, First Letter to Corinthians, 20–21.

3.2.1.3.1 Theological Unity of 1 Corinthians

While some scholars argue for the unity of 1 Corinthians using rhetorical analysis, others such as Malcolm, Ho, and Ciampa and Rosner have argued that there is a theological coherence in the letter, especially when it is viewed in the light of its Jewish character.[252] They do not dispute that the call to unity is important (as seen in Mitchell), but rather see disunity as one of "several behaviours that characterize the Corinthians as 'worldly,' as 'acting like mere human beings ([1 Cor] 3:3).'"[253] They believe that Paul's goal in the letter of 1 Corinthians is bigger than simply getting the Corinthians to live harmoniously,[254] and that Paul's most fundamental concern is with the "glory of God; that is, the church in Corinth might reflect the ultimate goal, 'that God may be all in all' (15:28)."[255]

Ciampa and Rosner argue that 1 Corinthians is "not an ad hoc reply to a series of distinct problems treated randomly or even in the order in which

---

252. Malcolm, "Paul and Rhetoric"; Ho, "Cleanse Out Old Leaven"; Ciampa, "Flee Sexual Immorality"; Ciampa and Rosner, "Structure and Argument"; *First Letter to Corinthians*; Rosner, "Logic and Arrangement". This view emerged strongly in the 2010 Moore Theological College, School of Theology annual lectures, which is now available as a book; *The Wisdom of the Cross: Exploring 1 Corinthians*, edited by Rosner (Published in 2011). It is worth noting that there are other scholars who argue for the theological unity of 1 Corinthians, but argue differently from those who will be presented in this section. Among these scholars are Barth and Thiselton; see Malcolm, "Paul and Rhetoric," 90–2; and "Structure and Theme," 259–61, for their contribution to this debate. According to Malcolm, Barth assumed that there was "some sort of Gnostic influence"; he characterised the core issue that Paul sought to address as "'unrestrained human vitality,' a theological issue that expresses itself in different ways throughout the letter until it is climactically answered in chapter 15." Malcolm, "Paul and Rhetoric," 90. Thiselton, on the other hand, thought that the causes of the problems in 1 Corinthian were over-realized eschatology by the Corinthians, a view that has been strongly rejected by Hays. Thiselton, "Realised Eschatology in Corinth," 510–26; "Book Review," 436–67. Hays rejects the notion that the issues that Paul is dealing with in 1 Corinthians arises from "explicit theological ideas" (emphasis original). Hays, *First Corinthians*, 8. He says it was "Paul who frames the issues in theological terms." He goes on to suggest that "the practices of the Corinthians were motivated by social and cultural factors – such as popular philosophy and rhetoric – that were not consciously theological at all." This point will be returned to, when this dissertation argues for the approach it will choose regarding the unity of 1 Corinthians. For now, it is worth mentioning that Thiselton has since modified his views from those of 1978, and now suggests that the problems at Corinth resulted from both the eschatological misperceptions and secular attitudes of the Corinthians. Thiselton, *First Epistle to Corinthians*, 40.

253. Ciampa and Rosner, "Structure and Argument," 207.
254. Ciampa and Rosner, 207.
255. Ciampa and Rosner, *First Letter to Corinthians*, 22.

they had come to Paul's attention."[256] They find 1 Corinthians to be a letter that has a biblical-theological framework, and they argue that Paul's main concern in 1 Corinthians is the purity of the church in the light of the two vices that dominated the Gentile world: idolatry and sexual immorality.[257] They view these vices to be of greater concern to Paul than communal harmony, as the outside influences upon the church could jeopardise "the health of the worshipping community."[258] They summarize the letter of 1 Corinthians as follows:

> Paul's attempt to tell the church of God in Corinth that they are part of the fulfilment of the Old Testament expectation of

---

256. Ciampa and Rosner, "Structure and Argument," 208, 218. This could be perceived as their response against Garland's thesis. Garland, 1 Corinthians, 21; see section 2.1.1 of this chapter (the traditional approach) for Garland's comment.

257. For primary sources regarding the Jewish perception of idolatry and sexual immorality being the vices that characterise the Gentiles, see: Wis. 13: 1–3; Sibylline, Or. 3.29–32; Testament of Naph. 3.3 (for idolatry) and Sibylline, Or. 3.185–6, 596–600, 764; 5.166, 387, 430 (for sexual immorality).

258. These views though are similar to those of Winter and Lieu. Winter, *After Paul Left Corinth*; Lieu, Christian Identity. Winter suggests that the problems at Corinth developed after "Paul's departure," the reason being that the Pauline community at Corinth were "cosmopolitan, i.e., citizens of this world and, in particular, citizens or residents of Roman Corinth" and thus "the primary influences on the responses of the Christians were derived principally from Romanitas" instead of their newly-found identity in Christ. Winter, 2, 27. Winter also adds sexual immorality as one of the cultural issues that influences the community. Lieu, on the other hand, working from a social identity perspective framework, states that in 1 Corinthians Paul was engaged in identity formation of the community, if identity "involves ideas of boundedness, of sameness and difference, of continuity, perhaps of a degree of homogeneity, and of recognition by self and by others." Lieu, 12. She goes on to suggest that Paul was using the framework that is found in the Jewish worldview: "the need to observe sacred boundaries, variously articulated, but in Judaism particularly through food and purity laws and the structuring of the Temple, correlates with the importance laid on well-defined and well-protected social boundaries." Lieu, 104. Lieu also speaks of "the pervasive rejection of the ways of the Gentiles, epitomized by idolatry and by a range of other 'vices' of sexual and intemperate behaviour." Lieu, 133. Seen globally a clear pattern emerges, that in 1 Corinthians Paul is concerned about the integrity of the identity of this community. This identity needs to be different from that of their previous identity as Roman citizens; that is, the vices that control their fellow citizens are not to be found in this new community. But this seems to suggest that once someone becomes a follower of Jesus, they need to cut ties with their "ethnic" identity and follow a new identity. Is this Paul's argument in 1 Corinthians? When Lieu talks of the "rejection of the ways of the Gentiles," does this refer to all the ways of the Gentiles or just the two vices which tended to characterise the Gentiles? This is where 1 Cor 7:17–24 comes in as some scholars view the references to circumcision and uncircumcision as identity markers. Punt, "1 Corinthians 7:17–24." Is the "pervasive rejection of the ways of the Gentiles" as suggested by Lieu consistent with Paul's view of how people in the Pauline community are not to seek to change their identity markers as articulated in 1 Cor 7:17–24?

worldwide worship of the God of Israel, and as God's eschatological temple they must act in a manner appropriate to their pure and holy status by becoming unified, shunning pagan vices, and glorifying God in obedience to the lordship of Jesus Christ.[259]

Thus, Ciampa and Rosner view the unity of 1 Corinthians as follows: 1 Corinthians 1–4 argues that the Corinthians must be united and that their unity is to be influenced by the cross, this section contains a negative treatment of worldly wisdom (1 Cor 1:10–2:5), followed by a positive treatment of the wisdom of the cross (1 Cor 2:6–4:17).[260] In 1 Corinthians 4:18–7:40, they say Paul deals with the issues of sexual immorality. This section is divided into two: first there is a negative treatment of the manifestation of sexual immorality in the Corinthian church (1 Cor 4:18–6:20) and then a positive treatment of marriage (1 Cor 7:1–40). They argue that chapters 8–14 deal with the issues of idolatry, and again here the section begins with the negative of its manifestation in Corinth (1 Cor 8:1–11:1) and then moves to the "positive treatment of the proper worship of the one true God" (1 Cor 11:2–14:40). Chapter 15 is seen as the climax which discusses the resurrection of the body which is an "ultimately ultimate triumph of Christ over all adversaries." 1 Corinthians 16 is then the close of the letter.

Arguing along similar lines is Ho, in his treatment of scholars such as Jonathan Klawans and Christine E. Hayes.[261] Ho's work is important for this dissertation as he is using social identity theory, a methodology that will also be incorporated in this study.[262] Ho in his thesis correctly shows that

---

259. Ciampa and Rosner, *First Letter to Corinthians*, 52.

260. Ciampa and Rosner, "Structure and Argument."

261. Ho, "Cleanse Out Old Leaven."

262. It is worth noting that in chapter 2 of his dissertation, Ho argues for the unity of 1 Corinthians, particularly 1 Cor 5–11:1, by using literary analysis (along a similar line to Mitchell). In fact, he says: "Margaret Mary Mitchell has pointed out the literary unity of 1 Cor 5–11:1. Her findings on the parallels between 1 Cor 5–7 and 1 Cor 8–11:1 can be taken as a starting point." Ho, 51. However, he does not agree with Mitchell that all issues dealt with in 1 Corinthians relate to unity. He states that 1 Corinthians 5–7 and 8–11 are to be read as a thematic unit, one inherited from Paul's Jewish tradition. Using social identity theory, he argues that in both sections (1 Cor 5–7 and 8–11) Paul seeks to distinguish insiders from the outsiders. In chapter 2 of his thesis, Ho argues that the phrase "imitate me" is a bracketing device (or Paul's design to frame 1 Cor 5–11:1) that is used both at the beginning and at the end of the sections of 1 Cor. 5–11:1 and thus this section is one of discourse. He also points to the numerous linguistic parallels and thematic parallels (an example of this is the mentioning of Satan in 1 Cor 5:5; 7:5: 10:20–21) between 1 Cor 5–7 and 8–11. He says that "readers are

1 Corinthians is not a letter concerned mainly with unity (as suggested by Mitchell) since there is no internal schism present in 1 Corinthians 5–11.[263] Ho makes similar assertions to those of Ciampa and Rosner that in 1 Corinthians, Paul was concerned with the purity of the community. He says that there is "one important Jewish concept that relates to" our study of 1 Corinthians, and that is "the idea of purity."[264] His particular interest in 1 Corinthians is the unity of 1 Corinthians 5:1–11:1, and he says the following concerning these chapters:[265]

> The concept of purity is repeated throughout 1 Cor. 5:1–11:1. Purity language or images such as "unleavened" (5:7), "washed and sanctified" (6:11; 7:14), "temple of the Holy Spirit" (6:19), "unclean" (7:14), "holy" (7:14, 34), "sin against" (8:12), "altar" (9:13), "baptised" (10:2), etc., permeate these six chapters.

Similarly to Ciampa and Rosner, Ho notes that "the concept of purity in Judaism of the first century is most probably shared by Paul and so it helps us understand Paul's purity language in 1 Corinthians."[266] Ho first analyses the work of Jonathan Klawans and Christine E. Hayes, who distinguish between two types of impurities that exist in the Hebrew scriptures: "ritual and moral impurity."[267] He states that "ritual impurity as indicated in Leviticus 15 is not

---

supposed to read 1 Cor 8–11 in the light of what Paul has said in 1 Cor. 5–7." Ho, 359. It is only after Ho has established the thematic unity between 1 Cor 5–7 and 8–11:1 that he then attempts to argue for the thematic unity of the whole letter. He does this by looking at the "in Christ (Christ/Jesus/Lord)" language. He notes that this language is dominant in 1 Cor 5–11:1 (5:4–5; 6:11, 13–14, 17; 7:10, 12, 17, 22, 25, 32, 34–45, 39; 8:6; 9:1–2, 5, 14; 10:21–22, 26) and at the same time is dominant also in the first section of 1 Corinthians. For example, in 1 Cor 1 "'Christ'" is used seventeen times," "twelve times in the first thirteen verses alone." Ho, 297. Ho then goes on to demonstrate that this "in Christ language" is used by Paul as an identity marker both for his identity and that of the Corinthians. Thus, Ho by showing that the "in Christ language" permeates the whole of 1 Corinthians, proves his thesis that 1 Corinthians is a unified letter. Our interest though in this section is on his first chapter, where he reviews scholars who argue for the unity of 1 Corinthians using theological analysis, as these scholars contribute to his final analysis that the structure of 1 Corinthians could be understood better in the light of Jewish traditions.

263. Ho, "Cleanse Out Old Leaven."
264. Ho, 1.
265. Ho, 16.
266. Ho, 16. See Ciampa and Rosner, "Structure and Argument."
267. Ho, "Cleanse Out Old Leaven," 16. It is worth noting that Hayes adds one further impurity alongside ritual and moral impurity of Klawans; "genealogical and carnal." These categorisations, she believes, were evident after the exile and they come through more clearly in

sinful and the sources of impurities are natural, unavoidable, contagious but not permanently defiling," while moral impurity on the other hand as "indicated in Lev 18 . . . is sinful and morally defiles the sinner, the land and the sanctuary. Moreover, the defilement effect is permanent (unless God intervenes). Sources of moral impurities are the three grave sins in the Hebrew Bible: idolatry, sexual sin, and bloodshed."[268] Thus, Ho adds a third category – bloodshed – to those of Ciampa and Rosner.[269] Moral impurity was taken very seriously by the Jewish people as it was perceived as the "grave sin against Yahweh" whose "final outcome for the people who committed moral impurities was expulsion from the land of Israel."[270] Using Klawans again, Ho argues that Paul and Jesus whenever they talk of impurity are concerned mainly with moral impurity rather than ritual impurity.[271] Since Paul is concerned about the moral impurity of his congregation at Corinth, Ho argues that there is a thematic unity that emerges in 1 Corinthians 5–7 and 8–11:1 "if Klawans' notion of the doctrine of moral defilement is correct."[272] He writes, "Paul likely understands this doctrine in the same way as other first century rabbis. He regards sexual sin and idol food issues in 1 Cor 5–11:1 as a matter of moral impurity. Those are sins against God, not just against Jewish traditions of propriety in worship." For Ho then, in 1 Corinthians 5, Paul's call that the Corinthian congregation should discipline and expel the brother who commits incest is not unusual, as according to the "ancient Jewish tradition, those who commit moral impurity should be expelled from the Promised Land."[273] He argues that since during Paul's time the Israelites were already in exile, "Paul may have transformed" the use of being expelled from the land or denied inheritance to "expulsion from the Kingdom of God." He goes on to

---

the books of Ezra-Nehemiah. She states that these impurities were considered to be intrinsic to Gentiles' identity by some Second Temple Jewish groups. Genealogical impurity is an impurity intrinsic to a nationality/race and cannot be cleansed through conversion or assimilation. The idea that Gentiles are intrinsically profane is introduced into Israelite ideology by Ezra, who conceives of all of Israel as a holy seed, a concept ascribed only to priests in the Torah and Ezekiel. For a criticism of Hayes, see Ho, 46–47.

268. Ho, 16. The aspect of bloodshed falls beyond the scope of this dissertation as it is dealt with under the issues surrounding food offered to idols.

269. Ciampa and Rosner, "Structure and Argument."

270. Ho, "Cleanse Out Old Leaven," 17.

271. Ho, 17–18.

272. Ho, 18.

273. Ho, 18.

say that "this may clarify Paul's requirement of sanctification and the lasting consequence of God's people committing vice in 1 Cor 6:9–10."[274]

Ho's distinctions between the two types of impurities that exist in the Hebrew Scriptures, "ritual and moral impurity" is important for our analysis of 1 Corinthians, because there seems to be this tension in the letter where on the one hand Paul calls upon the community to have "regular social intercourse with unbelievers (5:9–11; 7:12–16; 9:19–23; 10:27–33)," while at other times he calls them to be "counter-cultural (6:1–11; 7:10–11; 8:10–13; 10:1–13)."[275] Ho, however, correctly points out that what Paul is doing here is setting the boundaries for his community: they are to accept the good and reject the bad in the society around them. This community is not to be isolated from the communities around them as if that would make them holy and pure; "for moral impurity is not contagious through social contact with immoral people."[276] Paul does, "however, regard holiness as a filter with which to evaluate elements from surrounding culture."[277] After Ho highlights the shortcomings of scholars such as Klawans and Hayes, he goes on to argue for the unity of 1 Corinthians 5–11:1 using social identity theory. In chapter 2 of his paper, he argues that "Paul intends 1 Cor 5–11:1 to be regarded as one unit instead of two independent discourses." He goes on to state that "new insights will emerge if 1 Cor 8–11:1 is read in the light of 1 Cor 5–7, demonstrating that there are intra-textual echoes between them."[278]

The other scholar who argues for the unity of 1 Corinthians on theological grounds is Malcolm who asserts that 1 Corinthians is a unified letter that exhibits "*kerygmatic rhetoric of dual reversal* (emphasis original)."[279] For him, the rhetoric of "Jewish motif of dual reversal" serves as a key factor that can be used to account for the structure and concerns of the letter of 1 Corinthians. He says:[280]

---

274. Ho, 18.
275. Ho, 19.
276. Ho, 19.
277. Ho, 19.
278. Ho, 51.
279. Malcolm, "Paul and Rhetoric," 11; 62.
280. Malcolm, 11.

Historical and Literary Context of 1 Corinthians 139

My contention is that the varied issues of 1 Corinthians, which can be elucidated fruitfully by socio-historical studies, have been pastorally evaluated by Paul as collectively exhibiting the theologically presumptuous pursuit of human autonomy. Paul counters this perceived situation by allowing the pattern of his kerygma to give overall shape to his epistolary response. The Corinthians are summoned to find their identity and status in Christ, who remains especially known in the shame of the cross until the day that he will finally be revealed in resurrected glory. Thus the main body of the letter (1:10–15:58) proceeds from cross to resurrection (emphasis original).

In chapter 1,[281] Malcolm argues for a dual reversal based upon the "motif of the condemned boaster and the vindicated cruciform sufferer" (emphasis original).[282] He mentions that this kerygmatic rhetoric of reversal was a "pervasive motif in early Jewish liturgy, literature, and historical interpretation." To support this claim, he shows how ancient Jewish sources support the dual motif of the condemned boaster and the vindicated sufferer. Here, he gives examples of the portions of the Old Testament like Psalms and Daniel. He contends that this continues in the intertestamental literature such as Judith, Wisdom of Solomon, 2 Maccabees, 1 Enoch, Philo, and Josephus. He says that this did not actually end there, and proceeds to show that this continues within Christian literature such as the Gospel of Mark, Acts, in Paul's biography, and in letters such as Romans, 2 Corinthians, Philippians, and Colossians. Our main interest with his work is 1 Corinthians. He says that the dual motif of the condemned boaster and the vindicated sufferer is more evident in 1 Corinthians. He says that in 1 Corinthians 1–4, "Paul evaluates struggles over leadership in the Corinthian congregation as an implicit expression of human autonomy."[283] He says that Paul responds to this situation by calling the "Corinthians to identify with Christ, by forgoing the role of the boastful ruler and adopting the role of the cruciform sufferer" (emphasis original).[284] He writes that in 1 Corinthians 5–14, the believers are

---

281. Malcolm, 14–64.
282. Malcolm, 64.
283. Malcolm, 2.
284. Malcolm, 2; 47–48.

called to live out the cross. In this section, Malcolm notices that there is a progression in Paul's ethics.[285] Paul moves from correcting passionate desires such as "sexual immorality, impurity and greed of bodies (chapters 5–7)," to interpersonal service and love within the church (chapters 8–14). He says that the logic of Paul's ethics is as follow: "Those who are brought into union with Christ in his bodily accomplishments are called to offer their bodies selflessly to God through Christ, and participate lovingly within the body of Christ."[286] He sees 1 Corinthians 15 as the promise of reversal. For him, the resurrection functions as a climax to the macro-argumentation of the epistle since it is the ultimate expression of the gospel. With this as a backdrop, Malcolm notes that Paul is saying that the "Corinthians are summoned not only to emulate Christ as a great example" (by changing from playing the role of the boastful ruler and to taking the place of the cruciform sufferer), "but to recognise that their very life and identity comes from union with him (1 Cor 1:30)"; and they are thus to subject their conceptions of their own status, life, and conduct to an acknowledgement of his (crucified and exalted) identity."[287]

The scholars who have been considered in this section have all argued in various ways that there is theological coherence in 1 Corinthians. They have demonstrated in one way or another that Paul's views in 1 Corinthians are in line with Jewish understanding of purity, that is, God's people are to be different from those who are outside the covenantal community. They have demonstrated that, in his treatment of the two vices that the Jewish community perceived as the characteristics of the gentile identity, Paul wanted his congregation at Corinth to understand the implications of the gospel. We want to support the above scholars that in his theological argument in 1 Corinthians, Paul is concerned about identity formation. But this dissertation still has to investigate whether there was one or a number of issues behind the problems that surfaced in 1 Corinthians. It is to this investigation that we will now turn.

---

285. Malcolm, 98.
286. Malcolm, 194.
287. Malcolm, 48.

3.2.2 The Issues behind 1 Corinthians

Scholars generally agree that in 1 Corinthians 1–4, Paul deals with the issue of divisions (cf. 1 Cor 1:10) which arose as a result of a preference for particular leaders (1 Cor 1:12). But, there is no consensus among the scholars regarding the issues that Paul is seeking to address in the whole of 1 Corinthians, or the reasons that the Corinthians preferred one leader above others, and why some in the congregation rejected Paul as their leader, even though Paul had founded the congregation. Who is to be blamed for all the issues that arose after Paul left Corinth? Barnett notes that when Paul founded the Corinthian church, no conflict is recorded in Acts 18 within the congregation.[288] By the time Paul wrote 1 Corinthians in 55 CE, his letter indicates much conflict. He notes that the crisis reached a particularly heightened point by the time of writing 2 Corinthians in 56 CE. Several other letters that 1 and 2 Corinthians mention also indicate that all was not well in Corinth.[289] The nagging question that scholars have to deal with is, what went wrong in this congregation? Some scholars are of the view that the problems that Paul experienced in 1 Corinthians resulted from foreign teachers coming to Corinth, while others argue that Paul is also to be blamed.[290] Traditionally, when scholars consider this section, they tend to approach it theologically and seek to identify Paul's opponents in the Corinthian church, particularly those mentioned in 1 Corinthians 1–4. Scholars generally seek to find answers to questions such as, what was the "nature of their σοφία."[291] In trying to identify these opponents, scholars consider the catchphrases like "over-realized eschatology, proto-Gnosticism, Hellenistic Jewish wisdom tradition, the Petrine party, and rhetorical conventions."[292] Kwon lists the following scholars and their views regarding the identity of the opponents in 1 Corinthians.[293] He says that

---

288. Barnett, Corinthian Question, 15–20.
289. Cf. 1 Cor 5:9–10; 2 Cor 7:8.
290. For a summary treatment of scholars who represent both views, see Butarbutar, *Paul and Conflict Resolution*, 12–38. Barnett is among recent scholars who fall in the latter group of scholars who think that Paul is to be blamed for some of the problems that developed in Corinth after he left. He writes: "It seems the Corinthian crisis was a casualty of Paul's missionary methods." Barnett writes that if Paul had stayed in Corinth longer that would have created stability in the congregation, and the problems that later developed after his departure might have been avoided. Barnett, *Corinthian Question*, 210.
291. Kwon, 1 Corinthians *1–4*, 386.
292. Kwon, 386.
293. Kwon, 387.

the scholars who postulated the views regarding "over-realized eschatology" were Schweitzer, Dahl, Towner, Oropeza, Thiselton, and Hiigel, while those who proposed "proto (or incipient)-Gnosticism" were Schmithals, Wilckens, Georgi, Conzelmann, Albert, F. F. Bruce, Pagels, and Klutz. "Hellenistic Jewish wisdom tradition" was postulated by Pearson, Davis, and Horsley, while those who thought that it was the "Petrine party" are Baur, Lüdemann, and Goulder. In addition, "rhetorical conventions or patterns" were proposed by Winter, Marshall, Lim, Pogoloff, Witherington, Litfin, Smit, Given, Martin, and Hays.[294]

One of the problems, though, that one has to contend with when trying to identify the opponents of Paul in 1 Corinthians 1–4 is that, unlike 2 Corinthians and Galatians, there is a lack of clear organised opposition to Paul from the outside, or from inside for that matter, in 1 Corinthians. Even scholars such as Fee, who try to identify Paul's opponents in 1 Corinthians, have conceded that "quite in contrast to 2 Corinthians and Galatians, this letter (1 Corinthians) yields little or no evidence that the church has been invaded by the outsiders."[295] Due to this lack of opposition to Paul from the outside, scholars such as Mitchell have argued very strongly that "Pauline scholarship should not simply talk about Paul's 'opponents' in 1 Corinthians in the same way as is done in the case of 2 Corinthians or Galatians, where Paul's own description of the situation justifies such language."[296] Similarly, Hurd claims that there is no evidence of the existence of the opponents who came to the Corinthian congregation from the outside, as is the case in 2 Corinthians and Galatians.[297] As evidence for his views, Hurd points to the lack of the strong "language which Paul uses elsewhere to castigate his rivals."[298] Moreover, it is very evident in 2 Corinthians that Paul had clear opponents in mind in writing that letter(s); Paul explicitly uses words like – ψευδαπόστολοι, ἐργάται δόλιοι (2 Cor 11:13), and οἱ διάκονοι αὐτοῦ ("where αὐτοῦ refers to Satan, 11:15) – as well as implicit designations like οἱ τοιοῦτοι (2 Cor 11:13), οἱ πολλοί (2 Cor 2:17· 11:18), and τινες (2 Cor 3:1· 10:2, 12); ὁ τοιοῦτος (2 Cor 10:11), ὁ ἐρχόμενος (2 Cor 11:4), which Savage says refers to

---

294. See also Hurd for a list of scholars and the views they represent regarding the identity of Paul's opponents at Corinth. Hurd, *Origin of 1 Corinthians*, 95–113.
295. Fee, First Epistle *to Corinthians*.
296. Mitchell, *Paul and Rhetoric*, 302.
297. Hurd, *Origin of 1 Corinthians*, 110.
298. Hurd, 110–11.

ring-leaders among Paul's opponents.[299] What is interesting is that there is no evidence of this language in 1 Corinthians.

It is important that when scholars consider the issues behind 1 Corinthians, they must look at 1 Corinthians in its own context and do not impose the setting of other Pauline correspondence onto this letter. Walters has rightly observed that in 1 Corinthians, "there is curious lack of references to conflict with outsiders, even though reference to contact between insiders and outsiders are more common in 1 Corinthians than in any of Paul's other letters."[300] Walter observes that the Pauline community moved freely, and even received invitations to dine with people outside this community.[301] It also seems that the outsiders moved freely within this community as well (cf. 1 Cor 14:23–25). Is it therefore possible that the causes of the issues in 1 Corinthians is a result of this social interaction with the Greco-Roman world by the congregation? This dissertation will not consider the theology of Paul's opponents in 1 Corinthians, as there is no clear evidence of a unified opposition to Paul from outside or inside the congregation that can be articulated theologically. Instead of trying to identify the opponents, in this section we will frame the question as: What were the issues that Paul was dealing with in 1 Corinthians, that might have given rise to the tension between him and his congregation at Corinth?[302] What were the causes of division, or why did the Corinthians prefer one leader over the others? Also, is it possible that there is one root problem that caused all the issues in 1 Corinthians? As this study employs mostly a socioscientific approach, in this section attention will be paid mostly to the scholars who consider social factors that might have contributed to the issues that Paul sought to address in 1 Corinthians. This will be done by highlighting some of the issues that have been seen by different scholars as problems that Paul sought to address in this letter. This is done with the hope that a clear motif will emerge, which will help us see that at the core, issues that Paul sought to address in 1 Corinthians relate to the question of identity.

---

299. Savage, *Power through Weakness*, 4.

300. Walters, "Civic Identity in Roman," 397–99; cf. Barclay, "Thessalonica and Corinth," 49–73.

301. Cf. 1 Cor 8:7–13; 10:27–11:1.

302. 1 Cor 1:12; 4:3, 6, 18–20; 9:3; 10:29–30; 14:37. For a most recent review of this question, see Tucker, *You Belong to Christ*, 14–31.

As already noted above, scholars such as Mitchell thought that the main issue that Paul was dealing with in 1 Corinthians was discord, and that in the whole of 1 Corinthians, Paul sought to bring about unity within this divided community.[303] Mitchell, upon analysis of 1 Corinthians in the light of the ancient deliberative rhetoric, comes to the following conclusion: "1 Corinthians is a unified deliberative letter which throughout urges unity on the divided Corinthian church."[304]

Other scholars, however, are of the view that the fundamental issue that Paul is dealing with in 1 Corinthians is the secular influences of the previous gentile identity upon the Corinthian community. The case for secular influences as an underlying issue in the Corinthian problem seems to be gaining momentum among the Pauline scholars. In 1959, Munck argued that divisions in Corinth are understood best in the light of the social milieu of Roman Corinth.[305] He said that the issue behind 1 Corinthians was that the "Corinthians regarded the Christian message as wisdom like that of the Greeks, the Christian leaders as teachers of wisdom, themselves as wise, and all this as something to boast about." Munck contends that what Paul is doing in 1 Corinthians is to spell out the implications of the gospel, which is counter-cultural.[306] He says: "Paul asserts, on the contrary, that the Gospel is foolishness, that the Christian leaders are God's servants whom God will judge, that the Corinthians are of the flesh and therefore without wisdom, and that none of this redounds to the glory of any human being, but that he who boasts is to boast of the Lord."[307]

Winter on the other hand says the following regarding the root problem of the issues in 1 Corinthians:[308]

> In 1 Corinthians, Paul was responding to problems which were created by the influence of secular ethics or social conventions on this nascent Christian community. They may have crept into the church imperceptibly and grown with the passage of

---

303. Mitchell, *Paul and Rhetoric*.
304. Mitchell, 296.
305. Munck, "Church without Factions," 68–69.
306. Munck, 68.
307. Munck, 68.
308. Winter, *After Paul Left Corinth*, 4.

time. Some were already there just below the surface (e.g., 3:1). Others were a rapid reaction to a problem which arose unexpectedly and were resolved almost unthinkingly on the basis of the legal or cultural mores of this Roman colony. These were sometimes judged to have required no specifically "Christian" answer – hence the argument for cultural responses by the Christian community.

Tucker also argues that Paul's "main concern was the formation of the Christ-movement around the Mediterranean basin."[309] He goes on to say that the issue in 1 Corinthians is that "some in Corinth were continuing to identify primarily with key aspects of their Roman social identity rather than their 'in Christ' identity and this confusion over identity positions contributed to the problems within the community."[310]

Donahoe makes claims similar to Tucker and Winter when she says:[311]

Paul's correspondence with the Corinthian community reveals that its members did not automatically abandon the societal norms, values, and behaviours upon their conversion. The problem of "boasting" in the Corinthian community stems from the influence of worldly values of competition, self-aggrandizement, and social prominence among its members.

Savage can also be included among the scholars who see the root cause of the problems in the Pauline community at Corinth arising from the community's continuous conditioning by societal norms.[312] He says that:[313]

Boasting is a serious problem in the Corinthian church, ... This is due ... to the influence of secular values and attitudes among Corinthian Christians. They are showing the same obsession with self-exalting behaviour as their pagan counterparts, the same drive to excel their neighbour, the same regard for

---

309. Tucker, *You Belong to Christ*, 13.
310. Tucker, 13.
311. Donahoe, "From Self-Praise," xiv.
312. Savage, *Power through Weakness*, 64.
313. Savage, 64.

arrogance and contempt for humility and ultimately the same compulsion to boast.

Based on what these scholars have observed, it seems that the transmission of the secular cultural norms onto the Pauline community at Corinth had a devastating effect on the life of the community, and gave rise to all the issues that Paul had to address. Even scholars who had previously thought that the root cause of the problems in the Corinthian correspondence was mostly theological, have now conceded that secular influences also had a big role to play. As already noted above, Thiselton has now conceded that the problems in 1 Corinthians are a result of both secular influences upon the community and theological misconceptions.[314] Similarly, Garland argues that in 1 Corinthians, "Paul addresses the issue of the church's identity over against its cultural surroundings and seeks to stake out firm boundaries."[315] He goes on to say that "the problem was not that the church was in Corinth but that too much of Corinth was in the church."[316]

Most of the scholars who were considered above concerning the issues behind 1 Corinthians, tended to focus their attention on examining the influence of Greco-Roman society upon the Pauline community at Corinthian congregation in their use of social scientific approaches. These scholars sought to draw attention to the influence of Sophists, patronage, immorality, education, social standing, and secular leadership. These studies have helped in changing the perspective of viewing Paul's Corinthian opponents by rightly drawing attention away from Gnosticism; they have focused more on Greco-Roman backgrounds, and the social world of Paul. Barnett has added a new nuance to this approach, while he seeks to answer the same question that was raised by Winter: "what happened after Paul left Corinth?"[317] Barnett's actual question is: "why is it that the church, having been successfully founded by Paul, later opposed him almost to the point of rejecting him?"[318] Unlike

---

314. Thiselton, *First Epistle to Corinthians*, 40.

315. Garland, 1 Corinthians, 8.

316. Other scholars who also hold to the view that social or cultural factors might be among the underlying causes of the problems of the Pauline community at Corinth include Horrell, Theissen, and Clarke. Horrell, Social Ethos, 101; Theissen, Social Setting, 69; Clarke, *Secular and Christian Leadership*, 41–57.

317. Barnett, *Corinthian Question*; Winter, *After Paul Left Corinth*.

318. Barnett, 15.

Winter, who sought to address this question by considering the Greco-Roman cultural influences on the Pauline community, Barnett addresses the question by drawing attention to the actual texts of 1 and 2 Corinthians, together with the book of Acts and portions of the letter to the Romans.[319] For him, the issues in the Corinthians' correspondence arose as a result of changing church dynamics. He says: "the church membership changed in number and character in the years following Paul's departure."[320] He notes that at the beginning of Paul's ministry in Corinth, Paul enjoyed a good relationship with the members of the congregation. But after Paul left Corinth, the relationship started deteriorating. He writes that this deterioration happened gradually at first (between 52–54 CE), and then "it happened drastically following Timothy's negative report on the church's reception of 1 Corinthians" (between 55–56 CE).[321] Barnett proposes that this deterioration in the relationship between Paul and the Corinthians was a result of a combination of factors: Paul's absence, the presence of a succession of other preachers like Apollos and Cephas, and a band of travelling teachers carrying letters of recommendation, in the case of 2 Corinthians. He says that all of these factors resulted in the crisis that is seen in the Corinthian congregation. A couple of things are of great help in Barnett's linear approach. First, it helps us not to assume that the Corinthian church is the same throughout the seven years of Paul's known interaction with it; he helps us to see a change in dynamic that progressed over time, particularly in Paul's absence. This is indeed an undervalued viewpoint and deserves further attention in the study of the issues behind 1 Corinthians. His work also brings to the fore the role that visiting preachers like Apollos and Peter might have played in the change in dynamics between Paul and the Corinthian congregation. Barnett argues that when Paul first started the church it was small and supportive of his apostolic ministry but, after Paul left Corinth and Apollos arrived, the congregation experienced a number of substantial developments. Barnett argues that under the ministry of Apollos, the church experienced numerical growth. He writes: "it is possible that the church numbers had reached several hundred" due to Apollos's "capacity

---

319. Barnett, 15.
320. Barnett, 209.
321. Barnett, 65.

to refute Jewish opposition to the new church publicly."[322] The numerical growth of the congregation, he argues, led to some aspects of church life being altered. First, the increase in numbers in the Corinthian congregation meant that there was now an influx of people who had not benefited personally from Paul's ministry, and thus did not recognise his authority. This insight from Barnett helps us to see some of the dynamics that might have been a contributing factor in the first four chapters of 1 Corinthians. The second thing that Barnett says regarding the impact of the numerical growth in the Pauline community at Corinth after his departure was that as a result of the new members, a series of social problems ensued, especially involving social elitism and condescension towards "have-nots" such as Paul.[323] Ultimately though, Barnett thinks that Paul is to be blamed for the crisis that ensued at Corinth. He writes: "it seems the Corinthian crisis was a casualty of Paul's missionary methods."[324] He sees this as a result of Paul's short length of stay in Corinth and the lack of having Titus with him. But this conclusion is perhaps the weakness of Barnett's work. By placing the blame on Paul's missionary methods, Barnett seems to downplay the social make-up (that is, the worldview) of the Pauline community at Corinth. Scholars who have been considered above demonstrated that the Pauline community at Corinth faced strong influences of the previous social identities such as paganism, secularism, immorality, and idolatry. But nonetheless, his work still helps us to consider other dynamics that were at play in 1 Corinthians, that might have led to the issues that Paul sought to address in the letter.

The picture that emerges from the scholars who see secular influences as an underlying cause of the problems is that identity is the major issue with which the Corinthians were grappling, and their identity perception influenced their conduct. This is why this dissertation wants to investigate the interrelationship between identity and leadership, instead of just looking at 1 Corinthians 1–4 as dealing with identity and factionalism. As we saw in various scholars' criticism of Mitchell, it is difficult to sustain the argument that 1 Corinthians is all about a call to unity.[325] But if in 1 Corinthians Paul

---

322. Barnett, 81.
323. Barnett, 86–102.
324. Barnett, 210.
325. Mitchell, *Paul and Rhetoric*.

deals with the issues of identity, particularly Greco-Roman cultural influences upon the Pauline community, then Ciampa & Rosner are stating the same concern theologically when they say "[1] Corinth[ians] consists primarily of a confrontation with the church over purity concerns in general and two vices in particular."[326] Since sexual immorality and idolatry were the two vices that were perceived by the Jewish people as being consistent with the identity and the behaviour of Gentiles, it seems that the major issue in 1 Corinthians is about identity. Or, at the very least, in 1 Corinthians Paul responds theologically to culturally-driven issues. But what does Paul hope to achieve by his theological response to these social issues? The argument of this dissertation is that at the heart of Paul's response is his desire to see that the identity of this community at Corinth aligns itself with their identity in Christ, and that their perception of what constitutes good leadership needs to evaluated in the light of their identity in Christ.

3.3 The Approach of This Dissertation

This dissertation approaches the question regarding the issues behind 1 Corinthians along similar lines to Winter.[327] Winter's approach seeks to understand the "underlying causes of the various problems of Corinthian Christians."[328] Winter argues that in 1 Corinthians, "there are common prob-

---

326. Ciampa and Rosner, *First Letter to Corinthians*, 21.

327. Winter, "'Underlays' of Conflict."

328. Winter, 139. Winter does this by first looking at the number of lines (and percentages) in the P46 manuscript that are devoted to different discrete issues at the Corinthian congregation. However, he finds that counting the number of lines devoted to issues is not quite accurate. He then proposes that a word count will yield a better result. See Winter, 140–41. Winter argues that by taking the two approaches together one gets better results, but at the same time the results are surprising. For example, when one looks at Winter's tables based on word count and the number of lines devoted to issues, its seems that the main issues that Paul sought to address in 1 Corinthians are as follows: "spiritual gifts, loyalty to former leaders in the church, food offered to idols and questions surrounding the resurrection." Winter, 140–41. Paul devotes most of his time to these issues in terms of percentage count, instead of issues like "marriage, separation, and singleness (which occupy less attention when compared to the first ones in terms of the percentage count). In addition, "incest, litigation and fornication occupy the least space." Winter, 140. These findings seem to suggest that there is a flaw in the methodology, because if one analyses 1 Cor 6:18 as an example, incest, litigation, and fornication are "serious issues for they are sins against the person's own body." But if one uses the word and percentage count, one would think that these issues were not on Paul's priority list or Paul did not take them seriously as compared to the other issues to which he devoted most of his time. This conclusion, Winter argues, can only be arrived at if one: (1) thinks that "the amount of space devoted to

lems or clusters of issues in which the same symptoms manifest themselves in different situations."[329] These result from "two underlying cultural issues in the first century, namely that of conflict and compromise."[330] This researcher prefers Winter's approach because it firstly incorporates sociohistorical analysis that in many ways demonstrates how the Pauline community at Corinth continued to be influenced by their previous Greco-Roman cultural identity. Second, Winter's approach can accommodate some of the proposed theories by different scholars regarding the unity of 1 Corinthians. Third, his approach brings together in a clear way how the underlying issue and the different themes of 1 Corinthians link together. Thus, this dissertation hopes that by following similar lines to Winter it will be able to demonstrate that there is indeed an interrelationship between identity and leadership, and at the same time establish the unity of the letter of 1 Corinthians, particularly of chapters 1–6 and 7:17–24.[331]

As seen in the previous section, there is an overlap between the issue of the unity of 1 Corinthians and the issue of the underlying problem that Paul sought to address; in order to deal with the unity of the letter, one has to deal with the question of what the issue is that Paul sought to address in a particular section of the letter. Thus, if we can prove that there is a pattern or one underlying issue behind all the sections, then the unity of the letter will be established.

When we combine the findings of Winter and Tucker, the underlying issue in the Pauline community at Corinth becomes very clear: it is their continuing identification with their previous identities.[332] It seems that the Corinthian congregation failed to understand the implication of their new identity in

---

an issue was an indicator of its importance"; (2) assumes that each of the "issues addressed forms a discrete unit"; and (3) thinks that there "is no underlying problem or problems that surface in different situations, no overlap between one issue and another". But if one takes a view that there is one underlying issue behind all these issues or that the different issues are a symptom of one underlying problem, taking the two approaches (word count and number of lines devoted to issues) could yield good results for us.

329. Winter, 142.

330. Winter, 142.

331. This study will not try to argue here for the unity of 1 Corinthians, as it thinks that the scholars mentioned above have amply demonstrated the unity of the letter. Our focus here will be on showing the unity of the first seven chapters of the letter, as that is the main focus of this study.

332. Winter, *After Paul Left Corinth*; "'Underlays' of Conflict"; Tucker, *You Belong to Christ*.

Christ, particularly as it relates to the issues of leadership in 1 Corinthians 1–4, which resulted in the conflict within the congregation. Some people in the congregation boasted that they followed Paul while others boasted about following Apollos.[333] Most scholars agree that this conflict was a result of the so-called Greco-Roman cultural influences upon the community and that in 1 Corinthians, Paul sought to summon his community "away from error to

---

333. Winter notes that it seems that the Corinthians' boasting was mostly about Apollos and Paul at the expense of the others. Winter, "'Underlays' of Conflict,"149. Elsewhere, Winter argues that the members of the Corinthian congregation are in fact divided into two; those who prefer Paul and those who prefer Apollos. Winter, *Philo and Paul*, 176–79. He says: "In 1 Cor 1:12 Paul uses ἕκαστος to describe the groupings, but his choice of ἕτερος δέ in 3:4 and his inclusion of the additional term ζῆλος could suggest that the allegiance of members of the church is now in effect divided between two former teachers, himself and Apollos." Winter, *Philo and Paul*, 176–77. Winter is not alone in this view. Scholars such as Smit also think that the followers of Paul and Apollos are the main target of 1 Cor 1:10–14:21. Smit, "What Is Apollos?", 231. Mihaila, in his analysis of the issues in 1 Cor 1–4, says that the main issue was the influence of the worldly wisdom that resulted in the dissension in the community. Mihaila, *Paul-Apollos Relationship*, 69–118. For him, the main issue was between those in the Corinthian congregation who preferred Apollos and those who preferred Paul. He says that Apollos demonstrated the kind of worldly wisdom that some in the Corinthian congregation preferred and, as a result of this, there were some members of the community who started to see Paul and Apollos in competitive, instead of complementary, terms. Scholars such as Mihaila and Hurd say that division in 1 Cor 1:12 is about Paul and Apollos rather than about the other individuals that are mentioned in 1 Cor 1:12. Mihaila, 113; Hurd, *Origin of 1 Corinthians*, 105. First, they say that "the existence of the Christ-party at Corinth is extremely doubtful." Hurd, 105. To support this statement, they say that the Christ party is never mentioned again (besides its mention in 1 Cor 1:12), even when the other three parties are mentioned See Mitchell, *Paul and Rhetoric*, 89, and Dunn, 1 Corinthians, 30, for more on this. Also, Garland notes that "there is no hint in the text that some Corinthians are claiming a unique relationship with Christ." Garland, *1 Corinthians*, 49. Thus, scholars such as Mihaila conclude that the slogan of 1 Cor 1:12, "I am Christ's," is Paul's "own rhetorical invention for the purpose of showing the absurdity of claiming allegiance to human teachers." Mihaila, 114. Second, with regard to the Petrine party, these scholars are quick to point out that there is no evidence that supports Peter's visit to Corinth, even though the Corinthians might have known about him. Both Smit and Mihaila suggest that there was no real party in Corinth that claimed to follow Peter. Smit, "What Is Apollos?", 242–43; Mihaila, 115. Rather, Paul adds the name of Peter in order to avoid reducing the conflict to an alternative between himself and Apollos. Mihaila says that Paul also adds the name of Peter to show the "absurdity of claiming allegiance to baptizer, since Cephas did not baptize anyone in the Corinthian congregation." Mihaila, 115. Thus, many commentators tend to agree that the conflict in the Corinthian congregation (in 1 Cor 1–4) was between those who preferred Paul as their leader and those who preferred Apollos. See Hurd, 97–99, for the list of scholars who hold to this view. This study will not rehash the debate about the identity of the different groups that are mentioned in 1 Cor 1:12. Our interest here is on how this conflict over a preferred leader was a result of compromise or the failure of the Corinthians to understand their new identity in Christ, and in what ways Paul, in his response to these issues, reinforces their identity in Christ.

a steadfast adherence" to their identity in Christ.[334] Winter notes that some of the influential people in the congregation wrote and asked for a return of Apollos, something that Paul deals with only in the concluding section of the letter (1 Cor 16:12; Περὶ δὲ Ἀπολλῶ).[335] The extended discussion about Paul and Apollos in 1 Corinthians 1–4 and the return of Apollos in 1 Corinthians 16:12 can be seen as bookends of 1 Corinthians.

The Greco-Roman influences upon the Pauline community at Corinth led to a number of conflicts and compromises within the community.

3.3.1 Conflicts

The conflict and tension within the community manifested themselves in different ways, one of which was members of the community bringing litigation against each other (1 Corinthians 6:1–11).[336] Clarke notes that what happened in 1 Corinthians 6:1–11 was in line with secular understanding of leadership, and that as part of self-advancement people in Greco-Roman society took each other to court, as a way of showing that they were more powerful than those they took to court.[337] Winter notes that the decision handed down in these litigations would have made those who won feel like they were the "most powerful of the parties."[338] The result of the litigations would have created a new set of relationships within the community, a relationship of enmity. What is of interest here, though, is the shape of Paul's argument, which seems to present a sense of a boundary between the Corinthian congregation and the larger Greco-Roman world. He calls those who are part of his community ἀδελφοί while he refers to the secular judges as ἄπιστοί. He views the judges as people who should not be held in high esteem within his community (the ἐκκλησία). Tucker notes that "Paul's rationale for avoiding the local

---

334. Chapple, "Local Leadership," 303; Keay, "Paul the Spiritual Guide," 259; Tucker, *You Belong to Christ*, 13; Winter, *After Paul Left Corinth*, 4. See the following sections of 1 Cor: 1:10–13; 3:1–4,16–21; 4:7–8,4, 18–21; 5:1–13; 6:1–10, 18–9; 8:9–13; 10:1–22; 11:17–34; 12:1–3,14–26; 13:1–13; 14:20, 33b–38; 15:1–2, 12–19, 33–34.

335. Winter, "'Underlays' of Conflict," 149.

336. 1 Cor 6:1–11 has been a subject of fierce theological debate among biblical scholars. For a review of the debate, particularly concerning the meaning of δικαιόω in 1 Cor 6:11, see Chester, *Conversion at Corinth*, 125–46. This dissertation will consider this debate when it does the exegesis of 1 Cor 6:1–11.

337. Clarke, *Secular and Christian Leadership*, 111.

338. Winter, "'Underlays' of Conflict," 149.

courts was identity-driven, that is, Paul understands the Corinthians to be transformed "in Christ" and that has an impact on communal boundaries."[339] While 1 Corinthians 6:1–11 will be explored further in the next chapter, the preliminary reading of this chapter suggests that the way in which the Pauline community at Corinth was acting was in line with their previous identity rather than their new identity in Christ. In 1 Corinthians 6:8–11, Paul tells them that the way they act is not consistent with their new identity in Christ. He says: ἀλλὰ ὑμεῖς ἀδικεῖτε καὶ ἀποστερεῖτε, καὶ τοῦτο ἀδελφούς. In verse 11, he tells the community that this belongs to their former identity, not their new identity which is in Christ; καὶ ταῦτά τινες ἦτε· ἀλλὰ ἀπελούσασθε, ἀλλὰ ἡγιάσθητε, ἀλλὰ ἐδικαιώθητε ἐν τῷ ὀνόματι τοῦ κυρίου Ἰησοῦ καὶ ἐν τῷ πνεύματι τοῦ θεοῦ ἡμῶν. To drive the point home, in 1 Corinthians 6:2–3 Paul had reminded the congregation of their eschatological identity, that one day they would judge the angels. Therefore, their civil litigations are not consistent with their identity in Christ. Hence, Paul says that ἤδη μὲν οὖν ὅλως ἥττημα ὑμῖν ἐστιν ὅτι κρίματα ἔχετε μεθ' ἑαυτῶν.[340]

The conflicts over preferred leaders and between the members of the Pauline community (which manifested itself with them taking each other to court) also spilled over to the worshipping life of the congregation. The community was divided over the Lord's supper (1 Cor 11:17–34, see verse 18 where Paul says: γὰρ συνερχομένων ὑμῶν ἐν ἐκκλησίᾳ ἀκούω σχίσματα ἐν ὑμῖν ὑπάρχειν), and it was also divided on its use of spiritual gifts (1 Cor 12–14, see 1 Cor 12:25, where Paul says: ἵνα μὴ ᾖ σχίσμα ἐν τῷ σώματι, ἀλλὰ τὸ αὐτὸ ὑπὲρ ἀλλήλων μεριμνῶσι τὰ μέλη). Thus, altogether there are three conflicts that are easily identifiable in 1 Corinthians that were results of Greco-Roman cultural influences upon the congregation of Corinth:

---

339. Tucker, *Remain in Your Calling*, 214. In social identity theory, boundaries are an important part of identity formation, and thus Paul, by setting the boundaries between his community and those outside his community, was crafting a sense of identity for those people who are in his community; "us versus them." For more on this from social sciences and social identity, see Lamont and Molnár, "Study of Boundaries"; Jackson et al., "Achieving Positive Social Identity," 241–54; Turner, *Rediscovering Social Group*, 42–67; Tucker, *Remain in Your Calling*, 214–17.

340. When this work does the exegesis, it will consider whether the call of 1 Cor 6:7 (διὰ τί οὐχὶ μᾶλλον ἀδικεῖσθε; διὰ τί οὐχὶ μᾶλλον ἀποστερεῖσθε) is consistent with their new identity in Christ, particularly 1 Cor 1:18–31, where there is an inversion of human wisdom; what the world considers foolish is God's wisdom, and what the world considers powerless is God's power, the cross.

- Conflict 1: Division in the congregation over preferred leaders—1 Cor 1:10-4:21.
- Conflict 2: Litigation within the Pauline community at Corinth—1 Cor 6:1-11.
- Conflict 3: Division around the Lord's supper and the use of spiritual gifts—1 Cor 11:2-14:40.

3.3.2 Compromises

The Pauline community's failure to understand their identity in Christ can also be seen in the number of compromises that plagued the community, to the point that they started acting like the rest of the Greco-Roman world.

The first compromise that is presented in the case of incest in 1 Corinthians 5:1-13. This was not a standard practice within the larger Greco-Roman world, as the text itself suggests: "Ὅλως ἀκούεται ἐν ὑμῖν πορνεία, καὶ τοιαύτη πορνεία ἥτις οὐδὲ ἐν τοῖς ἔθνεσιν, ὥστε γυναῖκά τινα τοῦ πατρὸς ἔχειν" (1 Cor 5:1). The attitudes of the congregation, however, did reflect the attitudes of the larger Greco-Roman world. In 1 Corinthians 5:2a, the text says: καὶ ὑμεῖς πεφυσιωμένοι ἐστέ (see 1 Cor 5:6, where boasting is also mentioned). The attitude of boasting was something that was pervasive in all of Greco-Roman society, as scholars such as Donahoe, Clarke, and Winter have demonstrated.[341] These scholars contend that the Corinthian congregation was not boasting about the actual sin of incest, rather they were boasting about the social status of the man who was committing incest, and ignoring the actual sin. The Roman law prohibited incest; it was viewed as a criminal offence[342] that could result in those individuals who committed such an act being exiled and they could also lose their lives, citizenship, and property.[343] In general, the Greco-Roman world frowned upon the act of incest.[344] This has led to scholars

---

341. Donahoe, "From Self-Praise"; Clarke, *Secular and Christian Leadership*, 73–88; Winter, *After Paul Left Corinth*, 44–57.

342. Dio Cassius refers to a case of incest as "criminal relations." Dio Cassius, *Rom. Hist.* 58.22: 3.

343. Dio Cassius, *Rom. Hist.* 58.22; Paulus, *Opin.* 2.26; Clarke, *Secular and Christian Leadership*, 77–80; Winter, "'Underlays' of Conflict," 144; *After Paul Left Corinth*, 46–47. Tacitus describes a case of Sextus Marius, who was accused of committing incest. The emperor Tiberius punished him by throwing him headlong from the Tarpeian rock, and all of his property was forfeited to the State. Tacitus, *Ann.* 6.19.

344. Cicero, *Pro Cluentio* 5.15. Even in the fictional writings of Apuleius, incest was depicted as an abhorrent crime. Apuleius, *Metamorphoses* 10.2–12.

questioning the attitudes of the Corinthians. Why would the congregation boast in the midst of such a sin? Are they boasting about the man's sin or something else? As already mentioned, scholars such as Winter and Clarke have demonstrated that the congregation was boasting about the social status of the man and the fact that he was legally untouchable.[345] While this interpretation raises issues that still need to be investigated in the next chapter when it considers the exegesis of 1 Corinthians 5, it offers a workable solution on why the Corinthians were boasting in the midst of such a sin. For the sake of the argument of this study, it does demonstrate the interrelationship between leadership and identity. The congregation is so proud of the social status of the man, but they failed to see how his actions are not consistent with their identity in Christ. Moreover, it highlights the failure of the Pauline community leaders at Corinth in their duties to constantly remind the congregation of their identity in Christ, and to act in ways that protect and reinforce their identity in Christ. The leaders of the Corinthian congregation failed to discipline the man, which would have meant that he would be removed from their fellowship, but this failure also meant that their own identities in Christ were compromised and were at stake; Οὐ καλὸν τὸ καύχημα ὑμῶν. οὐκ οἴδατε ὅτι μικρὰ ζύμη ὅλον τὸ φύραμα ζυμοῖ (1 Cor 5:6). For now, it suffices to say that there is a thematic link between 1 Corinthians 1–4, 5, and 6, and that is, that the Pauline community at Corinth had not properly understood the implications of their new identity in Christ. They still viewed things in the light of their previous identities (those of the Greco-Roman world), the result of which was that there was division and compromise within the congregation.

The second compromise that is presented in 1 Corinthians can be seen in the case of sexual immorality, particularly visiting prostitutes in 1 Corinthians 6:12–20.[346] In the Greco-Roman world, there was a rite of passage from boyhood to manhood which was known as the toga virilis.[347] During this rite of passage sexual immorality was the norm among young men, who would sleep with prostitutes. The consequence of coming of age meant that the young

---

345. Winter, "'Underlays' of Conflict," 144; *After Paul Left Corinth*, 44–57; Clarke, *Secular and Christian Leadership*, 73–88.

346. This text will be dealt with in more detail in the following chapter. Our interest here is to demonstrate that it supports the notion that the main issue in the Corinthian congregation was their continued identification with their previous identities.

347. Plutarch, *Moralia*, 37 C–D; Winter, "'Underlays' of Conflict," 144.

men (around the age of eighteen years old) were now allowed to "recline at the banquets and were also exposed to 'its attendant perils.'"[348] These banquets were often marked by an unholy trinity of heavy drinking, eating, and sex. Winter (citing Xenophon) says, "'Hercules has reached the ephebic age' (which was equivalent to that of receiving the toga virilis), and he had the freedom of choice and must select 'between the joys of eating, drinking, and lovemaking . . . and edifying toil.'"[349]

In 1 Corinthians 6:16, Paul challenges this practice by reminding the young men that sleeping with a prostitute meant that one was united to her, and also that such actions were fornication (1 Cor 6:13). This would not have gone down well with the Corinthians who, according to Winter, defended their actions with the catch-cry "all things are permitted for me."[350] This catch-cry was a self-justifying maxim for "the notorious conduct of the Corinthian Christians at dinners, concerned the 'intimate and unholy trinity' of eating and drinking and sexual immorality," says Winter.[351] These dinners were characterized by gluttony, drunkenness, and sexual immorality. The wealthier the patron, the more extravagant the dinner would be. Winter tells a story of the banquet hosted by the president of the Isthmian Games, who made use of the travelling brothels to cater for the guests at his parties.[352] In elite parties, it was customary for the host not only to provide food for the appetites but also prostitutes for sexual appetites. According to 1 Corinthians 6:12–20, it seems that the Corinthians took part in these parties, and had sex with the prostitutes within a dining context.[353]

There are many references in 1 Corinthians 6 that are similar to the dining experiences that were given to the young men, according to Winter.[354] For example, Winter says that the reference "food for the stomach and the stomach for food" represents the "unholy trinity of eating, drinking and fornicating" that occurred in the dining experiences of the young men.[355] Sexual

---

348. Winter, *After Paul Left Corinth*, 89–90.
349. Winter, 90.
350. Winter, "'Underlays' of Conflict," 144.
351. Winter, *After Paul Left Corinth*, 88.
352. Winter, 88.
353. Winter, 88.
354. Winter, "'Underlays' of Conflict," 144.
355. Winter, 144.

freedom was defended philosophically in the Roman world by philosophers like Cicero who poured scorn on any call for sexual abstinence.[356] First Corinthians 6:12–20 therefore demonstrates the continued cultural influences of the Greco-Roman world upon the Pauline community at Corinth. As already seen above, what Winter calls the unholy trinity of food, sexual immorality, and alcohol consumption, is referred to by some scholars as characteristics of gentile identity, particularly the vice of sexual immorality.[357]

What becomes clear in 1 Corinthians 6:12–20 is that Paul desires the ἐκκλησία to understand the implications of their somatic and pneumatic identity in Christ.[358] In this section, Paul wants the Corinthians to understand that since their identity is in Christ, their bodies belong to Christ, and are identified with Christ.[359] What is fascinating in Paul's description of the Corinthians' identities here is that their bodies are not identified as the property of Christ, rather, they are the limbs of Christ (μέλη Χριστοῦ). This presents a strong link of the identity of the Corinthians and that of Christ; it is an intimate relationship.[360] Thus, their actions of visiting the prostitutes are not consistent with their identity in Christ. To drive home this point, Paul asks them a pertinent question: ἄρας οὖν τὰ μέλη τοῦ Χριστοῦ ποιήσω πόρνης μέλη? Since their identity is in Christ, their bodies are exclusively for his use, which does not allow them to visit prostitutes. Their "in Christ" identity is mutually exclusive of πορνεία. Thus, the second compromise of the Corinthians reveals that they have not understood the implications of their identity in Christ. Both the first and the second compromise reveal to us how the Greco-Roman world seems to continue to influence the Corinthian congregation; the vice of sexual immorality, which was a characteristic of gentile identity, seems to have had a grip on the Pauline community at Corinth.

The third compromise can be seen in 1 Corinthians 7, in the discussion about marriage and engagement. While in the first two compromises Paul

---

356. Winter, 144–45; Cicero, *Pro Caelio*, 20.48.

357. For more on this, see: Lieu, *Christian Identity*, 104; Ciampa, "Flee Sexual Immorality," 100–33; Ciampa and Rosner, *First Letter to Corinthians*; "Structure and Argument"; Ho, "Cleanse Out Old Leaven," 17–19.

358. May, *Body for the Lord*, 110.

359. οὐκ οἴδατε ὅτι τὰ σώματα ὑμῶν μέλη Χριστοῦ ἐστιν; ἄρας οὖν τὰ μέλη τοῦ Χριστοῦ ποιήσω πόρνης μέλη; μὴ γένοιτο, 1 Cor 6:15.

360. May, *Body for the Lord*, 110–11.

dealt with the negative treatment of sex, in this third compromise, he deals with the positive treatment of sex.[361] Regarding the previous compromise, Paul had spelt out for the Corinthians that their identity was intrinsically linked with Christ, that they were the metaphorical limbs of Christ. In 1 Corinthians 6:12–20, Paul made it clear that sexual immorality was not compatible with their identity in Christ. In 1 Corinthians 7, there is a positive treatment of sexuality, that is, within marriage couples can glorify God with their bodies.

Thus far, this study has observed, along similar lines to Winter, Tucker, and Clarke, that in 1 Corinthians Paul has been spelling out the implication of the Corinthians' identity in Christ.[362] He has been fighting secular influences upon his congregation, as his congregation was strongly identifying with their Greco-Roman identity instead of their "in Christ" identity. But this raises the question – is everything Gentile evil? Or is it just certain parts of Greco-Roman culture that are not consistent with the in Christ identity, that is, sexual immorality and drinking? Scholars such as Tucker and Pickett argue that there are parts of gentile culture that continue to be relevant for Gentiles who are now members of the Pauline community, and they are of the view that 1 Corinthians 7:17–24 argues for that continued relevance of the Greco-Roman culture in the Pauline community at Corinth.[363] But if what

---

361. See May for an extended treatment of establishing the link between 1 Cor 5, 6, and 7. May, *Body for the Lord*, 205–67. Some of his insights will be used in this study when we consider the exegesis of 1 Corinthians in the next chapter. Wenham thinks that part of the issue at Corinth might have stemmed from some in the congregation misunderstanding Paul's teachings, particularly when it comes to 1 Cor 7. Wenham, "Whatever Went Wrong?", 140. He says that the people who were "advocating for Christian celibacy," and recommending that those who were married should separate (i.e. 1 Cor 7:1, particularly if they were married to unbelievers, cf. 1 Cor 7:13–16) might have thought that they were following Paul's teachings of 2 Cor 6:14–7:1, where Paul taught that people should not be yoked with unbelievers. Wenham, 140. He also states that some in the Corinthian congregation might have advocated celibacy because they thought that what they were teaching was in line with Jesus's teachings in Luke 20:35. He says: "The Corinthians certainly thought that they have arrived at 'that age' [the age that is promised in Luke 20:35] (possibly even to the resurrection of the dead), and so it made sense to conclude that sex was no longer appropriate for people who were now 'in the Spirit' and for whom bodily life was unimportant." Whatever one chooses as a backdrop of 1 Cor 7, what becomes clear in this chapter is that Paul advocates for a positive view of sex within marriage, whether or not a believer is married to a nonbeliever. In fact, 1 Cor 7:2–5 makes it clear that sex within marriage is one of the ways that will help a married couple not to fall into the sin of sexual immorality.

362. Winter, "'Underlays' of Conflict"; Tucker, *You Belong to Christ*; Clarke, *Secular and Christian Leadership*.

363. Tucker, 9; Pickett, Cross in Corinth, 99–100.

Tucker and Pickett suggest is the case, then this raises more questions: How ought the Corinthian believers to understand their identity in Christ? How are they to view the Greco-Roman culture around them? This will be the subject of our investigation in the next chapter. For now, what is emerging is that Paul on the one hand is trying to instil in the Corinthian community a sense of separateness from Greco-Roman cultural identity, because a continuing identification with that identity has led to conflict and compromises within his community. On the other hand, this identity he sought to instil is not a reclusive identity. It is different from the surrounding cultures but at the same time allows for a continuation of some aspects of the previous identities.

3.4 Conclusion

In the light of the criticism against the use of social scientific approaches and social identity theory in the biblical studies that was dealt with in the previous chapter (particularly Edwin Judge's criticism that these approaches tended to be anachronistic as they tell us more about the modern sociological theories than actually offering us a better description of the early Pauline community at Corinth), this chapter has sought to avoid these anachronistic tendencies in two ways. First, it gave careful attention to the historical description of both Corinth and the Pauline community at Corinth, and second, it sought to deal with the literary issues surrounding 1 Corinthians, which is a primary document for our investigation.

Under the literary context, this chapter has dealt with different scholarly arguments for the unity of 1 Corinthians and, to a lesser degree, has dealt with the scholars who view 1 Corinthians as a composite document. Establishing the unity of 1 Corinthians is important for our analysis of the interrelationship between leadership and identity in 1 Corinthians, as the sections on which the study focuses are not normally identified as a single unit. All of this is done so that we can understand the social context of 1 Corinthians before we proceed to the exegesis of 1 Corinthians, which is the subject matter of the next chapter.

CHAPTER 4

Paul's Apostolic Defense: Group Prototypicality and Mimesis Tradition

4.1 Introduction

My thesis statement is that in 1 Corinthians 1–4, Pauline leadership is about identity formation, that is, Paul sets himself as a group prototype, whose leadership style is consistent with the group's identity "in Christ." Paul wanted the congregation at Corinth to draw their praxis from their "in Christ" identity.[1] If they did this, they would have a proper understanding and recognition of the roles of their leaders. But, before Paul can achieve this goal, he first has to convince the Corinthians about his legitimacy as their leader and that indeed his leadership and conduct is consistent with their identity as drawn from Christ.[2]

---

1. Harris has done a substantial amount of work on the significance of the preposition ἐν for the New Testament exegesis. Harris, *Prepositions and Theology*, 115–36. He notes that this is the most prominently used preposition in the whole of the New Testament. It accounts for 26.5% of proper prepositions used in the New Testament, and in its diverse use, it encroaches on other prepositions such as εἰς, διά, μετά, σύν, and κατά. Harris, 115, 117. Our interest in this chapter is to investigate its compound use as ἐν Χριστῷ (Ἰησοῦ) or ἐν (τῷ) κυρίῳ.

2. I am aware of the arguments by Schütz who sees the main issue regarding Paul's apostolic defence to be mostly concerned with authority rather than legitimacy. It is worth noting though that while Schütz argues that "legitimacy and authority are not the same thing," he later admits that these two words are interrelated. Schütz, *Paul*, 7. He writes; "authority and legitimacy are twin motifs, integrally related." Schütz, 9. Moreover, Schütz writes, "Paul's letters reflect a situation in which the Christian apostle is already something of an authority figure." Schütz, 8. Thus, for this study the main issue regarding Paul's apostleship is legitimacy, that is, does Paul meet the criteria for being an apostle? Only once Paul has established or convinced

In chapter 2, it was demonstrated that in order for one's leadership to be recognised by the group, one has to embody the values and the aspirations of the group, that is, a leader has to be a group prototype.[3] Reicher, Spears, and Haslam, and Van Knippenberg and Hogg have noted that leadership is easier where there is a positive social identification by the group members.[4] On the other hand, "where people do not share a common social identity, leadership over them is impossible – for where there are no agreed collective norms, values, and priorities that characterise the group, no-one can be entrusted to represent the group."[5] Below, I argue that this was indeed the case in 1 Corinthians.

In chapter 3, we saw that one of the problems with the Corinthians was that they had weak social boundaries, which made them susceptible to out-group influences. Walters has rightly observed that in 1 Corinthians "there is curious lack of references to conflict with outsiders, even though references to contact between insiders and outsiders are more common in 1 Corinthians than in any of Paul's other letters."[6] Walter observes that the Pauline community moved freely, and even received invitations to dine with people outside this community.[7] It also seems that the outsiders moved freely within this community as well (cf. 1 Cor 14:23–25). One suspects that it is possible that this social interaction with the Greco-Roman world by the congregation will have had a big influence on the congregation's praxis. Reicher, Spears, and Haslam note that under these circumstances, leadership can only be

---

the Corinthians about his apostleship can he exercise his authority. Schütz makes an interesting point about authority, particularly when he distinguishes it from leadership. He writes: "A leader functions as such so long as his followers will accede to his request; but one in authority has a 'right' to require obedience." Schütz, 9.

3. In chapter 2, I stated that while this study would be employing social identity theory in my analysis of the 1 Corinthians text, my approach would have components of sociohistorical approach. My social identity theoretical approach follows scholars such as Clarke and Tucker who argue that social identity theory is useful when it is merged together with the sociohistorical approach. Clarke and Tucker, "Social History," 41–58. They write; "Social theory provides a framework for interpreting the evidence that the historian finds, while social historians provide the evidence needed to substantiate purported theoretical claims." Tucker and Baker, "Introduction," 2.

4. Reicher, Spears, and Haslam, "Social Approach," 29; Van Knippenberg and Hogg, Leadership and Power.

5. Reicher, Spears, and Haslam, 29.

6. Walters, "Civic Identity in Roman," 397–99; cf. Barclay, "Thessalonica and Corinth," 49–73.

7. Cf. 1 Cor 8:7–13; 10:27–11:1.

achieved when the individual person is seen by the group "to be prototypical of the group."[8] The more the group notices this in that particular individual, the more likely it is that such a person will be seen as a leader and that person in return will "be able to influence other group members."[9] Paul's in-group prototypicality will be considered in this chapter in the light of his apostolic defence, particularly as it relates to his social identity agenda in 1 Corinthians 1–4.

Thus, this chapter will deal with four points that have an impact on Paul's apostolic defence and his identity formation agenda:

1. it will revisit the theoretical foundations of social identity theory, but now with particular attention being given to group prototypicality (section 4.2);
2. it will also revisit the debate that was raised in the previous chapter regarding the issues behind 1 Corinthians in relation to social identity theory (section 4.3);
3. it will review the debate regarding Paul's apostolic defence (section 4.4).
4. it will consider Paul's strategy in resolving the issue in 1 Corinthians 1–4. Our focus here will be on theoretical aspects of Paul's resocialisation strategy in using the "in Christ" idiom (section 4.5).

By dealing with these four points, this chapter seeks to demonstrate that Paul's apostolic defence/leadership discourse is intrinsically linked with his identity formation agenda.

4.2 The Leader as a Prototype of the In-group Identity: A Theoretical Framework

In the English language, according to Merriam-Webster, the term prototype carries with it three meanings:

(1) an original model on which something is patterned (meaning something is an archetype); (2) an individual that exhibits

---

8. Reicher, Spears, and Haslam, "Social Approach," 29.
9. Reicher, Spears, and Haslam, 29.

the essential features of a later type, and; (3) a standard or typical example.

Looking at these three definitions of the term prototype, it becomes clear that it will be anachronistic for this study to refer to Paul as an in-group prototype if by that we espouse the first meaning of the term prototype (if we mean Paul was the archetype of the Corinthian identity). The reason why it will be anachronistic is that both here in 1 Corinthians and elsewhere in Paul's letters, Paul never saw himself as the archetype of the early Jesus followers. In Scriptures such as Galatians 1:1 and Romans 1:5, Paul speaks of his apostleship as coming "through Jesus Christ and God the Father who raised him from the dead" and having received "grace and apostleship" through "Jesus Christ our Lord." Moreover, in both 1 and 2 Corinthians, Paul makes it clear that he was not one of the original apostles, and thus refers to himself as one who was abnormally born. Hence, in considering Paul's presentation of himself as a group prototype, it is important to emphasise that Paul saw himself as a group prototype in a way that is reminiscent of the mimesis tradition that will be explored in section 4.4.1.3.1 of this chapter. That is, he used his personal example as a moralistic device to be emulated by the Corinthians. An example of this can be seen in 1 Corinthians 8:1–11:1. First Corinthians 8:1–13 deals with how the exercising of "rights" by the strong who have knowledge is likely to make the weak betray their consciences. In 1 Corinthians 9:1–23, Paul tells the Corinthians that he also has "rights," but the Corinthians are to emulate him in how he exercises his own "rights." That is, they are to use their rights in order to advance the in-group. Similarly, as we will see shortly in section 4.4.1.3.1, personal imitation was a common practice in the ancient world, particularly in a context where the archetype is absent.[10] The archetype, by encouraging the imitation of God, exhorts his listeners to emulate those who exhibit values that are consistent with the character of God. Paul's presentation of himself as a group prototype needs to be looked at in light of that practice, in order for one to avoid anachronistic tendencies.

It is thus important to understand how a group prototype is perceived in social identity theory, which posits that leadership prototypicality can be defined as a leader's ability in "representing the unique qualities that define

---

10. See Quintilian, Inst. 1.8.5; 2.2.1–8; see also Philo, Spect. Leg. 4.73.

the group and what it means to be a member of this group. Embodying those core attributes of the group that make this group special as well as distinct from other groups. Being an exemplary and model member of the group" (emphasis original).[11] This study will consider Paul's group prototypicality along the lines of the second definition of prototype by the Merriam-Webster dictionary, in that he saw himself as one who embodied group values and norms. This will become clearer in section 5.3.3.1 of the next chapter, where it will be argued that in his missionary endeavours Paul opted for a missionary strategy that captured the essential aspects of the in-group identity.

In using social identity theory to look at the question of leadership and identity in the Pauline Corinthian correspondence, the emphasis (particularly with regard to identity) is on the social aspect of identity "as opposed to personal identity"; that is, identity defined in terms of belonging to a particular group.[12] Social identity theory approaches leadership as a group phenomenon, as opposed to the prevailing views of leadership studies where the emphasis tends to be on the persona and the charisma of the leader. Both Hogg and Lord et al. explain that abstract leadership category types are insufficient in explaining what makes a leader more effective in their communities, as they tend not to consider group dynamics.[13] Even those perspectives that are cognisant of the relational properties of leadership, do not pay enough attention to the cognitive processes involved in forming group identity. These sentiments come through strongly in the works of Turner and Haslam et al.[14] In particular, Turner has been very critical of the view that "particular personal characteristics" of a leader determine the leader's success. Social identity theory, especially under self-categorization theory, shows that different types of leaders will be better suited for different tasks. Personal characteristics need to align with the values and the identity of a given group, while identity embodiment and values of what is required in a leader will also be influenced

---

11. Steffens et al., "Leadership as Social Identity," 1002.

12. Horrell, "Becoming Christian," 311. A group here is defined as "a collection of individuals who perceive themselves to be members of the same social category, share some emotional involvement in this common definition of themselves, and achieve some degree of social consensus about the evaluation of their group and of their membership in it." Horrell, 312.

13. Hogg, Van Knippenberg, and Rast III, "Social Identity Theory," 189; Lord et al., "Contextual Constraints."

14. Turner, *Rediscovering Social Group*; Haslam, Psychology in Organizations; Haslam, Reicher, and Platow, *New Psychology of Leadership*.

by the context that the group faces. Under social categorization, social identity theory asserts that people or groups "generally want to have a clear sense that their ingroup is different from, and superior to, outgroups."[15]

What this means is that the members of the group who better capture the in-group identity (prototypicality), especially in comparison to the out-group are more likely to exert more influence on the group, and thus lead the group,[16] than those who do not embody the values of the group. This study's argument is that Paul, in his apostolic defence, is trying to show the Corinthians that he embodies the group norms and values and that their behaviour is not in line with their "in Christ" identity. Thus, Paul's focus on his own personal example serves as the measure for their behaviour. Steffens states that the person's "ability to influence other group members is argued to follow a gradient that is contingent on the degree to which he or she is perceived as *relative ingroup prototypical* of a social category" (emphasis original).[17] Haslam writes that the person who is an in-group prototype is that one who is most likely to influence the group; "as the (most) prototypical group member, the leader best epitomizes (in the dual sense both of *defining* and *being defined by*) the social category of which he or she is a member" (emphasis original).[18] Once the leader is viewed as "one of us," the in-group members will be more loyal to that person, as compared to someone who is viewed as "one of them."

This chapter then argues that Paul, in trying to help the Corinthians to act in the manner that is consistent with their identity in Christ, first has to convince them that he is indeed a group prototype. Only once Paul has succeeded in convincing the Corinthians that he embodies the group identity and that he has the best interests of the group at heart, can he proceed to correct their praxis and act as an entrepreneur of the group identity. Unless Paul persuades the group that he is the prototype of the in-group identity, he is going to be constantly rejected by the members of the group, as some in Corinth had already begun to question his apostleship.[19] This in turn would

---

15. Steffens, "Leaders' Personal Performance," 49; cf. Tajfel and Turner, "Integrative Theory."
16. This aspect of the process is sometimes referred to as leadership emergence.
17. Steffens, "Leaders' Personal Performance," 49–50.
18. Haslam, *Psychology in Organizations*, 45.
19. See 1 Cor 1:12; 3:4–5; 9:2.

make it impossible for him to have a long-lasting impact on the dynamics of the group.

Thus this chapter, in its treatment of Paul's apostolic defence in 1 Corinthians 1, deals with the scholarly debates regarding how Paul portrays himself as a group prototype. Linked with this is how Paul uses his teaching on leadership as a basis for his community identity management strategy. In 1 Corinthians 1–4, Paul uses many descriptors as the means by which he presents himself as a group prototype. First, he describes himself as "κλητὸς ἀπόστολος Χριστοῦ Ἰησοῦ διὰ θελήματος θεοῦ" (1 Cor 1.1). Second, he compares the message of the cross and the wisdom of the world, and states that the message of the cross is foolishness to those who are perishing (out-group) but it is the power of God and the wisdom of God to those who are being saved (in-group).[20] Thus he contrasts the in-group and the out-group. But, linked with this, he describes his approach when he came to the Corinthians: "Κἀγὼ ἐλθὼν πρὸς ὑμᾶς, ἀδελφοί, ἦλθον οὐ καθ' ὑπεροχὴν λόγου ἢ σοφίας καταγγέλλων ὑμῖν τὸ μαρτύριον τοῦ θεοῦ."[21] These texts support the position that in 1 Corinthians 1–2, Paul portrays himself as a group prototype and this finds its climax in his call to the community to imitate him, in 1 Corinthians 4:16 (cf. 1 Cor 11:1).[22]

However, before we deal with how Paul portrays himself as a group prototype, it is important first to revisit the debate regarding the issues behind the letter of 1 Corinthians. The main argument of the following section is that at the heart of the issues in 1 Corinthians is the question of belonging.

---

20. 1 Cor 1:18–31. Clarke calls this secular versus Christian leadership. *Secular and Christian Leadership*, 89–107.

21. 1 Cor 2:1–10; see particularly 1 Cor 2:1–4 where Paul aligns the wisdom he imparts with God's wisdom.

22. Paul's representation of himself as a group prototype will be developed in the next chapter. See particularly section 5.3.3.1 to 5.5 for the exegetical treatment of Paul's presentation of himself as a group prototype. The main concern of those sections is the question of Paul's missionary strategy. What becomes clear is that Paul chose a missionary strategy that demonstrates that he embodies the group values, a strategy that is aligned with how God works to bring about his purposes, which inverts human wisdom and power.

4.3 The Heart of Intragroup Conflict in 1 Corinthians 1–4 as a Quest for Belonging

The question regarding what was at the heart of the conflict in 1 Corinthians was first dealt with in chapter 3. Various propositions by scholars regarding the issues behind 1 Corinthians were addressed, and the question of belonging, while introduced, was not fully developed in that chapter. In chapter 3, we stated our preference for Winter's proposal of conflict and compromise as an underlying cause to all the issues in 1 Corinthians.[23] This section applies social identity theory in its analysis of those phenomena and seeks to demonstrate that at the core of conflict and compromise in 1 Corinthians was the quest for social belonging.

Scholars such as Tellbe and Punt have built on the findings of social conflict theorist Coser and demonstrated that group conflict or tension can have a positive social outcome for a social identity of a group, as this conflict or tension forces the group to engage on issues that are pertinent for their identity.[24] This becomes clearer in Tellbe who writes, citing Gager, that "all social conflicts serve 'a positive function in solidifying social groups and in shaping the complex symbolic and institutional apparatus needed to sustain them.'"[25] Coser on the other hand observes that conflict can help the group to "generate new norms," as conflicts allow for the "expression of hostility and the mending of strained relationships."[26] For him, conflicts between the members of the same group enable the group members to address and seek redress for the offended parties through the establishment of new norms or the affirmation of old ones. Hostility towards the out-group unifies the in-group as they deal with what is perceived as a common enemy/interest. Tellbe, building on Coser's theory, has observed and summarized four ways in which conflict can help the in-group with regard to its own identity:[27] "First, conflict may serve as a boundary-maintaining and group-binding function." On this point, Tellbe notes that inter/intra-group conflict forces the group to either establish or reaffirm the in-group identity and social boundaries.[28]

---

23. Winter, "'Underlays' of Conflict," 142.
24. Tellbe, *Christ-Believers in Ephesus*; Punt, "Identity Claims"; Coser, "Social Conflict."
25. Tellbe, 140.
26. Coser, "Social Conflict," 198.
27. Tellbe, *Christ-Believers in Ephesus*, 140; cf. Punt, "Identity Claims," 94.
28. Tellbe, 140.

"Secondly, the closer the relationship, the more intense the conflict seems to be. . . . Thirdly, conflicts may serve to define and strengthen group structures and may result in in-group solidarity, enhanced awareness of in-group identity and a tightening of the group boundaries. . . . Fourthly, ideology (the collective aims) that transcends personal interests will make struggles between competing groups more intense." Tellbe has observed that one of the positive outcomes of intergroup conflict is that it helps the in-group to better articulate what makes it distinct from other groups, while an intra-group conflict helps the in-group to revisit core aspects of in-group identity.[29] Thus, for scholars who employ a positive reading of Paul,[30] these conflicts in 1 Corinthians afforded Paul an opportunity to revisit and restate core identity issues. They also provided him with an opportunity to define the in-group boundary markers clearly.

Throughout 1 Corinthians, Paul deals with the issue of conflict that has engulfed the community.[31] In chapters 1–4, Paul deals with a report from Chloe's people who informed him about quarrels (ἔριδες, 1 Cor 1:11), which resulted in division because of the community's preference for one leader at the expense of the other.[32] In 1 Corinthians 3:3, Paul returns to the sub-

---

29. Tellbe, 140.

30. The term "positive reading of Paul" in this context is used because some scholars such as Schüssler Fiorenza, Shaw, Castelli, and Wanamaker are suspicious of Paul's apostolic discourse in 1 Cor 1–4. Fiorenza, "Rhetorical Situation," 396–97; Shaw, *Cost of Authority*; Castelli, *Imitating Paul*; Wanamaker, "Rhetoric of Power," 115–37. For Schüssler Fiorenza, Paul's apostolic defence is oppressive as Paul is "arrogating the authority of God, the 'Father,' for himself." Fiorenza, 397. Castelli exposes similar views, noticing that power dynamics are at play in 1 Cor 1–4 in Paul's use of mimesis discourse. She views Paul's argument in these chapters as his ways of consolidating power to himself (this idea will be revisited below). Similarly, Wanamaker who builds upon the findings of Castelli and incorporates the ideological perspectives of John Thompson, views Paul's rhetoric in 1 Cor 1–4 as "Paul's attempt to re-establish his authority as paterfamilias over the Corinthian community." Punt, "Foolish Rhetoric," 9; Wanamaker, 115–37. Footnote 171 below will revisit this subject of how Paul uses his apostolic discourse in 1 Corinthians. Scholars who employ a more positive reading of Paul's apostolic discourse in 1 Corinthians are Barentsen, Ehrensperger, and Tucker. Barentsen, *Emerging Leadership*; Ehrensperger, *Paul and Dynamics*; Tucker, *You Belong to Christ*.

31. For more on this, see section 3.2 of this study, where literary issues regarding 1 Corinthians were discussed. In that section, this dissertation argued for the literary integrity of 1 Corinthians. Section 3.2 of the dissertation also argued, using the findings of Winter, that conflict and compromise as the problem of the Corinthians can be seen throughout 1 Corinthians. Winter, *After Paul Left Corinth*.

32. 1 Cor 1:10–12, 12; 3:4–5. Scholars such as Donahoe and Birge believe that a misunderstanding of wisdom acted as a catalyst to the divisions within the community. Donahoe, "From Self-Praise"; Birge, *Language of Belonging*, 1. Finney and Meeks have argued

ject of division and quarrelling; ἐν ὑμῖν ζῆλος καὶ ἔρις. The argument of this study is that at the heart of the issues of division and quarrelling was an issue of identity and belonging.[33] This becomes apparent when we consider 1 Corinthians 1:12; λέγω δὲ τοῦτο ὅτι ἕκαστος ὑμῶν λέγει· Ἐγὼ μέν εἰμι Παύλου, Ἐγὼ δὲ Ἀπολλῶ, Ἐγὼ δὲ Κηφᾶ, Ἐγὼ δὲ Χριστοῦ.[34] Birge provides a rationale why Ἐγὼ δὲ could be translated as "I belong."[35] He writes that "the word belong is a dynamic equivalent for the verb 'to be' accompanied by a noun in the genitive case, e.g., · Ἐγὼ μέν εἰμι Παύλου, 'I belong to Paul' (3:4) . . . 'to express that a thing belongs to another.'" Thus, the issue here in 1 Corinthians 1:12 and in 1 Corinthians 3:4 (where Paul writes: ὅταν γὰρ λέγῃ τις· Ἐγὼ μέν εἰμι Παύλου [I belong to Paul], ἕτερος δέ· Ἐγὼ Ἀπολλῶ [I

---

that the unity of the community was a concern for diaspora synagogue leaders – a concern apparently inherited by Christ's early followers. Finney, *Honour and Conflict*, 69–70; Meeks, *First Urban Christians*, 108, 113, 166–67, 191. Outside the New Testament it can be observed in the works of the early church fathers such as Clement, who wrote extensively against factionalism. In his arguments he quoted 1 Corinthians extensively. See also 1 Clem 47. 1–5. See also Mitchell who also considers other early church fathers such as Ignatius in her analysis of 1 Corinthians 1:10. Mitchell, *Paul and Rhetoric*, 75–76.

33. Tucker, *You Belong to Christ*, 15. For a scholarly treatment of the various schools of thought regarding the problems behind 1 Cor 1–4, see Tucker, *You Belong to Christ*, 14–31; Thiselton, *First Epistle to Corinthians*, 123–33; and Clarke, *Secular and Christian Leadership*, 89–107. As demonstrated in chapter 3 of this study, the issues that lay behind 1 Corinthians were not theological in nature, but were rather the result of social influences upon the community, particularly the personality-cult that existed in the Greco-Roman world. See also Clarke, 90–95.

34. First Corinthians 1:12 mentions that division and quarrelling took the form of four groups. There were those who claimed to belong to Paul, while others claimed Apollos, and still others claimed to belong to Peter. There were also those who are viewed as Christ's party. In footnote 333 of chapter 3 of this study, I have done a comprehensible review of scholars' arguments regarding the actual number of parties present in 1 Corinthians. This research agrees with scholars such as Mihaila, Winter, Smit, and Hurd that the mention of the "Peter party" and the "Christ party" was Paul's rhetorical device in order to avoid reducing the conflict to an alternative between himself and Apollos. Mihaila, *Paul-Apollos Relationship*; Winter, *Philo and Paul*; "'Underlays' of Conflict"; Smit, "What Is Apollos?"; Hurd, *Origin of 1 Corinthians*. Thus, the conflict in 1 Cor 1–4 was between those who preferred Apollos as their leader and those who preferred Paul as their leader. Paul only mentions himself and Apollos when he discourses the party disputes further in 1 Cor 3:4, 21. See also Winter, *After Paul Left Corinth*, 176–77; Smit, 231. Our focus in this section will be to consider why some in the Corinthian ἐκκλησία preferred Apollos to Paul. For a view different to the one taken in this paper, see Odell-Scott who is of the view that there was indeed a "Christ" group in Corinth, and that this is the group that Paul was most concerned about. Odell-Scott, *Paul's Critique of Theocracy*, 59, 62. He writes that the people who declared, "I belong to Christ" (1 Cor 1:12) together with those who boasted "noble birth" (1 Cor 1:26) represented the claims of superiority of members of Jesus's family. He takes James, the brother of Jesus, and Peter as examples of the people who belonged to this group. Odell-Scott, 52. For a critique of Odell-Scott's argument, see Tucker, *You Belong to Christ*, 160–62.

35. Birge, *Language of Belonging*, 14.

belong to Apollos], οὐκ ἄνθρωποί ἐστε;") is that the community, rather than deriving their identity from Christ, were identifying with certain sub-groups within the community. Winter, Birge, and Malherbe observed that the cultural influences behind slogans "I belong to Paul" and "I belong to Apollos" (as an expression of loyalty for preferred leaders) were a result of continued Greco-Roman cultural influences upon the community.[36] Chong notes that the "term I belong" was used in the Greco-Roman world as a way of self-identification (emphasis original).[37] White suggests that the issue here was the power struggle between certain factions in the ἐκκλησία, in a way that is reminiscent of ancient political party politics.[38] Welborn adds that "political

---

36. Winter, *After Paul Left Corinth*; Birge, 10; Malherbe, *Social Aspects*, 69. Similar sentiments are also expressed by scholars such as White, Mitchell, and Welborn. White, *Where Is the Wise Man?*, 1; Mitchell, *Paul and Rhetoric*, 82–86; Welborn, "On the Discord," 90. Birge notes that several commentators have taken this slogan "I belong to" as "a representation of political parties or factions" (i.e. Clarke and Welborn). Birge, *Language of Belonging*, 10; Clarke, *Secular and Christian Leadership*, 94; Welborn, "On the Discord," 91. Mitchell, while agreeing that the Corinthians in their use of "I belong to" were influenced by the personality cult of the day, disagrees that this slogan was following a common formula of political self-identification in antiquity. Mitchell, 83–85. For views contra to this assertion by Birge, see Finney and Mitchell who demonstrate that there are verbal similarities between 1 Cor 1:10–4:21 and Greco-Roman political terms. Finney, *Honour and Conflict*, 72–76; Mitchell, 71–99. See also Welborn who analyses 1 Cor 1–4 in the light of the ancient politics. Welborn, 85–111. Birge, however, maintains that there is no "ancient political slogan which has the same formula (personal pronoun + εἰμί [or ellipsed] + genitive of a proper name)." Birge, 11. Birge suggests that the "closest formulaic parallel to the partisan phrase" that is found in 1 Cor 1:12; 3:4 is in Isa 44:5 (LXX), which is τοῦ θεοῦ εἰμί which corresponds to Acts 27:23 (τοῦ θεοῦ εἰμί ἐγώ). Birge, 11. Thus for her, the issue in 1 Cor 1:12 and 3:4 is the community's failure to grasp that they "belong to God alone and to claim otherwise is idolatry." Birge, 10–11. She sees Paul's enterprise in 1 Cor 1–4 as a criticism of the Corinthians' idolatrous behaviour which was influenced by his reading of Isa 44:5.

37. Chong, *Strategies in Church*, 31.

38. White, *Where Is the Wise Man?*, 1. White insists that the source of the problems in the Corinthian ἐκκλησία was due to the "Apollos party," which was insistent on judging Paul "according to the values found in the schools of oratory and philosophy, or, more generally, Graeco-Roman παιδεία." White, 2–3. This dissertation agrees with White in part that there were some in the ἐκκλησία who were judging Paul according to worldly wisdom (see also 1 Cor 1:26–31), and were hoping that Paul could employ "contemporary oratorical methods" (i.e. "wise speech," σοφία λόγου). However, the insistence that it was Apollos's group who is the main cause of the problems in 1 Corinthians is somewhat speculative. There is no way of knowing with certainty that people in "Paul's party" did not use secular wisdom in arguing that Paul is their legitimate leader, particularly if one looks at factions in the light of the Greco-Roman patronage system. Chong and Donahoe demonstrate how well-entrenched the patronage system was during Paul's day. Chong, *Strategies in Church*, 31; Donahoe, "From Self-Praise," 79–80. Chong notes that "belonging and loyalty to a certain oikos" could even "rival loyalty to the empire" as the *oikos* could offer more security to those who belong to it than the state. He also notes that "association with those of high rank and status was an important way of gaining benefits and

parties thus took the form of groups of clients and personal adherents pledged to particular leaders."³⁹ People were more concerned about the "personality-centred" politics than party ideology. Chong notes that the political parties were named after the individuals rather than "ideological beliefs."⁴⁰ He notes that in 1 Corinthians 1:12, Paul wants to bring about the unity of the community, and he wants to anchor that unity on the shared identity in Christ. Paul wants the Corinthians to realize that their true patron is Christ. This is why Paul frames his argument in 1 Corinthians 1:10 and 1 Corinthians 4:16 with an encouragement or an appeal to the Corinthians to be united.⁴¹

Scholars also debate the meaning of the phrase παρακαλῶ δὲ ὑμᾶς (1 Cor 1:10).⁴² Fitzmyer, who represents a dominant view regarding how Paul uses "παρακαλῶ," argues that Paul in his use of this term makes "an urgent appeal."⁴³ Ehrensperger argues that Paul uses this term in a relational way, where a situation requires a "cooperation, contribution or acceptance" by the recipient.⁴⁴ She argues, using the findings of Bjerkelund, that this term has its origins

---

status." Chong, 31. It is thus possible that some of those who claimed to belong to Paul did not do this out of "godly motive," but rather because they were influenced by secular Greco-Roman cultural values. It is possible that by claiming to belong to Paul, they wanted honour, prestige, and to ascend above others in terms of authority within the community, and thus they were equally guilty of bringing about disunity in the ἐκκλησία. See Donahoe who also argues that allegiances to different leaders was a means of "increasing one's social status." Donahoe, "From Self-Praise," 78. For more on the role that patronage played in the ancient voluntary associations, see Chester, *Conversion at Corinth*, 236–40. He demonstrates how in the ancient world backing the right patron (particularly if he/she wins and ascends into power) was a way of boosting one's own social status and prestige. Chester suggests that the rivalries between the groups that are mentioned in 1 Cor 1:12 are "best explained as a struggle for ascendency between their local leaders." Chester, 241. Thus, it seems wrong to assume that the people who were at fault are only the "Apollos party." It is possible that even those who were supporting Paul did so out of selfish ambition, (contra to Paul's stance in Phil 2:3), and hence in 1 Corinthians, he wants to pursue his social identity agenda, so that the community, rather than deriving their identity from their leaders, should derive their identity from Christ.

39. Welborn, "On the Discord," 90.
40. Chong, Strategies *in Church*, 32.
41. For the arguments concerning the unity of 1 Cor 1:10–4:21, see the previous chapter of this dissertation. See also Malcolm, Welborn, and Punt who have identified Παρακαλῶ δὲ ὑμᾶς of 1 Cor 1:10 and παρακαλῶ οὖν ὑμᾶς of 1 Cor 4:16 as literary devices that are used to mark the unity of these chapters. Malcolm, "Paul and Rhetoric," 128–57; Welborn, *Paul, the Fool of Christ*, 13; Punt, "Foolish Rhetoric," 2.
42. For an extended treatment of this debate, see Ehrensperger, *Paul and Dynamics*, 174–77.
43. Fitzmyer, *First Corinthians*, 140; cf. Tucker, *You Belong to Christ*, 154.
44. Ehrensperger, *Paul and Dynamics*, 175.

in first-century diplomatic context, where it is not used in a "paternalistic or ... authority-exercising" manner between the sender and the addressee. While Paul uses this term in an asymmetrical manner, he is nonetheless not threatening or dominating the Corinthians to succumb to his wish.[45] Rather, Paul exercises power in a compassionate way, as he wishes that the group "will follow his guidance and share his perceptions of the implications of the Christ-event."[46] This becomes clearer when one considers the presence of the sibling language that he uses to describe his relationship with the Corinthians.[47]

This dissertation, while agreeing that personality-centred cultural politics played a crucial role in the community's preference of one leader at the expense of the other, prefers the proposal by Winter, which takes the personality-centered cult a step further.[48] Winter suggests that the Corinthians were influenced by the Sophist tradition of teacher/pupils relationship of the Greco-Roman world.[49] He notes that during Paul's days, the Sophists were held in high honour by some and viewed as the skilful public speakers of the day.[50] They spoke in secular ἐκκλησία and had a large public following. Further, the Sophists ran very expensive public performance schools where "they trained the next generation of the social élite to argue in the criminal and civil courts and debate in the secular assemblies."[51] In these Sophist schools, pupils in expressing their belonging and loyalty to their teachers, modelled themselves after their Sophist teachers. This is because the student was seen as the disciple of the teacher. In this regard, they modelled themselves after their teachers, "not only in terms of the oratorical style of the

---

45. Contra Castelli, *Imitating Paul*.

46. Ehrensperger, *Paul and Dynamics*, 175.

47. See the following chapter regarding the importance of sibling language (ἀδελφός) as employed by Paul in his argument in 1 Corinthians.

48. Winter, *After Paul Left Corinth*.

49. Winter, 31–43.

50. It is worth noting that not everyone held Sophists in high regard. They were criticised and even despised by others. While some saw them as oratorically proficient, many others doubted their sincerity, and accused them of abusing rhetoric to get their way. Sophism got a bad reputation in some circles. For more literature regarding the distrust of the Sophists by some in the ancient world, see Plato's Gorgias.

51. Winter, *After Paul Left Corinth*, 33.

teacher but also in the way that the disciple spoke, dressed, and even walked."[52] Winter notes that the Corinthians applied to Paul, Apollos, and possibly Peter the same cultural norms that "governed the relationship of secular pupils and their elitist teacher."[53] Another important feature of the Sophist schools which must have influenced relationships within the ἐκκλησία at Corinth is that the students tended to play teachers against each other, and also teachers would compete against each other in order to win more disciples.[54] Students were encouraged to be loyal to their teachers and the way in which they expressed that loyalty was that they needed to be zealous for the honour of their teachers. They did this by promoting the oral attributes and "educational prowess" of their teachers.[55] This created strife, as the act of promoting one's teacher also meant that one had to highlight the deficiencies of the other teacher.[56] Scholars believe that Paul alludes to this cultural practice in 1 Corinthians 3:3 when he criticizes the Corinthians about their jealousy and strife. Hence, Paul views what the ἐκκλησία was doing in respect to claiming to belong to him or Apollos as "acting like mere human beings."[57] He views their behaviour as not consistent with their identity in Christ, and being worldly (ἔτι γὰρ σαρκικοί ἐστε), because they used secular Sophist categories in assessing him and Apollos. Strife in the community was also not only a result of the

---

52. Winter, 33. Winter's findings are important for this research as he observes the link between the Sophist school and imitation, which is an important aspect for the present argument. This research is of the view that in 1 Corinthians, Paul was calling upon the ἐκκλησία to imitate him as he follows Christ. This was not a unique thing in the ancient world, as this practice was common among the people who had disciples.

53. Winter, 31.

54. Winter, 36–37; cf. Chong, *Strategies in Church*, 32.

55. Winter, 39.

56. Part of ridiculing the deficiencies of other teachers included highlighting their grammatical mistakes or lisps in their speeches. This seems to be the cultural influence behind the Corinthians' criticism of Paul in 2 Cor 10:10, when they say: "His letters are weighty and forceful, but in person he is unimpressive and his speaking amounts to nothing."

57. 1 Cor 3:3–4. This dissertation agrees with Donahoe that Paul's strategy in his admonition in 1 Cor 1:10–4:21 and 5:1–13 is directed at criticizing the Corinthians' worldly wisdom, which is based on physical attributes and social status. Donahoe, "From Self-Praise," 78. What Paul wants to instil in the Corinthians is a standard that is set by the cross, which is an integral part of the group's identity in Christ, as this was the means by which they became members of the group.

community's preferences between Paul and Apollos; the previous social identity of the community might also have contributed in the division.[58]

The people in the Pauline community at Corinth came from diverse social backgrounds,[59] and as members of those previous different identity groups they held certain prejudices against each other. In social identity theory, one of the important aspects of group identity is that groups provide a sense of worth for the members of the in-group, and "positive group identity is maintained

---

58. White, *Where Is the Wise Man?*, x; Tidball, *Introduction to Sociology*, 99; Chong, *Strategies in Church*, 44; Chow, Patronage and Power, 105–10. See White who argues that the problems in 1 Cor 1–4 resulted from elite educated members of the ἐκκλησία who "preferred Apollos to Paul as a teacher since Apollos more closely resembled other teachers of higher studies." White, x. Based on this, it seems probable that the members of this group retained the elitist mind-set. Also, the elite in the Greco-Roman world did not socialise with the poor or see them as their equals. Therefore, it is possible that when these two groups become fellow Christ-followers, there might have been intragroup conflict or at the very least, the elite were still holding onto their group stereotypes regarding the poor. Tidball, 99. For more on the relationship between the elite and the poor in the Greco-Roman world, see Longenecker, Chow, and for more on the psychology of prejudice between in-groups and out-groups, see Brewer. Longenecker, *Remember*, 19–107; Chow, *Patronage and Power*; Brewer, "Psychology of Prejudice," 429–44. Brewer's study shows that while members of the in-group do not have to hate the members of the out-group, discrimination by members of the in-group, does occur against the members of the out-group, "motivated by preferential treatment of ingroup members." Brewer, 429. Scholars such as Tidball, Chong, Chow, and Marshall argue that the problems in 1 Corinthians were a result of the elite in the ἐκκλησία looking down on Paul and everyone else of lower social status and seeing themselves as being superior. They disrespected Paul because of his lack of rhetorical ability (see also 1 Cor 2:1–5; and 2 Cor 10:10), something that the elite prized as an important qualification for one to assume power, particularly in political pursuit. Tidball, *Introduction to Sociology*, 99; Chong, *Strategies in Church*, 44; Chow, 105–10; Marshall, *Enmity in Corinth*, 181. See Pliny the Younger, *Ep.* 2.9.4; 2.13.6–7; 3.2.3;7.22.2; who valued rhetorical abilities in the candidates he recommended for a job. See also Chow, 105. However, Tidball thinks that Paul received an elite education and had been trained in rhetoric. Tidball, 93. Porter argues that it is probable that Paul did receive or at the very least was exposed to Greco-Roman rhetoric but Porter also suggests that "The direct evidence from the New Testament regarding Paul's capability as a rhetoric is not great." Porter, "Paul of Tarsus," 533–37. He further suggests that there is insufficient evidence to reconstruct a hypothesis regarding Paul's Greco-Roman educational background. Porter, 537. Thus, for this study, at issue here in 1 Corinthians is not whether or not Paul was trained in elite schools or whether he was good at rhetoric, rather the issue is Paul's lack of use of such a skill. Both Chow and Marshall note that Paul's refusal of financial support from the Corinthian patrons might have worsened an already tense relationship between Paul and them. Chow, 105–10; Marshall, *Enmity in Corinth*, 251–53. Chow argues that during the Lord's Supper, the rich patrons provided better food that they shared with those with whom they shared the same social status, while they provided inferior and less food for the poor. He says it is probable that this is what Paul was referring to in 1 Cor 11:21 when he says that some are going hungry while others are getting drunk. Chow, 110–12. What becomes clear from all of this is that there was a myriad of issues that might have contributed to the intragroup conflict at Corinth for which Paul had to develop a strategy for resolution.

59. See 1 Cor 1:26–30.

by the process of comparison and evaluation against the out-groups."[60] In this process of evaluation, people ascribe positive attributes to their in-group and at times they can prejudice the out-groups. Social identity theory holds that individuals "strive for a positive self-concept,"[61] and in the effort to "achieve or to maintain positive social identity," they tend to discriminate against the members of the out-group.[62] In chapter 2, I argued that positive social identity happens when the individual perceives the in-group of which they are part to be superior to the out-group, and hence their membership of the group boosts their self-esteem. In this regard, it is possible that members of the Pauline community at Corinth were still holding on to their previous self-categorization, and this in turn might have also contributed to the strife in the community, and more than that this threatened the very existence of the group and also undermined what Christ has done for the group. Paul's role in this regard will need to involve a re-categorization process. Paul had to introduce new evaluation criteria to "diffuse or prevent any potential, perceived or real ingroup-outgroup differentiation and intergroup comparison."[63] Since the members of the community belonged to different social status groups, it would have been tempting to use the previous categories of social identity to evaluate each other, thereby dividing the community further. The argument of this dissertation is that, by using the "in Christ" idiom, Paul brings a new evaluation category into the community to help diffuse the tension that might have been caused by their previous social identities.[64] Further, this "in Christ" language would serve as the superordinate identity, which would help different group members to realize their common in-group identity.[65]

---

60. Lim, *Metaphors and Social Identity*, 36.
61. Haslam, *Psychology in Organizations*, 26.
62. Tajfel and Turner, "Social Identity Theory," 16.
63. Lim, *Metaphors and Social Identity*, 37.
64. Tidball puts the same idea this way: "Paul was not arguing that the social distinctions should be completely abandoned by Christians any more than the biological differences between sexes disappeared when people became Christians. However, he was arguing that the church was an alternative society, which operated on different principles from the normal society and enjoyed entirely new relationships. Within the church there must be acceptance and respect for people whatever their class background and the acknowledgement that God may use some prominently within the church who would not normally have risen to positions of leadership. In a word, the prominent members of the church at Corinth needed to repent of their snobbery and treat the ordinary members with more seriousness." Tidball, *Introduction to Sociology*, 99–100.
65. Lim, *Metaphors and Social Identity*, 37; cf. Tucker, *You Belong to Christ*, 80.

It is hoped that looking at Paul's emphasis on the superordinate identity in Christ, will result in the in-group becoming a cohesive group and that this will reduce intragroup "discrimination and bias," and that this "in-Christ" identity will now become an evaluative criterion for the in-group, not their wealth or ethnicity.[66]

Conflict and compromise are not limited only to 1 Corinthians 1–4, they also manifest themselves in 1 Corinthians 6:1–8 (civil litigation), 1 Corinthians 6:12; 8:1–11:1 (libertarianism), 1 Corinthians 11:3–16; 14:33–36 (gender disputes), and 1 Corinthians 11:17–34 (worship). All of this was because of the community's failure to understand the implications of their "in Christ" identity. There was a prevalence of the Greco-Roman social identity in the ἐκκλησία, rather than their "in Christ" social identity.[67]

What compounds the problems in the ἐκκλησία in 1 Corinthians is the fact that Paul's apostolic authority was challenged, and "not all Corinthians accepted Paul as their apostle, since some of them recognize such figures as Cephas and Apollos as their preferred leaders."[68] So, in 1 Corinthians Paul has to do two things: he has to counter the secular influences on Christ-followers in Corinth, and at the same time establish or defend his apostolic authority. In the light of the rejection by some members of the ἐκκλησία, Paul employs a rhetorical strategy where he brings his identity and that of the community together. In social identity theory terms, Paul has to both establish himself as an in-group prototype and at the same time, he has to act as a social identity entrepreneur of the in-group identity. The argument of this section, then, is that Paul, by using the "in Christ" idiom, is able to demonstrate that he is the group prototype and at the same time, he is able through the use of this terminology to re-socialise the Corinthians into the ethos of their new identity in Christ. De Silva contends that "the Corinthian believers have not been adequately socialized into the ethos of the new group."[69] Similarly, in his treatment of God as a benefactor, Neyrey looks at the role of God as a

---

66. Lim, 37.
67. Barclay, "Thessalonica and Corinth," 57–58; De Vos, Church and Community Conflicts; Clarke, *Secular and Christian Leadership*, 73–88; Donahoe, "From Self-Praise"; Winter, *After Paul Left Corinth*, 44–57; De Silva, Hope of Glory, 121; and Tucker, Remain *in Your Calling*.
68. Phua, *Idolatry and Authority*, 180. According to Chow, in his use of the verb ἀνακρίνω in 1 Cor 4:3 and 9:3, Paul demonstrates that he was probably being "examined or scrutinized" by some of the community members at this stage. Chow, *Patronage and Power*, 172–74.
69. De Silva, Hope of Glory, 121.

Father and makes the following observations regarding the rights and duties of a father: "The duties of a father include socialization of his children, protection and nurture of them, and the like."[70] While in 1 Corinthians, Paul argues that God is the ultimate benefactor of the community, he nonetheless presents himself as the father to the ἐκκλησία (1 Cor 4:15). Thus, Paul has to lay upon himself the responsibility of socializing the Corinthians with regard to their new identity "in Christ." The argument of this dissertation is that Paul's apostolic defence has to be seen in the light of his identity formation agenda in 1 Corinthians 1–4.

4.4 Scholarly Treatment regarding Paul's (Re)Presentation of Himself as a Group Prototype

In the previous section, we have mostly been considering Paul's apostolic defence in the light of social identity theory. However, in both chapters 1 and 2, it was argued that we will incorporate sociohistorical and socioscientific approaches in our analysis of the interrelationship between leadership and identity. In this section, we consider the findings of scholars who incorporate these methodologies in the analysis of Paul's apostolic defence.

Paul's presentation of himself as a group prototype is traditionally studied under two categories: (1) Paul's apostolic understanding, and (2) Paul's language of imitation. Hence, this section tries to merge these two ideas. It is important that before one does an analysis of Paul's apostolic defence and of how he presents himself as a group prototype, one must do a short summary first of recent scholarly approaches to this subject. Pauline scholars have dealt with the subject of Pauline apostleship in two ways: (1) The traditional approach, that tends to be theological by nature, and tends to focus mostly on the implications and the origins of Paul's use of the term apostle; (2) The socioscientific approaches, which are mostly concerned with how Paul asserts his authority. Here scholars are concerned with the power dynamic in Paul's use of the title apostle.

---

70. Neyrey, "God, Benefactor and Patron," 472; cf. Tucker, *Remain in Your Calling*, 67.

4.4.1 The Traditional Approach to Paul's Apostleship and Mimesis Tradition

As already stated above, traditionally, in dealing with the subject of the apostleship in Paul, scholars focus on the developments, origins, and the theological implications of the term. The origins of the ἀπόστολος terminology in Paul has been a subject of great debate among scholars particularly as it relates to how the word ἀπόστολος came to signify leadership among early Jesus followers. Scholars have focused on the linguistic problem of the origins of the term ἀπόστολος with the hope that by so doing, this will yield a better understanding of how the early Jesus movement understood the office of the apostles.[71] Sociohistorical studies of the term ἀπόστολος have revealed that it "has an obscure and unimpressive history in Greek literature" outside its use to describe leaders in the early Jesus movement.[72] Keay and Rengstorf suggest that the term was rarely used outside the early Jesus movement in the Greco-Roman world, and when it was employed it was used in an objective way to describe a cargo or merchant ship.[73] Afterwards, the lemma came to be used in reference to a convoy of a military expedition.[74] Still later, the term was applied to a group of men sent out for a specific purpose, such as admiral of a naval ship,[75] or a band of colonists and their settlement.[76] Due to a lack of correlation in how the term ἀπόστολος was used in antiquity, with how it has been used in the New Testament, scholars have sought to find out how it was used within the Pauline corpus. Here they pay careful attention to the development of how Paul used this term.

4.4.1.1 The Development of Paul's Use of ἀπόστολος

It seems that Paul, in his early use of ἀπόστολος, used the term very loosely to describe one sent by the ἐκκλησία; he used it in reference to himself and his

---

71. Schütz, *Paul*, 6.
72. Keay, "Paul the Spiritual Guide," 8. For sociohistorical use of the term outside its use by the early Jesus followers, see Keay and Rengstorf; see also Best and Agnew for a review of the scholarly discussions regarding the meaning and origins of the term ἀπόστολος. Keay, 8–14; Rengstorf, "ἀπόστολος", 398–447; Best, "Paul's Apostolic Authority"; Agnew, "Origin of NT Apostle-Concept," 75–96.
73. Keay, 8; Rengstorf, "ἀπόστολος", 407–08. See also Plato, *Epi.*, 7.346a.
74. Lysias, *Or.*, 19, 21; Demosthenes, *Or.*, 18, 107.
75. Diontsius, Ant. Rom., 9.59.2.
76. Rengstorf, 407–408; Keay, "Paul the Spiritual Guide," 9; Bertone, "Apostle."

co-workers. Best notes that in the New Testament, the term ἀπόστολος carried with it a variety of meanings but it "always retains some sense of being sent, whether by an individual, a group such as a church, or by Christ or God."[77] This has led some scholars to argue that it is possible that in his early use of the term, Paul simply used it to highlight the fact that both he and his co-workers had been sent by their representative churches for mission work. In this sense, the term apostle did not carry with it leadership authority within the ἐκκλησία, it simply represents a missionary activity.[78] As an example, scholars point to texts such as Acts 14:4, 14, where Paul and Barnabas are referred to twice as the ἀπόστολοι of the ἐκκλησία of Antioch.[79] Looking at these texts together with Galatians 2:1–10 and Acts 15:6–21, 29, Taylor notes that the significance of the use of the term is more on the message proclaimed (the ἀποστολή of the gospel) rather than the title of an individual ἀπόστολος.[80] Taylor notes that in this context the status and authority of an individual are not the main concern, and thus the term ἀπόστολος (in Acts 14 and 15) could be "applied to any person involved in ἀποστολή."[81] However, this raises the question of why Paul used the term ἀπόστολος in a restricted sense in letters such as Galatians and Corinthians. The answer provided by Taylor seems to be speculative at this point, when he writes, "Galatians . . . reflects Paul's reconstruction of his apostolic identity after ceasing to be a representative and a missionary of the church of Antioch."[82] A much more plausible explanation regarding Paul's maturation or evolution in his use of the term ἀπόστολος is

---

77. Best, "Paul's Apostolic Authority," 5.

78. It is worth noting though as Best has observed, that it would not be true to say that everyone "who carried out missionary work would have been called an apostle." Best, "Paul's Apostolic Authority," 4; see also, Phil 1:14–18. What is true is that the term is closely linked to being sent.

79. Taylor, "Apostolic Identity and Conflicts," 101.

80. Taylor, 102.

81. Taylor, 102–03.

82. Taylor, 103–04. While Taylor offers a plausible answer to why Paul argues forcibly in Galatians for divine origin of his apostolic commission, he unfortunately leaves more questions unanswered by asserting that Paul ceased "to be a representative and a missionary of the church of Antioch." Taylor, 104. Taylor does not answer the question; why did Paul cease to be a missionary of Antioch? Taylor, 104–05. Also, if Paul ceased to be an apostle from the church of Antioch, why does he continue to use Antioch as his home base when he returns from his missionary journeys, as depicted in the book of Acts? Further, while Taylor acknowledges the early use of the term ἀπόστολος in the Synoptic Gospels, he seems to allow too much of a difference in the use of the term between Acts and Synoptic Gospels. He acknowledges that in the Synoptic Gospels, the term ἀπόστολος is closely tied to authority in the ἐκκλησία, but

the one offered by Betz, namely that Paul's self-description and his concept of the term ἀπόστολος changed after his conflict in Antioch, presumably after his confrontation with Peter in Galatians 2:11–14.[83] For Betz,[84] this confrontation precipitated a change in "Paul's apostolic self-consciousness,"[85] causing him to reconsider his own apostleship status. Betz notes that after this confrontation with Peter, Paul's description of himself as an apostle became a norm in most of his epistolary prescript.[86]

Due to a lack of correlation between how the term ἀπόστολος was used in antiquity, and how it has been used in the New Testament, scholars have been concerned to explore the ideological influences on Paul in how he came to use this term.

4.4.1.2 The שָׁלוּחַ Tradition as an Ideological Influence on Paul's Apostolic Self-consciousness

In trying to find ideological influences on Paul's apostolic self-consciousness, scholars have paid attention to the institution of the שָׁלוּחַ in the Old Testament.[87] There has been a growing consensus among scholars that the use of the term ἀπόστολος in the New Testament has its roots in the Old Testament, and that in particular institution of the שָׁלוּחַ played a major role in Paul's apostolic understanding.[88] They note the similarities between the idea of an apostle as being someone sent to act on behalf of someone else or

---

in his treatment of Acts, he seems to suggest that authority was vested only in the particular ἐκκλησία that sends the apostle.

83. Betz, "Apostle," 310.

84. Betz, 310.

85. Keay, "Paul the Spiritual Guide," 16.

86. Betz, "Apostle," 310. See: Rom 1:1; 1 Cor 1:1; 2 Cor 1:1; Gal 1:1; Eph 1:1; Col 1:1; 2 Thess 1:1; 1 Tim 1:1; 2 Tim 1.1, 11; Tit 1:1.

87. For more on the institution of the Shaliach and its relationship with the apostolic tradition, see Barrett, "Shaliach and Apostle," 88–102.

88. Not all scholars agree though that the designation 'apostle' has its roots in the Old Testament institution of the שָׁלוּחַ. Gerhardsson has demonstrated that the relationship between the שָׁלוּחַ and the apostle is not that the latter is derived from the former, "but that both are rooted in the Old Testament sending convention and emerge separately and distinctly." Gerhardsson, *Memory and Manuscript*, 109–10; Keay, "Paul the Spiritual Guide," 13. A similar idea is found in Munck, who writes: "Far too much importance has for some time now been attached to these Jewish . . . The Christian apostles are part of something entirely new and dynamic in that the whole Christian religion is something to spread abroad." Munck, *Paul and Salvation of Mankind*, 100. According to these scholars both the idea of the apostle and the institution of the שָׁלוּחַ have their origin in the Old Testament. For these scholars, the institution of the

the ἐκκλησία in the New Testament, with the institution of the שָׁלוּחַ in the Old Testament.[89] This idea was first proposed by Lightfoot and was developed further by Rengstorf who argued that an apostle, just like the שָׁלוּחַ in ancient Judaism, was a representative of the one who had sent them.[90] More importantly for this research is the fact that, according to Rengstorf, an apostle of Jesus or שָׁלוּחַ in the Old Testament had to be a prototype of the one who sent them.[91] Thus, the "duty of being" an apostle was to be "Jesus-like." Similarly, scholars such as Käsemann, Ehrensperger, and Tucker write that the early Jesus followers' understanding of the term ἀπόστολος has its basis in the Hebrew Bible's concept of God's messenger.[92] Käsemann asserts that ἀπόστολος has its roots in the verbal form of the word ἀποστέλλω in the LXX.[93] He writes that, "it seems fairly certain that the Semitic idea of sending with an authoritative commission determines the NT understanding of apostle."[94] The term ἀπόστολος in its noun form is however used only once in 1 Kgdms 14:6, where it is used to refer to an ambassador or a delegate or a messenger. The verbal form of the term ἀποστέλλω is however used around 700 times in the LXX, most often to render the Hebrew equivalent שָׁלוּחַ. It is also used from time to time to refer to the authority of the prophet.[95] Thus, researchers such as Goodrich have concluded in their observations that there is a growing consensus among scholars since Lightfoot's (1865) first proposal that Paul's use of the term ἀπόστολος has its origin in the Jewish tradition of the office of the שָׁלוּחַ.[96] It is worth noting though that Käsemann thinks that

---

שָׁלוּחַ was developed in the second century by Jewish rabbis, separately from the Christian understanding of the apostle. Keay, "Paul the Spiritual Guide," 13.

89. Rengstorf sees the term שָׁלוּחַ as being synonymous with the word apostle. He based his findings on the translation of the term ἀπόστολος as "Slias" by the Syrian Church (which was connected to Jerome). He argues that this is just a Latinization of the Hebrew term שָׁלוּחַ by the Syrian Church. Rengstorf, *Apostolate and Ministry*, 29.

90. Lightfoot, Dissertations on Apostolic Age, 93; Rengstorf, Apostolate *and Ministry*.

91. Rengstorf, 30. Rengstorf does not actually use the term prototype, but this meaning could be construed from his emphasis that an apostle has to be like the one who sends him or her. Rengstorf, 30.

92. Käsemann, Commentary on Romans, 5; Ehrensperger, Paul and Dynamics; Tucker, *You Belong to Christ*, 134. See Isa 18:2; Jer 49:14.

93. Käsemann, 5.

94. Käsemann, 5.

95. Isa 6:8 in the LXX; Keay, "Paul the Spiritual Guide," 10; Bertone, "Apostle."

96. Goodrich, *Paul as an Administrator*, 3; Lightfoot, *Epistle of St. Paul*. For a helpful discussion on the institution of the Shaliah and apostle, see Barrett, "Shaliach and Apostle," 88–102.

the influence of the שָׁלִוּחַ institution is limited to the original twelve apostles, and that it should be restricted in its use to the events that are mentioned in Mark 6:7 and Luke 10:1, where Jesus sent out the apostles two by two.[97] Most scholars, however, maintain that the influence of the Jewish tradition of the office of the שָׁלִוּחַ extends to the use of ἀπόστολος throughout the New Testament. Barrett provides an incisive summary of the institution of the שָׁלִוּחַ and highlights five points about this institution:[98] (1) the one who is sent as a representative of the sender functions as his or her principal and is entitled to all to which the principal is entitled. (2) The function and entitlement is limited to the duration of his or her commission. (3) The commission "is not transferable." (4) "The shaliach is not a term of status but of function." And, (5) within a religious context the function of the shaliach "is exercised within the borders of Jewry," and not what is now considered "missionary activity." This insight by Manson is helpful in highlighting both the similarities between the institution of the שָׁלִוּחַ and the apostles. The significance of the institution of the שָׁלִוּחַ for our understanding of the term ἀπόστολος is well stated by Rengstorf.[99] He writes that the designation of the term שָׁלִוּחַ does not merely signify the act of sending nor "the indication of the task involved but simply the assertion of the form of sending, i.e., of authorization." The significance of the term is the fact that the person being sent has the authority to act on behalf of the one who is sending him or her. Rengstorf notes that the שָׁלִוּחַ is as good as the one sending him (the שָׁלַח),[100] and thus as the Rabbis used to say, "the one sent by a man [sic] is as the man himself."[101] It thus seems that the authority behind the term ἀπόστολος lies ultimately in the one who is performing the commissioning of the ἀπόστολος (that is, those commissioned by the Lord Jesus Christ will have significant or high authority in the ἐκκλησία in comparison to those commissioned by the ἐκκλησία). The emphasis on Paul's restrictive use of the term ἀπόστολος in 1 Corinthians 1 and 15 simply serves to highlight the source of the commission. And since the twelve apostles and Paul himself were commissioned by the Lord Jesus

---

97. Käsemann, Commentary on Romans, 6.
98. Barrett, "Shaliach and Apostle," 90.
99. Rengstorf, "ἀπόστολος", 414–415.
100. Rengstorf, 415.
101. Ber 5:5.

Christ, they have leadership authority in the ἐκκλησία by virtue of the One who commissioned them.

In this sense, it is possible to assume that when Paul described himself as the ἀπόστολος Χριστοῦ Ἰησοῦ in 1 Corinthians 1:1, he wanted the Corinthians to understand that he was a representative of Christ Jesus, that he had the authority to act on behalf of Christ Jesus. But, Paul's self-description as an apostle of Christ Jesus is not only significant in terms of his authority within the group, it also forms part of his own self-identity, which plays a key role "in his identity-forming agenda."[102] Taylor is of the view that much research is needed in order to analyse the impact of the title "apostle of Christ" in "Paul's self-identity."[103] Similarly, Rengstorf notes that being an apostle meant that the apostle's self-consciousness was always preoccupied about how to embody the values of Jesus Christ and act in accordance as his representative.[104]

Locating Paul's ideological influence on the institution of the שָׁלִיחַ has unfortunately resulted in unintended consequences. In focusing on this institution, scholars have tended to reduce Paul's apostolic consciousness to be only about gospel proclamation. Taylor for example, whose findings were considered above, is not alone in emphasising the proclamation aspect in the meaning of the term ἀπόστολος, particularly as it relates to the missionary activity among Jesus's followers.[105] Barrett argues that Paul "understood ἀπόστολος in the sense of a missionary – a sense that was ultimately to prevail."[106] Similarly, Rengstorf views the essence of apostolic consciousness as being a preoccupation with the preaching of the word of God.[107] He writes, "in the New Testament the dominant factor in the work of an apostle must lie in the proclamation of the Word" (emphasis original).[108] Further, Rengstorf argues that the preaching of the word and the demonstration of the power of the word were the objects of Paul's meditation, and that these two activities developed "a pronounced apostolic consciousness of office and

---

102. Tucker, *You Belong to Christ*, 134.
103. Taylor, "Apostolic Identity and Conflicts," 99.
104. Rengstorf, *Apostolate and Ministry*, 30–34.
105. Taylor, "Apostolic Identity and Conflicts."
106. Barrett, "Shaliach and Apostle," 98.
107. Rengstorf, Apostolate *and Ministry*, 32; 35.
108. Rengstorf, 32.

self-consciousness."[109] While these scholars have been effective in highlighting the centrality of preaching the word by Paul, their findings also tend to present an obscure picture of Paul's apostolic self-consciousness and ministry, as being "first and foremost in terms of missionary evangelism" and not as an establishment of early Jesus followers' communities.[110] Samra correctly observes that this led to scholars viewing "pastoral work," community care or community organization as being a distraction for Paul from his main activity, which was to preach the word.[111] These sentiments come across strongly in the works of Murphy-O'Connor, who describes Paul's self-consciousness as that of someone who "understood his mission as simple evangelization, to plant the gospel and march on; the watering of the seed was not his responsibility (1 Cor 1:17a)."[112] Murphy-O'Connor's statement directly contradicts what this research is arguing. While agreeing that the preaching of the word or gospel proclamation was an integral part of Paul's apostolic self-consciousness, this research argues that Paul's apostolic self-consciousness cannot be divorced from his identity formation agenda or "community maturation" agenda, in the words of Samra.[113] Take for example 1 Corinthians 1:17a, which Murphy-O'Connor alludes to when he writes; "the watering of the seed was not his responsibility." This reading of the text misses Paul's rhetorical strategy in 1 Corinthians 1, that is, his downplaying of his role in baptising some of the members of the community should not be seen as Paul being against pastoral work. Had Murphy-O'Connor considered Paul's statement on baptism in the light of social identity, he would have noticed why it was important for the Corinthians to identify who baptised whom. He would have seen that baptism in 1 Corinthians 1:14–17 does not just reflect pastoral work. The Corinthians used baptism as an identity category. This comes through more clearly in the work of Tucker, who argues that "a person who baptised an individual or a household" was interpreted as a patron of that person or household "in a manner that is similar to the way a dedicatory plaque served

---

109. Rengstorf, 35; See also: Rom 15:18–19; 1 Cor 2:4–5; 1 Thess 1:5.
110. Samra, Being Conformed to Christ, 35.
111. Samra, 34–36.
112. Murphy-O'Connor, *Paul*, 211.
113. Samra, *Being Conformed to Christ*, 36.

as a reminder of the importance and honour of the sponsor of the bath."[114] Thus, within the context of 1 Corinthians, this simple "Christian" rite was used to further fuel divisions within the community. Tucker has correctly observed that Paul's main issue around baptism is not that it is a distraction from his main task, which is to preach the gospel; rather, his main issue is that the Corinthians were failing to understand their primary identity, which is in Christ.[115] Hence, Paul asks the following three rhetorical questions in 1 Corinthians 1:13; "Is Christ divided? Was Paul crucified for you? Were you baptized in the name of Paul?"[116] Thus, as Tucker observes, the issue here is that the Corinthians were failing to understand the implication of their identity in Christ.[117] Instead of their primary loyalty being to Christ, they were identifying more with the "group leaders or prototypes." Paul's thankfulness in 1 Corinthians 1:14 is thus to be understood as his gratefulness to God that he did not "inadvertently contribute to the division within the community."[118] This has led to scholars such as Samra[119] and Aernie to argue that Paul's ideological influences come from Moses, rather than from the שָׁלוּחַ tradition.[120] Samra's proposition seems to offer a much more probable source for Paul's

---

114. Tucker, "Baths, Baptism, and Patronage," 183–88. Clarke expresses similar views, when he writes, "Paul points out his thankfulness that few can look to him as their figure head through his baptizing them, 1 Cor 1:14–16. It was actions like these which were interpreted in the Christian community as indicative of patronal relationships." Clarke, *Secular and Christian Leadership*, 92. Samra notes that what Paul is doing in 1 Cor 1:17 "is simply distancing himself from anything which might be seen as supporting the factionalism in Corinth." Samra, *Being Conformed to Christ*, 47. For more on the baptism and the patronage connection, see Tucker. Tucker, 173–88.

115. Tucker, "Baths," 184.

116. NIV.

117. Tucker, "Baths, Baptism and Patronage," 184.

118. Tucker, 184.

119. He lists eight reasons why Moses was the primary influence for Paul's understanding of his ministry. He does this by pointing to the number of parallels that existed between Paul's ministry and Moses's ministry, one of them being the fact that "Moses' legitimacy as leader was called into question in Exod. 17:1–7; Numbers 14 and Numbers 16–17." He notes that Moses had to demonstrate through performing miraculous signs that God had chosen him as a preferred leader for his people. Samra notes that Paul in a similar way in 2 Cor 10–13 had to demonstrate that he was chosen by God. Samra, *Being Conformed to Christ*, 48–49. For more on the issues surrounding 2 Corinthians, see Sindo, where I have argued for the literary integrity of 2 Corinthians and also that the motivation for Paul to write 2 Corinthians was that his personality and integrity were being attacked by the false apostles. Sindo, "Socio-Rhetorical Approach," 79–105.

120. Samra, *Being Conformed to Christ*, 49–51; Aernie, *Is Paul Also among Prophets?*, 113–33.

ideological influences, as it encompasses both aspects of Paul's concerns in his letters, which was the gospel proclamation and maturation or identity formation of his congregations.[121]

4.4.1.3 The Mimesis Tradition and Group Prototypicality

As a group prototype, Paul is traditionally studied under the category of imitation (mimesis).[122] Studies that deal with the metaphor of Paul as the father of the Corinthians fall under this category as well. The subject of imitation has received considerable attention among the New Testament scholars and it has been a subject of extensive debate.[123] Clarke and Samra note that the imitation motif in the New Testament appears mostly in the letters of Paul.[124] Eight out of the eleven times that the noun [συμ]μιμητής ("imitator") together with the verb μιμέομαι ("to imitate") are used, occur in the Pauline letters.[125] Even though eight uses of a term might appear to be relatively insignificant in the light of the Pauline corpus as a whole, Hooker writes, "the notion of imitation is much more significant in Pauline thought than has often been allowed."[126] What is striking in Paul's use of the imitation language is that he predominantly calls communities that he has established to imitate himself, rather than calling them to imitate Christ.[127] Ehrensperger writes that the

---

121. Samra, *Being Conformed to Christ*.

122. For more on Paul setting himself up as a group prototype, see Chong's work on Paul as a paradigm and father. Chong, *Strategies in Church*, 51–84. While Chong does not use the term group prototype, the idea as we will see shortly is the same. Fiore, in his treatment of the topic of exemplification and imitation, does consider imitation as prototype (albeit that he does not fully develop this idea). Under imitation as a prototype, he says that the emphasis "centres on the person or thing that imitates or copies the prototype, or that at least strives to fashion itself after the model." Fiore, *Function of Personal Example*, 236.

123. For a historical treatment of this debate, see Dodd, Clarke, De Boer, and for the summary of the debate, see Samra. Dodd, Paul's Paradigmatic "I," 13–32; Clarke, "'Be Imitators of Me,'" 329–60; De Boer, Imitation of Paul, 1–12; Samra, *Being Conformed to Christ*, 125–30.

124. Clarke, 329–31; Samra, 125.

125. 1 Cor 4:16; 11:1; Eph 5:1; Phil 3:17; 1 Thess 1:6; 2:14; 2 Thess 3:7, 9. The following appear outside the Pauline corpus; Heb 6:12; 13:7; 3 John 1:11. For an exegesis of all these texts, see De Boer, *Imitation of Paul*, 92–205 who also does exegesis of Acts 20:35; 1 Tim 1:16; 2 Tim 1:13; 3.10.

126. Hooker, "Partner in the Gospel," 92. Of particular interest for Hooker is imitation of Christ by Paul and Christians at large.

127. Clarke, "'Be Imitators of Me,'" 331; More, "Is Jesus King?", 288. Clarke notes that, "with regard to the congregations which he has not founded, he does, nonetheless, enjoin imitation of Christ (Rom 15:2–3)." Clarke, 331, citing Best. It is worth noting though that sometimes even among the congregations that Paul has established, he does encourage imitation

reason that Paul does not call for a direct imitation of Christ but for the believers to imitate him is because "it is only in μιμεῖσθαι of the apostle, that is, in obedience in accordance with the apostolic παρακαλεῖν that there is true μίμησις τοῦ Χριστοῦ."[128]

4.4.1.3.1 Personal Imitation in the Ancient World: A Short Survey

In order to understand the significance of the imitation language in Paul, scholars have often considered the Greek theory of mimesis, with particular interest in how the imitation language was used in antiquity.[129] Both Dodd and Samra observed that there are at least six ways in which personal imitation functioned in the ancient world:[130]

(a) Mimesis as Moralistic Device

Scholars have observed that in the ancient world, personal examples were used as a moralistic device where ethical emulation of good people was encouraged.[131] Sometimes personal examples were used negatively to highlight the errors of other people that are to be avoided.[132] Samra notes that in this use, "personal example, ethical model, and mimesis are often found together" in antiquity.[133]

---

of members within the congregation who embody group values, and he also encourages imitation of other congregations τοῦ θεοῦ (i.e. 1 Thess 1:6; 2:14; 1 Tim 4:12).

128. Ehrensperger, Paul and Dynamics, 137, using the findings of Betz, "Apostle," 1967.

129. For the use of mimesis as a rhetorical device in the Greco-Roman world, see Fiore. Fiore, *Function of Personal Example*, 228–37. It is worth noting that most of the ancient sources that Fiore considers, deal mostly with the importance of examples, rather than exclusively dealing with mimesis. In his defence, he does state that imitation or mimesis is associated with example. Fiore, 230.

130. Dodd, *Paul's Paradigmatic "I,"* 18–29; Samra, *Being Conformed to Christ*, 127–28. For more on imitation in the ancient world, see De Boer, *Imitation of Paul*, 1–12; 17–20; 24–50; Fiore, 45–163; and Castelli, Imitating *Paul*, 59–87. Dodd summarises the ancient sources through his review of Michaelis, Stanley, De Boer, and Fiore. Dodd, 16–29; Michaelis, "μιμέομαι, μιμητής, συμμιμητής"; Stanley, "'Become Imitators of Me'"; De Boer, *Imitation of Paul*; Fiore, *Function of Personal Example*. Even though this section is listed under the traditional approach, some scholars in this section employ socioscientific approaches in their analysis of Paul's use of the mimesis language. Our focus when it comes to the ancient sources is on those in which the use of mimesis terminology is similar to Paul's.

131. See Democritus, *Frag.* 39; Xenophon, *Mem.* 1.2.3; Isocrates, *Ad Dem.* 9–11; Quintilian, *Inst.* 1.1.35. This can also be seen in the works of Polybius X.21; Strabo, *Geog.* VII.3.9.; Dionysius of Halicarnassus, *Pomp.* 6.

132. Anaximenes, *Rhet. ad Alex.* 8[1429a.29-31] and 14[1431a.26-27].

133. Samra, *Being Conformed to Christ*, 127.

(b) Mimesis as a Replacement of Unavailable Models

Scholars such as Samra have observed that in the ancient world, when a model for imitation was unavailable, imitation of known persons who embodied the values of the unavailable model is often encouraged.[134] This comes across more clearly in Quintilian who writes: "For however many models for imitation he may give them from the authors they are reading, it will still be found that fuller nourishment is provided by the living voice."[135]

(c) Mimesis as a Practical Application of Moralistic Lesson

Samra also notes that imitation language is used for "moral progress, perfection, and blamelessness."[136] This comes up more forcefully in the works of Seneca, who is described by Fiore as "a spiritual guide par excellence."[137] For Seneca, examples played three roles: (1) In terms of morality teaching, they helped the audience to conceptualize virtues;[138] (2) They show a doubting person that moral life can be achieved;[139] (3) Examples "become companions and guardians for individual's self-examination and moral progress."[140]

(d) "Mimesis" Is Not the Same as "Mimicking"

Imitation is not the same as mimicking, as it is tied to "recontextualization of attitudes."[141] Samra provides an example of how, both in the works of Plutarch and Dio Chrysostom, Socrates is said "to be an imitator of Homer," even though they had not met personally and had different professions.[142] Dio Chrysostom observed that what led to Socrates being viewed as an imitator

---

134. Samra, 127. In the works of Anaximenes, which is mostly concerned with examples in legislative and forensic speeches, replacement of historical examples with recent examples that are known to the hearers, is encouraged. Anaximenes, *Rhet. ad Alex.* 8[1430a.7–9] and 32[1439a.1–5]. See Fiore, *Function of Personal Example*, 229; 249.

135. Quintilian, *Inst.* 2.2.8; cf. Quintilian, *Inst.* 1.8.5; 2.2.1–8; Horace, *Ars* 333–40; *Carm.* 3.3.1–4; Diodorus Siculus, 12.13.2.

136. Samra, *Being Conformed to Christ*, 127; Plutarch, *Mor. Prog.* 84–85.

137. Fiore, *Function of Personal Example*, 235.

138. Seneca, *Ep.* 102.30.

139. Seneca, *Ep.* 72.22.

140. Seneca, *Ep.* 104.21; cf. Fiore, *Function of Personal Example*, 135–37.

141. Dio Chrysostom, *Disc.* 55.4.

142. Samra, *Being Conformed to Christ*, 127; Plutarch, *Mor. Prog.* 85B–C and Dio Chrysostom, *Disc.* 55.4, 7–9.

of Homer was that his character (which was marked by humility and lack of boasting) was similar to that of Homer.[143]

(e) Imitation of God and Human Beings Are Not Mutually Exclusive
In antiquity, people were often encouraged to imitate God; Castelli notes that this idea appears mostly in the work of Philo.[144] Samra notes that while people are encouraged to imitate God, the call to imitate God is given in the context where people are also "instructed to imitate" fellow human beings as well.[145] These two ideas are well presented in Seneca. He exhorts his readers to imitate the gods.[146] Yet, a close object of imitation is the teacher, who provides a paradigm for moral life.[147] The teacher offers security to those who look to him or her for guidance.[148] In Seneca, the teachers or sages "were born to be a pattern" particularly as they suffer for their cause. In this fifth scenario, imitating God does not exclude imitating fellow human beings. In fact, fellow human beings become examples that show us that virtuous life is possible. What is interesting in Philo's use of the imitation motif in imitating God is the "analogy between parental relationship to children and God's relationship to the world."[149] One of the clearest uses of this in the New Testament is in John 5:17–30, particularly verses 19–20.[150] Jesus's claims of God being his Father and him seeing and doing what the Father does is analogous with how the imitation motif was used in the Greco-Roman world and Jewish writings.[151] In Proverbs 23:26, the son is to learn by watching his father's ways. Likewise, in Sirach 30.3–4 the idea of the son listening, doing what the father teaches, and thus becoming like him is present. Similarly, Dio Chrysostom demonstrates

---

143. Dio Chrysostom, *Disc.* 55.7.

144. Castelli, *Imitating Paul*, 77; Philo, *Spec. Leg.* 4.73; Philo, *Fug.* 63; Philo, *Virt.* 168; Philo, *Leg. All.* 1.48.

145. Samra, *Being Conformed to Christ*, 127–28.

146. Seneca, *Ben.* 4.25.1; 7.31.5.

147. Similar views are found in Dio Chrysostom, *Or.* 55.4–5, and Epictetus *Diat.* 3.22.45–50.

148. Seneca, *Ep.* 11.8–10; cf. Seneca, *Ep.* 22.5–6; 32.1; 52.8–10; 94.40–41.

149. Castelli, Imitating *Paul*, 77. For more on ancient sources that encourage the imitation of God, see Castelli, 74–8.

150. For an analysis of John 5 in the light of ancient imitation discourse, see Witmer, *Divine Instruction in Early Christianity*, 87–107.

151. Witmer, 96.

that Socrates was a disciple or a student of Homer by highlighting a number of resemblances between them.[152]

(f) The Relationship between Imitation and Discipleship and Love
Lastly, "imitation is tied with discipleship and love."[153] This is a debated point among the scholars. Section 4.4.2 of this chapter will expound upon this. This study is of the view that the link between mimesis language and love, and how it often functioned in antiquity has been overlooked in recent studies in their analysis of the imitation language in Paul, particularly so in the work of Castelli.[154]

4.4.1.3.1 Scholarly Debate regarding Paul's Use of the Imitation Motif

Besides these six observations on how the imitation motif was used in ancient sources, there are three contrasting views in recent scholarship regarding how the imitation motif functions in Paul.[155] It is to this that we now turn.

(a) Imitation and Obedience
Some scholars argue that imitation is used by Paul as a means of demanding obedience to himself and to his gospel. This view is expressed particularly by Michaelis who writes that imitation in Paul primarily means "recognise my authority."[156] He writes further that imitation in Paul "is not repetition of a model. It is an expression of obedience." Michaelis sees 1 Corinthians 4:16 as referring to Paul's authority, taking the meaning of "παρακαλῶ οὖν ὑμᾶς, μιμηταί μου γίνεσθε" as "Be told, take it to heart, keep it, be obedient."[157] He argues further that in 1 Corinthians 11:1, Paul "does not refer to examples to be emulated, let alone to models to whom one is to become similar or equal by imitation, but to authorities whose command and admonition

---

152. Dio Chrysostom, *Or.* 55.4–5. See also Philo, *Virt.* 66; Philo, *Sacr.* 65. In paragraph 68, this is connected with the imitation of God.
153. Samra, *Being Conformed to Christ*, 128.
154. Castelli, Imitating *Paul*.
155. Clarke, "'Be Imitators of Me,'" 331; Samra, *Being Conformed to Christ*, 128.
156. Michaelis, "μιμέομαι, μιμητής, συμμιμητής," 668. According to Dodd, Michaelis identifies three uses of μιμέομαι in Paul. These are: (1) simple comparison (i.e. 1 Thess 1:6; 2:14); (2) following an example (Phil 3:17; 2 Thess 3:7, 9); and (3) obedience to the apostolic authority. Dodd, *Paul's Paradigmatic "I"*; Michaelis, 661–78. For Michaelis, the third use is the dominant one in Paul. Michaelis, 668.
157. Michaelis, 668.

are to be obeyed." The problem with Michaelis's approach has been highlighted by Dodd and Fiore, who note that the major problem for Michaelis is that he struggles to understand the notion of imitating an ethical example.[158] Michaelis writes: "It may be asked how far it is advisable to speak of imitating an example at all."[159] Fiore has correctly observed that "the notion of obedience advanced by Michaelis finds no precedent in the theoretical works surveyed earlier" (that is, the ancient use of the imitation language).[160]

(b) Imitation as Power Manipulation
Recent scholarship, particularly Shaw, Wanamaker, and Castelli, has argued that the imitation motif in Paul is not specific regarding what aspects of imitation Paul wants his congregation to follow. Castelli argues that the imitation motif acts as a rhetorical device that is employed by "Paul to reinforce his power and thereby define his group's identity."[161] While this dissertation agrees with Castelli regarding Paul's use of imitation as a rhetorical devise, it nonetheless disagrees with her conclusions. Reasons for disagreement with her will be expounded upon in section 4.4.2 of this chapter.

(c) Imitation as Discipleship
Both Samra and Belleville admit that it is difficult to establish verbal links between the discipleship (μαθητής) language that is found in the Gospels and Acts, and Paul's imitation language.[162] Both, however, maintain that this difficulty does not mean that there is no overlap in ideological meaning of the two terms. Belleville notes that, throughout his letters, Paul consistently "devotes a major segment to spelling out for his readers what it means to live a life worthy of the gospel."[163] He notes further that Paul constantly presents himself, Jesus, and other churches to his congregations as models that ought to be copied – "as models of discipleship." However, one still has to account for the lack of the μαθητής language. Why did Paul not use this language?

---

158. Dodd, *Paul's Paradigmatic "I"*, 19; Fiore, *Function of Personal Example*, 168.

159. Michaelis, "μιμέομαι, μιμητής, συμμιμητής," 671.

160. Fiore, *Function of Personal Example*, 168. For more on this, see De Boer's work, which demonstrates how the μιμέομαι and τύπος terminology were used in the Hellenist and Jewish world to mean following the example of someone. De Boer, *Imitation of Paul*, 1–50.

161. Clarke, "'Be Imitators of Me,'" 331.

162. Samra, *Being Conformed to Christ*, 129; Belleville, "Imitate Me," 120.

163. Belleville, 120.

Scholars such as Longenecker and Samra argue that Paul did not use this language because his audiences were more familiar with imitation language than discipleship language.[164] Longenecker for example notes that even Luke in his use of the μαθητής language, uses it to describe the relationship between Jesus and his followers (particularly in the gospel of Luke), while he uses "brother" and "sister" to describe the relationship between the believers.[165] He writes that perhaps the reason Luke does this is because "the term 'disciple,' while carrying many important nuances, also suggested ideas about subordination and inequality, whereas 'brother' carried more the nuances of familial oneness and equality." Samra notes that the reason that Paul did not use the μαθητής language might also be because his audiences were not familiar with its use in a religious context, and thus Paul used a term with which they were more familiar, "imitation," to convey the same idea.[166]

4.4.2 Social-scientific Approaches: Apostleship and Power Dynamics

Over the years, there have been a number of studies on Paul's apostolic (re)presentation from a social-scientific perspective. These studies utilise mostly modern-day social-scientific theories, and they focus on detecting, comparing, and assessing Paul's use of power and authority.[167] According to Goodrich, Holmberg is accredited with ushering in the use of sociological studies in Paul.[168] Also, Goodrich is grateful to him for being the first to analyse Paul's apostolic representation in terms of power relations rather than just theologically.[169] We have given a detailed review of Holmberg's work in chapter 2. While it has been praised for helping scholars to look beyond the theological presentation of Paul's apostleship, Holmberg's work has also been criticised and accused of being anachronistic in its imposition of foreign "models onto the ancient text."[170] There have been other studies

---

164. Longenecker, "Taking Up the Cross," 72–73; Samra, *Being Conformed to Christ*, 129.
165. Longenecker, 72.
166. Samra, *Being Conformed to Christ*, 129.
167. Goodrich, *Paul as an Administrator*, 5.
168. Goodrich, 5; Holmberg, *Paul and Power*.
169. Goodrich, 5.
170. Goodrich, 5; Judge, "Social Identity," 210; Clarke, *Secular and Christian Leadership*, 3–6.

since Holmberg's work that have also sought to incorporate social-scientific approaches in their analysis of Paul. Among these are those by Castelli, Polaski, and Ehrensperger.[171]

---

171. Castelli, *Imitating Paul*; Polaski, *Paul and Discourse of Power*; Ehrensperger, *Paul and Dynamics*. Our focus in this section will be on the work of Castelli, as her work served as a great influence on both Polaski and Ehrensperger, even though they do not entirely agree with her. Polaski, like Castelli, employs Foucault's post-structuralist perspective in analysing Paul's discourse on power. Polaski, 13–22. The difference between the two though is that in her approach, Polaski is hoping not to do a "hostile reading" of Paul, nor does she seek to "vilify Paul's claim to power" or "to dismiss them as deceitfully self-serving." Polaski, 21. She describes her approach as "hermeneutics of suspicion," where she reads the "New Testament texts" looking for the "evidence of power relations which the surface meaning of the text may mask." For her, Paul's perspective is mostly "theological, that is, he writes to focus his readers' attention on God," so that Paul's discourse on power must be seen in the light of the "divine interest and intervention in human affairs." Polaski, 22. She notes, however, that the way in which Paul presents himself as God's ambassador, who speaks on God's behalf and "acts on God's power" provides him with incredible powers within the community. Disobeying Paul's word means that one is disobeying the word of God, and such action might lead to someone being treated as an outsider within the community. Polaski, 24–25. For a critique of the hermeneutics of suspicion and how at times it can give a distorted picture regarding how Paul used his authority in 1 Corinthians, see Dunn, *Theology of Apostle Paul*, 575. It is clear in 1 Corinthians that there are asymmetrical aspects in Paul's use of authority. For example, in 1 Cor 1:10, Paul uses the verb παρακαλῶ to appeal for unity in the community. Dunn demonstrates how the verb παρακαλῶ carries authority, and how it is often used in cases of a superior addressing an inferior. Dunn, *Theology of Apostle Paul*, 574. Similarly, in 1 Cor 2:6–3:2, in his rebuke to the Corinthians, Paul assumes a role of a pneumatic mature person addressing the people who are "worldly" and "mere infants in Christ" (1 Cor 3:1). He assumes the role of a father who is to be modelled by his children in 1 Cor 4:15–17 and 11:1 (for more examples that demonstrate the asymmetrical nature of Paul's relationship with the Corinthians, see Dunn, 574. However, Dunn also provides examples of how Paul demonstrates restraint in the exercise of his authority, something that is at times missed by the scholars who employ the hermeneutic of suspicion, such as Polaski and Shaw. Dunn, 575; Polaski, *Paul and Discourse of Power*; Shaw, *Cost of Authority*. Dunn notes, for example, that in texts such as 1 Cor 7:6, 19, 25; 14:37, Paul distinguishes between the Lord's commands and his own advice. Dunn, 575–76. All of this demonstrates that Paul wanted the Corinthians to obey God ultimately, rather than himself. For a detailed review of Ehrensperger's work, see Punt, "Review: Kathy Ehrensperger," 150–51. Again, what comes up in Ehrensperger's work is a positive treatment of Paul's discourse on power, which she describes as transformative power. However, she also follows a similar path as Dunn and Tucker, concluding that there were asymmetrical hierarchical aspects in Paul's use of power. Ehrensperger, *Paul and Dynamics*, 61; Dunn, *Theology of Apostle Paul*; Tucker, *You Belong to Christ*. Unlike Castelli, Ehrensperger sees the power relations in Paul beginning from a voluntary relationship of trust. Ehrensperger, 136. Castelli, *Imitating Paul*. For Ehrensperger, "trust is the essential basis for transformative relation . . . Paul emphasizes again and again that the aim of his teaching is to empower those within his communities to support each other. He acts as a parent-teacher, using power over them to empower them and thus render himself, and the power-over exercised in this role, obsolete." Ehrensperger, *Paul and the Dynamics of Power*, 136. It is on this last point, regarding the statement that Paul sought to eradicate ecclesiastical hierarchy, that Ehrensperger has received major criticism from scholars such as Goodrich, who says that it is at this point that Ehrensperger goes beyond what the evidence of the text allows. Goodrich, *Paul as an Administrator*, 10.

In her analysis of the Pauline motif, "be imitators of me," Castelli employs Michael Foucault's post-structuralist perspective.[172] Her methodological approach has been summarised well by Clarke when he writes that in the "Foucauldian post-structuralist perspective" the recovery of authorial intent is impossible, and thus *the* truth is relative.[173] The text is viewed as "coercive force on social relations" and it is suggested that it should "be analysed for its effect, rather than its meaning."[174] For Castelli, the "text should be taken as a univocal signifier of authority, rather than as a site at which power is negotiated, brokered, or inscribed";[175] thus the text should indeed be analysed for its effect rather than its meaning.[176] Castelli sees the imitation motif in Paul as a power relation that is designed to maintain Paul's privileged position within the community,[177] and also to enforce sameness of the group.[178] For her, Paul is concerned with imposing his powers and eliminating deviancy. She writes, "sameness is not simple social expediency but is tied to salvation of the community. By implication, difference is cast in stark contrast to the community's salvation."[179] Her views of imitation as sameness have been well-critiqued by scholars such as Ehrensperger and Samra on two grounds:[180]

---

172. Castelli, *Imitating Paul*.

173. Clarke, "'Be Imitators of Me,'" 332. Castelli makes this clear when she writes, "Whether Paul *meant* or *intended* that his discourse be understood in this way I have argued is not a question that I have answered . . . I have bracketed the whole matter of conscious authorial intent – the motives residing in the mind of the writer [are] unattainable because it involves inaccessible aspects of the author's psychology" (emphasis original). Castelli, *Imitating Paul*, 120. Thiselton provides a critical assessment of Castelli's use of the Foucauldian theory. Thiselton, *Interpreting God*, 140–44. His findings are that far from Paul using the imitation motif for manipulation and control, he was hoping to achieve the opposite. He writes, "Paul's call to the community to imitate a pattern of humility and servanthood is not for the purpose of 'conformity' or 'control.' It is precisely to protect those who might otherwise be despised or considered socially inferior; in other words, precisely to protect the 'social deviant' for whom Foucault shows concern." Thiselton, 142.

174. Clarke, "'Be Imitators of Me,'" 332.

175. Castelli, *Imitating Paul*, 24.

176. Clarke, "'Be Imitators of Me,'" 332.

177. Castelli, *Imitating Paul*, 95–117.

178. Castelli, 120. She writes that mimesis "must be understood in its larger context, as a notion that places sameness at a premium and imbues the model with a privileged and unattainable status." Castelli, 89.

179. Castelli, 113–14.

180. Ehrensperger, *Paul and Dynamics*, 139–42; Samra, *Being Conformed to Christ*, 128–29.

(1) Her focus exclusively on the word μίμησις from the Greco-Roman world perspective have made her miss the nuances of how the idea was used in the LXX.[181] Ehrensperger points out that in the LXX the idea of imitation does not imply sameness, rather it is used to call a person to live their life in a way that is analogous to their relationship with God.[182] Similarly, Samra points out that "it is incorrect to understand 'imitation' as requiring uniformity or sameness."[183] He points to examples such as Romans 14, 1 Corinthians 7, 8, and 10:15 where Paul does allow the believers to make decisions for themselves; also in 1 Corinthians 14, Paul encourages diversity. Also, scholars such as Clarke have observed that in texts such as 1 Thessalonians, Paul encourages the imitation of models other than himself.[184] This has led scholars such as Clarke to conclude that there is no clear evidence that Paul uses the imitation language in a manipulative way for his exclusive advantage.[185] For example, in 1 Thessalonians, "Paul's emphasis throughout the letter is on the equality,

---

181. Castelli is not the only one to ignore the OT in considering the influences upon Paul's understanding of the imitation motif. Michaelis argues that the concept of "imitation is foreign to the OT," particularly the idea of imitating God. He writes that in the OT, the idea of imitating God is inconceivable. Michaelis, "μιμέομαι, μιμητής, συμμιμητής," 663; see also Clarke, "'Be Imitators of Me,'" 330. Michaelis and Clarke argue that the imitation language appears only in the apocryphal writings of the LXX (4 Mac 9:23; 13:9; Wis 4:2; 9:8; 15:9). Michaelis, 663; Clarke, "'Be Imitators of Me,'" 330. Scholars such as Dodd, De Boer, and Ehrensperger have argued that while the exact word μιμέομαι might be absent in the OT, the imitation motif is present, particularly if one considers associated terminology such as ὁδός "way"' and περιπατέω "walk," which Paul uses in association with the imitation motif (Judg 2:17; 1 Sam 8:3; 1 Kgs 3:14; 9:4; 11:33, 38; see also 1 Cor 4:16–17; Phil 3:17; 2 Thess 3:6–9). Dodd, *Paul's Paradigmatic "I"*, 17; De Boer, *Imitation of Paul*, 29–41; Ehrensperger, Paul and Dynamics of Power, 140—42. Dodd and Ehrensperger argue that even the idea of imitating God is present in the OT, particularly in the Levitical tradition which attributes God as saying: "Be holy as I am holy (i.e. Lev 1:45; 11:44; 19:2; 20:26). Dodd, 17; Ehrensperger, 139–42. Commenting on these verses, Ehrensperger notes that "what people ought to become is comparatively related to God via the causal particle ὅτι. Ehrensperger, 140. The term used for what they ought to become is the same term which refers to a dimension of God." Ehrensperger observes that this does not imply sameness, in the sense that they should be identical with God. She notes that the language of imitation in the OT denotes how people ought to live in a way that is consistent with their relationship with God (see also Lev 19:2, 8; and Num 15:40). Thus, for Ehrensperger the language of imitation in the OT is "towards a relational comparative dimension of imitation rather than a dimension of copying." Ehrensperger, 140. For Ehrensperger, the call to imitate God means that a person lives their life in a way that is analogous to God's character. Ehrensperger, 141.

182. Ehrensperger, 139–42.

183. Samra, *Being Conformed to Christ*, 128–29.

184. Clarke, "'Be Imitators of Me,'" 339–40.

185. Clarke, 340.

mutuality, and reciprocity of the relationship between him(self) and his converts."[186]

(2) The other thing that Castelli notes regarding the imitation motif is that any notion of fatherly warmth is out of place in how mimesis worked in antiquity. Here, she is critical of scholars such as Conzelmann, Sanders, De Boer, and Fiore in their presentation of Paul's imitation language as paternal love and concern for the Corinthians.[187] She says that their position is no longer justifiable in the light of how paternal relationships functioned in the Greco-Roman world. She insists that even when Paul uses the "image of the father," it must be read in the light of the Greco-Roman world in which it was analogous with military context – "which is a role of possessing total authority over children."[188] She draws this conclusion after her analysis of a passage from Epictetus.[189] Citing scholars such as Williams and Holmberg, she writes that the father image in the Greco-Roman world assumed "the authoritarian position of a father-teacher," that the relationship was "one of obligation on the part of the child."[190] However, when one looks at the variety of texts in antiquity, one discovers that the mimesis motif is sometimes linked to a mutual reciprocal love between a disciple and the teacher whom the disciple ought to imitate. This idea is strong in the works of Philo in his description of the friendship between Moses and Joshua. He describes their friendship as being different from how other friendships are made; their friendship was "by the rapturous love, which is of heaven, all pure and truly from God, from which in fact all virtues spring."[191] Philo states that what qualified Joshua as a leader was that he was Moses's disciple, he "modelled himself on his master's characteristics with the love which they deserve."[192] This action by Joshua is

---

186. Clarke, 340. Unfortunately, Castelli simply dismisses the teaching of 1 Thessalonians on the mimetic relationships as not revealing "the clearly-defined relations of power evident in other texts involving mimesis." Castelli, *Imitating Paul*, 95.

187. Castelli, 100. She views the position as a "naïve and utopian reading of Paul." Castelli, 101. Her focus in this section is on 1 Cor 4:14–17, where Paul links his appeal to the congregation to imitate him to his role as their father.

188. Castelli, 101.

189. Epictetus, *Diss*, 3.22.95ff.

190. Castelli, *Imitating Paul*, 101.

191. Philo, *Virt*. 55.

192. Philo, *Virt*. 66.

what got him the approval of the Divine, according to Philo.[193] Interestingly, Philo then adds that Moses was not depressed, as others might be, because God chose his nephew instead of his sons.[194] Rather, Moses had incredible joy because the nation was going to have a leader who excelled in every way. Further, Philo notes, when Moses was about to die, he addressed Joshua and told him "to be of good courage and might in wise policy, initiate good plans of action and carry out his decisions with strong and resolute thinking." At this point, Philo makes an interesting comment – that Joshua did not really need such an exhortation. Rather, Moses realised how important it was to relate on a personal level, and so he did not conceal his feeling of "mutual affection (τό φιλάλληλον) and patriotism which urged him like a spur to lay bare what he thought would be profitable."[195] Interestingly though, Philo writes that Moses is the archetype and the model for all future leaders, and their success as leaders will depend on how they model themselves after the archetype, which is Moses. In *On Virtues* 52—53, Philo describes Moses's choice of "Joshua as his successor as one of the achievements of his uninterrupted and continuous nobleness of life." In summary, in Philo the imitation language is linked to discipleship and love. Joshua was chosen because he modelled his life after Moses, who was an archetype of leadership. Moses and Joshua's relationship was a relationship that was marked by mutual love. Thus, not all sources from antiquity support Castelli's presentation of mimesis as being just exercises of power devoid of warm feeling.[196] Moreover, Samra has correctly observed that it is incorrect to view imitation in Paul as requiring "rigid uniformity or sameness," as Castelli argues.[197] He also notes that Castelli ignores classical data,[198] which demonstrates what people ought to imitate, that is, "attitudes and virtues, not specific actions." Therefore, it is important that one should be careful not to impose on Paul modern theories on how

---

193. Philo, *Virt.* 66.

194. Philo, *Virt.* 67.

195. Philo, *Virt.* 69.

196. In criticising Castelli, one can also add the insight from social identity theory that was explained in chapter 2 of this dissertation regarding why people join groups.

197. Samra, *Being Conformed to Christ*, 128–29.

198. The classical data that Castelli is accused of ignoring is *Epic. Dis.* 2.14.11–13. Interestingly, Castelli does refer to this text in her work but skips over the middle part of the quotation, which states, "the imitator must be free as the deity is free." Castelli, *Imitating Paul*, 79.

paternal imitation functioned in antiquity; nor should one impose modern expectations of paternal relationships on those of antiquity.

This study has looked at different scholarly approaches, in how apostolic discourse functions in Paul. We saw that there are two dominant approaches to this subject; on the one hand, we have scholars who are mostly concerned with the theological implications of Paul's apostolic language. Their emphasis tends to be on describing and constructing Paul's apostolic understanding. On the other hand, there are scholars who are mostly concerned with how Paul asserts his authority in his apostolic discourse. They tend to employ socioscientific theories in their analysis of Paul's apostolic discourse. While both approaches have their strengths and weaknesses, we have demonstrated in sections 4.4.1 to 4.4.2 that there are hermeneutical shortcomings in both approaches. In its quest to synthesise all of Paul's arguments concerning his apostolic defence, the traditional approach tends to pay too little attention to the whole argument of Paul's letters in a given context, particularly in the light of its historical context. Similarly, the socioscientific approaches tend to place too much focus on modern theories rather than on the original context of the text. Goodrich writes that scholars who employ modern theories are "prone to identify power claims without adequately demonstrating" that such notions are indeed supported by historical data.[199] The next chapter seeks to analyse Paul's apostolic defence in the light of his overall argument in the given context of 1 Corinthians 1–4. Our focus here will be the text of 1 Corinthians 1–4.

4.5 Theoretical Considerations for Paul's Resocialisation of the Corinthians

Up to this point, this chapter has demonstrated that one of the issues that besieged the community was their social identity. They were struggling to understand the implications of the gospel, particularly how the gospel ought to change the way they view themselves, their leaders, and the way they act. In the words of De Silva, we saw that "the Corinthian believers have not been adequately socialized into the ethos of the new group."[200] Paul's apos-

---

199. Goodrich, *Paul as an Administrator*, 11.
200. De Silva, Hope of Glory, 121.

tolic defence thus needs to be seen in the light of his quest to resocialize the Corinthians with regard to their new identity in Christ.

As seen above, the Pauline community at Corinth was experiencing many quarrels and divisions, with some not recognising Paul as their leader. In order for Paul to bring about unity in the ἐκκλησία, he had to remind them of their shared beliefs and shared identity in Christ, with a view that by so doing the members of the ἐκκλησία would agree about the issues that were relevant for their identity in Christ, so that the consensualization process might begin. According to Sania and Reicher, "consensualization" is a generic psychological process that seeks consensus rather than focus on its achievement.[201] They argue that if a topic is viewed by the group as constituting the essence of group identity, people are more likely to reach an agreement about the issues and thus able to reach a consensus; but if the topic is perceived as irrelevant for group identity people are likely to move towards dissension. Thus, it could be argued that Paul, by employing the "in Christ" language, was trying to draw the ἐκκλησία into the conversation so that all could see that his argument was fundamentally an argument about the group identity at its core. He is trying to prove to the Corinthians that his identity is part of the in-group identity and that his conduct is in line with their shared identity in Christ.[202] As already stated above in section 4.3, the issue in 1 Corinthians was not only about division and quarrelling over preferred leaders, but rather, some in the ἐκκλησία had begun questioning Paul's apostolic credibility in 1 Corinthians 9:1–2. In the light of this division and rejection of Paul by some in the ἐκκλησία, Paul had to develop a strategy, not only to bring about unity in the community, but also to establish his credibility as an apostle. This strategy becomes apparent when it is considered in the light of the findings from the field of social psychology.

Scholars in the field of the social sciences, particularly social psychology and developmental psychology, have demonstrated the importance of shared group beliefs[203] and religion in the social identity formation of small groups

---

201. Sani and Reicher, "Identity, Argument and Schism," 280.

202. This will be developed further in chapter 5.

203. Bar-Tal notes that the new line of research in the social psychological tradition prefers to use the term "shared cognition" rather than "shared beliefs." Bar-Tal, *Shared Beliefs in a Society*, 28. For a review of social psychology scholars who argue for the significance of shared beliefs in social identity formation, see Bar-Tal, 15–38.

and voluntary associations.[204] According to social psychological scholars such as Fraser and Gaskell, "shared attitudes and beliefs play an important role in defining groups and group behaviours, in the formation and maintenance of social identities, and more broadly in collective realities."[205] Social psychology scholars define "group beliefs as the conviction that group members (a) are aware that they share and (b) considered defining their groupness."[206] Bar-Tal further states that these shared beliefs then provide the group collective identity and the purpose of the group's existence.[207] Shared beliefs also provide the basis for which one can become a member of the group, as "they explicitly and specifically express the particular contents that group members have to hold."[208] He continues to write that shared beliefs help the group by defining "the essence of the group and supply the rationale for the sense of belonging to the group."[209] Thus, shared beliefs are the glue that bonds the group together, and justifies the group's existence. Similar conclusions are found in scholars such as King, who argues, using the findings of Erikson, that religious beliefs influence the person's self-concept, and provides people with a "transcendent worldview that grounds moral beliefs and behavioural norms in an ideological base," and thus helps them make sense of the world.[210] She further notes that once an individual internalises the religious commitment of the group, that individual tends to act in ways that are consistent with group identity. In addition, the internalisation of the group beliefs creates a sense of "shared vision or shared worldview, beliefs, values, and goals" within the group regardless of gender or age.[211] In this way, group beliefs act as an epistemic basis that unites the group. Oppong argues that there is a strong link

---

204. Bar-Tal, Group Beliefs; King, "Religion and Identity"; Oppong, "Religion and Identity." This dissertation hopes that by using some of the findings by these scholars, Paul's rhetorical strategy will become apparent.

205. Fraser and Gaskell, Social Psychological Study, 8.

206. Bar-Tal, *Shared Beliefs in a Society*, 35; cf. Tucker, *You Belong to Christ*, 129. This definition also appears in his earlier work. Bar-Tal, Group Beliefs, 36.

207. Bar-Tal, *Shared Beliefs in a Society*, 35.

208. Bar-Tal, 35.

209. Bar-Tal, 35.

210. King, "Religion and Identity," 197–98. King focuses on the role that religion plays in the development of identity among adolescents.

211. King, 198–99.

between religion and identity formation; he argues that religion can create a deep sense of unity among the members of the same group.[212]

This then raises a question for this study: what is Paul hoping to achieve by his use of the "in Christ" idiom in 1 Corinthians 1:1–9, and in what ways does this terminology help him in his quest to present himself as the group prototype? In chapter 3, we argued that in 1 Corinthians Paul was fighting secular influences in the ἐκκλησία, as the ἐκκλησία was strongly identifying with their Greco-Roman identity instead of their "in Christ" identity. The argument of this dissertation is that by using the "in Christ" language in 1 Corinthians 1:1–9, Paul is trying to foster a sense of group unity in Corinth.[213] In addition, by using this "in Christ" language, he is able to present himself as the prototype of the in-group identity. Thus, using social identity theory, our focus in the first nine verses of 1 Corinthians is first on investigating in what ways Paul, from the onset of the letter, creates a sense of shared identity of the group and also presents himself as a group prototype of Christ's followers in Corinth.

As already seen above, scholars such as Sani and Reicher have observed the importance of salience in-group identity.[214] People tend to agree with their in-group members on identity-related topics, and thus Paul, by using the "in Christ" language, hopes that the group will agree with his point of view. When one considers the findings of Nicklas and Schlögel regarding the significance of the "in Christ" idiom in the whole of the Pauline corpus, one gets a better understanding of what Paul is hoping to achieve by using that idiom in the light of the intragroup conflict.[215]

Nicklas and Schlögel observe the following regarding the significance of the "in Christ" language in Paul as it relates to identity formation.[216] First, the "in Christ" language changes the believer's self-perception and "radically

---

212. Oppong, "Religion and Identity."
213. The "in Christ" idiom, which sometimes expresses with the singular term "Lord" permeates the whole of 1 Corinthians. In 1 Cor 1–4, Paul refers to "Christ" or "Christ Jesus" seventeen times, while he refers to him as "Lord" five times in 1 Cor 1–4. In the first nine verses of 1 Cor 1, he refers to Jesus Christ nine times. Outside the first four chapters of 1 Corinthians, see: 1 Cor 5:4–5; 6:11, 13–14, 17; 7:10, 12, 17, 22, 25, 32, 34–45, 39; 8:6; 9:1–2, 5, 14; 10:21–22, 26.
214. Sani and Reicher, "Identity, Argument and Schism," 280.
215. Nicklas and Schlögel, "Mission to the Gentiles."
216. Nicklas and Schlögel, 3.

changes the believer's existence,"[217] in that the believer is now identified as

---

217. For the use of believer (πιστ-word group) as a designation for all of Christ's followers and its significance, see Trebilco, *Self-Designation*, 68–121. He notes that in the New Testament, besides the Pauline use, the term "believers" as the designation for all of Christ's followers is used seventy-nine times. He writes that πιστεύω in the "present, aorist, or perfect participle" is used substantively sixty-five times while the adjective πιστός is used fourteen times. Trebilco, 68. He further notes that the πιστ-word group is very significant for Paul. He writes that Paul uses πίστις 101 times, while he uses πιστεύω 46 times and πιστός is used 14 times. Trebilco, 72. The significance of the believer designation is that these are people whose identity is derived from their faith in Christ Jesus. An example of this is 1 Cor 1:21, where those who are saved or are part of Christ's followers are described in terms of them having accepted or believed the kerygma of Christ's followers. In this verse, Paul draws a clear contrast between insiders of the community and outsiders. The insiders are those who believe, while the outsiders are those who reject the gospel and consider it foolish. Paul uses many other terms in 1 Corinthians to draw a boundary between the in-group and the out-group. In this footnote, we have considered the believer designation as the term that is used for the in-group. This term can be contrasted with unbeliever (ὁ ἄπιστος), the designation of the outsider, as οἱ ἄπιστος is used multiple times by Paul in 1 Corinthians. It appears in 1 Cor 6:6; 7:12, 13, and twice in 14, 15; 10:27; 14:22. This insider (believers) and outsider (unbelievers) designation is very important for Paul's identity formation agenda. He uses it, first, to show the contrast between the in-group and the out-group. It is worth noting here that when Paul uses οἱ ἄπιστος to describe the out-group, this does not mean that the out-group does not believe in anything; this is an insider label for the outsider. Trebilco correctly observes that οἱ ἄπιστος would have been surprised to hear that they are described as unbelievers. οἱ ἄπιστος is a label constructed by the in-group to distinguish itself from the out-group. Trebilco, *Outsider Designation*, 50. As Hogg has observed, "groups exist by the virtue of there being out-groups." He further notes that social groups are categories of people and thus a "social category acquires its meaning by contrast with other categories." Hogg, "Social Categorization," 56. Groups identify themselves by comparing their group with other groups; "identity is constructed through opposition." Trebilco, *Outsider Designation*, 2. Thus, Paul's use of οἱ πιστός versus οἱ ἄπιστος language shows us that believing in Christ is a key aspect of the in-group identity. See also Trebilco, 50. Paul uses ἄπιστος in order to highlight that the outsiders do not have a key component of our salient identity; the distinguishing feature of the group is stated positively in that they are believers, where the out-group is stated negatively as being unbelievers. The in-group has something that the out-group does not possess, that is, faith in Jesus Christ. By stating the positive attributes of the in-group identity, Paul raises the group boundaries and wants the members of the group to feel positive about their group membership. As already stated above, people join groups because as individuals we "strive for a positive self-concept." Haslam, *Psychology in Organizations*, 26. In the previous chapter, it was stated that there was too much of "Corinth" or "secular values" among Christ's followers. The Corinthians had what is called "weak social and ideological boundaries." By using the πιστ-word group as a designation for the in-group and ἄπιστος as the designation for the out-group, Paul is in fact raising the group boundaries, to highlight "them" from "us." See also Trebilco, *Outsider Designation*, 51. There are other terms that Paul uses to show a contrast between the in-group and the out-group in 1 Corinthians. He refers to the in-group sometimes as οἱ ἀδελφοί (i.e. 1 Cor 6:6; 7:12, 14, 15), οἱ ἅγιοι (1 Cor 1:2; 6:1–2; and 2 Cor 1:1); and ἡ ἐκκλησία τοῦ θεοῦ (1 Cor 1:2; 11:18, and is implied in verse 20; 10:32; 12:27–28; 16:9). Paul uses these positive self-designations of the in-group to remind his audience of their privileged position as a people of God. Trebilco, *Self-Designation*, 129. For more on the term that Paul uses to describe the outsiders in 1 Corinthians, see Trebilco, *Outsider Designation*, 209. This footnote has not dealt with the debate regarding the translation of πιστοῖς for two reasons: (1) It is not used in 1 Cor 1–4, which is our main focus. (2) Scholars such as O'Brien, Best, and Campbell

being part of Christ and Christ as part of him or her. Hence, Paul can write in Galatians 2:20 ζῶ δὲ οὐκέτι ἐγώ, ζῇ δὲ ἐν ἐμοὶ Χριστός.[218] The believer's identity is bound up with the identity of Christ. Hence in a passage like Romans 6:1–10, Paul appropriates the events that Christ went through for the lives of believers, as if they themselves experienced what Christ experienced, that is, in Romans 6:4 Paul refers to believers as "co-buried with Christ through their baptism" and refers to baptism as "baptism into his death."

Second, Nicklas and Schlögel observe another significance of the "in Christ" language in the life of the believer when they say that being "in Christ" "renews and redefines the believer's relationships to his or her fellow believers," who are also "in Christ."[219] They argue further that the language of being "in Christ" "should not be misunderstood as something that addresses mainly the believing individual. Being "in Christ" always means sharing this "identity in relationship" with others. In other words, being "in Christ" means being part of a community of believers who are a "body of Christ" (1 Cor 12:12–31, esp. 12:27; Rom 12:4–5) and who call each other "brothers" and "sisters.""[220]

Third, Nicklas and Schlögel note that the "in Christ" language in Paul serves as a boundary marker that distinguishes the in-group from the out-group.[221] It creates a sense of us versus them. This study will approach the "in Christ" language of 1 Corinthians as Paul's way of reminding the Pauline community at Corinth of their common salient identity in Christ Jesus, which distinguishes them from those who are not "in Christ."

The findings of Nicklas and Schlögel offer great insight into the significance of the "in Christ" idiom on identity-related issues.[222] Its major weakness, however, is that they consider Paul's use of the term broadly, and tend to miss the nuances of how Paul uses this term in the light of a given passage

---

have convincingly argued that it is best to translate πιστοῖς as believers instead of faithful ones, as the term believers is in keeping with Paul's substantive use, which highlights the contrast to unbelievers (i.e. 2 Cor 6:15; 1 Tim 4:10,12; 5:16; and Tit 1:6). O'Brien, *Letter to Ephesians*, 87; Best, *Ephesians*, 101; and Campbell, *Paul and Union*, 112.

218. This is of course hyperbolic language, by means of which Paul wants to emphasize Christ's lordship over him. It does not mean that as a person Paul ceases to exist, but that his life is now grounded "in Christ"; it just means that Christ is the one who comes first in his life.

219. Nicklas and Schlögel, "Mission to Gentiles," 3–4.

220. Nicklas and Schlögel, 3.

221. Nicklas and Schlögel, 3.

222. Nicklas and Schlögel, "Mission to Gentiles."

such as 1 Corinthians 1–4. Basically, Nicklas and Schlögel have not properly integrated the findings of scholars such as Dunn and Campbell which emphasise the significance of a given context, and argue that Paul's use of the "in Christ" idiom needs to be understood in the light of the overall argument of a given text.[223] It is therefore important for us at this juncture to do an exegesis of Paul's use of the "in Christ" idiom in the light of his overall argument of 1 Corinthians 1–4. Our focus in the next chapter will be on the opening verses of the book of 1 Corinthians.

4.6 Conclusion

This chapter has sought to lay the groundwork for the exegesis that follows in the next chapter. It revisited the discussion that was raised in chapter 3 regarding the issues behind 1 Corinthians and analysed them in the light of social identity theory. It demonstrated that at the heart of the issues in 1 Corinthians 1–4, particularly behind the slogan "I follow Paul, I follow Apollos, I follow Christ, and I follow Peter" was a quest for identity. The problem with the Corinthians was that they were identifying themselves in terms of their factions rather than drawing their identity from Christ. In 1 Corinthians Paul had to resocialise them, and remind them of their salient identity in Christ. But, this would prove to be a problem, as some of the members of the community were questioning his credibility as their apostle. So, Paul first had to prove that he is the prototype of the in-group identity, and also he had to employ a strategy that would make those who no longer regarded him as their apostle, listen to him. The argument of this chapter is that the "in Christ" idiom served that purpose within the argument of 1 Corinthians 1–4. This will become clearer in chapter 5.

The subject of Paul and group prototypicality is traditionally centered around the debate regarding Paul's apostolic defence, which has received a considerable amount of analysis from sociohistorical and socioscientific scholars. In chapter 2, we pointed out that the study will incorporate sociohistorical approaches in its use of social identity theory, thus this chapter engaged with the sociohistorical scholars who have debated Paul's apostolic defence. It highlighted that the traditional approach to Paul's apostolic

---

223. Dunn, *Theology of Apostle Paul*; Campbell, "Paul and Union."

defence, in its emphasis on the centrality of preaching in Paul, tended to overlook Paul's identity formation agenda in 1 Corinthians, particularly in 1 Corinthians 1:13–7.

The scholars who employ social-scientific approaches in their analysis of Paul's discourse on power help us to see the power dynamics in Paul's apostolic defence, but they also tended to be overcritical in their analysis and tended to present Paul as an egomaniac who wanted to consolidate all authority to himself.

The argument of this chapter was that Paul's apostolic defence needs to be seen in the light of his social identity formation agenda. The following chapter will now focus on the exegesis of 1 Corinthians 1–4. It will pay careful attention to the first nine verses of 1 Corinthians, particularly the "in Christ" idiom.

CHAPTER 5

Exegesis of 1 Corinthians 1–4 (with Focus on 1:1–9)

5.1 Introduction

This chapter attempts to demonstrate that there is an interrelationship between leadership and identity in 1 Corinthians 1–4. This will be done by revisiting the discussion that was raised in chapter 4 regarding the resocialisation process of the Corinthians, and our focus will be on the significance of the "in Christ" and the κλῆσις idiom in the argument of 1 Corinthians 1–4, with special attention being given to 1 Corinthians 1.

The main argument regarding these terms is that by using them, Paul links his identity and that of the Corinthians together, and thus hopes, as it was stated in chapter 4, that the consensualization process might begin. Also, in so doing, Paul presents himself as the group prototype. While theoretical considerations regarding the use of these terminologies in the argument of 1 Corinthians 1 will be considered, the main focus of this chapter is on the exegesis of the text of 1 Corinthians. The focus of the next section will be on the first nine verses of 1 Corinthians. In these verses, we will focus on establishing that Paul was concerned about identity formation among the Corinthians. By such means, this dissertation hopes to be able to demonstrate that there is indeed an interrelationship between leadership and identity in 1 Corinthians.

The leadership aspect in the discourse of 1 Corinthians 1–4 is assumed in this chapter, as scholars such as Savage, Hooker, Clarke, and Carson have demonstrated that these four chapters deal with leadership-related issues.[1] These scholars do however tend to highlight the fact that Paul's presentation of leadership in these chapters contrasts sharply with the prevailing views regarding leadership in the Greco-Roman world.

The leadership discourse concerning 1 Corinthians 1–4 can also be seen in the work of scholars such as Barentsen, Tucker, and Holmberg, who incorporate social-scientific approaches in their analyses, which includes social identity theory.[2] They tend to focus on the power dynamic and identity-related issues in their treatment of leadership issues in 1 Corinthians 1–4. While this dissertation will follow along a similar line of thought to these scholars, the present task is to prove that identity discourse is an integral part of the discourse of 1 Corinthians 1–4. While the focus of the next section is mostly on 1 Corinthians 1:1–9, this dissertation is cognisant that this section forms part of the broader section which is 1 Corinthians 1–4. The reason for the specific focus on 1 Corinthians 1:1–9 is that the argument of this section is indicative of the broader argument of 1 Corinthians 1–4. Where appropriate, reference will be made to the broader section.

5.2 The Letter's Opening and Paul's Resocialization Agenda in 1 Corinthians 1:1–9

Chapter 3 of this dissertation has already argued for the literary integrity of 1 Corinthians. Our interest in 1 Corinthians is on the first four chapters of the letter. In chapter 3, we argued that 1 Corinthians 1:10–4:3 forms a single unit which deals with the issue of division in the congregation over preferred leaders. First Corinthians 1:1–9 follows a general pattern found in the opening sections of Greco-Roman letters of the day. This comprises epistolary conventions, that is: (1) a sender (1 Cor 1:1), (2) recipients (1 Cor 1:2), (3) greetings (1 Cor 1:3), and (4) thanksgiving (1 Cor 1:4).[3] First Corinthians 1:1–3 is an

---

1. Savage, *Power through Weakness*; Hooker, "Partner in the Gospel"; Clarke, *Serve the Community*; "Another Corinthian Erastus Inscription"; Carson, *Cross and Christian Ministry*.

2. Barentsen, *Emerging Leadership*; Tucker, *You Belong to Christ*; Holmberg, *Paul and Power*.

3. Horsley, *1 Corinthians*, 39; Jervis, *Purpose of Romans*, 69–72. Jervis notes that this threefold Pauline letter opening formula is "the most consistent of formal features of a Pauline letter." Jervis, 69. This can be seen clearly in the following letters: Rom 1:1–7; 2 Cor 1:1–2; Gal 1:1–5; Eph 1:1–2; Phil 1:1–2; Col 1:1–2; 1 Thess 1:1; 2 Thess 1:1–2; 1 Tim 1:1–2; 2 Tim 1:1–2;

epistolary prescript of the letter, while 1 Corinthians 1:4–9 forms an epistolary thanksgiving.[4] However, there is more to this epistolary prescript than just the conventional statement of ancient Greco-Roman letter writing. Porter observes a number of formal features regarding the epistolary opening of the letter, which he views as performing key functions in the letter, "such as establishing and maintaining contact between the sender and recipients and clarifying their respective statuses and relationships."[5]

While agreeing with Porter, this study wants to emphasise that in 1 Corinthians 1:1–3 Paul also sets the agenda for the whole epistle. In these verses, he reminds the Corinthians about the salient aspects of their group identity, and also of his status as an apostle.[6] Horsley notes that the opening and thanksgiving section of Paul's letters do not merely follow ancient letter writing conventions, but also contain Paul's extended rhetoric that introduces the major themes of the argument to be expounded in the body of the letter.[7] From the outset, Paul invites the Corinthians to participate in the conversation about his identity formation agenda. This becomes clear when we consider

---

Titus 1:1–4; Phlm 1–3. For more on the comparison on Paul's epistolary style, see Jervis, 69–80. For more on ancient letter openings and their similarities and differences with Paul's letter opening, see: Exler, *Form of Ancient Greek*, 23–68; White, *Where Is the Wise Man?*, 198–200; see also Miller on the history of scholarship of ancient letters written in different languages. Miller, "Performance of Ancient Jewish," 12–29. For more on the characteristics and the function of the introductory thanksgiving in Paul's letters, particularly 1 Corinthians, see O'Brien, *Introductory Thanksgiving*, 107–40.

    4. Here, this dissertation follows the structure of Mitchell regarding the first nine verses of 1 Corinthians. Mitchell, *Paul and Rhetoric*, 22. Scholars such as Witherington, Mitchell, and Snyman, using rhetorical analysis, read 1 Cor 1:4–9 as the exordium of the letter. Witherington, *Conflict and Community in Corinth*, 78–94; Mitchell, 192; Snyman, "Persuasion in 1 Corinthians 1:1–9," 2. Snyman, using insight from Watson regarding the function of the exordium, observes that the aim of the exordium is generally viewed as a way for the speaker to prepare the audience psychologically for his or her case, and thus it acts as preparation "for the real arguments" that are to follow in the letter. Snyman, 2; Watson, "Rhetorical Analysis of Philippians," 62. Snyman has correctly observed that this has led to scholarship generally overlooking the argument of 1 Cor 1:1–9 as it is normally viewed as general letter opening remarks and the focus of the scholarship tends to be on the probation of the letter (1 Cor 1:18–16:2). Snyman, 2. This dissertation shares similar sentiments to that of Snyman, who views this section as Paul's preference of stating his best argument first at the beginning of the letter. Snyman, 2.

    5. Porter, "Paul of Tarsus," 569; cf. White, *Where Is the Wise Man?*, 198–200.

    6. According to Tucker, "salient social identity describes a situation in which an identity is switched on, is in the dominant position in the identity hierarchy, and thus represents that component of identity that is most likely to impact behaviour." Tucker, *You Belong to Christ*, 153.

    7. Horsley, 1 Corinthians, 39; cf. Tucker, *You Belong to Christ*, 130. See Tucker, who argues that "[1 Corinthians] 1:1–9 contains similar themes, which are explicated throughout the letter."

the "in Christ" and the "calling" idioms that Paul uses in 1 Corinthians 1:1–9 as the basis of the salient in-group identity.

In the epistolary prescript of 1 Corinthians 1:1–3, Paul describes his identity and that of his recipients in Christ terms.[8] In the previous chapter, we argued that Paul sought to distinguish insiders from outsiders in 1 Corinthians. One of the ways he makes this distinction is by using "in Christ" language as an identity marker for both himself and his community at Corinth.[9] In addition, in the previous chapter, we showed that in

---

8. Ho, "Cleanse Out Old Leaven," 297.

9. It is worth noting that not all scholars consider the "in Christ" idiom as a boundary marker of Christ's followers. A minority of scholars argue against such a reading; among these are Kim and Odell-Scott. Kim, *Christ's Body in Corinth*, 33–38; Odell-Scott, *Paul's Critique of Theocracy*, 98–107. For a review of Odell-Scott's work, see Nanos, "Review: David Odell-Scott," 438–41; Baird, "Review: David Odell-Scott," 332–34; and Winter, "Review: David Odell-Scott," 105–06. Basically, Odell-Scott's argument is that texts such as 1 Cor 2:6–15 and 3:16–17 (among other passages), which are traditionally viewed as acting as the boundary markers of early Christ's followers, are actually not Paul's words at all. Rather in these texts, Paul is simply quoting the words of his opponents, which are represented by the Christ party of 1 Cor 1:12. According to Odell-Scott, this Christ's party of 1 Cor 1:12 is the same as those who boast of "noble birth" in 1 Cor 1:26, and this group represents the claims of superiority of the members of Jesus's family. Odell-Scott, 50. He contends that the slogan "I belong to Christ" is a self-declaration of a domestic association, which "refers to the household of the Lord." Odell-Scott, 50. He further argues that 1 Cor 1:12 refers to anyone who is associated with the household of Christ. This can include the Lord's mother, brother, and even cousins. However, he argues that the identity of those of "noble birth" is restricted to the Lord's family, which is mostly represented by James, who, according to Gal 2:9, is mentioned as a pillar of the community. Odell-Scott, 50–51; 179. For Odell-Scott, the Lord's household claimed theocratic significance within the early Christ movement, and Paul sought to confront and deconstruct such theocratic authority. Odell-Scott, 179. He writes: "One primary purpose of Paul's letters to the Corinthians and the Galatians is to persuade [them] . . . not to engage, or cease engaging or to reject those who do engage, in using wisdom, authority and natural family connections to establish the authority of those who belong to Christ." Odell-Scott, 51. Nanos has highlighted major weaknesses in Odell-Scott's work, of which one is worth repeating here. Nanos, "Review," 440–41. "When Paul claims to speak for God (e.g. when declaring his apostleship is 'not from humans or through humans, but through Jesus Christ' [Gal 1:1]), is not Paul guilty of the same propositional fault that Odell-Scott suggests Paul seeks to subvert in the Christ faction's claim to speak from direct relationship to Jesus?" This study follows the majority reading of "in Christ" idiom, and texts such as 1 Cor 2:6–15 and 3:16–7 as being used as the boundary markers of Christ's followers. Kim's main objection regarding viewing the "in Christ" idiom as a boundary marker is that such a reading tends to focus narrowly on group unity at the expense of diversity among the group members. Kim, *Christ's Body in Corinth*, 34. He views the argument that is proposed in this dissertation of "in Christ" idiom as identity marker as being "an arrogant and exclusivist claim." Kim, 2). He is writing against the third race theory that was looked at in chapter 1 of this study, which featured the accusation of cultural imperialism. While this study is critical of the third race theory, particularly its cultural imperialism, it nonetheless disagrees with Kim's and Odell-Scott's reading of the "in Christ" or 'in the Lord" terminologies. Kim, 35; Odell-Scott, *Paul*. For Kim, the call to concord and unity was a tool of the political elite that was used to

1 Corinthians 1, Paul uses the noun "Christ" seventeen times with the bulk of its appearances in the first thirteen verses. If one takes Paul's use of the singular "Lord" to be referring to Christ, the reference to Christ appears twelve times in the first thirteen verses of 1 Corinthians.[10] So, why does Paul use this idiom so many times in the opening verses of 1 Corinthians? One thing that is clear is that "in Christ" was special for Paul. He uses it and other Christ language to describe his identity and that of his community at Corinth.

While our focus in this chapter is on the significance of "in Christ" and κλῆσις terminologies, it is worth noting that in his description of his own and the Corinthians' identities, Paul also uses other metaphors that highlight their common identity in Christ. Of particular interest for us is his use of sibling language; ἀδελφός (brother and sister).[11] The first time in 1 Corinthians that Paul uses this term is in 1 Corinthians 1:1, where it is used to describe Sosthenes. He writes, Σωσθένης ὁ ἀδελφός. Scholars generally agree that Paul mentioned Sosthenes because the community at Corinth knew him, but there is much debate about why Paul singles out Sosthenes as a brother,[12] as within

---

advocate for hegemonic unity. Kim, 39–49. He writes that the problem with this is that "the politics of the hegemonic body does not consider the voices of the lowly, and its philosophical, ideological basis is in hierarchical dualism, assuring that the low class will serve the high class." Kim, 49. Kim presents Paul as someone who sought to give voice to the marginalized and expose the abuse of power by the social elite. Kim, 51–54. Thus for Kim, the "in Christ" idiom should not be viewed as the "unity-based" or "belonging-centered" (i.e. identity) terminology as that would privilege the political elite. Kim, 36–38. Rather, he argues that this language should be read "modally," that is, "a way of life manifested in and associated with Christ's life and sacrifice." Kim, 37. Sweatman has correctly observed two major weaknesses in Kim's work; (1) Kim has overlooked scholarly treatment of unity that allows for diversity. Sweatman, "Review: Yung Suk Kim," 312; cf. Snyder, "Review," 98. Sweatman provides an example of Volf's work, "Exclusion and Embrace," where a balance is maintained between unity and diversity. Sweatman, "Review," 312. (2) Kim downplays texts such as 1 Cor 1:10 which call for unity and harmony, and 1 Cor 12:27 which argues for diversity within the unified community. Cf. Wenham, "Review," 94. The argument of this dissertation is that Paul uses the "in Christ" idiom as boundary marker. However, this does not mean that this dissertation agrees entirely with the third race theory, which is the theory that tends to embrace the use of "in Christ" idiom as the identity marker of the Pauline community. The problems that this study has with some aspects of the third race theory have been presented in chapter 1. We have argued that there are elements of the continuation of previous identities "in Christ," but these identities have been radically transformed by the Christ event, contrary to the views of the third race theory, which tends not to allow for the continuation of previous identities.

10. See Ho, "Cleanse Out Old Leaven," 297.

11. For a defence of why ἀδελφός should be translated as brother and sister, see Tucker, *You Belong to Christ*, 154–55.

12. There is also debate regarding the identity of Sosthenes. Scholars such as Calvin, Fee, Collins, and Barentsen argue that this is the same Sosthenes who is mentioned by Luke in Acts

1 Corinthians there is clear evidence that there are others who were known by the Corinthians, whom Paul could also have mentioned in 1 Corinthians 1:1.[13] Byrskog has provided a much more plausible answer to this question.[14] He argues that the reason that Paul referred to Sosthenes at the beginning of the letter is that he wanted to "establish or maintain good relations with the recipients of the letter . . . if Sosthenes was known as a respected citizen of Corinth, he may also have provided some important weight to the letter itself." While Sosthenes's identity and the reasons why he is mentioned may be a subject of debate, what is clear is that Paul uses sibling language to describe himself and the Corinthians.[15] Collins notes that by using ἀδελφός, Paul is doing more than "merely" identifying Sosthenes; he is also "introducing the 'kinship language, the language of belonging" from the onset of the letter.[16] Scholars such as Tucker and Trebilco have also observed that ἀδελφός in Paul acts as a key group identifier of those whom Paul regards as believers,[17] while Collins adds that this sibling "language emphasizes the bonds that bind Christians to one another as members of the same family."[18] The sibling language is appropriate for a divided community to foster unity.[19] Aasgaard notes that there are 122 instances of the ἀδελφ- lemma in Paul.[20] Of particular

---

18:17, who was the ruler of the synagogue in Corinth, and who is now a member of the Christ followers in Corinth. Calvin, *Commentary on Epistle of Paul*, 17; Fee, *First Epistle to Corinthians*, 30–31; Collins, *First Corinthians*, 51; Barentsen, *Emerging Leadership*, 87. Scholars such as Horsley and Conzelmann have rejected this view as being speculation. Horsley, *1 Corinthians*, 40; Conzelmann, *1 Corinthians*, 20. For more on the debate regarding the identity of Sosthenes, see Thiselton, *First Epistle to Corinthians*, 69–72.

13. See also 1 Cor 16:15–19; Trebilco, *Early Christians in Ephesus*, 54. Much work has been done by scholars on Paul's relationship with his co-workers and the social status of his coworker; for more on this, see Barentsen, *Emerging Leadership*, 86–89, and Clarke, *Secular and Christian Leadership*, 41–56. Barentsen, for example, argues that Paul's coworkers tended to be wealthy patrons in comparison to the majority of Christ's followers in Corinth (1 Cor 1:26) and that they used their wealth to exact influence within the community. For Barentsen, the Sosthenes of 1 Cor 1:1 is the same individual as that of Acts 18:17. Barentsen, *Emerging Leadership*, 87. Unfortunately, Barentsen is too quick in talking about Paul and his coworker and does not provide any reason for Paul singling out Sosthenes in 1 Cor 1:1.

14. Byrskog, *Jesus the Only Teacher*, 240. See also Trebilco, *Early Christians in Ephesus*, 54.

15. See, 1 Cor 1:10, 11, 26; 2:1; 3:1; 16:12.

16. Collins, *First Corinthians*, 45.

17. Tucker, *You Belong to Christ*, 154–55; Trebilco, *Self-Designation*, 21–50.

18. Collins, *First Corinthians*, 45. For an extended treatment of the ἀδελφός metaphor in Paul and for a rhetorical function of this term in Paul, see Aasgaard, *My Beloved*.

19. See Collins, First Corinthians, 45.

20. Aasgaard, My Beloved.

interest for this study is the fact that most of their uses in 1 Corinthians are concentrated in the first six chapters. In the first four chapters, where Paul deals with the issue of division within the community (1 Cor 1:10–13), he uses ἀδελφός seven times,[21] mostly to describe community members.[22] At the beginning of the section where Paul deals with the subject and quarrelling, he repeatedly addresses the Corinthians as ἀδελφοί. He uses this term to highlight that the addressees belong together as a family. It is a diverse family that comes from different sociopolitical and ethnic backgrounds (1 Cor 1:26). What brings them together is what God has done in Christ (1 Cor 1:30), which at its core is counter cultural (1 Cor 1:27–29). What makes them a family is that, unlike everyone else, they value the cross of Christ. For them, the crucified Christ is both the "power of God and the wisdom of God" (1 Cor 1:23–24), while he is a "stumbling-block to Jews and foolishness to Gentiles." We can thus say that the ἀδελφ- terminology acts as a boundary marker that distinguishes who are members of the community and who are not. This terminology also highlights the "unity and solidarity" which should be characteristic of ἀδελφοί. In fact, in 1 Corinthians 1:10 Paul begins his urgent appeal on how the community is to act using this sibling language. So, why is Paul beginning his appeal this way? The argument that this dissertation is making is that Paul is hoping, by using "in Christ" and the κλῆσις language together with the sibling suggestions, to begin a consensualization process (for more on this see section 5.1.2 below). It is also important though to point out that there is more to the ἀδελφ- terminology than a call to unity, or using it so that the consensualization process might begin. Paul also uses ἀδελφοί as a boundary-marking term to distinguish who is a member of the community (cf. 1 Cor 1). In 1 Corinthians 5 and 6, Paul also uses ἀδελφ- terminology to make a contrast between those who are part of the community of ἀδελφοί and those who are ἄπιστος (1Cor 6:6). He also uses the term to mark behaviour that is in line with the community's identity in Christ. For example, in 1 Corinthians 5:11 someone who used to be a member of the community but does not act in line with what this community represents is to be denied the privileges that come from being a member of a family.

---

21. 1 Cor 1:1, 10, 11, 26; 2:1; 3:1; 4:6.
22. Trebilco, *Self-Designation*, 32; Tucker, *You Belong to Christ*, 154.

5.3 Scholarly Treatment of the "in Christ" Idiom

The aim of this section is to investigate the significance of the "in Christ"[23] idiom particularly as it relates to the identity formation of the Pauline community at Corinth.[24] Section 4.5 of the previous chapter introduced the scholarly treatment of the "in Christ" idiom, but the focus of that chapter was on scholars who employ social identity theory in their approach. In this chapter, the focus will be on both the scholars who employ the sociohistorical approach and those who focus on grammatical analysis of the "in Christ" idiom. The reason for the inclusion of these scholars is the methodological stance of this dissertation, which was presented in chapter 2. In that chapter, it was argued that this dissertation would incorporate both social identity theory with the sociohistorical approach and grammatical analysis of the Greek text to establish the interrelationship between leadership and identity in 1 Corinth. Thus, this section seeks to establish that balance by revisiting the scholarly treatment of "in Christ" idiom in Paul, paying particular attention to the context of 1 Corinthians. The scholars that are going to be looked at in this section are mostly those who use a sociohistorical approach along with grammatical analysis in their consideration of Paul's "in Christ" idiom in Paul. The idiom "in Christ"[25] has been analysed extensively. Campbell

---

23. For a statistical analysis regarding the prevalence of this and other terms associated with ἐν Χριστῷ such as ἐν κυρίῳ, ἐν αὐτῷ, διὰ Χριστοῦ, σὺν Χριστῷ, σὺν αὐτῷ, in Paul, see Dunn and the previous chapter of this study. Dunn, *Theology of Apostle Paul*, 396–97. For different nuances on how scholars approach the ἐν Χριστῷ terminology, see Tucker, *You Belong to Christ*, 83–87. For example, Horrell argues that ἐν Χριστῷ terminology in Paul needs to be seen in the light of the Jewish symbolic universe. He writes that Paul, by employing this language, wants to build "a positive social identity for members of his "in Christ" groups." He argues that Paul achieves this by "transferring to them (Gentiles) the positive labels of Israel, the people of God: the identity designations of the parent community are claimed for the new grouping." Horrell, "No Longer Jew or Greek," 15. For Horrell, Paul believed "that the people of God – the true Israel – find their identity in Christ alone." While this dissertation appreciates his argument that the ἐν Χριστῷ terminology needs to be understood in the light of the Jewish symbolic universe, the point of divergence from Horrell is on his views that theology precedes identity formation. Cf. Tucker, *You Belong to Christ*, 85; Horrell, "Introduction"; "No Longer Jew or Greek." While this dissertation follows the work of Campbell on the ἐν Χριστῷ terminology, it is reluctant to agree with him that identity is a precursor to theology. Thus this dissertation prefers a hybrid understanding and interaction between theology and identity. Tucker, *You Belong to Christ*, 85–86; Campbell, *Paul and Creation*, 52.

24. For the significance of the preposition ἐν for identification, see Turner, Grammatical Insights, 118–22.

25. For a review of a historical treatment of this subject in the twentieth century until 2012, see Campbell, *Paul and Union*, 31–64. See also the extended treatment of this subject

does a survey of scholars from 1892 until the time of his publication in which he highlights the main arguments and the contributions of the following scholars:[26] Deissmann (1892), Bousset (1913), Schweitzer (1930), Bultmann (1948–1953), Murray (1955), Wikenhauser (1960), Neugebauer (1961), Bouttier (1962), Barth (1932–1968), Tannehill (1967), Davies (1970), Sanders (1977), Gaffin (1978), Dunn (1998), Horton (2007), and Gorman (2009). He then produces a synthesis of his findings.[27] He notes that in the first half of the twentieth century, Deissman, Bousset, and Bultmann tended to look at Paul's theology of union with Christ (which is covered by the idiom "in Christ") in the light of Hellenistic religious mysticism. Campbell demonstrates how these scholars' proposals are actually anachronistic, and that Paul's argument regarding union with Christ is actually the opposite of how the Hellenistic religious mysticism functioned; this particular insight actually came from Schweitzer, who pointed to Jewish eschatology for a parallel to Paul's concept of union with Christ. Campbell notes that these scholars have failed to determine what ἐν Χριστῷ actually means.[28] He notes that the "in Christ" language can have a multifaceted function in Paul, and maintains that the idiom acts like a "'webbing' that holds" all of Paul's concepts together.[29] He argues that the idiom "in Christ" is woven into other elements of Christ's work in Paul's thought, such as: "salvation, redemption, reconciliation, creation, election, predestination, adoption, sanctification, headship, provision, his death, resurrection, ascension . . . eternal life, the Spirit, . . . and the fulfilment of God's promises."[30] He argues that, "Virtually every element of Christ's work that is of interest to Paul is connected in some way to union with Christ."[31]

---

in the collection of essays edited by Thate, Vanhoozer, and Campbell. Thate, Vanhoozer, and Campbell, "In Christ" in Paul, 3–558.

    26. Campbell, *Paul and Union*. This section will follow his argument closely as his book has been considered to be the "authoritative book on the subject for decades to come" by scholars such as Johnson and Bird. Johnson, "Review: Constantine R. Campbell," 431; Bird, endorsement of *Paul and Union*, on back cover.

    27. Campbell, Paul and Union, 58–64.

    28. Campbell, 60.

    29. Campbell, 441.

    30. Campbell, 331--32.

    31. Campbell, 331.

In his synthesis of scholarly contributions, Campbell recognizes that there are five ways that the "in Christ" language functions in Paul:[32] (1) Union with Christ is a "local" conception; that is, it "encapsulates a spatial-spiritual relationship, whereby Paul is 'in Christ,' and Christ is 'in' Paul."[33] (2) Union with Christ is a "relational conception"; here it refers to spiritual harmony with the nature and work of the Holy Spirit. (3) Union with Christ is an "eschatological" formulation; the emphasis here is the believers' connection to the risen Christ, and an anticipation of the new age. (4) Union with Christ refers to a Trinitarian fellowship; here, Campbell emphasises the union within the Godhead, not just the relationship between Christ and believers. He writes that in this aspect, union with Christ "refers to the Father's relationship with the Son, and their union in the Spirit."[34] Thus, Christ is primarily identified by the fact that God was in Christ, and our relationship with "Christ stems from the mutual indwelling of Father and Son within the Godhead."[35] The Father acts through the person of the Son "by the virtue of his union with him" to bring about salvation for humanity.[36] This Trinitarian fellowship also governs believers' fellowship with Christ, just "as the Father indwells the Son, so the Son indwells his people."[37] Campbell makes an interesting point at this juncture, when he notes that this mutual indwelling does not mean that the believers lose their identity and thus become divine; they still retain their personhood, in the same way that Christ retains his, even though he is indwelt by the Father. (5) Union with Christ as an existential model or spiritual reality. Here the emphasis is on solidarity with Christ, particularly "what Christ experienced becomes part of the 'experience' of the believer."[38] These five findings of Campbell help us to be aware of the many concepts that are covered by the idiom "in Christ." Therefore, Campbell proposes that the following terms must be adopted into our understanding of the "in Christ" idiom: "union, participation, identification, incorporation" (emphasis original).[39] He argues

---

32. Campbell, 60–61.
33. Campbell, 60.
34. Campbell, 409.
35. Campbell, 12, 61.
36. Campbell, 409.
37. Campbell, 410.
38. Campbell, 60–61.
39. Campbell, 29; cf. Vanhoozer, "From 'Blessed in Christ,'" 25.

that these four terms span the full range of all that Paul sought to achieve when he used the "prepositional phraseology, metaphorical conceptualisation, and theological interaction" to describe the believers' union/participation/identification/incorporation with Christ, which is encapsulated by ἐν Χριστῷ.[40]

Dunn highlights three ways in which "in Christ" functions in Paul.[41] (1) Paul uses "in Christ" language in an "objective" manner. He refers "to the redemptive act which has happened "in Christ" or depends on what Christ is yet to do." An example is τῇ χάριτι τοῦ θεοῦ τῇ δοθείσῃ ὑμῖν ἐν Χριστῷ Ἰησοῦ in 1 Corinthians 1:4.[42] (2) Paul uses "in Christ" in a subjective way in 1 Corinthians 1:2, where he "speaks of believers as being "in Christ" or "in the Lord." Dunn writes that an example of this is when believers are described as those ἡγιασμένοις ἐν Χριστῷ. Looking at this category, one might consider the social implications of the gospel (that is, "the outworking of the objective aspect of Christ's redemption").[43] We will, later in this chapter, argue that the ἐκκλησία at Corinth was struggling to understand the social implications of their identity "in Christ," and that Paul's subjective use of "in Christ" is his way of resocialising the community. He wants to help them understand the implications of their social identity "in Christ." The emphasis here will be on the significance of Paul's describing the community as ἡγιασμένοις ἐν Χριστῷ and also κλητοῖς ἁγίοις. (3) Paul uses "in Christ" language to describe his ministry activity. This is seen in his discussions on topics such as his Jewishness, apostleship, and his ongoing relationship with the early followers of Jesus. He also uses "in Christ" language when exhorting believers to adopt a particular lifestyle or course of action. We can say that here Paul uses the term in relation to his identity formation agenda. When one considers the "in Christ" idiom in the light of the findings of both Campbell and Dunn, Paul's identity formation agenda in 1 Corinthians 1–4 becomes apparent. The findings of these scholars also help us in our exegesis to be sensitive about the different uses of the prepositional phrase ἐν Χριστῷ, as they highlight that there are nuances in how Paul uses this term.

---

40. Campbell, 29; cf. Vanhoozer, 24–25.

41. Dunn, *Theology of Apostle Paul*. Vanhoozer has a similar conceptual framework, but his third use is intersubjective, which focuses on the union of those who are in Christ. "From 'Blessed in Christ,'" 24.

42. Dunn, 397.

43. Cf. Tucker, *You Belong to Christ*, 82.

This study, in considering the "in Christ" idiom, is particularly interested in attempting to answer the following questions: first, what was Paul anticipating to accomplish by employing "in Christ" idiom (what was the rhetorical purpose of the term)? Second, in what ways does this idiom contribute to the argument of this dissertation regarding the interrelationship between leadership and identity in 1 Corinthians?

Paul describes himself as the ἀπόστολος Χριστοῦ Ἰησοῦ and he describes the ἐκκλησία in Corinth as ἡγιασμένοις ἐν Χριστῷ Ἰησοῦ. This description is not limited to Paul and the Corinthians, it is used as an identity marker of everyone who calls on the name of Christ Jesus (1 Cor 1:2). Thus, it could be argued that Paul uses the "in Christ" idiom as a social identity that "connects the Corinthian Christ-followers to the broader Christ-movement throughout the Roman Empire" and that in this manner the "in Christ" idiom acts a superordinate identity for all of Christ's followers.[44] Our interest in the following section will be on how "in Christ" idiom functions in the argument of 1 Corinthians 1:1–9.

5.3.1 The Function of the "in Christ" Idiom in the Argument of 1 Corinthians 1:1–9

The previous section was concerned mostly with the scholarly treatment of the "in Christ" language. While there is an element of overlap with this section, the main consideration is now with the grammatical analysis of the Greek text, that is, with the function of the "in Christ" language of a particular verse, especially as it pertains to identity foundations of the Pauline community. The historical context of the Pauline community in Corinth was dealt with in chapter 3. The concern of this chapter is with the identity foundation of this group. What is it that made this community unique compared to other voluntary associations of the time?[45] What did they consider to be their in-group identity? The focus of our discussion here will be the text of 1 Corinthians, particularly the text where Paul builds his argument on their

---

44. Tucker, *Remain in Your Calling*, 73.

45. There is a growing interest among scholars in analysing the New Testament in the light of the Greco-Roman voluntary association. Among those who take this approach are Meeks; see also the book edited by Kloppenborg and Wilson for more scholars who follow this approach; Meeks, *First Urban Christians*; Kloppenborg and Wilson, *Voluntary Associations*; see also Macrae, "Eating with Honor," 165–81.

assumed identity. He employs different strategies in 1 Corinthians to reinforce the Corinthians' unique identity in Christ.[46]

As seen above, Pauline scholars note that the frequency with which Paul uses the prepositional phrase ἐν Χριστῷ Ἰησοῦ is not accidental. However, it remains a struggle to get to grips with the exact meaning of ἐν Χριστῷ Ἰησοῦ. For example, while acknowledging the prevalence of Paul's use of ἐν Χριστῷ Ἰησοῦ, Brookins and Longenecker argue that the term is used "loosely in Paul's writings."[47] Similar sentiments are shared by Blass and Debrunner, who wrote that "ἐν Χριστῷ is copiously appended by Paul to the most varied concepts, [and] utterly defies definite interpretation."[48] BDAG argues that ἐν Χριστῷ Ἰησοῦ is used by Paul and John "to designate a close personal relation in which" Christ Jesus "is viewed as the controlling influence."[49] This dissertation follows similar lines to Campbell who, while conceding that the meaning of the prepositional phrase ἐν Χριστῷ cannot have one single meaning due to the variety of its lexical possibilities, it is, nonetheless, an idiom that Paul likes to use to describe the believer's identity in Christ.[50] Paul tends to use the idiom "in reference to things achieved for/given to people, believers' actions, characteristics of believers, faith in Christ, justification, and new status."[51] Campbell observes that the prepositional phrase ἐν Χριστῷ is used twenty times by Paul; out of which it is used instrumentally eight times.[52] The other uses fall beyond the scope of this dissertation as they do not deal with 1 Corinthians.[53]

---

46. Section 5.1 above, mentioned Paul's use of the sibling metaphor in fostering group identity.

47. Longenecker, Epistle to Romans, 4.

48. Blass and Debrunner, Greek Grammar, §§219.4.

49. Bauer, Walter, and William F. Arndt. *A Greek-English Lexicon of the New Testament and Other Early Christian Literature* (BDAG), s.v. "ἐν Χριστῷ Ἰησοῦ."

50. Campbell, *Paul and Union*, 199.

51. Campbell, 199.

52. Campbell, 94. See Rom 6:23; 1 Cor 1:2,4; 2 Cor 5:19; Gal 3:14; Eph 1:3; 2:10; 2 Tim 1:9.

53. There is a debate among the scholars regarding exactly how many times Paul uses the phrase "in Christ." Campbell says it is used 20 but his focus is only on "ἐν Χριστῷ," while Vanhoozer says Paul uses it 73 times. Campbell, 94; Vanhoozer, "From 'Blessed in Christ,'" 13. This dissertation is more inclined to agree with Vanhoozer. Scholars note that the enquiry into Paul's use of the "in Christ" idiom should not be limited to the term ἐν Χριστῷ; they suggest that other associated prepositional phrases with ἐν Χριστῷ, such as ἐν κυρίῳ, ἐν αὐτῷ, διὰ Χριστοῦ, σὺν Χριστῷ, σὺν αὐτῷ should also be considered. Vanhoozer, 13–14; Campbell. When one adds these other prepositional phrases with the "in Christ" idiom to express the

Some scholars refer to the prepositional phrase ἐν Χριστῷ Ἰησοῦ as a Pauline formula. However, Campbell has correctly observed that it is best to describe this prepositional phrase as a Pauline idiom.[54] The problem with using the term formula in describing this prepositional phrase is that it suggests that the meaning of this phrase is static, but as Campbell has demonstrated, the meaning is actually elastic and it depends on how the preposition ἐν is used in any given context.[55] This is something that is missed by some of the scholars who apply social identity theory to the "in Christ" idiom.[56]

An example of how the preposition ἐν affects the meaning of ἐν Χριστῷ Ἰησοῦ can be seen in our text of 1 Corinthians 1:2, which reads: τῇ ἐκκλησίᾳ τοῦ θεοῦ, ἡγιασμένοις ἐν Χριστῷ Ἰησοῦ, τῇ οὔσῃ ἐν Κορίνθῳ, κλητοῖς ἁγίοις, σὺν πᾶσιν τοῖς ἐπικαλουμένοις τὸ ὄνομα τοῦ κυρίου ἡμῶν Ἰησοῦ Χριστοῦ ἐν παντὶ τόπῳ αὐτῶν καὶ ἡμῶν. There are four ways in which the preposition ἐν can function in 1 Corinthians 1:2.[57] The scholars argue that ἐν Χριστῷ can function as (1) a locative dative; (2) instrumental dative; (3) dative of agency; and (4) causal dative. Of the four possibilities, scholarship seems to have been mostly concerned with the first two,[58] even though there is a strong grammatical ground for the third option.[59] The causal dative aspect is not really relevant for the text of 1 Corinthians 1:1–9. It is to these four possible aspects of the propositional dative that we now turn.

(1) ἐν Χριστῷ Ἰησοῦ as a locative dative: The emphasis here is on where something is being done, that is, sanctified in the sphere of Christ, or Paul/Corinthians is/are "in Christ."[60] This use of the preposition deals mostly

---

idea of union/participation/identification/incorporation with Christ, the number of instances that Paul uses the terminology jumps to a staggering 164 appearances, besides the Pastoral epistles, Colossians, and Ephesians.

54. Campbell, 25. Idiom suggests that this phrase is used flexibly.

55. Campbell, 25–27.

56. See Nicklas and Schlögel, "Mission to Gentiles"; Barentsen, *Emerging Leadership*; and to a limited extent, Ho, "Cleanse Out Old Leaven."

57. Campbell, *Paul and Union*, 76–77; Vanhoozer, "From 'Blessed in Christ,'" 13–16. See Vanhoozer for a historical review of how different scholars interpreted the preposition ἐν, from the time of Luther to recent scholars. Vanhoozer, 13–16.

58. Vanhoozer, 14; Campbell, 76–77.

59. Campbell, 76.

60. Blass and Debrunner argue that this use of the dative is "extremely limited in the classic period," and that it is not used in the New Testament. Blass and Debrunner, *Greek Grammar*, §§199. In recent years however, this understanding of the dative has been in ascendency;

with the subject of incorporation; the believer being incorporated within the Godhead.[61] According to Hoehner, Deissmann first proposed this reading of the "in Christ" idiom. He gave the preposition ἐν Χριστῷ a mystical sense that sought to demonstrate the intimate fellowship between Christ's followers and "the living 'spiritual Christ.'"[62] Deissmann and Wilson wrote: "Christ is Spirit; therefore He can live in Paul and Paul in Him. Just as the air which we breathe, is 'in' us and fills us, and yet at the same time we live in this air and breathe it, so it is also with . . . Paul: Christ in him, he in Christ."[63] Scholars such as Hoehner and Campbell have criticised Deissman on two grounds:[64] First, he failed to appreciate the areas of differences between Paul and the Hellenistic religious mysticism. Second, in his presentation of Christ, Deissman tends to present an "impersonal Christ."[65] Fee, Conzelman, and Campbell have rejected the locative use of the preposition ἐν, as being the least likely in the context of 1 Corinthians.[66] Allan also rejects its use in the context of Ephesians, while Hoehner argues that the locative use makes "the best sense in" the context of Ephesians 1.[67] In recent years, some scholars of 1 Corinthians have argued for the locative use in 1 Corinthians 1:2. Among them is Ho, who writes that the phrase ἐν Χριστῷ Ἰησοῦ is placed between the phrase ἐν Κορίνθῳ and ἐν παντὶ τόπῳ in 1 Corinthians 1:2, and that the position of ἐν Χριστῷ Ἰησοῦ in the structure of the sentence makes

---

see Hoehner, *Ephesians*, 170; Ho, "Cleanse Out Old Leaven," 297; Thate, "Paul, φρόνησις, and Participation," 303–04; and Vanhoozer, "From 'Blessed in Christ,'" 29.

61. Hoehner, *Ephesians*, 171.

62. Hoehner, 170.

63. Deissmann and Wilson, St. Paul, 172. See also Campbell, Paul and Union, 32; Hoehner, 170.

64. Hoehner, 170; Campbell, 59–60.

65. Hoehner, 171.

66. Fee, *First Epistle to Corinthians*, 32; Conzelman, 1 Corinthians, 21; Campbell, Paul and Union, 76. Conzelmann rejects the mystical reading of ἐν Χριστῷ and contends that the phrase should be read as "objective saving work" of Christ. Conzelmann, *Outline of Theology*, 209–10. Arguing his case in the light of 2 Cor 5:17–21, Conzelmann writes: "One fact which tells against this mystical interpretation is that the phrase ἐν Χριστῷ appears in the very passage where 'reconciliation' is spoken of in juridical, objective terms . . . moreover, πίστις and ἐν Χριστῷ are connected." Conzelmann, 208–09. While Conzelmann does admit that there are instances in which ἐν Χριστῷ seems to "have a mystical ring" to it, he nonetheless dismisses the mystical reading and explains these passages (i.e. Gal 2:20; Rom 8:9) in non-mystical terms. Conzelmann, 209, 211. He argues that the emphasis of these passages is on the fact that "Christ is 'there for' believers in the sense that he intercedes for them." Conzelmann, 211; Colijn, "Paul's Use," 21.

67. Hoehner, *Ephesians*, 172.

it a locative dative.[68] That is, the Corinthians "are referred to as a group of people literally situated within the same place of Christ." Similar views are also held by Turner, Porter, and Vanhoozer.[69] All three scholars argue that ἐν Χριστῷ can be taken as locative dative, but with a major difference to Deissman's views: they argue, respectively, that believers' incorporation with Christ should not be viewed as a physical locative metaphor (that is, "spatially the way coins are in a piggy bank"[70]) but "spherically", that is, "one is in the sphere of Christ's control."[71] In this use – proposed by Porter[72] – the emphasis on the use of the preposition is more in the realm to which the believers belong. While this makes sense, particularly if one is using social identity, as it will highlight the differences between those who belong to Christ and those who do not, the argument of this dissertation is that, in the light of the argument of 1 Corinthians 1:1–3, it is an improbable use of the preposition. In fact, Vanhoozer admits that "the force of the locative sense of "in Christ" is less obvious," while Turner relies on the gospel of John to make his case.[73] Moreover, Vanhoozer also argues that the context in which the prepositional phrase is used must take precedence over any meaning one might be tempted to assign to it.[74] Thus far, this dissertation has sought to demonstrate why it disagrees with the scholars who take the locative view of the prepositional phrase ἐν Χριστῷ in 1 Corinthians 1:2. We now consider the other views regarding how ἐν Χριστῷ functions in 1 Corinthians 1:2.

(2) ἐν Χριστῷ has been seen as an instrumental dative, that is, sanctified through Christ. According to Battle, an instrumental dative "describes the means, cause, or manner of action."[75] In section 5.2.2, this dissertation will follow scholars such as Campbell, Conzelmann and Fee in arguing that this is how ἐν Χριστῷ Ἰησοῦ functions in the argument of 1 Corinthians 1:2.[76]

---

68. Ho, "Cleanse Out Old Leaven," 297.

69. Turner, *Grammatical Insights*, 121; Porter, *Idioms of Greek*, 159; Vanhoozer, "From 'Blessed in Christ,'" 28–29.

70. Vanhoozer, 28.

71. Porter, *Idioms of Greek*, 159.

72. Porter, 159.

73. Vanhoozer, "From 'Blessed in Christ,'" 14; Turner, Grammatical *Insights*, 120.

74. Vanhoozer, 14.

75. Battle, "Notes on Greek Syntax."

76. Campbell, Paul and Union, 76; Conzelmann, Outline *of Theology*, 210–11, and Fee, *First Epistle*, 32. It is worth noting that this position has been severely criticised by Turner, who

(3) ἐν Χριστῷ Ἰησοῦ as a dative of agency (sanctified by Christ): Wallace defines the dative of agency as "the agent (personal) by whom something is done."[77] He notes further that "the only difference between means and agency is that means is impersonal, agency is personal."[78] In section 5.3.2 this dissertation will consider the findings of Wallace regarding how the dative of agency works in a given context. This dissertation argues that, based on 1 Corinthians 1:2 alone, ἐν Χριστῷ Ἰησοῦ could probably be read as a dative of agency, even though Wallace advises against this, when he writes that, "when the dative follows a preposition, you should not attempt to identify the datives' function by case usage alone."[79] This study will consider the possibility that ἐν Χριστῷ Ἰησοῦ can be defined as the pure dative, because there is a problem concerning the understanding of the meaning of the prepositional phrase ἐν. Vanhoozer has highlighted this problem when he argues that, "biblical prepositions alone are [also] insufficient to determine meaning."[80] This will be done even though for this study, in the light of the overall argument of 1 Corinthians 1:1-3, the instrumental dative is preferable.

(4) ἐν Χριστῷ Ἰησοῦ as a causal dative – sanctified because of Christ: Scholars such as Campbell and Vanhoozer argue that this use of the dative is not applicable in the context of 1 Corinthians.[81] For Campbell this is the least likely because 1 Corinthians 1:4 together with 1 Corinthians 1:1 and 1:2 make it clear that calling, sanctification, and grace originate with God, that is, verse 2 could be read as sanctified in Christ because of God.

Of these four possible uses of the prepositional phrase ἐν Χριστῷ, the one that is argued for in this dissertation is the instrumental use. While thus far, arguments for and against ἐν Χριστῷ as a locative dative were considered, the following section will argue for the instrumental use of this dative.

---

writes that ἐν as "having merely an instrumental meaning (i.e. 'by' or 'with') should be resisted, for the predominant meaning is still 'in,' 'within,' 'in the sphere of.'" Turner, *Grammatical Insights*, 120-21.

77. Wallace, *Greek Grammar*, 373, citing Williams.

78. Wallace, 373, citing Williams. Due to the similarity between means and agency, in section 5.3.2 the two meanings will from time to time be used interchangeably. However, this dissertation is by no means implying that Christ is an impersonal agent, rather theologically speaking, one can argue that Christ is the means by which God achieves his purposes.

79. Wallace, 175.

80. Vanhoozer, "From 'Blessed in Christ,'" 14.

81. Campbell, *Paul and Union*, 76-78; Vanhoozer, 28-29.

5.3.2 The Function of the Instrumental Dative ἐν Χριστῷ in Paul's Social Identity Agenda

The previous section in this chapter dealt mostly with the debate regarding ἐν Χριστῷ as a locative dative; even though the other three grammatical possibilities regarding the meaning of ἐν Χριστῷ Ἰησοῦ were mentioned, we did not deal with them in-depth. This section will now first consider ἐν Χριστῷ Ἰησοῦ as a dative of agency before it deals with the justification for taking ἐν Χριστῷ as an instrumental dative. Ἐν Χριστῷ Ἰησοῦ as a causal dative falls beyond the scope of this dissertation and thus will not be considered.

At first glance, one might be tempted to think that ἐν Χριστῷ Ἰησοῦ in 1 Corinthians 1:2 indicates the agency by which the Corinthians are sanctified, that is, they have been sanctified by Christ Jesus. This view is strong, particularly in the light of Wallace's argument regarding the dative of agency (i.e., by or through).[82] Wallace notes that this dative is "used to indicate the personal agent by whom the action of the verb is accomplished" and he notes that this case "is an extremely rare category in the NT" (emphasis original).[83] He writes that there are four keys to identifying the dative of agency, all of which are present in 1 Corinthians 1:2. Wallace writes:[84] (1) the noun in the dative must be personal; in our case Christ Jesus. (2) The person specified by the dative noun must be portrayed as exercising volition; this is assumed in the context of 1 Corinthians (for example in 1 Cor 1:4, Paul is thankful to God for the Corinthians because of God's grace in Christ).[85] (3) Grammatically, the text has to include "a perfect passive verb"; this is found in verse 2 in ἡγιασμένοις. (4) The "agent of the passive verb can become the subject of an active verb"; again this criterion is met in this verse as Christ could be viewed as the one doing the action of sanctification with the Corinthians being the objects or the recipients of Christ's sanctifying actions.[86] When one weighs Wallace's rules regarding the dative of agency, one might conclude that ἐν Χριστῷ Ἰησοῦ in 1 Corinthians 1:2 acts as a dative agency. However, this is

---

82. Wallace, Greek *Grammar*, 163. This study is grateful for the insight of Campbell regarding the nuances of Wallace's argument regarding the dative of agency. Campbell, *Paul and Union*, 77.
83. Wallace, 163.
84. Wallace, 163–64.
85. See Campbell, Paul and Union, 77.
86. See Campbell, 77.

where the argument of this dissertation comes in; that the context in which the dative ἐν Χριστῷ Ἰησοῦ is used needs to be paramount in our thinking before we make general statements regarding the function of ἐν Χριστῷ Ἰησοῦ.

When one considers 1 Corinthians 1:2 within its context, particularly verse 1, one soon realises that it is improbable that ἐν Χριστῷ Ἰησοῦ can function as a dative of agency in this specific context. In verse 1, Paul makes it clear that it is God who has called him, that is, God is the ultimate agent in calling him and the Corinthians.[87] The idea of God as an active agent is not limited only to the first three verses of 1 Corinthians. Throughout 1 Corinthians 1, Paul repeatedly reminds the Corinthians of what God has done. In 1 Corinthians 1:19, God destroyed the wisdom of the wise and frustrated the intelligence of the intelligent. In 1 Corinthians 1:20, God made foolish the wisdom of the world, and saved those who believe (1 Cor 1:21). First Corinthians 1:27–28 repeatedly speaks of God's choice: God chose the foolish and weak things of the world in order to shame the wise and the strong. Further, in 1 Corinthians 1:30, it is because of God that the Corinthians are in Christ Jesus. Thus, the argument of 1 Corinthians 1 makes it clear that God is the active and ultimate agent in the formation of the identity of the Corinthians in Christ; Christ is the instrument by which God achieves his purposes. Fee, Conzelman, and Campbell argue that the phrase ἐν Χριστῷ Ἰησοῦ acts in an instrumental manner,[88] that is, it is "by what God has accomplished through Christ" that the community is sanctified.[89] Further, Campbell correctly observes that the key in understanding 1 Corinthians 1:1–2 is the calling language, meaning that both Paul's calling to be an apostle and the Corinthians' being set apart as people of God, have their origin in God.[90] As already stated above, by representing his identity and apostleship in terms of being called by the will of God, and the Corinthians' calling and sanctification having its origin in the divine plan of God, Paul intertwines his identity with that of the Corinthians.

---

87. "Agent" in this context is used in terms of divine agency, a theological construct that was proposed by Leydecker, which focuses on the decision of God. Leydecker argues that "the act of God as Spirit by which he has by himself established from eternity most freely and wisely what and how everything in time will be unto his glory." Bac, *Perfect Will Theology*, 1. For more on the concept of divine agency, see Bac, *Perfect Will Theology*.

88. Fee, *First Epistle to Corinthians*, 32; Conzelman, *1 Corinthians*, 21; Campbell, *Paul and Union*, 76.

89. Fee, 32.

90. Campbell, *Paul and Union*, 77.

Moreover, by highlighting their identity in terms of God's agency in the person of Christ, he makes the group aware of their salient identity in Christ that has its origin in God's calling. In so doing Paul is also simultaneously presenting himself as a group prototype, that is, his identity and apostleship are rooted in the work of God in Christ, which is a core feature of the in-group identity. Also, by phrasing his identity and that of the Corinthians in terms of what God has done in Christ for them, Paul hopes for consensualization with(in) the group.[91] Further, it could also be argued that the prepositional phrase ἐν Χριστῷ Ἰησοῦ in 1 Corinthians functions "as means of a social cognition and serves as the foundation" of the in-group identity.[92] Thus, "in Christ" idiom in 1 Corinthians functions as a lens through which the in-group perceives its real identity (that is, as a worldview). This will become clearer in section 5.3 below when we consider the implication of the calling language in 1 Corinthians. For now, though, it will suffice to say that the "in Christ" idiom in Paul acts as a foundational and resocialising category for the in-group identity. Paul employs the "in Christ" idiom in order to bring about positive identification of the group, and more than that, in order to help the group to have a proper regard for its leaders. The following section will now focus on expounding the meaning of this statement. Up to this point, this chapter has been primarily concerned with the grammatical analysis of the "in Christ" idiom. This was done in line with the argument of chapter 2, that is, in order for social identity theory not to be anachronistic, it needs to be sensitive to the grammatical argument of the given text and the sociohistorical context. The following section now seeks to connect how grammatical analysis complements the social identity theory, as the grammatical analysis provides us with the raw data that can be interpreted using social identity theory.

5.3.3 "in Christ" idiom as Installation of Positive Identity

This section will now incorporate the grammatical findings that were uncovered above by social identity theory. Tajfel recognises that there are three features that make a group function well, namely (1) cognitive – the sense of the knowledge that one belongs to a group; (2) evaluation – the connotations of the values attached to belonging to such a group – whether positive

---

91. See the previous chapter of this study in terms of how this works.
92. Tucker, *You Belong to Christ*, 80.

or negative; and (3) emotional – the sense that the cognitive and evaluative aspects may be accompanied by emotions.[93] Social identity theory concerns itself with "how a group installs its distinctive identity on individual members" of the group.[94] What is clear in 1 Corinthians 1:2 is that Paul wants the group to know (cognitive aspect of identity) that they belong to God and that God acted in Christ to make them his.[95] In social identity theory terms, what Paul is doing here is installing group norm or identity descriptors.[96] Group norms are concerned with "generating and inculcating" a positive social identity, they tell "group members what patterns of thinking and feeling and behaving are required if they are to belong to the group and share its identity."[97] This is exactly what Paul is doing in 1 Corinthians 1:2. He does not only describe the group in terms of what God has done for them in Christ, he also describes the Corinthians as the ἐκκλησία τοῦ θεοῦ. Moreover, by using the genitive of source τοῦ θεοῦ, which shows that they are a church that has its origin in the call of God, this means that they are also dependent on God for their existence.[98] Dunn notes the following regarding the significance of the ἐκκλησία τοῦ θεοῦ in Paul.[99] He writes, "ἐκκλησία is the single most frequent term used by Paul to refer to the groups of those who met in the name of Christ . . . 'church' is the term with which Paul most regularly conceptualized

---

93. Tajfel, *Differentiation between Social Groups*, 28.

94. Esler, "Prototypes, Antitypes," 128.

95. This is a crucial part of social identity theory; Esler notes that in social identity theory, group members are "told who they should be and who they should not be." Esler, 4.

96. Esler, *Conflict and Identity*, 20.

97. Esler, "Prototypes, Antitypes," 128; *Conflict and Identity*, 20. Esler notes that group norms are broader than ethics, and hence in some instances peace and joy are viewed as group norms even though they are not ethics. He writes that group norms or identity descriptors "bring order and predictability to the environment, especially by narrowing down personal and social dispositions and moral choices from the vast range of possibilities on offer to those that accord with the group's sense of who and what it is." Esler, "Prototypes, Antitypes," 4; *Conflict and Identity*, 20–21. Similarly, Koelen and Van den Ban describe group norms as "a set of values which defines a range of acceptable and unacceptable attitudes and behaviours for members of a social unit." Contrary to ethics, scholars, by using the term "group norms," hope to capture three aspects in terms of what it means to be a group member: behaviour (how one should act as a group member), attitude (how one ought to feel and evaluate things), and beliefs (what we hold to be true and how we interpret the world). Koelen and Van den Ban, *Health Education*, 245.

98. Brookins and Longenecker, *1 Corinthians 1–9*, 4.

99. Dunn, *Theology of Apostle Paul*, 537.

the corporate identity of those converted in the Gentile mission."[100] When Paul first describes the Corinthians as the ἐκκλησία τοῦ θεοῦ... ἐν Κορίνθῳ, he speaks of them as an independent, autonomous entity that is located in Corinth, thus the locative dative is only for ἐν Κορίνθῳ in this verse (contrary to Ho's analysis, which extends the locative dative to refer also to ἐν Χριστῷ Ἰησοῦ). The fact that Paul emphasises to the Corinthians that they are the ἐκκλησία τοῦ θεοῦ is significant, particularly in the light of the identity issues that were facing the community in 1 Corinthians 1:10–12. In its analysis of these verses in section 4.3 of the previous chapter, this dissertation argued that at the heart of the intragroup conflict was the quest for belonging – social identity. The community was in conflict because different members of the group derived their identity from their preferred leaders. When Paul describes them as the ἐκκλησία τοῦ θεοῦ, ἡγιασμένοις ἐν Χριστῷ Ἰησοῦ, κλητοῖς ἁγίοις, he is doing more than just reminding them about their salient identity, he is also engaging in identity entrepreneurship.[101] The following section will now briefly consider this entrepreneurial enterprise in 1 Corinthians 1–4.

5.3.3.1 A Synopsis of Paul's Use of "in Christ" idiom as a Tool in His In-group Entrepreneurial Enterprise

Chapter 2 argued that for a leader to exert influence on the group, he or she has to do more than just be a prototype of in-group identity; the leader also has to be an entrepreneur of the in-group identity. He or she has to embody the group values and norms but also create a sense of "us." This section will now consider the interplay between these two roles in Paul – group prototype and entrepreneur of in-group identity – in the argument of 1 Corinthians 1–4. In chapter 2, leadership identity entrepreneurship was defined as the leader's ability to create a sense of shared identity, where a leader is able

---

100. Dunn, 537. For more on ἐκκλησία as a self-designation and group identity of Christ followers, see Trebilco, *Self-Designation*, 170–207. He notes that when it is used together with the genitive τοῦ θεοῦ, it stresses "God's initiative." Trebilco, 205. Linked with this and similar to Dunn's definition, Trebilco writes that in his use of the term ἐκκλησία, Paul: "sees all the assemblies as interconnected... he commends one assembly to another (1 Thess 1:7); he encourages one assembly to provide hospitality for visitors from other assemblies (Rom 12:13); he speaks of 'my rule in all the assemblies' (1 Cor 7:17) and of customs in 'the assemblies of God' (1 Cor 11:16)... and he can write of a common policy in all assemblies (1 Cor 4:17; 14:33)." Trebilco, 179–80.

101. For more on the idea of a leader as an entrepreneur of the in-group identity section, see chapter 2.

to make "different people all feel that they are part of the same group and increase cohesion and inclusiveness within the group."[102] In the ἐκκλησία that comprised people from different socioeconomic statuses,[103] Paul wants the in-group to draw their identity from God, not from their social or religious status.[104]

Paul further wants them to recognise that they are a part of a worldwide movement that has a unique identity, which he labels as "in Christ." Horrell correctly observes that this label "in Christ" is applied both to individuals, that is, Paul in 1 Corinthians 1:1, and to the group – ἡγιασμένοις ἐν Χριστῷ Ἰησοῦ, which in 1 Corinthians 1:2b is restricted to those that are geographically in Corinth.[105] However, in 1 Corinthians 1:2c, the "in Christ" label is used and also becomes the functional equivalent of the group identity – σὺν πᾶσιν τοῖς ἐπικαλουμένοις τὸ ὄνομα τοῦ κυρίου ἡμῶν Ἰησοῦ Χριστοῦ ἐν παντὶ τόπῳ αὐτῶν καὶ ἡμῶν.[106] The "in Christ" idiom also helps Paul in his entrepreneurial enterprise, particularly as it relates to the cognitive aspects of his identity formation agenda which is not limited only to 1 Corinthians 1:1–3, where he emphasises aspects of group identity. While space does not allow us to do an in-depth analysis of this phenomenon in 1 Corinthians 1–4, a short summary of Paul's group entrepreneurial enterprise will suffice for now.

From 1 Corinthians 1:18–31, Paul counters the Corinthians' preoccupation with wisdom and power, which has led to division in the ἐκκλησία, by reminding them of the gospel he proclaimed. The gospel that Paul has preached, by which the Corinthians came to be members of Christ's community, is about Christ crucified on behalf of others, thus an antithesis to their preoccupation with power and wisdom. The gospel was the antithesis of the secular wisdom and power as both the Jews and the Gentiles considered it weak and foolish. Thus, Paul's group entrepreneurial strategy targets both the cognitive aspect and evaluative aspect of the group's identity. This becomes

---

102. Steffens et al., "Leadership as Social Identity," 1004.

103. For more regarding the socioeconomic status of the early Christ followers at Corinth, see chapter 3 of this study. See also Punt, "1 Corinthians 7:17–24," 3; Meeks, *First Urban Christians*, 17–118; and Theissen, *Miracle Stories*, 106–10.

104. By religious statuses, this dissertation refers to the Jew-Gentile relationships that are the subject of 1 Cor 7. For more regarding that debate, see Punt's treatment of κλῆσις and related terminology in the argument of 1 Cor 7. Punt, "1 Corinthians 7:17–24," 3–9.

105. Horrell, "No Longer Jew or Greek," 15.

106. Horrell, 15.

apparent if one considers Paul's argument in 1 Corinthians 1–4 in the light of the salient social identity, as espoused by Tucker.[107] Paul's strategy here is to remind the Corinthians of God's rhetoric of reversal, where the patterns of worldly wisdom and power are reversed.[108] In 1 Corinthians 1:25, Paul reminds them that τὸ μωρὸν τοῦ θεοῦ σοφώτερον τῶν ἀνθρώπων ἐστίν, καὶ τὸ ἀσθενὲς τοῦ θεοῦ ἰσχυρότερον τῶν ἀνθρώπων. Further, in 1 Corinthians 1:26–31 Paul reminds the Corinthians how God used this rhetoric of reversal in bringing them to himself. In 1 Corinthians 1:26, he reminds them of their social status when God called them; ὅτι οὐ πολλοὶ σοφοὶ κατὰ σάρκα, οὐ πολλοὶ δυνατοί, οὐ πολλοὶ εὐγενεῖς. Of course, this does not mean that there were no members in the community that were wealthy or of noble birth,[109] rather, in his rhetorical strategy, Paul reminds the majority of the congregation about their social status prior to God's calling. Paul uses this rhetoric of reversal showing that τὰ μωρὰ τοῦ κόσμου ἐξελέξατο ὁ θεός, ἵνα καταισχύνῃ τοὺς σοφούς, καὶ τὰ ἀσθενῆ τοῦ κόσμου ἐξελέξατο ὁ θεός, ἵνα καταισχύνῃ τὰ ἰσχυρά. In this ἐκκλησία that was struggling with its sense of identity, Paul counters the temptation to derive their social identity from human patrons by reminding them how they became part of the community of God's people. It was through the preaching of the message about Christ crucified, the message that both Jews and Gentiles consider weak and foolish. But this message for the in-group is the power of God, and it is because of their acceptance of this message that they are the ἐκκλησία τοῦ θεοῦ. The fact that God chose or called mostly the people from poor socioeconomic backgrounds is in itself a demonstration of God's inversion of the human conventions of social status. What matters most is not one's social status, rather how one views

---

107. Tucker, *You Belong to Christ*, 153. For more on this, see footnote 23 of this chapter of this dissertation.

108. Malcolm, "Paul and Rhetoric," 160–63; Ellington, "Impulse towards Disadvantaged," 3.

109. See chapter 3 of this dissertation regarding the social status of the Pauline community at Corinth. See also Punt, "1 Corinthians 7:17–24," 3; Meeks, *First Urban Christians*, 117–18; Theissen, *Miracle Stories*, 106–10. The argument in that section was that the Pauline community at Corinth was composed of people from various socioeconomic and religious backgrounds, with the majority being people from the poor socioeconomic background, and fewer who were wealthy and powerful; hence, Paul uses the phrase "οὐ πολλοὶ" in his description of the community, in 1 Cor 1:26. These few wealthy and powerful members seem to have dominated the discourse within the ἐκκλησία, and Paul has to counter the influence of this group by reminding them how God works in calling people to himself. For more on the influence of the minority of wealthy and powerful members, see the previous chapter of this dissertation.

the cross. Pickett observes that Paul's message regarding the inversion of human wisdom and power was not only aimed at those who were from the lower socioeconomic bracket, it was also aimed at the minority of the community who were "wise" and "strong."[110] They may have engaged in hubristic activity. In a sense, they were engaging "in shaming and dishonouring those members of the community that they consider socially inferior (behaviour which is attested to by their criticism of Paul)."[111] What Paul is doing by using the rhetoric of reversal is in fact turning the tables on this group by showing that their actions were κατὰ σάρκα and belong to the category that has been shamed and annulled by God.[112] Due to the way in which Paul describes how God operates by using the shameful cross to accomplish his purposes, and in the process inverting the value system of the world, there are no grounds for boasting (1 Cor 1:29) except boasting in the Lord (1 Cor 1:31), for "God has undermined all grounds of human boasting."[113]

The other aspect of Paul's entrepreneurial strategy is evident in 1 Corinthians 3:5–7, regarding the way the group ought to perceive those in leadership positions. In 1 Corinthians 1:12, we read that the community was divided over preferences for different leaders, particularly, between Paul and Apollos. In 1 Corinthians 3:5–7, Paul corrects the wrong behaviour by reminding the ἐκκλησία that they belong neither to Paul nor to Apollos, since both of them count for nothing, as it is God who caused them to grow. Paul's use of the agricultural image brings this meaning to the fore, as, by describing his role as planting and Apollos's as watering, he drives home the point that it is God who causes the seed to germinate and, thus, he reduces the role that these leaders have in the ἐκκλησία. The agricultural metaphor evokes the reality of human agents in the identity formation of God's people, that is, they, "like agricultural laborers [sic], perform tasks which remain conditions for growth (not sources of growth)" (emphasis original).[114] The success of Paul and Apollos is entirely dependent on the life that God alone can give.[115] They are simply labourers, while God is the one who determines results.

---

110. Pickett, Cross in Corinth, 73.
111. Pickett, 73.
112. Pickett, 73.
113. Pickett, 74.
114. Thiselton, First Epistle to Corinthians, 302.
115. Button, "Leadership and Gospel," 45.

Paul's entrepreneurial strategy applied to how the Corinthians are to perceive their leaders comes to a conclusion in 1 Corinthians 4:1, where he writes: Οὕτως ἡμᾶς λογιζέσθω ἄνθρωπος ὡς ὑπηρέτας Χριστοῦ καὶ οἰκονόμους μυστηρίων θεοῦ (emphasis added). Thus, Paul wants the community cognitively to know (λογιζέσθω[116]) that they belong to God, and not to human leaders. They are the ἐκκλησία τοῦ θεοῦ, and the leaders are simply the labourers, servants, and stewards (1 Cor 3:5–9). The implication of this is that it will be foolish for the members of the community to derive their identity from the human leaders, or to continue in their factional behaviour, since it is God who ultimately caused them to become members of the group. To continue such behaviour would mean that the members of the community are not acting and thinking like members of the in-group, as that behaviour is in line with the characteristics of the out-group. In 1 Corinthians 3, Paul uses contrasting terms to distinguish in-group and out-group behaviour. The in-group behaviour is marked by being spiritual and being in Christ (1 Cor 3:1), while the out-group is marked as being human, worldly, childish, and fleshly. If the community continues in its factional battle regarding Paul and Apollos, that will mean that they are not acting in a manner that is consistent with their identity in Christ. It means that their behaviour will be more characteristic of Corinthian society – hence Paul will describe them as κατὰ ἄνθρωπον περιπατεῖτε, as being νηπίοις and σαρκικοί (1 Cor 3:1–3).[117]

This agricultural metaphor, together with the rhetoric of the cross as the inversion of human wisdom, is also related to the argument that was advanced by this dissertation in section 4.4 of chapter 4, regarding Paul's (re)presentation as a group prototype. While some members of the community apparently reject Paul's apostleship as it does not square up with their cultural expectations,[118] Paul's argument, particularly regarding the inversion of the human wisdom and power, is that at the core of the secular cultural value system is rejection of a fundamental aspect of their in-group identity. Thus, if

---

116. Brookins and Longenecker observe that this verb is used mostly as a verb "pertaining to mental activity." Brookins and Longenecker, *1 Corinthians 1–9*, 9.

117. For more on this factional behaviour as a characteristic of the out-group, see Winter, *After Paul Left Corinth*, 40–43.

118. Both section 4.3 and section 3.2.2 of this study dealt with the reasons why some members of ἐκκλησία in Corinth rejected Paul's apostleship. A major contributing factor to their rejection of Paul as their apostle resulted from the prevailing secular cultural influences upon the life of the ἐκκλησία.

anyone keeps insisting on judging Paul using a criterion which undermines a fundamental aspect of the in-group identity, that particular person might be in danger of losing his/her group membership, as such criteria have been nullified by God.[119] This becomes clearer when one considers Paul's evangelistic strategy that resulted in the formation of this community, which we encounter in 1 Corinthians 2:1–5. Winter notes that Paul's use of κἀγώ in 1 Corinthians 2:1 and 2:3 refers to his evangelism strategy, while Ciampa and Rosner note that the last time that Paul used the first-person singular in 1 Corinthians was in 1 Corinthians 1:17 when describing the gospel that he preached to the Corinthians.[120] For Ciampa and Rosner, what Paul is doing in 1 Corinthians 2:1–5 is simply picking up where he left off, and thus, 1 Corinthians 2:1–5 is viewed as forming a part of a long section that begins in 1 Corinthians 1:18 and ends in 1 Corinthians 2:16.[121] In 1 Corinthians 2:1–5, Paul argues that when he came to Corinth, he resolved to know nothing except Christ, and him crucified (1 Cor 2:2). Scholars such as Ciampa and Rosner, Thiselton, Winter, and Button have observed that Paul is being deliberate in 1 Corinthians 2:1–4 in contrasting his method of evangelism with that of the rhetoric and popular philosophy of the Sophists.[122] The Sophists were known for drawing attention to themselves and for trying to outwit each other with their rhetorical prowess. Paul chooses a different strategy; his emphasis is on Christ, and not even the glorified but the crucified Christ. There are two reasons that Paul chose this strategy, as given in 1 Corinthians 2:4–5: καὶ ὁ λόγος μου καὶ τὸ κήρυγμά μου οὐκ ἐν πειθοῖ σοφίας ἀλλ' ἐν ἀποδείξει πνεύματος καὶ δυνάμεως, 5 ἵνα ἡ πίστις ὑμῶν μὴ ᾖ ἐν σοφίᾳ ἀνθρώπων ἀλλ' ἐν δυνάμει θεοῦ (1 Cor 2:4–5, emphasis added). The first reason Paul chooses an evangelical strategy that endorses weakness, and not the words of wisdom, is that this strategy is in line with the in-group identity. In 1 Corinthians 1:18–31, Paul had already told the Corinthians that the message of the cross is foolishness to the out-group, but for the in-group it is the power of God. Paul does not use πειθοῖ σοφίας λόγοις because to use them would mean adopting a method

---

119. 1 Cor 1:20; 28.
120. Winter, *Philo and Paul*, 155; Ciampa and Rosner, First Letter *to Corinthians*, 113.
121. Ciampa and Rosner, 113.
122. Ciampa and Rosner, 114; Thiselton, *First Epistle to Corinthians*, 204; Winter, *Philo and Paul*, 155; Button, "Leadership and Gospel," 47.

that has been nullified by God (1 Cor 1:28),[123] the very same thing of which the Corinthians were guilty.[124] Worldly wisdom is not an acceptable strategy for Paul because it stands in opposition to the key tenets of the in-group, since people become members of the in-group through their acceptance of the message of Christ crucified.

The second reason that Paul chooses to know nothing except the crucified Christ when he comes to the Corinthians, is actually related to the imagery of agricultural labour that we have dealt with in this section. It was demonstrated that the growth of the community was entirely dependent on God, and not on the human leaders (1 Cor 3:5–7). Paul's strategy of coming in weakness and preaching about the crucified Christ serves to imply that the Corinthians' faith and identity may not rest on human wisdom, but on the power of God.[125] Incidentally, while Paul's evangelistic strategy may not be appealing to the world, it ought to have an opposite effect on the in-group, as it is in line with how God works. Paul's coming to the Corinthians in weakness (1 Cor 2:3) is actually in line with God's inversion of human wisdom and power. Since the cross is "folly" (1 Cor 1:18) and "an affront" (1 Cor 1:23), Paul, by embracing its weakness and adopting that weakness in his evangelical strategy, becomes an embodiment of the group core identity – thus a prototype of the in-group identity.

Thus far, this dissertation has argued that Paul, by using the "in Christ" language, has sought to bring about unity between himself and the group members – consensualization. In his use of this language, Paul sought to help the members of the community at Corinth to be aware of their salient identity "in Christ." More than this, Paul also uses the "in Christ" idiom as a means of presenting himself as a group prototype, and also as a tool towards his entrepreneurial enterprise. The "in Christ" vocabulary is not the only terminology that Paul employs to bring about positive self-identity in the group; as seen in

---

123. See Winter who argues that this is a reference to the philosophical tradition of the Sophists. Winter, *Philo and Paul*, 155–62.

124. See Witherington, who argues that the problem in Corinth was that the Corinthians thought that they could use the secular rhetorical categories to judge Paul, as this was a common practice for the Sophist philosophers. Witherington, *Conflict and Community in Corinth*, 47. Similarly, Pickett argues that the problem in the Corinthian ἐκκλησία was a result of the few members of the community who were wealthy and powerful, who insisted on judging Paul κατὰ σάρκα (1 Cor 3:1–4). Pickett, *Cross in Corinth*, 72–74.

125. Thiselton, *First Epistle to Corinthians*, 220; Button, "Leadership and Gospel," 47.

the first section of this chapter, Paul also draws on the sibling terminology to bring about the same desired outcome. The following section will investigate one more term that Paul employs to bring about positive social identity of the in-group, which aids him in his group entrepreneurial enterprise; this is the καλέω/κλῆσις terminology.

5.4 The Transition from "in Christ" idiom to the καλέω/ κλῆσις Terminologies in the Argument of 1 Corinthians 1:1–9

The focus of the previous section was on how the "in Christ" idiom functioned in the argument of 1 Corinthians 1:1–3, with particular attention being given to its grammatical function. The argument of this study is that Paul uses the instrumental dative ἐν Χριστῷ for the following reasons: (1) To remind the group about their salient identity in Christ. (2) To bring his identity and that of the Corinthians together by using the same identity descriptors. Previously, we have argued that in the context where there is conflict in the group, consensualization is possible if the members consider a topic to be dealing with core aspects of the in-group identity. Paul counters the whole issue of division in the community by using the ἐν Χριστῷ terminology. This allows him to draw into the discussion even the members of the community who no longer recognise him as their apostle. (3) The ἐν Χριστῷ terminology also helps Paul in his group identity entrepreneurial enterprise, as he uses this term to help the group know that they belong to God, not the human leaders. This section will now consider other identity descriptors that Paul uses to influence the group identity, particularly the καλέω/κλῆσις terminology. Again, our focus in the following section will be on the smaller section of 1 Corinthians 1:1–9, which is a representative section of the argument of 1 Corinthians 1–4.

In 1 Corinthians 1:2, we start to see the introduction of a further set of terminology that Paul uses to remind the ἐκκλησία of their in-group identity, namely the calling language. First Corinthians 1:2 reads: τῇ ἐκκλησίᾳ τοῦ θεοῦ, ἡγιασμένοις ἐν Χριστῷ Ἰησοῦ, τῇ οὔσῃ ἐν Κορίνθῳ, κλητοῖς ἁγίοις, σὺν πᾶσιν τοῖς ἐπικαλουμένοις τὸ ὄνομα τοῦ κυρίου ἡμῶν Ἰησοῦ Χριστοῦ ἐν παντὶ τόπῳ αὐτῶν καὶ ἡμῶν (emphasis added). There is a debate among scholars regarding how Paul uses κλῆσις/καλέω in his argument in 1 Corinthians. Is it intended in the theological sense (that is, referring only to what God has done for the group), in a social sense or both theologically and socially?[126] The stance assumed by this dissertation is that Paul uses the language both theologically and socially, It is to this dual use that we now turn. There are two significant points that scholars have noticed regarding Paul's use of the κλῆσις terminology in 1 Corinthians 1:2:

The first point has been observed by Fee, who argues that by using the calling language to describe the Corinthians, Paul is broadening their self-perspective.[127] Paul wants them to know that they are part of a bigger movement. By using the calling language, which echoes the Old Testament,[128] Paul wants the Corinthians to know that they are the eschatological people of God.[129] Fee writes that, "'calling on Yahweh' was a distinguishing feature of the people of God."[130] Here in 1 Corinthians 1:2 Paul changes the characteristics of the people of God from people who call on the "name of the Yahweh" to people who now call on the "name of Lord Jesus Christ."[131] What distinguishes the in-group (people who belong to God) now is that God has called them and that they also call on the name of the Lord Jesus Christ. In 1 Corinthians 1:10, Paul resorts to using the "name of the Lord Jesus Christ" as the basis of his appeal that the Corinthians should agree with one another and avoid division. This use of the "name of our Lord Jesus Christ" functions as the authority behind Paul's appeal.[132]

Second, by using the calling language in 1 Corinthians 1:2, Paul wants the group to evaluate their actions in the light of their salient identity in Christ. While the group is described according to what God has done in Christ,

---

126. For more details regarding this debate, see Punt, "1 Corinthians 7:17–24," 3–5; Plank, *Paul and Irony*, 24–31; Thiselton, *Thiselton on Hermeneutics*, 110–13; Ellington, "Impulse towards Disadvantaged." Punt and Ellington have correctly observed the weaknesses of the arguments by scholars who tend to emphasise the theological aspect of the calling language, that is, they drive "an unwarranted disjuncture between theological obedience and social responsibility." Punt, 3–4; Ellington, "Impulse towards Disadvantaged." Theological emphasis at the expense of social responsibilities can also be attributed to the negative application of the "third race theory" which was considered in chapter 1 of this dissertation.

127. Fee, *Pauline Christology*, 127–28.

128. Fee notes that in the Old Testament, "calling on the Lord's name" in the LXX was a reference to Yahweh, the God of Israel. Fee observes that Paul transfers this reference to the God of Israel to Christ (1 Cor 1:10; 5:3–4). Fee, *Pauline Christology*, 135.

129. Fee, 128; cf. Ho, "Cleanse Out Old Leaven," 298.

130. Gen 4:26; 12:8; 13:4; Joel 3:5 (both texts in the LXX).

131. Fee, *Pauline Christology*, 129.

132. Fee, 129.

that is, ἡγιασμένοις (perfect passive participle, meaning those that have been and continue to be sanctified)[133] ἐν Χριστῷ, Paul also adds a verbal adjective κλητοῖς [called to be[134]] ἁγίοις (saints). It is clear from these phrases that Paul wants the Corinthians to evaluate their conduct in line with their identity in Christ. Chester observes that the phrase "κλητοῖς ἁγίοις" has both cultic and ethical dimensions to it.[135] By cultic he refers to the process by which God sets people apart as his.[136] Thus, in this sense κλητοῖς ἁγίοις refers to the identity of the people. He argues that in the Old Testament, being called by God was intrinsically linked to being different from other people. They are called out or set apart by God to be his own people, who are to be different from others – they are called to be holy. Both Tucker and Ehrensperger argue that Paul's use of the "calling language as the language of community formation" signifies that the community is called by God to be in a relationship with himself, and to be in a relationship with the members of the in-group who are also called by God.[137] Tucker writes that Paul uses this language as an aid for his identity formation agenda, while Ehrensperger argues that Paul uses the calling language to remind and to inspire (in this case the Roman) believers to live holy lives, as they now belong to God who is holy

---

133. Systematic theological scholars are embroiled in a debate regarding the meaning of the perfect passive participle ἡγιασμένοις. For a systematic treatment of the debate, see Peterson, *Possessed by God*, 11–49. While there are important aspects of the doctrine of sanctification for this study, as "sanctification has to do with the identity and status of those who are 'in Christ,'" we are not going to engage in greater detail with this field of research as it extends beyond the current scope of this dissertation. Peterson, *Possessed*, 40. For now, we will simply highlight some of Peterson's insights into this field. Peterson notes the relationship between identity and the doctrine of sanctification when he writes that the doctrine of sanctification "also points to the lifestyle that is consistent with God's calling." Peterson, 40. The debate regarding sanctification is whether this is a once-off event or a continuous event. For example, how do we translate ἡγιασμένοις? Is it "'being sanctified,' which suggests an action in the past" (i.e. Collins) or is it "those who have been or continue to be sanctified" (Brookins and Longenecker)? Collins, *First Corinthians*, 46; Brookins and Longenecker, *1 Corinthians 1–9*, 4. Here, this dissertation follows Campbell's classification of the perfect participle as following an imperfective aspect; that is, as a process (i.e. Matt 5:10; Luke 6:25; and 19, 24), contra to the traditional view which sees sanctification as static, that is, the static aspect of the perfect passive participle ἡγιασμένοις. Brookins and Longenecker, 1 Corinthians, 4; Campbell, *Basics of Verbal Aspect*, 124.

134. For a defence of reading κλητοῖς as a verbal force that acts in a similar manner as a participle, see Brookins and Longenecker, 1 Corinthians *1–9*, 5.

135. Chester, *Conversion at Corinth*, 87–90.

136. Chester, 88.

137. Tucker, *Remain in Your Calling*, 67; Ehrensperger, "'Called to be Saints,'" 102.

(cf. Lev 19:2).[138] She writes, "One of the basic requirements of 'holiness' is separation and distinctive behaviour in relation to other peoples." She argues that Paul uses the calling language to remind the community of Christ-followers to develop an identity that is "distinct from this world." "Called to be saints" now becomes an identity marker that distinguishes Christ-followers from the rest of the world.[139] Thus, in 1 Corinthians 1:2, two identity-related issues are present: (1) Paul describes and reminds the community who they are, that is, they are "in Christ" and belong to Christ (this is predominantly how the "in Christ" language functions). (2) Paul also uses another identity descriptor, calling, but there is more to this language than just identity description; it also has aspects of entrepreneurship to it.[140] By employing the calling language, particularly the phrase κλητοῖς ἁγίοις, Paul brings to the fore behavioural aspects that are meant to be prominent characteristic features of the in-group identity. Finney has observed that Paul is unique among the New Testament authors in describing Christ's followers as the ἐκκλησία τοῦ θεοῦ.[141] This of course raises a question of what he is hoping to achieve by using such a description when referring to the Corinthians. For Finney, the significance of the calling language, as it relates to identity formation, is as follows: It is the call of God, mediated through the apostle, which establishes the Corinthian ἐκκλησία as an alternative society whose values are to "be understood only in relation to God himself."[142] This alternative society "represents his new

---

138. Tucker, 67; Ehrensperger, 102.

139. The social implications of the calling language together with the "in Christ" language are articulated well by Chester. Chester, *Conversion at Corinth*, 111–12. He writes, "The self-understanding urged on them by Paul, in which both they [Gentile Christians] and Jewish Christians had been called into fellowship with Christ, replaced ethnicity with faith in Christ as the boundary which defined the community. The alien other was no longer Jewish but unbelieving... The presumption is established that ethnic differences must not divide those who are in Christ." Chester, 111–12.

140. For more on a leader as the entrepreneur of the in-group identity, see section 2.5.3. There it was argued, using the findings of Haslam, that one of the key features of a leader is that he/she needs to be "an active constituent of the group, who is simultaneously involved in the defining of and defined by the group." Haslam, *Psychology in Organizations*, 47 (emphasis original). The argument this study is making here is that this is precisely what Paul is doing by employing the calling language.

141. Finney, "Christ Crucified and Inversion," 27. 1 Cor 1:2; 2 Cor 1:1.

142. Finney, 27–28.

creation and delineates the very matrix of his people" which stands "in stark opposition to the pax Romana (Roman peace)."[143]

The ethical implications (or observable norms)[144] of the calling language in 1 Corinthians 1:2 have been made clear by Thiselton.[145] He makes the following analogy in order to bring out the nuance of this phrase κλητοῖς ἁγίοις, when he writes: "Just as Joshua was called to 'possess' the land because he 'possessed' it as a divine gift (Josh 1:11–12), so believers are called to a lifestyle which reflects their already given status" (emphasis original).[146] Below, in section 5.5, we will revisit the significance of the calling language in Paul in conjunction with the ἐν Χριστῷ emphasis. It is worth noting for now that Paul employs this language, together with the "in Christ" idiom, as a boundary marker that separates the in-group from the out-group. Chester notes that by using the calling language, Paul "has developed a powerful conceptual tool by which to maintain the boundaries of the Christian community."[147] He further notes that this language acts as a tie that binds together the members of the in-group and which is stronger than any ties that the in-group might have with the out-group.[148]

At this juncture, it is important for us to lift out the key points of the argument that has been advanced in this section in the light of Tajfel's description of a group. In doing this summary, we hope that Paul's social identity formation agenda will become apparent. First, Paul wants the Corinthians to recognise (cognitive aspect) their identity in Christ in terms of what God has done for them in Christ. Second, he wants them to evaluate (the evaluative aspect) their lifestyle in line with what God has done for them in Christ. Third, by framing their identity in terms of what God has done for them in Christ, which is what sets them apart from other groups, we can say that he wanted them to connect emotionally with that identity. They have something

---

143. Finney, 27–28.

144. Observable norms are sometimes referred to as behaviour norms, and are defined as "*norms about* observable *behaviour (as opposed to attitudes, goals and beliefs, which are not directly observable, but can only be attributed to others on the basis of their behaviour)*" (emphasis original). Roitto, *Behaving as Christ-Believers*, 21.

145. Thiselton, *First Epistle to Corinthians*, 77.

146. Thiselton, 77.

147. Chester, *Conversion at Corinth*, 112.

148. Chester, 112.

that the rest of humanity does not have[149]; they are the people who have faith in God through Christ, they are the people who have their origins in God's action plan. They are special, because they are the recipients of God's grace (1 Cor 1:4) and also they have been called to have fellowship with the Son of God, Jesus Christ (1 Cor 1:9). According to the findings of social identity theory, the more an individual identifies with the group identity, the more likely he or she is to act in accordance with the group norms. Thus, it is very interesting to see that before Paul corrects the praxis of the Corinthians, he first reminds them who they are in Christ. He wants them to identify with Christ and be Christ-like. The emphasis of this dissertation thus far has been on the instrumental dative ἐν Χριστῷ. Our particular focus has been on how Paul, in his use of this instrumental dative, helps the in-group to be aware of their salient identity "in Christ." While the locative reading of the dative ἐν Χριστῷ has been rejected on grammatical grounds in this study, this does not mean that there is no aspect of association in Paul's use of ἐν Χριστῷ. As Tucker has correctly observed, the more the individual is aware of his/her salient identity, and the salient identity is rendered active, the more likely that salient identity will impact on that individual's behaviour.[150] Thus, the more the Corinthians are aware of what God has done for them through Christ, the more likely does it become that they are going to identify with their "in Christ" identity. Samra's work is helpful at this point regarding the nuances of how we ought to use the term "identify with Christ."[151] To identify with Christ does not mean that Paul wants the believers to "equate" themselves with Christ or consider themselves "identical" with Christ. Rather, identifying with Christ is used "in the sense of 'associating [oneself] very closely or inseparably with,' so that 'identifying with Christ' indicates a process of strengthening one's conscious association with Christ or strengthening one's self-categorization as a believer in Christ and a member of the Christ-group." Samra's point here, while it might appear to support the locative use of the dative ἐν Χριστῷ, actually works for the instrumental use as well, if one considers the fact that Paul's purpose in using this instrumental dative is so that the community

---

149. For more on this, see see footnote 217 of page 203 in chapter 4 of this dissertation which talks about Paul's use of the πιστ-word group. It was argued there that Paul uses that word group as a designation of the in-group identity.

150. Tucker, *You Belong to Christ*, 153.

151. Samra, *Being Conformed to Christ*, 113.

might be aware of their salient in-group identity. Thus, if the group's salient identity in Christ is activated, that will result in "one's conscious association with Christ" being strengthened. Samra further argues that Paul does not want the Corinthians to "think of themselves as Christ, but to be unable or unwilling to conceive of themselves without also thinking of Christ and their relationship to Christ and other believers in Christ."[152] This way of thinking was obviously absent in the Corinthians' thinking, and Paul has to remind them of who they are in Christ. In his closing argument of 1 Corinthians 2, he reminds them that they have the mind of Christ.

5.4.1 The Significance of καλέω/κλῆσις Terminology in the Argument of 1 Corinthians

In the previous section, we considered the idea that Paul uses both the "in Christ" and the κλῆσις terminology as boundary markers for the in-group. This section will investigate further the significance of the κλῆσις terminology for his identity formation agenda in 1 Corinthians. Both Finney and Chester note that Paul uses a variety of terminologies to denote the new identity in Christ, with the κλῆσις terminology apparently dominating the words that he uses to describe the new identity in Christ.[153] They note that the κλῆσις terminology occurs around 37 times in the "uncontested Pauline letters". The verb καλέω appears 27 times (including the one instance where it refers to an invitation to a meal, in 1 Corinthians 10:27); the noun κλῆσις appears 4 times;[154] and the adjective κλητός appears 7 times.[155] The major-

---

152. Samra, 113.
153. Finney, "Conflict in Corinth," 27–32; Chester, *Conversion at Corinth*, 59–112.
154. Rom 11:29; 1 Cor 1:6; 7:20; and Phil 3:14.
155. Rom 1:1; 1:6; 1:7; 8:28; 1 Cor 1:1; 1:2; and 1:24; Chester, *Conversion at Corinth*, 60. Donahoe provides a wonderful summary of Chester's extensive work on the different uses of καλέω, κλητός, and κλῆσις in Paul. Donahoe, "From Self-Praise," 80; Chester, 59–112. She notes that Paul primarily uses words such as καλέω, κλητός, and κλῆσις in reference to the divine calling, "with an emphasis on God's initiative." In texts such as Rom 1:1, 6, 7; 8:28; 1 Cor 1:1, 2, 24, Paul uses κλητός to refer to God's calling of people to be something else, that is, saints or an apostle. κλῆσις is used for the divine call (Rom 11:29; Eph 1:18; 4:1; Phil 3:14; 2 Thess 1:11; 2 Tim 1:9) or to a station in life (1 Cor 7:20). On the other hand, while Καλέω does refer to the divine calling, its "meaning extends beyond the divine." She also notes that: "It speaks of the act of God's calling (Rom 4:17; 8:30; 9:12, 24, 25; 1 Cor 1:9; Gal 1:6, 15; 5:8; Eph 4:4; 1 Thess 4:7; 5:24; 2 Thess 2:14; 2 Tim 1:9) and can carry the implication to live a certain lifestyle (1 Cor 7:15, 17; Gal 5:13; Eph 4:1; Col 3:15; 1 Thess 2:12; 1 Tim 6:12)." Donahoe, "From Self-Praise," 80. Another important meaning of καλέω and κλῆσις for this dissertation is that it is also used to refer to the religious or socioeconomic situation of the called individual (1 Cor 7:18, 20–22, 24).

ity of the κλῆσις terminology appears in 1 Corinthians, 16 times to be precise.[156] Looking at this statistical analysis, we can see that the bulk of the use of the κλῆσις terminology appears mostly in 1 Corinthians 1 and 7.[157] Our focus in this dissertation on Paul's use of the κλῆσις terminology will be on 1 Corinthians 1. In 1 Corinthians 1:1–2 we see that the κλῆσις terminology is a key identity descriptor of Paul and of the Corinthians. It is what sets the in-group apart from the out-group. Tucker notes that the κλῆσις terminology in 1 Corinthians 1:1–2 is a "foundational ordering principle in the formation of a salient identity 'in Christ.'"[158] Paul's vocation as an apostle, as well as his self-identity as well as that of the Corinthians, is established in God's calling. Horrell notes that in 1 Corinthians 9:1; 15:8; and Galatians 1:12–6, Paul links his calling, which is a foundation for his commissioning as an apostle to the Gentiles, with him seeing the risen Christ.[159] Using the finding of Stendahl, Horrell is quick to point out that Paul's calling must not be understood as conversion, as if he changed one religion for the other, but should rather be seen in the light of vocational commissioning, in the same vein as those of Jeremiah and Isaiah.[160] Horrell's contention is that the κλῆσις terminologies in Paul need to be understood in the light of the Jewish symbolic universe.

The following section will investigate in what ways God's calling has influenced Paul's apostolic self-consciousness. In the previous chapter, it was observed that some scholars, for example Castelli, are very critical of Paul's apostolic defence and his call to the community to imitate him.[161] Castelli presents Paul as if he were an egomaniac who wanted to centralise power to

---

This last meaning is especially important in our discussion of κλῆσις in 1 Cor 1:26 since it refers to the social status of the Corinthians at the time of their calling. This is important as it raises a question whether previous identities have any role to play in the new identity that is defined by being in Christ (cf. 1 Cor 7:17–24).

156. Chester, *Conversion at Corinth*, 60. See 1 Cor 1:1, 2, 6, 9, 24, 26; 7:15, 17, 18 (twice), 20–22 (twice), 24; 15:9.

157. With regard to the use of the κλῆσις terminology in 1 Cor 7, this study agrees with Tucker that Paul's use of this language in this chapter signifies that the previous existing identities are not completely obliterated by the new identity in Christ, rather they continue in "a transformed manner." Tucker, *You Belong to Christ*, 131.

158. Tucker, 131.

159. Horrell, "Paul," 262.

160. Horrell, 262; Stendahl, *Paul among Jews and Gentiles*, 7–23. See Isa 49:1–6; Jer 1:5; cf. Gal 1:12–16. For more on the discussion regarding whether κλῆσις is used by Paul to refer to his conversion, see Appendix 2.

161. Castelli, Imitating *Paul*.

himself, and did not allow dissension within his community. Sections 4.4.1.1 to 4.4.1.3.2 dealt with the scholars who were critical of Paul's apostolic discourse, and in those sections it was argued that a positive reading of Paul's apostolic discourse would be adopted in this study.

This study is of the view that Paul is far from being an egomaniac in his apostolic discourse, as the motivation for his apostolic defence is not power or greed, but the gospel. Thus, the following section revisits the discussion of section 4.4.2, with the view of demonstrating that there is indeed an interrelationship between leadership and identity in 1 Corinthians 1–4. This interrelationship is much more prominent in Paul's apostolic defence. However, since the scholars who are critical of Paul's apostolic discourse also allude to other Pauline texts to make their case, it is critical for the following section also to do a cross-reference to Galatians so that it can establish that this interrelationship is not an isolated occurrence in 1 Corinthians. First Corinthians and Galatians are the two texts where Paul defends his apostleship energetically. The argument of this section is that Paul had to defend his apostleship because the identity of Jesus's followers was at stake. In both these texts, the community was facing outside influences, which in Paul's opinion led to a compromise of their identity in Christ.

5.5 The Influence of the ἐν Χριστῷ and κλῆσις Terminologies in Paul's Apostolic Self-consciousness in Galatians and 1 Corinthians

Scholars such as Best and Keay have indicated texts such as Galatians 1:1 and 1 Corinthians 1:1; 15, in which Paul argues vigorously that his apostleship did not derive from any human commissioning.[162] Paul writes: Παῦλος ἀπόστολος, οὐκ ἀπ' ἀνθρώπων οὐδὲ δι' ἀνθρώπου ἀλλὰ διὰ Ἰησοῦ Χριστοῦ καὶ θεοῦ πατρὸς τοῦ ἐγείραντος αὐτὸν ἐκ νεκρῶν (Gal 1:1).

It is worth noting at this point that there is a debate regarding why, in Galatians 1:1, Paul stresses the divine origins of his apostolic calling. Both Keay and Taylor suggest that this statement means that at this point Paul ceased to be an apostle of the Antioch ἐκκλησία.[163] In section 4.4.1, we pro-

---

162. Best, "Paul Apostolic Authority," 3–25; Keay, "Paul the Spiritual Guide," 16.
163. Keay, 16; Taylor, "Apostolic Identity and Conflicts," 103–04.

vided reasons why it disagrees with their assertion. This dissertation is of the view that what motivated Paul to defend his apostleship is not the fact that he had ceased to be an apostle of the ἐκκλησία of Antioch,[164] but the conflicts, both the ones reported in Galatians and in 1 and 2 Corinthians, which stemmed from the community's failure to understand their identity in Christ. In both conflicts, Paul is not primarily concerned to establish his authority with the ἐκκλησία (contrary to Taylor);[165] rather he is concerned with defending his apostolic identity, as it is linked to his personal identity and that of his community, which is in line with the in-group ideological belief system. Brinsmead, for example, argues convincingly that in Galatians Paul is not only concerned with establishing his authority, but also with defending the authenticity of the gospel that he preaches.[166]

While the focus of this study is on 1 Corinthians, Galatians is also being considered for two reasons: (1) Most scholars who are critical of Paul's apostolic defence and who tend to present Paul as an egomaniac, use Galatians as well in their analysis, and argue that in both 1 Corinthians and Galatians, Paul uses his apostolic defence to suppress dissension. (2) Galatians is important for this dissertation in order to demonstrate that the interrelationship between leadership and identity is not an isolated occurrence that is present only in 1 Corinthians, but recurs in other parts of the Pauline corpus. Thus, the present interest in Galatians is to demonstrate that there is a link between leadership and identity, particularly as it relates to Paul's apostolic consciousness. Moreover, in both 1 Corinthians and Galatians what becomes apparent is that Paul views both his identity and commissioning to be an apostle, as having their origin in God.

In section 5.3.3 of this chapter, we demonstrated that one of Paul's points of emphasis in 1 Corinthians 1:1–3 is that Christ's followers at Corinth also have their origins in the call of God. Thus, we see this link between Paul's identity and apostolic defence, and the identity of Christ's followers. A similar

---

164. Halcomb suggests that Paul wrote Galatians while he was in Antioch, and that Paul's phrase καὶ οἱ σὺν ἐμοὶ πάντες ἀδελφοί in Gal 1:2 should be seen as Paul claiming that the church in Antioch can "vouch for him, that is, he is an apostle sent by God and that what follows in the letter is true." Halcomb, *Paul the Change Agent*, 104.

165. Taylor, "Apostolic Identity and Conflicts"; "Conflict as Context."

166. Brinsmead, *Galatians*, 50–51. Brinsmead writes, "throughout the letter, arguments about the gospel are bound up with arguments about apostleship, and the two cannot be separated." Brinsmead, 50.

pattern of thinking can also be observed in Galatians. In this letter it is clear that Paul argues that his identity, the gospel that he preaches, as well his apostleship have their origin in God and not κατά ἄνθρωπον (Gal 1:1; 1:11). Paul is not an egomaniac who has to defend his apostolic authority (contrary to Castelli);[167] rather he has to defend his apostleship because that is bound up together with the gospel he preaches, and the identity of his community.

A similar point was argued for in section 5.3.3.1 when this dissertation considered Paul's evangelistic strategy in 1 Corinthians 2:1–5. Paul demonstrates that, while his evangelistic modus operandi might be rejected by those on the outside (because he came to the Corinthians in weakness and did not use words of wisdom), it is actually in line with how God works in saving his people, which is through the foolishness of the preaching of the message of the cross.[168] It will be amiss, however, for this study to focus on 1 Corinthians 1:10–4:21 as if it deals only with Paul's apostolic modus operandi. Such an emphasis, which views 1 Corinthians 1:10–4:21 as Paul's apologia, is the hallmark of the older scholars such as Dahl, Carter, and Fee.[169] In this chapter, we have argued that in 1 Corinthians 1:10–4:21 Paul also seeks to present himself as a group prototype, and that pointing the Corinthians to his modus operandi serves the similar purpose.

Donahoe correctly observes that in 1 Corinthians 1:10–4:21, Paul does not only present himself as the group example [prototype], he also presents Apollos as one.[170] She further argues that the reason that Paul presents himself and Apollos as the group examples is to counteract the Corinthians' "improper 'boasting' and divisive allegiance to specific leaders."[171] Donahoe's observations tally with recent scholarly developments, which have observed that in 1 Corinthians Paul is dealing with broader issues, which are crucial for the group to function well. Primarily among these is the issue of group unity.[172]

White and Donahoe, in agreement with chapter 3 of this dissertation, have argued that the reasons for the schism in the community are the influence

---

167. Castelli, *Imitating Paul*.
168. 1 Cor 1:18–31.
169. Dahl, *Studies in Paul*, 313–35; Carter, "Big Men in Corinth," 45–71; Fee, *First Epistle to Corinthians*, 156.
170. Donahoe, "From Self-Praise," 76.
171. Donahoe, 76.
172. 1 Cor 1:10–12; Donahoe, 75.

of the general Greek Roman culture among the members of the community.[173] Paul seeks to counteract this cultural influence upon the group life by reminding the Corinthians of the message that he has preached, and which is the foundation on which they became members of the group. However, in reminding them of his gospel message in 1 Corinthians 1:18–31, Paul also establishes a link between his gospel message and the identity of the Corinthians. The message that Paul preaches, and which the Corinthians accept, is, however, at odds with ἡ σοφία τοῦ κόσμου, as the world considers foolishness ὁ λόγος ὁ τοῦ σταυροῦ. By implication, a continuous use of ἡ σοφία τοῦ κόσμου in judging group leaders (cf. 1 Cor 4:8–13) is at odds with the community's identity "in Christ," because the ἡ σοφία τοῦ κόσμου has been nullified by God (1 Cor 1:20).

The argument of this dissertation has been that Paul's apostolic defence in 1 Corinthians needs to be seen in the light of his identity formation agenda, where Paul helps the Corinthians by reminding them of the salient features of their group identity. To that end, Paul used terminology such as ἐν Χριστῷ, κλῆσις, and ὁ λόγος ὁ τοῦ σταυροῦ. However, these three identity descriptors, used to remind the Corinthians who they are so that they can evaluate whether their actions are in line with their identity, are intrinsically linked with Paul's own apostolic identity. God, in Jesus Christ, called Paul to preach a message, the core aspect of which was about Christ crucified. The Corinthians accepted the message as the power of God, but the world rejected it as foolishness. Paul's weakness, according to the world's standard, actually does not discredit him, as it is in line with how God operates. Thus, Paul's apostleship is actually in line with the in-group identity as they are both (his evangelistic strategy and the message he preaches) considered foolish by the world.

While the ἐκκλησία in Galatians was facing a different situation to that of the one in Corinth, there are areas of similarity when it comes to Paul's apostolic defence. The issue in Galatians is that the opponents of Paul not only discredit his apostleship, they also do not accept the gospel that Paul preaches, which is the same gospel that is taught by the Jerusalem believers.[174] Du Toit notes that throughout Galatians, Paul juxtaposes the authentic "gospel"

---

173. White, *Where Is the Wise Man?*, 71; Donahoe, 75–76.
174. See: Gal 2:15–21; Brinsmead, Galatians, 50.

(εὐαγγέλιον) and a false or contrary "gospel."[175] God's calling "in the grace of Christ" (1.6), "the gospel of Christ" (1:7) or "the gospel that was preached by me" (1:11) is juxtaposed against "a different gospel" (1:6), "a gospel contrary to the one we preached to you" (1:8), the gospel "you received" (1:9) or "man's gospel" (1:11). While in Galatians there is juxtaposition between the authentic gospel and the false one, in 1 Corinthians 1:18–31 and 4:8–13, Paul's juxtaposition is between σοφία and μωρία and their diverse associations.[176] As already observed, in these passages Paul distinguishes between "worldly wisdom," "worldly power," and "God's wisdom" and "God's power" (1 Cor 1:18–31).

Paul's motivation for his apostolic defences in Galatians and 1 Corinthians for that matter are linked to his desire that Christ-followers should live according to the gospel or act in a manner that is consistent with their "in Christ" identity. The argument of this dissertation is that Paul's apostolic defence is intertwined with his identity formation agenda. Scholars such as Hall, Hester, Kennedy, and Smit have also adequately demonstrated that in Galatians Paul is seeking to persuade the Galatians to conform to his interpretation of the gospel,[177] while Aune and Lyons argue that in Galatians he seeks to portray himself as a group example.[178] A group example and the group prototype are similarly aligned. We have argued that Paul, in his use of the "in Christ" and calling language, sought to present himself as a group prototype; more than that, he also uses this language to shape the group behaviour. Thus, it could be argued that both in 1 Corinthians and in Galatians Paul's strategy is to present himself as a group prototype and as the entrepreneur of the in-group identity.

Paul's defence of his apostolic identity and his gospel are important for his identity formation agenda, as the gospel is the basis by which people become members of the community, and apostleship is linked to Paul's group prototypicality. In 1 Corinthians, Paul centres his identity formation agenda around the "in Christ" idiom, i.e., those who are "in Christ" (insiders) over against those who consider the Christ event as foolishness (outsiders), while in Galatians the contrast between the insiders and the outsiders is described in terms of the "Spirit–flesh" contrast, "God–man" contrast, and "faith-works"

---

175. Du Toit, "Galatians 3," 20; Gal 1:6–11.

176. Whites, *Where Is the Wise Man?*, 71.

177. Hall, "Historical Inference"; Hester, "Placing the Blame," 282; Kennedy, *New Testament Interpretation*, 146; Smit, "Letter of Paul," 23.

178. Aune, *New Testament*, 189–90; Lyons, *Pauline Autobiography*, 175–76; cf. Gal 4:12–20.

contrast.[179] Du Toit notes that, "The Spirit-flesh contrast, which converges with the faith-works contrast as well as the contrast between the new era in Christ and the old era under the Law, is (sic) argued to be the controlling paradigm for determining identity and covenant membership in the letter."[180] Both 1 Corinthians 1:1 and Galatians 1:1 are important for Paul's apostolic self-consciousness and his identity formation agenda. In both texts, Paul understood his apostolic identity as having its origin in Christ Jesus, also that the identity of his audience has its origin in God's calling through Christ Jesus.

In Galatians 1:1, Paul is emphatic in his statement about his apostolic call/commissioning. He first puts it negatively; twice Paul emphasises his apostleship is οὐκ ἀπ' ἀνθρώπων and οὐδὲ δι' ἀνθρώπου. In the first part of verse 1, Paul uses two different propositions (ἀπ' ἀνθρώπων and δι' ἀνθρώπου) which introduces his denial that his apostleship has its origins in human beings (οὐκ ἀπ' ἀνθρώπων). He also denies that his apostolic mission was mediated through any human beings (οὐδὲ δι' ἀνθρώπου).[181] Paul then adds ἀλλὰ, which acts as a strong contrast in order to highlight the origins and agency of his apostleship. Then he states his identity positively: διὰ Ἰησοῦ Χριστοῦ καὶ θεοῦ πατρὸς τοῦ ἐγείραντος αὐτὸν ἐκ νεκρῶν. It has its origin [διὰ] θεοῦ πατρὸς, and was achieved διὰ Ἰησοῦ Χριστοῦ. While the negative emphasis is absent in 1 Corinthians, in 1 Corinthians 1:1, nonetheless Paul states his identity positively and emphatically, that κλητὸς ἀπόστολος Χριστοῦ Ἰησοῦ διὰ θελήματος θεοῦ.[182] Incidentally, while in 1 Corinthians Paul mentions God's will in relation to his being called to be an apostle, in Galatians God's will is mentioned with regard to God our Father's ultimate agency in the saving work that is done by Jesus Christ, even though in Galatians 1:3–5 the emphasis is on Christ's sacrificial self-giving of himself for our sins. Best observes that the phrase "Christ gave himself up" is analogous to the Christological statement of Galatians 1:1, which focuses on what God the Father has done to Jesus.[183] Hence, the argument that was made earlier in this dissertation

---

179. Du Toit, "Galatians 3," 1; Lyons, 125.

180. Du Toit, 1.

181. De Silva, Galatians, 2.

182. See Brookins and Longenecker, who observe that κλητὸς together with διὰ θελήματος θεοῦ indicates that there is a verbal force in κλητὸς. Brookins and Longenecker, *1 Corinthians 1–9*, 1–2.

183. Best, "Paul's Apostolic Authority," 3–25.

regarding Christ as an instrument that God uses to achieve his purposes still stands even here in Galatians. Both Galatians 1:1 and 1:4 emphasise that what Christ has done was κατὰ τὸ θέλημα τοῦ θεοῦ καὶ πατρὸς ἡμῶν. Thus, both 1 Corinthians 1:1–3 and Galatians 1:1–4 highlight the divine origin of Paul's apostleship and the Pauline community in both places. Section 5.4 of this dissertation, using Tajfel's observations regarding what makes groups function well, argue that the divine origins of the group identity has enormous impact on both the cognitive and evaluative aspects of group membership. It makes the members of the in-group feel special, as they view themselves as people whose identity originates in God. A similar point could also be argued regarding Galatians 1:1–4.

Particularly in its analysis of 1 Corinthians, this dissertation has striven towards establishing the link between Paul's apostolic defence and his identity formation agenda. A similar point could also be made regarding Galatians. There are features in Galatians that demonstrate that Paul's apostolic defence needs to be seen in the light of his identity formation agenda.[184] Lyons notes that, "the underlying 'God – man [sic]' contrast is a significant antithesis throughout the letter."[185] What is interesting in Galatians is that Paul uses similar words to define both his apostolic identity and the gospel he preached.[186]

In Galatians 1:11–12, Paul asserts:

Γνωρίζω γὰρ ὑμῖν, ἀδελφοί, τὸ εὐαγγέλιον τὸ εὐαγγελισθὲν ὑπ' ἐμοῦ ὅτι οὐκ ἔστιν κατὰ ἄνθρωπον·οὐδὲ γὰρ ἐγὼ παρὰ ἀνθρώπου παρέλαβον αὐτό, οὔτε ἐδιδάχθην, ἀλλὰ δι' ἀποκαλύψεως Ἰησοῦ Χριστοῦ.

Both his gospel and his apostleship originate from God and thus the two are bound together. More than this, Paul wants the Galatians to know that their identity in Christ has its origin in God.

---

184. Appendix 3 considers Paul's apostolic defence in Galatians in greater detail, particularly in the light of the problems that besieged the community.

185. Lyons, *Pauline Autobiography*, 125.

186. Mitchell makes a correct observation that Paul uses the term gospel as shorthand rhetorical technique, which captures all that God has done for his people in Christ. Mitchell, "Rhetorical Shorthand," 64–69. The term gospel encapsulates central elements of Christ's work on behalf of his people, such as "Christ's suffering and death; his sacrifice 'for us'; his cross; his being raised from the dead (or rising from the dead); his appearance; his coming again in the future." Koester, *Ancient Christian Gospel*, 6–7.

5.6 Conclusion

The main objective of this chapter was to do an exegesis of 1 Corinthians 1–4, in order to demonstrate that there is an interrelationship between leadership and identity. While the focus of this chapter was on 1 Corinthians 1, this study was cognisant that 1 Corinthians 1 forms part of the broader section of 1 Corinthians 1–4. The reason that this dissertation focuses mostly on 1 Corinthians 1 was that the argument of this section is indicative of the broader argument of 1 Corinthians 1–4, and when appropriate, we demonstrated this point by looking at the broader section which is 1 Corinthians 1–4.

The reason that we scrutinised the Greek grammatical analysis in 1 Corinthians 1:1–9 was that, as has been argued in section 5.2, these verses do not merely act as a letter opening, but also contain the material that Paul unpacks in the rest of the letter. As such, when this dissertation isolated a theme in these verses, a concerted effort was made to show how that particular theme was developed through the rest of the letter.

This study observed that in the opening verses of 1 Corinthians 1, there are three identity descriptors that Paul employs. These are ἀδελφός, ἐν Χριστῷ Ἰησοῦ, and κλῆσις terminologies. We argued that these identity descriptors accord well with the three features that Tajfel considers necessary in order for the group to function well, which are cognitive, evaluation, and emotional factors.[187]

Paul also uses these three identity descriptors in order for the consensualization process to take place. This process in his social identity agenda was first introduced in this dissertation in chapter 4, where it was argued that Paul uses the identity descriptors in order to draw the members of the group into the conversation, which is about group identity. It is important for Paul to capture the attention of group members and for him to use terminology that draws in the group members from the beginning of the letter, as some members of the group had already rejected him as their apostle.

This chapter reviewed the scholarly treatment of the ἐν Χριστῷ Ἰησοῦ terminologies extensively, as also the grammatical analysis of 1 Corinthians 1:1–3, particularly as it relates to ἐν Χριστῷ Ἰησοῦ terminologies and to a limited extent the κλῆσις terminologies. The reason for this strong focus

---

187. Tajfel, *Differentiation between Social Groups*, 28.

on the ἐν Χριστῷ Ἰησοῦ terminologies is that they provide the key to Paul's social identity agenda.

This dissertation argued that ἐν Χριστῷ Ἰησοῦ functions as an instrumental dative in the argument of 1 Corinthians 1, and it highlights God's plan in forming this community and using Christ in achieving his purposes. By highlighting God's activity in the identity formation of the community, Paul seeks to bring about positive feelings regarding group membership. These are special people who have been chosen by God in Christ Jesus, and they constitute a group that has something that the rest of humanity does not have, viz., faith in Jesus Christ. While this group comprises mostly people from poorer social economic backgrounds, they are on the right side of history because they are on the side that understands how God operates. Through the cross of Jesus, God rejected human wisdom and power; in fact, the cross nullified them. The ἐν Χριστῷ Ἰησοῦ terminology, together with the message about the cross, becomes a tool in Paul's social identity agenda. Paul uses the cross and the ἐν Χριστῷ Ἰησοῦ terminology in order to show which values are acceptable within the community, and thus he uses them for his identity entrepreneurial enterprise.

While Galatians is not the main focus of this dissertation, a comparative look at Paul's apostolic defence in this letter was necessary for this dissertation, on two grounds: (1) It assists in framing my position which counteracts the view that seems to be gaining traction in scholarship, which tends to present Paul as an egomaniac whose interest is to suppress dissension. (2) Galatians was important in order to validate the argument of this dissertation that there is an interrelationship between leadership and identity. Both 1 Corinthians 1–4 and Galatians demonstrate that the motivation for Paul's apostolic defence was that some members of the community were beginning to challenge his apostleship, but in so doing they were unfortunately using categories that were not in line with the "in Christ" identity. In his defence, Paul reminds them of their salient identity "in Christ," an identity that has its origins in the call of God, which was achieved through the cross, something that both Jews and Gentiles consider foolish. However, the in-group members consider the cross to be the wisdom of God and the power of God. If the people keep on judging Paul using the value systems of the world, they put the community's well-being at risk, as God has nullified and shamed the wisdom of the world.

CHAPTER 6

Summary and Conclusion

This study has argued that there is an interrelationship between leadership and identity in 1 Corinthians 1–4. In order to argue for that hypothesis, this study was placed within the context of the current studies that have been done on the subject of leadership and identity in Paul. This was the focus of chapter 1. The following section will now do a brief synopsis of chapter 1 and subsequent chapters, and highlight some of the findings that were observed.

6.1 Summary and Findings of Chapter 1

In building its case regarding the interrelationship between leadership and identity, chapter 1 proposed a rationale for the entire study, in order to argue for the position it took concerning the subject of leadership and identity in 1 Corinthians 1–4. This study ventured into an interface between two fields of studies – leadership studies and identity studies. Thus, chapter 1 had two major sections: leadership in Paul (section 1.2.1), and identity formation in Paul (section 1.2.2).

6.1.1 Current Trends in Leadership Studies

The first section focused first on the current trends in leadership studies in general, and a number of observations were made regarding the nature of leadership studies:

(1) Western scholars with a Western worldview dominate leadership studies. The result of this is that leadership studies tend to be anthropocentric by nature, to the extent that they exaggerate the role of a leader and diminish the role of God. While the role of a leader is important, there seems

to be a level of incongruence between current leadership theories and the teachings of the apostle Paul on this matter. For example, in his teachings Paul tends to exaggerate the role of God in the formation of the life of the group, while downplaying the role of human leaders, himself included.[1] This emerges clearly when one considers the centrality of the "in Christ" identity in the argument of Paul, and also when one considers the inversion of human wisdom and power in Paul's emphasis on the centrality of the cross for the identity of the Corinthians, which was part of the main argument of chapter 5. Thus, Paul's teachings tend to be theocentric by nature, while current theories tend to be essentially anthropocentric. This difference in emphasis between Paul's theocentrically styled leadership and twenty-first century leadership theories, however, is not an occurrence resulting from (post)modern day thinking by twenty-first century scholars. Clarke has observed that this difference in emphasis existed between Paul's leadership approaches and those of his contemporaries in the Greco-Roman world.[2] Thus, for Clarke, Paul's leadership needs to be viewed through the lens of Paul being against "worldly" leadership, that is, Paul wanted to counter the secular influences upon the life of the congregation.[3] While we agree with some aspects of Clarke's analysis, we argue that, rather than Paul simply wanting to counter secular influences upon the life of the ἐκκλησία τοῦ θεοῦ, his leadership emphasis needs to be seen in light of his identity formation agenda. Hence, the emphasis of this study is on the interrelationship between leadership and identity.

(2) The second observation that was made in chapter 1 is that in its approach to the subject of leadership in Paul, biblical scholarship tends to get bogged down with word studies approaches. Biblical scholarship tends to look at the absence or the limited use of the Greek words, such as ἄρχων, ἡγούμενος, στρατήγιον, and προστάτης, together with their compounds in the Pauline corpus, and debate whether it is appropriate to talk about leadership in the Pauline corpus, since Paul seldom used these Greek terms to describe leaders in the early Jesus Christ movement. The argument that was made was that the lack of Paul's use of the equivalent Greek terms regarding leadership, does not mean that Paul does not deal with the subject of leadership.

---

1. 1 Cor 1:26–31; 2:1–5; 3:5–23; 4:1–7.
2. Clarke, *Secular and Christian Leadership*, 109.
3. Clarke, 109.

(3) The third observation of chapter 1 concerned the scholarly approaches to the subject of leadership in Paul. It was observed that scholars adopt three approaches, and their strengths and weaknesses were highlighted. These approaches are: (a) the traditional approach, which is also known as the Holtzmann-Sohm hypothesis; (b) the socioscientific approach; and (c) the integrated, group-based approaches, which incorporates the findings of both the traditional and the socioscientific approach. In its methodology, this dissertation follows the integrated group-based approach, with an emphasis on the socioscientific approaches, which also incorporates social identity theory. However, this presents a problem for this dissertation as it is in danger of incorporating the same weaknesses that have been observed regarding the socioscientific approaches, particularly the fact that its findings can be anachronistic. In order to avoid the anachronistic tendencies of socioscientific approaches, chapter 2 detailed exactly how socioscientific approaches will be utilised in this dissertation (we will return to this point shortly). Still, under the integrated, group-based approaches, it was observed that these approaches integrate both the social (historical) and the ideological (psychological) factors in their analysis of Paul's argument, and the main interest is not simply on the content of Paul's teachings about leadership, but is also on the "how" and "why" of the Pauline leadership strategy.[4] This approach is important for this study since a major component of its research has been on the significance of ἐν Χριστῷ, κλῆσις, ἀδελφός and related terminologies, in the argument of 1 Corinthians 1–4. The emphasis of this study is on why Paul uses such terminologies, and how he uses them in his argument in 1 Corinthians 1–4. This became a major point of focus in chapters 4 and 5.

6.1.2 Paul and the Formation of Identity

The second section of chapter 1 continued with the approach that has been adopted by this dissertation, which is the integrated, group-based approaches. It was observed that in relation to identity aspects, two positions dominate scholarship. The first position adopts a universalistic stance, also referred to as the third race theory, because the majority of scholars who hold this view see the early Christ followers as constituting a "third race," a move away from both their own ethnicities as well as the Jewish traditions which saw and

---

4. Lowery, "Review: Jack Barentsen."

divided ethnicity in terms of being Jewish and Gentile. With a universalistic approach, scholars emphasise the newness of one's identity in Christ. At times, the continued presence of previous identities (prior to one's being a member of the Christ community) is dismissed as having no role to play under the new found identity in Christ, or is simply ignored. The third race theory has been criticised severely by scholars who belonged to the "Beyond the New Perspective on Paul" (BNP), as being imperialistic, and as having tendencies of giving an impression of the sameness of different ethnic groups that might be present among Christ followers. Scholars who hold to the third race theory in their emphasis on passages such as Galatians 3:28 and Colossians 3:11, which talk about the concept of there being neither Jew nor Greek in Christ, and unity passages like 1 Corinthians 12:13 and 2 Corinthians 5:17, tend to be racially biased in that they tend to endorse Western values and traditions as being Christian. Conversely, other values and traditions, which are not Western, but that might be present within the community, are sometimes dismissed as being "non-Christian" or are not considered at all in the discourse of group identity. On the other hand, in their emphasis on Scriptures such as 1 Corinthians 7:17–24, scholars who endorse the BNP, tend to allow for too much of the continuation of the previous identities, without paying attention to how those identities have been disrupted by the Christ event. The approach of this dissertation has been to argue for a mediating position between these two extremes. In its approach to the question regarding the role that previous identity plays among the members of Christ's community, this dissertation is of the view that such previous identities are not completely obliterated by the newfound identity in Christ. Rather, they continue in "a transformed manner," as the cross event provides a new dimension in how we consider human wisdom and power.[5] The arguments considered in section 1.2.2 of this dissertation have direct bearing on our analysis of how Paul uses the κλῆσις terminology for his identity formation agenda in texts such as 1 Corinthians 1:1–3; 1:26–31; and 7:17–24, which was the main subject of the investigation in chapter 5.

There were aspects of the debate regarding identity that were alluded to throughout this study, which, while crucial for our understanding of Paul's identity formation agenda, proved difficult to incorporate into the main

---

5. Tucker, *You Belong to Christ*, 131.

argument of this study. This was because they would have required a standalone section, or proved to be too much of a detour and thus break the flow of the argument.

One of these was the question of how we translate the term Ἰουδαῖοι? The second was how the κλῆσις terminology functions in Paul's self-understanding. Both these identity-related terms have been the subject of great debate among the New Testament scholarship, and it was important for this dissertation to engage with that debate without digressing too much from the main argument. We opted to engage with this debate in the form of appendices in order to demonstrate that we are aware of the debate, and also provide a rationale for the stance we took.

Appendix 1 deals with the debate regarding the translation of the term Ἰουδαῖοι and argues that it will translate Ἰουδαῖοι as Jew. This option was chosen as it carries both religious and ethnic undertones to it. This study is of the view that both aspects are evident in Paul's use of the term Ἰουδαῖοι.

Appendix 2 on the other hand deals with the debate regarding Paul's use of κλῆσις terminology in relation to his self-understanding. Did Paul use this term to speak about his conversion as it was traditionally argued? The argument that is made by this dissertation in appendix 2 is that this term should not be primarily understood as referring to Paul's conversion, as the term conversion implies that Paul changed from one religion to another. However, this is not to deny that there was a radical change in Paul's self-understanding and his understanding of who God is during his Damascus road experience.

6.2 Summary and Findings of Chapter 2

In chapter 1, we stated that we would employ a variety of methodological approaches (that is, social scientific, social identity, and historical-critical grammatical approaches) in our analysis of the interrelationship between leadership and identity formation in the Corinthian correspondence.

The primary aim of chapter 2 was to outline the key aspects of these methodologies and address the objections that have been made regarding the use of social scientific approach and social identity theory in New Testament studies. This was done with the view of contributing or adding nuance to how social identity theory could be applied to the reading of leadership and identity in the Pauline correspondence of 1 Corinthians 1–4. In this chapter, the study picked up the question of methodology that was raised in chapter 1. We weighed the advantages and disadvantages of using social scientific methodologies for the analysis of the biblical texts, arguing that, while there is a danger that scholars who used social scientific approaches can deliver findings that are anachronistic, that danger can be circumvented by incorporating historical-critical methods in their analysis, as the latter help one to gather the data that can be interpreted using social-scientific approaches. This, together with the Greek-grammatical analysis which was argued for in chapter 1, can help us to understand Paul's argument in 1 Corinthians 1–4 more thoroughly.

Scholars in the field of social identity theory have observed a number of factors that have an impact on leadership success, two of which have direct relevance for the argument of this dissertation. These are group prototypicality and group entrepreneurship.

(1) Social identity theory scholars have observed that leadership success is dependent on the leader's ability to capture and represent the group values and norm; this ability is called group prototypicality. It is argued that the more an individual exhibits the group values and norms, the more likely it is that that individual will assume leadership within the group. However, social identity theory scholars have not investigated one question regarding group prototypically, viz., what happens to the group in the event that the group as a collective loses sight of their core identity? Is there a way for people who are members of the in-group and who are still holding firm to the core features of the identity, to assume leadership positions within the group, even if they are not recognised by the group to be prototypical, since the group has gone rogue by abandoning its salient identity features?

The argument of this dissertation has been that this was the case in the Pauline community at Corinth. The group had gone rogue or failed to understand how the core identity ought to influence how they perceived reality; as a result, some members of the group rejected Paul's apostleship, even though Paul's leadership style was in line with the core features of the in-group identity. One inevitable consequence of this ἐκκλησία failure to be true to its in-Christ identity is that it is inclined to choose inappropriate leaders, which means that one of Paul's many tasks in the letter is to steer them in the direction of more suitable leaders. But this means challenging the strong influence of the Corinthian culture, which is perhaps why he leaves this almost to the end of the letter, where he gives them counter-cultural indications of what to look for in their leaders, for example Stephanas in 1 Corinthians 16:15–16. However, this dissertation did not focus on other leaders like Stephanas and Apollos as that was beyond its scope and focused instead on Paul himself.

The special area of interest for this dissertation has been an investigation into the means of asserting a leader's prototypically, and that this is exactly what Paul seeks to do. This is one of the subjects of our investigation in chapters 4 and 5, that is, how does Paul present himself as group prototype to a community, some of whom have rejected him? This fits in with the second finding by scholars in the field of social identity theory.

(2) Social identity theorists argue that in order to be a great leader, one has to be a group entrepreneur, that is, one has to create a sense of "us." Again, this is what this dissertation argued for in its main arguments in chapters 4 and 5. In chapter 4, we argued that by using ἐν Χριστῷ and κλῆσις terminologies, Paul was in fact killing two birds with one stone, in that he was using these terminologies to remind the group about their salient identity "in Christ." Simultaneously, he was also using this terminology to present himself as a group prototype. Further, Paul used these terminologies to shape (entrepreneur) the group identity, as he was able to demonstrate to the group what behaviour is aligned with the in-group identity.

In chapter 4, to which we will turn shortly, we argued that in order for Paul to get a hearing with those who did not consider him to be their apostle, he had to frame his argument using terms that would signify to the group that what he was talking about was relevant and important for key aspects of the group identity; in social identity theory this process is called a consensualization process. Using the findings of scholars such as Sania and Reicher, we argued in chapter 4 that if a topic is viewed by the group as constituting the essence of group identity, people are more likely to reach an agreement about the issues and thus able to reach consensus.[6] It was argued in chapter 4 that by using ἐν Χριστῷ and κλῆσις terminologies at the beginning of the letter, Paul was hoping that the consensualization process might begin. He did this in order to overcome the hurdle of being rejected by some in the group. The ἐν Χριστῷ terminology, in particular, allowed Paul an opportunity to remind the group about their salient identity "in Christ." But in so doing, Paul also seized

---

6. Sani and Reicher, "Identity Approach," 280.

the opportunity to demonstrate to the group that his apostleship is actually in line with an in-group identity, thus inserting himself as a group prototype.

Paul also used the ἐν Χριστῷ and κλῆσις terminologies for his group entrepreneur strategy, by reminding the group about how their identity "in Christ" is diametrically opposed to the world's wisdom and power, the same categories that they were using to judge him. All of this was the subject of investigation in chapters 4 and 5. For now, it is important for us to turn our attention to how chapter 3 was situated in the overall logic of this dissertation and how it helped us establish the interrelationship between leadership and identity.

6.3 Summary and Findings of Chapter 3

Chapter 3 sought to achieve three goals:

(1) It offered a description of the social context of Corinth and the Corinthian Christian-movement. This was considered necessary particularly in light of the criticism against the use of social scientific approaches and social identity theory that we dealt with in chapter 2, also considered Edwin Judge's criticism that these approaches tended to be anachronistic, yielding more about the modern sociological theories, than actually offering us a better description of the early Pauline community at Corinth. This chapter has sought to avoid these anachronistic tendencies by paying careful attention to the historical description of both Corinth and the Pauline community at Corinth. This was done with the view that it would yield data that we can utilise to understand the social influences that were at play in the Pauline community at Corinth. This was in line with the methodological framework that was proposed in chapters 1 and 2, which argued that social identity theory needs to incorporate historical critical methods, as historical critical methods help us unearth the data that we can then analyse or interpret using social scientific approaches such as social identity theory.

(2) Chapter 3 also argued for the literary integrity of 1 Corinthians. Discussing 1 Corinthians' literary context, this chapter dealt with different scholarly arguments for the unity of 1 Corinthians and, to a less degree, dealt with the scholars who view 1 Corinthians as a composite document. Establishing the unity of 1 Corinthians is important for an analysis of the interrelationship between leadership and identity in 1 Corinthians. This is because the key terminologies that this study uses to build its argument appear

in different sections of the letter, which are not normally identified as a single unit by the scholars who argue that 1 Corinthians is a composite document. For example, Paul's call for the community to imitate him, which chapter 4 of this study argues represents a climax of Paul's presentation of himself as a group prototype, appears in 1 Corinthians 4:16 and in 1 Corinthians 11:1. Similarly, the κλῆσις terminology that Paul uses in 1 Corinthians 1 is also used in 1 Corinthians 7. Because this study holds to the unity of 1 Corinthians, it became apparent that the κλῆσις terminology has both theological and social implications in Paul's argument. This realisation further strengthens the case that this study first made in chapter 1 regarding the role of people's previous identity, now that they are "in Christ." It enabled us to establish that, while there is a new dispensation that has been ushered in by the Christ event, that reality does not entirely erase people's previous identities, rather it transforms them and radically changes the areas of that previous identity that are inconsistent with the new-found identity "in Christ." This becomes clear when one asserts the unity of 1 Corinthians, and harmonises the use of the κλῆσις terminology both in 1 Corinthians 1 and 7.

One of the areas that chapter 5 argued for regarding the change that has been brought by the newfound identity "in Christ" is how one perceives and evaluates leaders within the ἐκκλησία. In chapter 5, it was argued that the cross brings about the inversion of human wisdom and power, as it nullifies them. The result is that human wisdom and power are invalid categories to judge leaders like Paul, because ἐμώρανεν ὁ θεὸς τὴν σοφίαν τοῦ κόσμου. This helps Paul in his case of presenting himself as a group prototype, because his behaviour is aligned with the cross. Establishing the literary integrity of 1 Corinthians together with the historical context was thus done so that we can understand both the social context and the overall argument of 1 Corinthians.

(3) Linked with the argument regarding the literary integrity of 1 Corinthians, in this chapter we finally sought to identify the underlying cause of the problems in 1 Corinthians. The reason that this chapter was concerned with both the literary issues and identifying the underlying causes of the problems in 1 Corinthians was to avoid the dangers that were observed in the previous chapters, regarding the anachronistic tendencies among scholars who employ social scientific approaches. In looking for the underlying causes of the problems in 1 Corinthians, we argued that the major cause of the issues

in Corinth was the community's failure to understand their identity in Christ. This becomes clearer in chapter 4, which employed social identity theory in its analysis of the motive behind the slogans that are found in 1 Corinthians 1:12, "I belong to Paul"; "I belong to Apollos"; "I belong to Cephas"; and "I belong to Christ."

6.4 Summary and Findings of Chapter 4

Chapter 4 sought to lay the groundwork for the exegesis that followed in chapter 5. It revisited the discussion that was raised in chapter 3 regarding the issues behind 1 Corinthians and analysed them in the light of social identity theory. It demonstrated that, at the heart of the issues in 1 Corinthians 1–4, particularly behind the slogans "I belong to Paul," "I belong to Apollos," "I belong to Christ," and "I belong to Peter," was a quest for identity. The problem with the Corinthians was that they were identifying themselves in terms of their factions rather than drawing their identity from Christ. In 1 Corinthians, Paul had to resocialise them, and remind them of their salient identity in Christ. However, this would prove to be a problem, as some of the members of the community were questioning his credibility as their apostle. So Paul first had to prove that he was the prototype of the in-group identity, and he also had to employ a strategy that would make those who no longer regarded him as their apostle listen to him. The argument of this chapter is that the "in Christ" idiom served that purpose within the argument of 1 Corinthians 1–4. This becomes still clearer in chapter 5.

The subject of Paul and group prototypicality traditionally falls under the debate regarding Paul's apostolic defence, which has received a considerable amount of analysis from sociohistorical and socioscientific scholars. In chapter 2, we argued that we will incorporate sociohistorical approaches in our use of social identity theory, thus this chapter had to engage with the sociohistorical scholars who have debated Paul's apostolic defence. We highlighted that the traditional approach to Paul's apostolic defence, in its emphasis on the centrality of preaching in Paul, tended to overlook Paul's identity formation agenda in 1 Corinthians, particularly in 1 Corinthians 1:13–17.

The scholars who employ social scientific approaches in their analysis of Paul's discourse on power help us to see the power dynamics in Paul's apostolic defence, but they also tend to be overcritical in their analysis and present Paul as an egomaniac who wants to consolidate all authority to himself. In chapter 4, we engaged with some of the scholars who hold this view, and argued that there is enough historical evidence, particularly the mimesis tradition, which supports the positive reading of Paul's apostolic defence. His presenting himself as a group prototype needs to be seen in light of his genuine concern for the group identity, not as group manipulation. Perhaps 2 Corinthians 11:2–3 better captures what this dissertation has been arguing for regarding Paul's apostolic defence and identity formation, when in 2 Corinthians 11:2–3 Paul writes:[7]

ζηλῶ γὰρ ὑμᾶς θεοῦ ζήλῳ, ἡρμοσάμην γὰρ ὑμᾶς ἑνὶ ἀνδρὶ παρθένον ἁγνὴν παραστῆσαι τῷ Χριστῷ·φοβοῦμαι δὲ μή πως, ὡς ὁ ὄφις ἐξηπάτησεν Εὕαν ἐν τῇ πανουργίᾳ αὐτοῦ, φθαρῇ τὰ νοήματα ὑμῶν ἀπὸ τῆς ἁπλότητος καὶ τῆς ἁγνότητος τῆς εἰς τὸν Χριστόν.

Thus, the argument in chapter 4 was that Paul's apostolic defence needs to be viewed in the light of his efforts to help the group understand their identity in Christ. After all, his apostolic defence and the group identity are intertwined, as they both have their origin in God through Christ.

6.5 Summary and Findings of Chapter 5

The main aim of chapter 5 of this dissertation was to do an exegesis of 1 Corinthians 1–4, in order to investigate the interrelationship between leadership and identity. While the focus of this chapter was on 1 Corinthians 1, this dissertation was cognisant that 1 Corinthians 1 forms part of the broader section of 1 Corinthians 1–4. The reason this dissertation focuses mostly on 1 Corinthians 1 was that the argument of this section is indicative of the broader argument of 1 Corinthians 1–4, and when it was appropriate this point was demonstrated by looking at the broader pericope.

The reason for focusing on the Greek grammatical analysis in 1 Corinthians 1:1–9 was that, as was argued in section 5.2 of chapter 5, these verses do not merely act as a letter opening, they also contain the material that Paul unpacks in the rest of the letter. As such, when we picked up a theme in these verses, a

---

7. "For I feel a divine jealousy for you, since I betrothed you to one husband, to present you as a pure virgin to Christ. But I am afraid that as the serpent deceived Eve by his cunning, your thoughts will be led astray from a sincere and pure devotion to Christ" (ESV).

concerted effort was made to show how that particular theme was developed through the rest of the letter.

This dissertation observed that in the opening verses of 1 Corinthians 1, Paul employs three identity descriptors. These are expressed through ἀδελφός, ἐν Χριστῷ Ἰησοῦ, and κλῆσις terminologies. We argued that these identity descriptors fit in well with the three features that Tajfel identified as requirements for the group to function well, which are the cognitive, evaluation and emotional aspects.[8]

Paul also used these three identity descriptors in order for the consensualization process to take place. This process in Paul's social identity agenda was first introduced in chapter 4, where it was argued that Paul uses the identity descriptors in order to draw the members of the group into the conversation, which is about group identity. It is important for Paul to capture the attention of group members and for him to use terminology that draws in the members of the group from the beginning of the letter, as some had already rejected him as their apostle. This chapter reviewed the scholarly treatment of the ἐν Χριστῷ Ἰησοῦ terminologies extensively, and conducted grammatical analysis of 1 Corinthians 1:1–3, particularly as it relates to ἐν Χριστῷ Ἰησοῦ terminologies and to a limited extent the κλῆσις terminologies. The reason for this strong focus on the ἐν Χριστῷ Ἰησοῦ terminologies is that this terminology is key to Paul's social identity agenda. We argued that ἐν Χριστῷ Ἰησοῦ functions as an instrumental dative in the argument of 1 Corinthians 1, and it highlights God's plan in forming this community and using Christ to achieve his purposes. By highlighting God's activity in the identity formation of the community, Paul sought to bring about positive feelings regarding group membership. People who have been chosen by God in Christ Jesus, constitute a group that has something that the rest of humanity does not; they have faith in Jesus Christ. While this group comprises mostly of people from poorer social economic backgrounds, they are on the right side of history because they are on the side that understands how God operates. Through the cross of Jesus, God rejected human wisdom and power; in fact, the cross nullified them. The ἐν Χριστῷ Ἰησοῦ terminology, together with the message about the cross, becomes a tool in Paul's social identity agenda. Paul uses the cross and the ἐν Χριστῷ Ἰησοῦ terminology in order to show which values are

---

8. Tajfel, *Differentiation between Social Groups*, 28.

acceptable within the community, and thus he applies them for his identity entrepreneurial enterprise.

While Galatians is not the focus of this study, in the final stages of its argument a comparative look at Paul's apostolic defence in this letter was necessary (this was done in appendix 3). It was necessary on two grounds: (1) It assisted in framing my position which counteracts the view that seems to be gaining traction in scholarship, which tends to present Paul as an egomaniac whose interest is to suppress dissention. (2) Galatians was important in order to validate the argument of this dissertation that there is an interrelationship between leadership and identity. Both 1 Corinthians 1–4 and Galatians demonstrate that the motivation for Paul's apostolic defence was that some members of the community were beginning to challenge his apostleship, but in so doing they were unfortunately using categories that were not in line with the "in Christ" identity. In his defence, Paul reminds them of their salient identity "in Christ," an identity that has its origins in the call of God, which was achieved through the cross, something that both Jews and Gentiles consider foolish. However, the in-group members consider the cross to be the wisdom of God and the power of God. If the people keep on judging Paul using the value systems of the world, they put the community's well-being at risk, as God has nullified and shamed the wisdom of the world.

6.6 Conclusion

The ἐν Χριστῷ Ἰησοῦ terminology is the key terminology on which this dissertation relied to establish the interrelationship between leadership and identity in 1 Corinthians. In using this terminology to frame his argument in 1 Corinthians 1–4, Paul was able, first, to get a group of people, some of whom had rejected him, to listen to him. As the use of ἐν Χριστῷ Ἰησοῦ terminology at the beginning of the letter signalled to the group that the subject matter that Paul was writing about was at the core related to in-group identity, ἐν Χριστῷ Ἰησοῦ terminology helped Paul in the consensualization process. Second, the use of the ἐν Χριστῷ Ἰησοῦ terminology allowed Paul to present himself as a group prototype. While again some members of the community had rejected him due to the Greco-Roman cultural influences on their perception of a leader, by using the ἐν Χριστῷ Ἰησοῦ terminology Paul reminded the in-group members of their salient identity "in Christ." As was observed in chapter 5, when the salient identity is activated, people are more likely to act in a manner that is consistent with it.

However, Paul did not only use the ἐν Χριστῷ Ἰησοῦ terminology to remind the in-group about their salient identity, he also used this terminology to explain to the group the implication of the fact that their identity was achieved through the death of Jesus Christ on the cross. He explained that the cross meant that worldly categories of selecting leaders had been nullified. By setting himself as a group prototype, Paul demonstrated to the Corinthians how his leadership approach was actually in line with the in-group identity, while at the same time highlighting to them that their worldly approaches were not in line with the in-group identity. Paul's teachings, particularly around the inversion of human wisdom and power, actually aided him in his social identity enterprise of the in-group identity, as he was able to demonstrate on which value system the in-group identity was built. Thus as used by Paul, the ἐν Χριστῷ Ἰησοῦ terminology enables this dissertation to demonstrate that there is indeed an interrelationship between leadership and identity.

6.7 The Significance of the ἐν Χριστῷ Ἰησοῦ, and κλῆσις Terminologies for the South African Christian Context

While the main concern of this dissertation has been to investigate how the ἐν Χριστῷ Ἰησοῦ, and κλῆσις terminologies help us to establish the interrelationship between identity and leadership in Paul, it will be amiss for this dissertation not to seek to apply these findings to the South African context, albeit to a limited extent.

The South African Institute of Race Relations, in investigating the state of race relations in South Africa, has observed an increase in racist incidents reported in the media. The Institute seems to place the blame on politicians' divisive rhetoric. This political rhetoric tends to divide people based on their skin colour, which in turn fuels racial tensions in South Africa. Paul's teaching about the significance of the ἐν Χριστῷ Ἰησοῦ, and κλῆσις terminologies can help South African pastors in building a united church, whose identity is based on what Christ has done for us. It seems that South African Christian leaders need to follow a similar strategy to Paul, who, in counteracting the schism that was in the church, reminded the church about what Christ has done for them. He also spelt out for the church how they ought to live in light of who they are in Christ.

6.8 Areas for Further Research

One of the major areas to which this dissertation has sought to contribute is the conversation regarding the nuances that are needed in the use of social identity theory in New Testament studies. Linked with that is the need to incorporate the identity agenda in Pauline discussion about leadership. It sought to contribute by focusing on the aspect of group prototypicality in this theory. However, one of the major hurdles regarding the prototypical leader is that, according to social identity theory, that person has to be a member of the group, and his or her activities need to be noticed and assessed by the group. If they see him or her as embodying their norms and values, the group gives him or her a leadership role by accepting his or her influence in and over the group and allowing him or her to represent the group.

One of the areas that invites further research is in what ways Paul, who was not physically present in the group, steers the group members towards some members of the community, whom he considers group prototypical. For example, these would be leaders like Stephanas (16:15–16) and Apollos (3:5, 8–9), whom Paul considered to be committed to διακονία, people who work together (συνεργοί) and who work hard (κόπος). It is clear, for example, that Paul considered Apollos to be a group prototype in 1 Corinthians 4:6. It was beyond the scope of this dissertation to investigate in what ways Apollos is a group prototype, thus further investigation is needed.

Another area that invites further investigation is the question of different levels or kinds of leadership roles within the Pauline community. The obvious difference between Paul's leadership and that of those like Stephanas and Apollos is that Paul insists that his leadership does not come from the church, but from the Lord. This is the main point of his argument in 1 Corinthians 1:1, where he emphasises that his apostleship was the result of the will of God,[9] which was a major focus of discussion in chapters 4 and 5. However, at the same time in texts such as 1 Corinthians 3:5, 9–11, and 4:1–3, Paul insists that Apollos and himself are both servants of Christ. Does this mean that Paul

---

9. See also Gal 1:1.

saw no difference between his leadership task of being an apostle, and the leadership task of Apollos, who was an ordinary member of the community and who in part received his teaching from people like Priscilla and Aquila (Acts 18:26)? Further investigation is needed to determine exactly Apollos's group prototypically, as that might have a direct bearing on how we are to apply Paul's group prototypicality to (post)modern day leadership in the church, as most church leaders do not see their leadership task as being on the same level as that of Paul.

Appendix 1

Debate on the Translation of Ἰουδαῖοι

There is a debate among scholars regarding the best way to translate Ἰουδαῖοι. Some scholars prefer to translate it to mean Judeans.[1] Others say that it is best to leave the term untranslated.[2] It is worth noting that Hodge was among the first scholars to argue for the term Ἰουδαῖοι to be translated as Judeans.[3] She has since reevaluated her position regarding this translation, and now thinks that it is best to leave the term untranslated. Her reasons for choosing to leave the term untranslated is that she feels that there is a drive among some scholars to undermine the heritage of present-day Jews. The scholars who choose to translate the term Ἰουδαῖοι as Judeans instead of Jews, do this for two reasons. First, they state that "designations such as 'Jews' and 'Judaism' in relation to New Testament scholarship have contributed to prejudice against modern Jews."[4] These sentiments come through very strongly in the works of scholars such as Danker and Esler,[5] with Esler emotionally stating: "It is arguable that translating Ἰουδαῖοι as 'Jews' is not only intellectually

---

1. Hays, *From Every People*, 141–46; "Paul and Multi-Ethnic," 77; Mason, "Jews, Judaeans," 457–512; Baker, "From Every Nation'," 83–84; and Du Toit, "Was Paul Torah Observant," 21–45.

2. Hodge, *If Sons Then Heirs*, 11–15.

3. Hodge, 11–14.

4. Du Toit, "Paul and Israel," 6; cf. Campbell, *Paul and Creation*, 2. For more on the biblical scholarship prejudice against modern Jews, see Du Toit, "Paul and Israel," 1–5; Esler, *Conflict and Identity*, 66–68.

5. Danker, *Greek-English Lexicon of the New Testament and Other Early Christian Literature*, 478; Esler, 66–68.

indefensible... but also morally questionable. To honor the memory of these first-century people it is necessary to call them by a name that accords with their own sense of identity. 'Jews' does not suit this purpose... 'Judeans' is the only apt rendering in English of Ἰουδαῖοι."[6] The second reason why these scholars chose to translate Ἰουδαῖοι as Judeans instead of Jew is because the term Ἰουδαῖοι as used in the Greco-Roman world did not have any religious undertones to it, as it was used with reference to an "ethnic group comparable to other ethnic groups, with their distinctive laws, traditions, customs, and God."[7] They say that at the heart of the ethnic description of the term Ἰουδαῖοι was where they came from (i.e. the homeland). They say that this is how ancient people perceived their identities. Thus, for Baker, Hodge, and Mason, it is better to translate the term Ἰουδαῖοι as "Judeans" instead of Jews.[8] They say that this will help to distinguish the Ἰουδαῖοι in Paul's time from the modern-day Jews (as most of them will trace their roots to Europe). There are two objections that can be raised regarding this translation. First, if the term is translated as "Judeans," does this not restrict its use to a geographical location? What about those people who were not staying in the territory of Judea but still viewed themselves as members of the covenant with Abraham, and still claimed loyalty to the God of Israel? Also, if the term Ἰουδαῖοι is translated as meaning "Judeans," does that impose a foreign identity onto the people who lived in Judea but did not claim loyalty to the God of Israel? Second, it can be argued that translating Ἰουδαῖοι as "Judeans" allows for too great a distance between modern day Jews and Judeans in Paul's time, something Campbell has described as "denying to post-New Testament Jews the heritage of Israel."[9] Similarly, Miller, citing Levine, argues that when "the Jew is replaced with the Judean... we have a Judenrein, ('Jew free') text, a text purified of Jews. Complimenting this erasure, scholars then proclaim that Jesus is neither Jew nor even Judean, but Galilean... once Jesus is not a Jew or a Judean, but a Galilean, it is also an easy step to make him an Aryan."[10] This dissertation is of the view that when one translates the term Ἰουδαῖοι,

---

6. Esler, 68.

7. Baker, "From Every Nation"; Esler, 62–74; Mason, "Jews, Judaeans," 457.

8. Baker, 83–84; Hodge, *If Sons Then Heirs*, 12; Mason, 457.

9. Campbell, *Paul and Creation*, 3. See also, Hodge who shares similar sentiments. Hodge, *If Sons Then Heirs*, 13–14.

10. Miller, "Meaning of Ioudaios," 99.

one has to consider how the term was used in its original context, and we should not let the abuse of the term in the twentieth century affect how we interpret in its original context. In our translation of the term, one also has to ask whether the term is used by the insider (those who are part of the Ἰουδαῖοι community) or by outsiders. In doing this, this dissertation will briefly consider how Paul uses the term Ἰουδαῖοι. Paul seems to use the term Ἰουδαῖοι differently, depending on the context.[11] While in John's and Luke's gospels, the term Ἰουδαῖοι is mostly used in the negative sense (i.e. those who stood in opposition to Christ), in the Pauline correspondence the term Ἰουδαῖοι is used both positively and negatively.[12] Paul, for example, in 1 Thessalonians 2:14 uses the term Ἰουδαῖος in a negative manner to describe the geographical location of Christ's believers ἐν τῇ Ἰουδαίᾳ ("Judea"), but Paul also uses the term to describe his ethnicity (Rom 9:4–13) or as an antithesis between Ἰουδαῖοι and Ἕλληνες.[13] Paul also uses the term Ἰουδαῖος to describe a true Ἰουδαῖος, not only someone who is outwardly a Ἰουδαῖος. In Romans 2:28–9 we read: 28 οὐ γὰρ ὁ ἐν τῷ φανερῷ Ἰουδαῖός ἐστιν, οὐδὲ ἡ ἐν τῷ φανερῷ ἐν σαρκὶ περιτομή· 29 ἀλλ' ὁ ἐν τῷ κρυπτῷ Ἰουδαῖος, καὶ περιτομὴ καρδίας ἐν πνεύματι οὐ γράμματι, οὗ ὁ ἔπαινος οὐκ ἐξ ἀνθρώπων ἀλλ' ἐκ τοῦ θεοῦ. According to the context of these verses, a true Ἰουδαῖος is someone who not only knows the Law and boasts about it, it is someone who obeys the Law.[14] This suggests that the term in Paul's use also has religious undertones; this comes through very strongly in Romans 2:29, where the term Ἰουδαῖοι is used synonymously with circumcision, which is a covenantal sign of God's people; a sign that was given to Abraham. What is interesting in Paul's use of the term here is that he does not only limit it to its ethnic use (i.e. a function of birth and/or geography) but rather he adds religious use. Scholars such as Longenecker have observed that in Romans 2:17–20, Paul uses a diatribe with five statements regarding the self-identity and self-consciousness of the Ἰουδαῖος of his day.[15] This diatribe is introduced by a

---

11. For more on this, see Harvey, *True Israel*, 68–78; BDAG, s.v. "Ἰουδαῖοι" in Paul.

12. For an extended treatment regarding John's use of the term Ἰουδαῖοι, see the papers presented in Leuven Colloquium, 2000, in Bieringer, Pollefeyt, and Vandecasteele-Vanneuville, *Anti-Judaism*.

13. Rom 1:16; 2:9–10; 9:24.

14. Rom 2:17; cf. BDAG.

15. Longenecker, *Epistle to Romans*, 298.

conditional participle εἰ. In Romans 2:17a, Paul provides the first statement, "Εἰ δὲ σὺ Ἰουδαῖος ἐπονομάζῃ." This first statement can be interpreted in two ways. First, the verb ἐπονομάζῃ can be seen as either a middle voice "you call yourself" (meaning, in view is a self-identification by Jewish people themselves) or a passive voice "you are called" (meaning how people from the outside perceive the Jews). Longenecker correctly observes that the context requires "that it be understood as in the middle voice" meaning that this is how the Ἰουδαῖοι perceived their own identity.[16] The conditioning particle εἰ at the beginning of Romans 2:17a tells us that all that is said in the five statements regarding what it means to be Ἰουδαῖοι is to be affirmed, meaning that this was a Jewish self-understanding.[17] Thus, the Jewish people boasted about their relationship with God and relied upon the law (Rom 2:17b); they regarded themselves as people who knew the will of God and who were able to discern the things that are superior because they were instructed in the law (Rom 2:18). They were convinced that they were guides for the blind, a light for those who are in the dark (Rom 2:19); and they considered themselves as instructors of the foolish, teachers of infants, because they have a law, the embodiment of knowledge and truth (Rom 2:20). What Paul does in Romans 2:25–29 is to demonstrate that a Ἰουδαῖος is not just someone who talks the talk, but someone who walks the walk. It is not just about physical symbols and association, it is about how one lives their life. Thus, a proper Ἰουδαῖος is someone who keeps the law. Scholars such as Middendorf have demonstrated that what Paul regarded as a true Ἰουδαῖοι is someone who obeys the law.[18] Paul's views in Romans 2 is not something that he invented, it is an idea that can be found in the Hebrew Scriptures of the Old Testament. We can thus see in Romans 2 that the Ἰουδαῖοι self-designation was not only limited in its use to ethnic identity, it also had religious meaning in it. Thus, this study translates the term Ἰουδαῖος as "Jew" to capture the religious use of the term, particularly by Paul. For more on the defence of the use of this term in this way, see Longenecker and Skarsaune.[19] It is worth noting though that this dissertation, by translating Ἰουδαῖοι as Jews, is by no means saying

---

16. Longenecker, 299.
17. Longenecker, 298.
18. Middendorf, *Romans 1–8*, 211–15.
19. Longenecker, *Epistle to Romans*, 298–304; Skarsaune, "Jewish Believers in Jesus," 7–16.

that the Jewish religion during Paul's day was monolithic. Far from it, there were different strands of Judaism during the first century (i.e. Essenes, Pharisees, Sadducees, Sacarii, and Zealots), but there was nonetheless a convergence of belief within these strands, they saw themselves as separate from the Gentiles. They believed that they were the chosen people of God (with the law that sets them apart from those around them), they believed that there is one God, the God, a covenantal God, with circumcision being a sign of the covenant.

Appendix 2

Does κλῆσις Refer to Paul's Conversion?

Paul establishes his apostleship on his Damascus road experience in both Galatians 1:15–6 and 1 Corinthians 9:1; 15:8–9. His apostleship is linked to his call by the will of God.[1] Traditionally, Paul's Damascus road experience is viewed as his conversion. It is this view that Horrell challenges.[2] In recent years, the traditional interpretation has been a subject of great debate among Pauline scholars. Stendahl questions the appropriateness of using the term "conversion" as it implies that Paul converted from one religion to another.[3] He notes that it is better to understand the Damascus road experience as a calling or a commissioning, not conversion.[4] This study, while it prefers to use the term "calling" or "commissioning" to refer to Paul's Damascus road experience, nonetheless agrees with Du Toit that conversion does not imply that Christ's followers, particularly those from the Jewish background, "converted from one religious system to another" (that is, from "Judaism" to "Christianity").[5] However, conversion does indicate the acquisition of a new core identity in Christ. The argument of this dissertation is that previous identities are not necessarily obliterated, but that they are no longer the

---

1. Gal 1:13–17; 1 Cor 1:1; 2 Cor 1:1; see also: Keay, "Paul the Spiritual Guide," 16; Esler, Galatians, 120.
2. Horrell, "Paul," 262.
3. Stendahl, *Paul among Jews and Gentiles*, 3–27.
4. See, Esler, Galatians, 120–21; Du Toit, "Paul and Israel," 3.
5. Du Toit, 110.

primary categories of identifying the people of God. For example, in Galatians 1:13–15 Paul makes it clear that after receiving the call from God, there was a radical difference between his former way of life in Judaism and his new identity as an apostle to the Gentiles. In Galatians 1:13–4, Paul speaks of his former way of life in Judaism, as having been marked by extreme zeal "for the traditions of his fathers" (NIVUK). Scholars such as Bell, Malcolm, and Hengel have observed that zeal for the purification of Israel was a pervasive radical Jewish identity that was influenced by the Phineas tradition.[6] Hengel writes:[7]

> Zeal for God's cause ... was a phenomenon that had characterized the whole of Palestinian Judaism in general from the time of the Maccabees and in particular the groups of Essenes and Pharisees who had emerged from the Hasidim. Even early Christianity had been at least to some extent influenced by its Jewish inheritance. This "zeal" was based on a consciousness of Israel's election and separateness and it was therefore experienced in a completely positive way.

People such as Saul who followed this school of thought, deemed it their duty to cleanse Israel by any means possible – including the use of violence against those who were perceived to be disloyal to the Torah and the God of Israel.[8] They thought that by their actions they were going to bring about the eschatological day of the Lord who was going to come and deliver Israel from its enemies. In the case of Paul, he saw the early Christ-followers as people who were polluting Israel, people who needed to be dealt with, thus he persecuted them. Paul's encounter with or calling by the risen Lord made it clear to him that his actions had thus far been presumptuous. He "came to perceive that in zealously pursuing the purity of Israel, he had been effectively pursuing a manifest 'reversal' that had in fact already been initiated by God in a hidden way, in Christ."[9] Thus, God's calling of Paul revealed to him that he was on the wrong side of what God was doing, and hence there was a fundamental change that needed to take place in his life from then

---

6. Bell, Provoked to Jealousy, 306; Malcolm, "Paul and Rhetoric," 46; Hengel, *Zealots*, 224.
7. Hengel, 224.
8. Wright, *What Saint Paul*, 35.
9. Malcolm, "Paul and Rhetoric," 46.

on. Paul, to mark this significant shift in the way he related to God, used an adversative conjunction δὲ in Galatians 1:15. This of course does not mean that Paul converted from one religion to a new religion or worshiped a new God after his Damascus road experience. Rather, after that experience he came to a fuller realisation of who God is and what God has done in Christ.[10] Moreover, throughout Galatians Paul still relies on Hebrew Scripture and theology to build his argument, and at times comes across as someone who has not relinquished his Jewish identity.[11] Yet it is equally clear in Galatians that Paul has reinterpreted Hebrew Scriptures in the light of what Christ Jesus has done for the community. See for example Galatians 3:6–9 and 4:28 where Paul appropriates the Jewish identity to those who now believe in Christ by faith. In Galatians 3, he argues that the Gentile believers are also children of Abraham, as they are saved in the same way as Abraham, that is, through faith. For more on this see Punt, who demonstrates how Paul "claimed Abraham as ancestor of all Jesus-followers."[12] Punt argues that Paul does not primarily use Abraham as an example of faith, in Galatians; rather, he uses Abraham as "patrilineal ancestor of many nations."[13] According to Galatians 3:7, 16, 29; 4:28, the children of Abraham are now constituted not in terms of biological links but through the Spirit. Du Toit argues for this when he writes, "the only way one can partake in the promise to Abraham is through faith."[14] Similarly, "the only way one can be Abraham's offspring and heir according to the promise, is by belonging to Christ (ὑμεῖς Χριστοῦ (Gal 3:29)), which implies faith in Christ"[15]. Crucially, Du Toit observes that, "since faith in Christ is set over against the works of the Law, it can be concluded that even Judaeans 'now'[16] become Abraham's offspring or God's children by faith only."[17]

---

10. See: Dunn, *Epistle to Galatians*, 63; Wright, *What Saint Paul*, 35–37; Malcolm, 46–47.
11. Gal 2:15; Phil 3:5; see Punt, "Identity Claims," 92.
12. Punt, "Identity Claims."
13. Punt, 91.
14. Du Toit, "Galatians 3," 14–15; Gal 3:22.
15. Du Toit, 15; Gal 3:22, 26.
16. νῦν, 1:23; 2:20; 4:9, 25; δέ, 3:16, 25.
17. Du Toit, "Galatians 3," 15.

Appendix 3

The Interrelationship between Paul's Apostolic Calling, His Gospel and the Identity of the Galatians

The main aim of this dissertation has been to establish that there is an interrelationship between leadership and identity in 1 Corinthians. This emerges clearly when one considers Paul's apostolic defence. He tends to argue very strongly that his apostleship and the gospel originated in God the Father through Jesus Christ. But what is the significance of Paul's apostleship and his gospel having its origins in God? To answer this question this dissertation will consider the argument of Galatians, in this appendix.

The argument of this dissertation is that Paul's discourse about the fact that his apostleship and his gospel originate in God is a heuristic device that serves his identity formation agenda, both in Galatians and in 1 Corinthians. This becomes apparent when one considers the findings of scholars such as Esler, Gaventa, and Barram.[1] Esler notes that Galatians 1:11–2:14 deals mostly with the important theme of the genuine gospel.[2] Paul writes Galatians to deal with what he perceives to be a major crisis that has fallen upon the community: Θαυμάζω ὅτι οὕτως ταχέως μετατίθεσθε ἀπὸ τοῦ καλέσαντος

---

1. Esler, *Galatians*, 118–20; Gaventa, "Maternity of Paul"; Barram, "Mission and Moral Reflection," 118–21.
2. Esler, 118.

ὑμᾶς ἐν χάριτι Χριστοῦ εἰς ἕτερον εὐαγγέλιον (Gal 1:6).[3] Paul expresses grave discontent about the Galatians' failure to adhere to the true gospel; they have quickly turned to a different gospel, which is not a gospel at all (Gal 1:7). Lyons notes that at issue in Galatians is the community's "relationship with Paul and the gospel he preached to them."[4] The Galatians are in the process of straying from the gospel, but there are implications for turning away from the gospel that Paul preached.[5] Abandoning the true gospel means turning away ἀπὸ τοῦ καλέσαντος ὑμᾶς ἐν χάριτι Χριστοῦ εἰς ἕτερον εὐαγγέλιον. What is interesting about Galatians 1:6-7 is the link between the gospel and the identity of the Galatians; turning away from the gospel that Paul preached is viewed as turning away from Christ Jesus himself.[6] Paul uses very strong language in Galatians 1:8–9; he says that anyone who preaches a gospel that is contrary to that which he preached, is to be accursed. Paul does not view a different gospel from his as a trivial departure; he takes it very seriously, as a different gospel has a direct bearing on the "in Christ" identity of the Galatians, which is now threatened by the current situation.[7] A different gospel has direct bearing on the identity of the Galatians. In verses 8–9, Paul uses a conditional clause καὶ ἐὰν to include both himself and the angels (not that he and the angels ever preached a different gospel) to highlight the unchanging nature of the gospel. The gospel is unchanging, because it has its origins in God (Gal 1:11–12), but it is mediated through Paul's apostolic ministry via the gospel he preached. The link between Paul's apostleship and his gospel is well articulated by Lyons who argues that turning away from Paul's gospel, and Paul, is equivalent to turning away from God (Gal 1:6), since God's call to the Galatians was mediated through the apostle Paul.[8]

---

3. See Lyons, who says that the Galatians turning to a different gospel served as the impetus for Paul to write the letter to the Galatians. Lyons, *Pauline Autobiography*, 126.

4. Lyons, 126; cf. Gal 1:8–9; 3:1–5; 4:11–20; 5:7–12.

5. Schreiner notes that the Galatians are "on the verge of apostasy" (cf. Gal 5:2-4), contrary to Longenecker who focuses much on the fact that μετατίθεσθε is in a present tense and thus the Galatians were "in the very act of turning" away. Schreiner, *Galatians*, 84–85; Longenecker, *Galatians*, 14. The context of all of Galatians suggests that the Galatians are in the process of turning away but have not done so yet.

6. Compare Gal 3:1–5; 4:8–11; 5:4–6, 7–11.

7. Compare Gal 3:1–4; 4:9–11,17–19; 5:2–4.

8. Lyons, *Pauline Autobiography*, 125. See Gal 4:14.

At the core of this dissertation seems to be the Galatians' acceptance of circumcision.[9] The present tense suggests that this is currently happening in the community.[10] However, this raises a question: why are the Galatians doing such a thing, particularly in the light of the fact that Paul says that the Galatians started on the right path? This dissertation is of the view that at the core of the Galatians' acceptance of circumcision is the question of social identity. However, before expanding on this, we first need to observe a few things regarding Paul's apostolic defence in Galatians 1.

Halcomb notes that there is a sort of hierarchy present in Paul's apostolic presentation in Galatians 1:1; that is: God – Jesus – Paul/ apostles.[11] This hierarchy is clearer in Galatians 1:3–4 where things go according to the will of God our Father (τοῦ θεοῦ καὶ πατρὸς is a subjective genitive in verse 4). In Galatians 1:3, God our Father and κυρίου ἡμῶν Ἰησοῦ Χριστοῦ are the source of grace, which is expressed in Christ's sacrificial giving of himself for our sins in verse 4. It is worth noting that while verses 1, 3–4 establish a hierarchy, which highlights that there is an asymmetrical relationship between Paul and Galatians, this does not mean that Paul has absolute power within the community. God our Father and our Lord Jesus Christ are the ones who yield absolute authority, which is expressed through the agency of Paul. Moreover, in Galatians 1:2 Paul makes it clear that he is not writing the letter alone, rather he is writing οἱ σὺν ἐμοὶ πάντες ἀδελφοί. Both Witherington III and Halcomb agree that in this verse Paul expresses the idea that there are other believers who agree with Paul's letter and the content of his gospel.[12] Similarly, Bruce writes, "Paul wishes to indicate to the Galatians" that he is not merely mentioning his own viewpoints; rather the content of what he is writing about is "shared by his colleagues."[13] Moreover, while in Galatians 1:11 Paul indicated that the gospel he "preached is not of human origins" (NIVUK), Galatians 2:2 makes it clear that Paul was not above human accountability. Galatians 2:2 needs to be seen in the light of the fact that Paul, in Galatians 1:11–24, where he was acknowledging the authority of the Jerusalem apostles

---

9. Gal 2:3, 7–9, 12; 5:2–3, 6, 11; 6:12–15.
10. Gal 1:6–7; 3:3; 4:16–18; 6:12–13.
11. Halcomb, Paul the Change Agent, 104.
12. Witherington III, *Acts of the Apostles*, 74–75; Halcomb, *Paul the Change Agent*, 102–3.
13. Bruce, *Epistle to Galatians*, 74.

among the Jewish believers, nonetheless did not see his mission to the Gentiles as contingent on their approval. He was aware of "the divine providence of his calling to the Gentile mission."[14] What is evident in Galatians 1:11–24 is that Paul viewed himself as an authentic and autonomous[15] apostle in the same calibre as the other apostles such as Peter, James,[16] and John who were perceived to be leaders of the church in Jerusalem. However, in Galatians 2:2 he writes, "ἀνέβην δὲ κατὰ ἀποκάλυψιν· καὶ ἀνεθέμην αὐτοῖς τὸ εὐαγγέλιον ὃ κηρύσσω ἐν τοῖς ἔθνεσιν, κατ' ἰδίαν δὲ τοῖς δοκοῦσιν, μή πως εἰς κενὸν τρέχω ἢ ἔδραμον." The first thing that Paul establishes in Galatians 2:2 is that he is going to Jerusalem for the second time, not because he was summoned by the church there; rather it was a response to a revelation. Scholars speculate regarding what this revelation might be.[17] The emphasis of this verse though is that it is God's revelation that initiated Paul's visit to Jerusalem. Galatians 2:2 raises questions regarding the meaning of the phrase μή πως εἰς κενὸν τρέχω ἢ ἔδραμον. Does this phrase mean that Paul sought the approval of the Jerusalem church, which would be contrary to what he had already said in Galatians 1:11–21? Upon analysing Paul's use of εἰς κενὸν in other texts such as 1 Thessalonians 3:5 and Philippians 2:16a, both Bruce and Asano conclude that, while he was not seeking "validation of his gospel" [because it had divine assurance],[18] Paul was seeking "its practicability."[19] They argue that Paul wanted to make sure that there was continuous harmony and unity between the gospel he preached and that of the ἐκκλησίαις τῆς Ἰουδαίας, so that there should be no division with the ἐκκλησία.[20] What all of this demonstrates is

---

14. Asano, *Community*, 81.

15. In Gal 1:12, Paul was emphatic that the gospel he preached had not been received from any human being, nor had he been taught it by anyone. There is, however, a debate among the scholars regarding Paul's use of the term Ἱεροσόλυμα in Gal 1:18. Did he go to Jerusalem in order to have his gospel authenticated by the apostles there? Asano correctly observes that this would be contrary to the argument of Gal 1:12. Asano, 91. It seems clear that Paul, in his account of the first visit to Jerusalem after his calling, emphasized his autonomy as an apostle to the Gentiles.

16. The status of James as an apostle is intentionally ambiguous on Paul's part, according to Asano and Bruce. Asano, 90; Bruce, *Epistle to Galatians*, 100–1.

17. For a summary of different views, see Asano, *Community*, 91–93, and Bruce, *Epistle to Galatians*, 108–11.

18. Bruce, 110–11; Asano, 93–94.

19. Bruce, 111.

20. Scholars such as Wan and Punt observe that while Paul viewed the members of the Jerusalem ἐκκλησία as members of the same community as the Galatians through what God

that while Paul acknowledges the divine origins of his apostleship and his gospel, he does not act as a lone ranger who is above everyone else. He has a community of believers around him, who can vouch for his gospel, and he is also willing to work with other apostles, so that the ἐκκλησία will not be divided. This is crucial in the light of what this dissertation has already established regarding what was happening in the ἐκκλησία.

The Galatians were struggling to understand their "in Christ" identity, and thus, to understand the social implications of the gospel they had received from Paul. This struggle can also be seen in the false brothers "ψευδαδέλφους" (Gal 2:4) or the agitators "οἱ ἀναστατοῦντες"(Gal 5:12). These false brothers who have infiltrated the community seem to have failed to comprehend what God has done in Christ in creating this new community; they seem to be stuck in the ethnocentric way of relating to God.[21] These false brothers were persuading the Galatians, particularly the Gentiles in the community, to be Torah-observant and insisted that they should keep the Jewish customs of circumcision and dietary laws. These principles were at the core of Jewish identity, acting as a boundary marker to distinguish the members of the in-group from the out-group.[22]

Circumcision among the Jews was a sign that they were God's covenantal people, and thus it was a sign of their corporate identity.[23] It symbolised

---

has done for all of them in Christ (Gal 2:6–10), Paul's description of his encounter with them is less than favourable (Gal 2:11–14). Wan, "Letter to Galatians," 262; Punt, "Identity," 93.

21. This comes up more clearly in the work of Hansen, "All of You," 28–30, and Esler, *Galatians*, 118–21.

22. Scholars such as Viljoen, Wright, and De Silva observe that there were five Jewish boundary markers that distinguished the Jews from other people groups. These were Torah observance, circumcision, keeping the Sabbath, dietary laws, and purity. The latter four aspects are in real terms a way of doing the first, which is Torah observance. Viljoen, "Matthew and Torah," 3–5; Wright, "Jewish Identity," and De Silva, "Jews in Diaspora," 283–88. De Silva notes that the Jewish people were "connected by an ethnic bond," in the fact that their lineage could be traced to one ancestor – Jacob. De Silva, 283–84. Their identity was broader than just an ethnic identity; it was also a way of life that was encapsulated in these Jewish boundary markers.

23. See Gen 17:9–12; Faulkner, "Jewish Identity," 4–8; Hansen, "All of You," 28. It is important to note though, that circumcision was not unique to the Israelites. Jer 9:25–26 makes it clear that circumcision was also practiced by other nations such as Egypt, Judah, Edom, Ammon, and Moab. Similarly, Wright provides other archaeological evidence that shows how widespread the practice of circumcision was in the ancient world. Nevertheless, there was a fundamental difference in why the Israelites practiced circumcision as compared to other nations. Wright, "Jewish Identity," 312. For example, Herodotus writes that the reason why the Egyptians practised circumcision was "for cleanliness' sake; for they would rather be clean than more becoming." Herodotus, *Hist.* 2.37. For the Israelites, circumcision had its roots

that the circumcision bearer was a worshipper of the one true God, and a "spiritual descendent" of the patriarch Abraham. Similarly, the dietary laws were another important Jewish identity boundary marker (cf. Lev 11:1–47; Deut 14:2–20). At the core of the dietary laws was the matter of covenantal purity (Lev 11:45 provides a key to all dietary laws; the motivation is holiness because God is holy). Leviticus 11:20–47 provides a list of creatures that might make an individual ritually unclean, also the "cooking practices that result in the ritual impurity of a vessel."[24] Viljoen notes that within the Jewish community, dining with others was "strictly regulated," as sharing a meal was seen as "binding the community together by confirming" their identity.[25] Both Wright and Viljoen note that eating with Gentiles was taboo for the Jews.[26] Wright observes that eating with Gentiles was tolerated only on two bases: (1) if the Jew is the host; (2) if the Jew brings his own food when the Gentile invites him or her.[27] Even under these strict circumstances, the Jews would not sit at the same table as the Gentiles, but would have a separate table with their distinct foods.[28] The Gentile saw this practice by the Jews as anti-social behaviour,[29] and it led to the Gentiles hating the Jews due to their religious distinctions.[30] Dietary laws and other Jewish boundary markers such

---

in the covenant that God established with Abraham in Gen 17. God demanded that every male be circumcised in order to be part of the covenant. This was done on the eighth day after a male child was born. Circumcision was also required for male individuals who were not biological descendants of Abraham, who wanted to assimilate into the Jewish religion. Wright, 311–14. Circumcision was very important for the Jewish identity, and its importance can be seen in the Dead Sea Scrolls. According to 1 QH 14.20, the uncircumcised may not walk on God's holy path, and 4Q458 declares that the uncircumcised will be destroyed in the last days. Wright, 314. Wright observes that during the period of 1 Maccabees, faithful Jews saw circumcision as being synonymous with covenantal faithfulness. Wright, 313; 1 Macc 1:15; cf. Josephus, *Ant.* 12.241. What this footnote hopes to demonstrate is how important circumcision was for Jewish identity, particularly as a boundary marker that distinguished the insiders from the outsiders. This sheds greater light on the social identity crisis that was facing the Galatians: for example, what are the Jewish-Christ believers to do with Gentile-Christ believers? Are the Gentiles expected to follow the stipulations of the old covenant in order for them to be in-group members of the Christ-followers?

24. Wright, "Jewish Identity," 314–15.
25. Viljoen, "Matthew and Torah," 4.
26. Wright, "Jewish Identity," 35; Viljoen, 4.
27. Wright, 315; compare. Jdt. 12:1–4, 19; Add. Esth 14:17; Josephus, *Vit.*14.
28. Josephus, *Jos. Asen.* 7.1; Dan 1:8; Tacitus, *Hist.* 5.5.
29. Philostratus, *Vit. Apol.* 33.
30. 3 Macc 3:4. It is worth noting though that some Gentiles found these Jewish social identity boundary markers to be attractive. For more on this, see Collins, *Invention of Judaism*,

as circumcision were very effective in reinforcing Jewish in-group identity and accentuating out-group differences. This can be seen in ancient sources such as Diodorus Siculus, Tacitus, Philostratus, and 3 Maccabees.[31] These boundary makers fostered strong social cohesion or strong in-group identity among the Jews, with their distinctiveness observable by the outsiders. At times this distinctiveness resulted in the Jews being ridiculed and criticised for their boundary markers.[32] De Silva notes that the practice of circumcision was "denounced as barbaric mutilation" by some of the Gentiles.[33] Jewish authors such as Josephus and Philo acknowledge this ridicule of the Jews by Gentiles.[34] Identity markers were an integral part of Jewish identity, as they encapsulated who they were as the people of God. The problem for the early Christ followers, particularly those from the Jewish background in Galatia, was to understand in what ways the Gentiles could be counted as people of God.[35] Did they need to assimilate into the Jewish identity by accepting the typical identity markers? Scholars such as Asano are of the view that Gentile "incorporation into a large Jewish commonwealth" was the issue that led to the conflict in Galatians 2:1–14.[36] In Galatians, it is clear that even Peter struggled to understand how this new identity in Christ relates to the

---

165—68; Josephus, *Ant.* 20.2.3-4; 24-48. The works of Josephus already reveal two quite different attitudes regarding the conversion of Gentiles to Judaism. On the one hand, there was Ananias who, after the conversion of the crown prince Izates, did not insist that Izates needed to be circumcised. For Ananias, the most important thing was for Izates to be devoted to the worship of God even if he was not circumcised. On the other hand, there was another Jewish teacher, Eleazar from Galilee, who according to Collins "was strict about the Law, and persuaded Izates that circumcision was indeed necessary." Collins, 167. Collins demonstrates that this was a raging debate among the Jewish leaders, but it seems that Eleazar's views regarding the importance of circumcision for proselytes dominated in the Jewish diaspora context. Collins, 167–71.

31. Diodorus Siculus, *Lib. Hist.* 34.1.1–4; 40.3–4; Tacitus, *Hist.* 5.5.1–2; Philostratus, *Vit. Apol.* 33; and 3 Macc. 3:33–37.

32. Josephus, *Ag. Ap.* 2.137; Tacitus, *Hist.* 5.4.2–3; Juvenal, *Sat.* 6.160; 14.98–104.

33. De Silva, "Jews in Diaspora," 287.

34. Josephus, *Ag. Ap.* 2.137; Philo, *Spec.*1.1–3. See also, Tacitus, *Hist.* 5.5.2; Strabo, and Juvenal, *Sat.* 14.104.

35. Within the Pauline scholarship, this question has been a matter of great debate, particularly among the New Perspective (NPP) and the Radical New Perspective (RNPP) on Paul. Unfortunately, this debate falls outside the scope of this dissertation. For a summary evaluation of both perspectives and their relation to the Galatians debate, see Du Toit and Collins. Du Toit, "Galatians 3," 41–67; Collins, *Invention of Judaism*, 159–82. Collins's work also focuses on Romans and 1 Corinthians.

36. Asano, *Community*, 78.

Jewish boundary markers. This becomes clear when one considers Paul's confrontation with Peter in Galatians 2:14. Paul writes: ἀλλ' ὅτε εἶδον ὅτι οὐκ ὀρθοποδοῦσιν πρὸς τὴν ἀλήθειαν τοῦ εὐαγγελίου, εἶπον τῷ Κηφᾷ ἔμπροσθεν πάντων· Εἰ σὺ Ἰουδαῖος ὑπάρχων ἐθνικῶς καὶ οὐκ Ἰουδαϊκῶς ζῇς, πῶς τὰ ἔθνη ἀναγκάζεις Ἰουδαΐζειν. It is worth noting that Peter does not fall under the same category as the agitator (οἱ ἀναστατοῦντες) of Galatians 5:12. In Galatians 2:13, Paul calls Peter a hypocrite (ὑπόκρισις), on the grounds of two reasons: (1) Peter was happy to have table fellowship with the Gentiles (Gal 2:11–12) until certain men came from Jerusalem. Moreover, his reason for withdrawing from eating with the Gentiles was not motivated by the gospel, but was to save face with "those who belonged to the circumcision group" (Gal 2:12, NIVUK). (2) Peter is called a hypocrite because he knew better. This becomes clear in Paul's question to him in Galatians 2:14; "You are a Jew, yet you live like a Gentile and not like a Jew. How is it, then, that you force Gentiles to follow Jewish customs?" (NIVUK).

Paul's apostolic defence and his identity formation agenda in Galatians need to be understood in the light of this problem of the Jewish identity markers. These identifying markers are what made the Jews, as the people of God, distinct from other nations, enabling "the Jews to acculturate to the Greek environment to a high degree without fear of losing their distinctiveness as members of the historical people of God."[37]

This then raises a question for those who were Gentiles, who are now part of the Jesus movement, who claim the same identity of being the children of God and to whom Paul appropriates the Abrahamic covenant as their identity. How are they to relate with the law and the Jewish social boundary markers? Wan has made helpful observations regarding Paul's argument in Galatians, which show how Paul deals with this question. Wan places Paul's argument in Galatians in the light of the inter-Jewish debate and in the light of the tension with the Jesus-movement.[38] He argues that there was a tension within the Jesus-movement, particularly, between the Jerusalem-Antioch faction and the apostle Paul. This tension centred on two things: authority and identity. He writes:[39]

---

37. De Silva, "Jews in Diaspora," 284.
38. Wan, "Letter to Galatians," 262.
39. Wan, 262.

> The Jerusalem-Antioch leaders saw themselves as the centre of the Jesus movement and thus constructed a narrative that . . . bolstered their authority. In their response to imperial pressure, they adopted a rigid ethnic boundary between themselves and outsiders. Paul . . . elected to embrace a universalism that would extend the "Jewish" borders to the ends of the earth.

Wan's insight regarding the tension with the early Jesus-followers clarifies the significance of why Paul has to defend his apostolic status and at the same time formulate his understanding of what constitutes the identity of Christ's followers. To counter the dominant perspective of the Jerusalem-Antioch alliance, it is crucial for Paul to establish his rightful place within the community. That is, he is an "ἀπόστολος, οὐκ ἀπ' ἀνθρώπων οὐδὲ δι' ἀνθρώπου ἀλλὰ διὰ Ἰησοῦ Χριστοῦ καὶ θεοῦ πατρὸς τοῦ" (Gal 1:1). His apostleship is not inferior to that of those who are δοκούντων εἶναί in Jerusalem (Gal 2:2; 6), nor is his gospel inferior to or different from theirs (Gal 1:11; 2:6–7). Once Paul has established his rightful position within the community, he can then counteract the use of ethnic binaries, which threaten to enslave the members of the community, particularly those who come from the Gentile background (Gal 2:4). Paul's fight for liberation is not only for Gentile believers, it is also for the Jewish believers, as the alternative would mean that they will become slaves once again to the ἔργων νόμου. The conflict in Galatians, both with the outsiders trying to force Jewish identity onto the Gentiles, and the tension within the community, particularly the Jerusalem-Antioch alliance, forced Paul to spell out the identity and the boundaries of this community in Christ. Thus, both in Galatians as in 1 Corinthians there is a strong interrelationship between leadership and identity. Paul's apostolic defence needs to be seen as a polemic strategy "directed at the community, plotting their identity and working towards their cohesion."[40] Both in 1 Corinthians and Galatians, conflict within and outside community "served an important purpose" for Paul in his identity formation agenda.[41] These conflicts helped Paul to clarify the boundary lines, and also helped him to restate or revisit core aspects of in-group identity, such as the identity "in Christ."

---

40. Punt, "Identity Claims," 93.

41. This section did not revisit the issue of conflict in Corinth as it was dealt with in both chapters 3 and 4 of this study, and to a limited extent in 5.3.3.

Bibliography

Aasgaard, Reider. *My Beloved Brothers and Sisters: Christian Siblingship in the Apostle Paul*. London: T&T Clark, 2004.

Ackerman, David A. *Lo, I Tell You a Mystery: Cross, Resurrection, and Paraenesis in the Rhetoric of 1 Corinthians*. Eugene: Pickwick, 2006.

Adams, Edward. "First-Century Models for Paul's Churches: Selected Scholarly Developments Since Meeks." In *After the First Urban Christians: The Social-Scientific Study of Pauline Christianity Twenty-five Years Later*, edited by Todd D. Still and David G. Horrell. London: T&T Clark (Continuum), 2009.

Adams, Edward, and David G. Horrell. *Christianity at Corinth: The Quest for the Pauline Church*. Louisville: John Knox, 2004

Aernie, Jeffery W. *Is Paul Also among the Prophets?: An Examination of the Relationship Between Paul and Old Testament Prophetic Tradition in 2 Corinthians*. London: T&T Clark, 2012.

Africa, Thomas W. "Psychohistory, Ancient History, and Freud: The Descent into Avernus." *Arethusa* (1979): 5–33.

Agnew, Francis H. "The Origin of the NT Apostle-Concept: A Review of Research." *Journal of Biblical Literature* 101, no. 1 (1986): 75–96.

Allan, John A. "The 'in Christ' Formula in Ephesians." *New Testament Studies* 5, no. 1 (1958): 54–62.

Allport, Floyd. *Social Psychology*. Boston: Houghton Mifflin, 1924.

Asano, Atsuhiro. *Community – Identity Construction in Galatians: Exegetical, Social-Anthropological and Socio-Historical Studies*. London: T&T Clark, 2005.

Ashley, Evelyn. "Paul's Paradigm for Ministry in 2 Corinthians: Christ's Death and Resurrection." PhD diss., Murdoch University, 2006.

Aune, David E. *The New Testament in Its Literary Environment*. Cambridge: Clarke, 1987.

Ayers, Michale. "Toward a Theology of Leadership." *Journal of Biblical Perspectives in Leadership* 1, no. 1 (2006): 3–27.

Bac, J. Martin. *Perfect Will Theology: Divine Agency in Reformed Scholasticism as against Suárez, Episcopius, Descartes, and Spinoza*. Boston: Brill, 2010.

Bailey, Kenneth E. *Poet & Peasant and through Peasant Eyes: A Literary-Cultural Approach to the Parables of Luke*. Grand Rapids: Eerdmans, 1983.

Baird, William. "One Against the Other: Intra-Church Conflict in 1 Corinthians." In *The Conversation Continues: Studies in Paul and John in Honor of J. Louis Marty*, edited by Robert T. Fortna and Beverly R. Gaventa, 116–36. Nashville: Abingdon, 1990.

———. "Review: David Odell-Scott, Paul's Critique of Theocracy: A/Theocracy in Corinth and Galatians." *ENC* 67, no. 3 (2006): 332–34.

Baker, Coleman. "Early Christian Identity Formation: From Ethnicity and Theology to Socio-Narrative Criticism." *Currents in Biblical Research*, no. 9 (2011): 228–37.

———. Identity, Memory, and Narrative in Early Christianity: Peter, Paul, and Categorization in the Book of Acts. Eugene: Pickwick, 2011.

———. "Social Identity and Biblical Interpretation." *Biblical Theology Bulletin* 42, no. 3 (2012): 129–38.

Baker, Cynthia M. "'From Every Nation Under Heaven': Jewish Ethnicities in the Greco-Roman World.'" In *Prejudice and Christian Beginnings: Investigating Race, Gender, and Ethnicity in Early Christian Studies*, edited by Elisabeth Schussler Fiorenza and Laura Nasrallah, 79–99. Minnesota: Fortress Press, 2009.

Banks, Robert J. *Paul's Idea of Community*. Rev. ed. Peabody: Hendrickson, 1994.

Barclay, John M. G. "Thessalonica and Corinth: Social Contrast in Pauline Christianity." *Journal for the Study of the New Testament*, no. 47 (1992): 49–74.

Barentsen, Jack. *Emerging Leadership in the Pauline Mission: A Social Identity Perspective on Local Leadership Development in Corinth and Ephesus*. Princeton Theological Monograph Series 168. Eugene: Pickwick, 2011.

Barna, George. *Leaders on Leadership: Wisdom, Advice and Encouragement on the Art of Leading God's People*. Ventura: Regal, 1997.

Barnett, Paul W. *The Corinthian Question: Why Did the Church Oppose Paul?* Nottingham: Apollos, 2011.

Barr, James. *The Semantics of Biblical Language*. Oxford: Oxford University Press, 1961.

Barraclough, Geoffrey. *Main Trends in History*. New York: Holmes & Meier, 1978/1991.

Barram, Michael D. *Mission and Moral Reflection in Paul*. Oxford: Peter Lang, 2006.

Barrett, Charles K. "Shaliach and Apostle." In *Donum Gentilicium: New Testament Studies in Honour of David Daube*, edited by Ernst Bammel, Charles K. Barrett, and William D. Davies, 88–102. Oxford: Oxford University Press, 1978.

Bibliography

Barth, Markus. *Ephesians 1–3: A New Translation with Introduction and Commentary.* New York: Doubleday, 1974.

Bar-Tal, Daniel. *Shared Beliefs in a Society: Social Psychological Analysis.* London: Sage, 2000.

Barton, David. *The Cambridge Companion to Biblical Interpretation.* Cambridge: Cambridge University Press, 1998.

Barton, Stephen C. "Social-Scientific Criticism." In *Handbook to Exegesis of the New Testament*, edited by Stanley E. Porter. Leiden: Brill, 1997/2002.

Batluck, Mark. "Paul, Timothy, and Pauline Individualism: A Response to Bruce Malina." In *Paul and His Social Relations*, edited by Stanley E. Porter and Christopher D. Land, 35–56. Boston: Brill, 2013.

Battle, John A. "Notes on the Greek Syntax." 2018. Accessed on 26 June 2018. wrs.edu/Materials_for_Web_Site/Courses/Intermediate_Greek/Syntax_notes.pdf

Bell, Richard H. *Provoked to Jealousy.* Tübingen: Mohr Siebeck, 1994.

Belleville, Linda L. "Imitate Me, Just as I Imitate Christ: Discipleship in the Corinthian Correspondence." In *Patterns of Discipleship in the New Testament*, edited by Richard N. Longenecker, 120–43. Grand Rapids: Eerdmans, 1996.

Berding, Kenneth. "The Hermeneutical Framework of Social-Scientific Criticism: How Much Can Evangelicals Get Involved?" *Evangelical Quarterly* 75, no. 1 (2003): 3–22.

Bertone, J. A. "Apostle." In *The Encyclopedia of Christian Civilization*, 2012. Accessed on 15 September 2017. https://www.credoreference.com/content/topic/apostles.embed.

Best, Ernest. *Ephesians: A Critical and Exegetical Commentary.* London: T&T Clark, 1998.

———. "Paul's Apostolic Authority." *Journal for the Study of the New Testament*, no. 27 (1986): 3–25.

Betz, Hans D. "Apostle." In *The Anchor Bible Dictionary*, Vol. 1, edited by David N. Freedman, Gary A. Herion, David F. Graf, and John D. Pleins, 309–11. New York: Doubleday, 1992.

Bieringer, Reimund, Didier Pollefeyt, and Frederique Vandecasteele-Vanneuville, eds. *Anti-Judaism and the Fourth Gospel: Papers of the Leuven Colloquim, 2000.* Asscn: Royal Van Gorcum, 2001.

Birge, Mary K. *The Language of Belonging: A Rhetorical Analysis of Kinship Language in First Corinthians.* Dudley: Peeters, 2002.

Blass, Friedrich, and Albert Debrunner. *A Greek Grammar of the New Testament and Other Early Christian Literature.* Translated by Robert W. Funk. Chicago: The University of Chicago Press, 1961.

Boff, Leonardo. *Church, Charism and Power: Liberation Theology and the Institutional Church.* Translated by John W. Diercksmeier. New York: Crossroad, 1981.

Bookidis, Nancy. "Religion in Corinth: 146 B.C.E. to 100 C.E." In *Urban Religion in Roman Corinth: Interdisciplinary Approaches*, edited by David N. Schowalter and Steven J. Friesen, 141–64. Cambridge: Harvard Theological Studies, 2005.

Brawley, Robert L. "From Reflex to Reflection? Identity in Philippians 2:6-11 and Its Context." In *Reading Paul in Context: Explorations in Identity Formation, Essays in Honour of William S. Campbell*, edited by J. Brian Tucker and Kathy Ehrensperger, 128–46. London: T&T Clark, 2010.

Brewer, Marilynn B. "The Psychology of Prejudice: Ingroup Love or Outgroup Hate?" *Journal of Social Issues* 55, no. 3 (1999): 429–44.

Brinsmead, Bernard H. *Galatians – Dialogical Response to Opponents*. Chico: Scholars, 1982.

Brockhaus, Ulrich. *Carisma und amt: Die paulinische charismenlehre auf dem hintergrund der frühchristlichen gemeindefunktionen*. Wuppertal: Theologisher Verlag Brockhaus, 1972.

Brookins, Timothy A., and Bruce W. Longenecker. *1 Corinthians 1-9: A Handbook of the Greek Text*. Waco: Baylor University Press, 2016.

Bruce, Frederick F. "Christianity Under Claudius." *Bulletin of the John Rylands Library*, no. 44 (1962): 309–26.

———. *Epistle to the Galatians*. Grand Rapids: Eerdmans, 2013.

———. "A Review of the New Testament World: Insights from Cultural Anthropology." *Journal for the Study of the New Testament*, no. 21 (1984): 111–12.

———. *Romans*. Grand Rapids: Eerdmans, 1985.

Bryskog, Samuel. "Co-Senders, Co-Authors and Paul's Use of the First Person Plural." *Zeitschrift fur die Neutestamentliche Wissenschaft und die Kunde des Urchristentums*, no. 87 (1996): 230–50.

Bultmann, Rudolf. "θάνατος, θνῄσκω, ἀποθνῄσκω, συναποθνῄσκω." In *Theological Dictionary of the New Testament*, Vol. 3, edited by Gerhard Kittel. Edited and Translated by Geoffrey W. Bromiley, 7–25. Grand Rapids: Eerdmans, 1964–76.

Bünker, M. *Briefformular und Rhetorische Disposition im 1. Korintherbrief*. Göttingen Theological Works 28. Göttingen: Vandenhoeck & Ruprecht, 1983.

Burke, Peter J., and Jan E. Stets. "Identity Theory and Social Identity Theory." *Social Psychology Quarterly* 3, no. 63 (2000): 224–37.

Burtchaell, James T. *From Synagogue to Church: Public Services and Offices in the Earliest Christian Communities*. Cambridge: Cambridge University Press, 1992.

Butarbutar, Robinson. *Paul and Conflict Resolution: An Exegetical Study of Paul's Apostolic Paradigm in 1 Corinthians 9*. Milton Keynes: Paternoster, 2007.

Button, M. B. "Leadership and Gospel in the Early Pauline Churches." PhD diss., North-West University, 2014.

Byrskog, Samuel. *Jesus the Only Teacher: Didactic Authority and Transmission in Ancient Israel, Ancient Judaism and the Matthean Community*. Stockholm: Almqvist & Wiksell, 1994.

Campbell, Constantine R. *Basics of Verbal Aspect in Biblical Greek*. Grand Rapids: Zondervan, 2008.

———. *Paul and Union with Christ: An Exegetical and Theological Study*. Grand Rapids: Zondervan, 2012.

Campbell, R. Alastair. *The Elders: Seniority within Earliest Christianity*. London: T&T Clark, 1994 [2004].

Campbell, William S. *Paul and the Creation of Christian Identity*. London: T&T Clark, 2006.

———. "The Rationale for the Gentile Inclusion and Identity in Paul." *Concordia Theological Review* 9, no. 2 (2012) :23–38.

Campenhausen, Hans V. *Ecclesiastical Authority and Spiritual Power in the Church of the First Three Centuries*. Translated by J. A. Baker. London: Adam & Charles Black, 1953.

Candice, K. "Of God: Karl Barth and the Coherence of 1 Corinthians." In *The Wisdom of the Cross: Exploring 1 Corinthians*, edited by Brian S. Rosner, 32–56. Nottingham: Apollos, 2011.

Cadbury, Henry J. "Erastus of Corinth." *Journal of Biblical Literature* 50, no. 2 (1931): 42–58.

Carson, Donald A. *The Cross and Christian Ministry: Leadership Lessons from 1 Corinthians*. Grand Rapids: Baker Books, 2004.

Carson, Donald A., Douglas J. Moo, and Leon Morris. *An Introduction to the New Testament*. Grand Rapids: Zondervan, 1992.

Carter, R. F. "Big Men in Corinth." *Journal for the Study of the New Testament*, no. 66 (1997): 45–71.

Castelli, Elizabeth A. *Imitating Paul: A Discourse of Power*. Louisville: John Knox, 1991.

Chae, Daniel J-S. *Paul as Apostle to the Gentiles: His Apostolic Self-Awareness and Its Influence on the Soteriological Argument in Romans*. Milton Keynes: Paternoster, 1997.

Chapple, Allan L. "Local leadership in the Pauline Churches: Theological and Social Factors in Its Development; A Study on 1 Thessalonians, 1 Corinthians and Philippians." PhD diss., University of Durham, 1984.

Chester, Stephen J. *Conversion at Corinth: Perspectives on Conversion in Paul's Theology and the Corinthian Church*. New York: T&T Clark, 2003.

Chow, John K. *Patronage and Power: A Study of Social Networks in Corinth*. Sheffield: Sheffield Academic Press, 1992.

Ciampa, Roy E. "Flee Sexual Immorality: Sex and the City of Corinth." In *The Wisdom of the Cross: Exploring 1 Corinthians*, edited by Brian S. Rosner, 100–33. Nottingham: Apollos, 2011.

Ciampa, Roy E., and Brian S. Rosner. *The First Letter to the Corinthians*. Grand Rapids: Eerdmans, 2010.

———. "The Structure and Argument of 1 Corinthians: A Biblical/Jewish Approach." *New Testament Studies*, no. 52 (2006): 205–18.

Cicero, Lavinia, Antonio Pierro, and Daan Van Knippenberg. "Leadership and Uncertainty: How Role Ambiguity Affects the Relationship between Leader Group Prototypicality and Leadership Effectiveness." *British Journal of Management* 21, no. 2 (2010): 411–21.

Cicero, Lavinia, Marino M. Bonaiuto, Antonio Pierro, and Daan van Knippenberg. "Employees' Work Effort as a Function of Leader Group Prototypicality: The Moderating Role of Team Identification." *European Review of Applied Psychology* 58, no. 2 (2008): 117–24.

Clarke, Andrew D. "Another Corinthian Erastus Inscription." *Tyndale Bulletin* 42, no. 1 (1991): 146–51.

———. "'Be Imitators of Me': Paul's Model of Leadership." *Tyndale Bulletin* 49, no. 2 (1998): 329–60.

———. *A Pauline Theology of Church Leadership*. London: T&T Clark, 2008.

———. *Secular and Christian Leadership in Corinth: A Socio-Historical and Exegetical Study of 1 Corinthians 1–6*. New York: Brill, 1993.

———. *Serve the Community of the Church: Christians as Leaders and Ministers*. Grand Rapids: Eerdmans, 2000.

Clarke, Andrew D., and J. Brian Tucker. "Social History and Social Theory in the Study of Social Identity." In *T&T Clark Handbook to Social Identity in the New Testament*, edited by J. Brian Tucker and Coleman A. Baker, 41–58. London: Bloomsbury, 2014.

Cohen, Shaye J. D. *Beginnings of Jewishness: Boundaries, Varieties, Uncertainties*. Berkeley: University of California Press, 1999.

Colijn, Brenda B. "Paul's Use of the 'in Christ' Formula." *Ashland Theological Journal*, no. 23 (1991): 9–26.

Collins, John J. *The Invention of Judaism: Torah and Jewish Identity from Deuteronomy to Paul*. Oakland: University of California Press, 2017.

Collins, Raymond F. *First Corinthians*. Collegeville: Liturgical Press, 1999.

Conzelmann, Hans. *1 Corinthians*. Translated by J. W. Leitch. Minneapolis: Fortress, 1991.

———. *An Outline of the Theology of the New Testament*. London: SCM, 1969.

Coser, Lewis A. *The Function of Social Conflict: An Examination of the Concept of Social Conflict and Its Use in Empirical Sociological Research*. New York: The Free Press, 1956.

———. "Social Conflict and the Theory of Social Change." *The British Journal of Sociology* 8, no. 3 (1957): 197–207.

Cunningham, Philip A. *Jewish Apostle to the Gentiles: Paul as He Saw Himself*. Mystic: Twenty-Third Publications, 1986.

Dahl, Nils A. *Studies in Paul: Theology for the Early Christian Mission*. Minneapolis: Augsburg, 1977.

Danker, Frederick W., Walter Bauer, William F. Arndt, and F. Wilbur Gingrich. *Greek-English Lexicon of the New Testament and Other Early Christian Literature*. 3rd ed. Chicago: University of Chicago Press, 2000.

De Boer, Willis P. *The Imitation of Paul: An Exegetical Study*. Kampen: Kok, 1962.

De Cremer, David, and Daan van Knippenberg. "Cooperation as a Function of Leader Self-Sacrifice, Trust, and Identification." *Leadership & Organization Development Journal*, no. 26 (2005): 355–69.

Deissmann, Gustav A. *Light from the Ancient East: The New Testament Illustrated by Recently Discovered Texts of the Graeco-Roman World*. London: Hodder & Stoughton, 1910.

Deissmann, Gustav A., and William E. Wilson. *St. Paul: A Study in Social and Religious History*. London: Hodder & Stoughton, 1926.

De Silva, David A. *Galatians: A Handbook on the Greek Text*. Waco: Baylor University Press, 2014.

———. *The Hope of Glory: Honor Discourse and New Testament Interpretation*. Collegeville: Liturgical Press, 1999.

———. "Jews in the Diaspora." In *The World of the New Testament: Cultural, Social, and Historical Context*, edited by Joel B. Green and Lee M. McDonald, 272–90. Grand Rapids: Baker, 2013.

———. "Let the One Who Claims Honor Establish That Claim in the Lord: Honor Discourse in the Corinthian Correspondence." *Biblical Theology Bulletin* 28, no. 2 (1998): 61–74.

De Vos, Craig S. *Church and Community Conflicts: The Relationships of the Thessalonian, Corinthian, and Philippian Churches with Their Wider Civic Communities*. SBLDS, 168. Atlanta: Scholars Press, 1999.

Desrochers, Stephen, Jeanine Andreassi, and Cynthia Thompson. "Identity Theory." In *A Sloan Work and Family Encyclopedia Entry*. Chestnut Hill: Boston College, 2002.

Dietrich, Donald J., and Michael J. Himes. *The Legacy of the Tübingen School: The Relevance of Nineteenth-Century Theology for the Twenty-First Century*. New York: Crossroad, 1997.

Dissmann, Adolf, and William E. Wilson. *The Religion of Jesus and the Faith of Paul: The Selly Oak Lectures, 1923, On the Communion of Jesus with God & the Communion of Paul with Christ*. London: Hodder, 1926.

Dodd, Brian. *Paul's Paradigmatic "I": Personal Examples as Literary Strategy.* Sheffield: Sheffield Academic Press, 1999.

Donahoe, Kate C. "From Self-Praise to Self-Boasting: Paul's Unmasking of the Conflicting Rhetoric-Linguistic Phenomena in 1 Corinthians." PhD diss., St. Andrews University, 2008.

Doughty, Darrell J. "Luke's Story of Paul in Corinth: Fictional History in Acts 18." *Journal of Higher Criticism* 4, no. 1 (1997): 3–54.

Dunn, James D. G. *1 Corinthians.* Sheffield: Sheffield Academic Press, 1995.

———. *The Epistle to the Galatians.* Peabody: Hendrickson Publisher, 1993.

———. *Neither Jew Nor Greek: A Contested Identity. Christianity in the Making, Volume 3.* Grand Rapids: Eerdmans, 2015.

———. *The New Perspective on Paul.* Rev. ed. Cambridge: Eerdmans, 2005/1983.

———. *Romans 9–16.* Dallas: Word, 1988.

———. *The Theology of the Apostle Paul.* Grand Rapids: Eerdmans, 1998.

Du Plooy, Andries Le R. "Die betekenis van charisma en amp vir die kerkregering." In *die Skriflig* 39, no. 3 (2005): 555–67.

Du Rand, J. A. "Charisma en amp – 'n Pauliniese eksegetiese verkenning." In *Gereformeerde ampsbediening*, edited by P. J. Rossouw, 75–94. Pretoria: NG Kerkboekhandel, 1988.

Du Toit, Philip La G. "Galatians 3 and the Redefinition of the Criteria of Covenant Membership in the New Faith-Era in Christ." *Neotestamentica* 52, no. 1 (2018): 41–67.

———. "Paul and Israel: Flesh, Spirit and Identity." PhD diss., Stellenbosch University, 2013.

———. "Was Paul Torah Observant? Perspectives on 1 Corinthians 7:19." Paper presented at New Testament Seminar, Stellenbosch University, 2015.

Dvorak, James D. "John H. Elliott's Social-Scientific Criticism." *Trinity Journal* 28, no. 2 (2007): 251–78.

Edsall, B. A. *Paul's Witness to Formative Early Christian Instruction.* Tübingen: Mohr Siebeck, 2014.

Ehrensperger, Kathy. "'Called to Be Saints' – The Identity-Shaping Dimension of Paul's Priestly Discourse in Romans." In *Reading Paul in Context: Explorations in Identity Formation. Essays in Honour of William S. Campbell*, edited by Kathy Ehrensperger and J. Brian Tucker, 90–109. London: Bloomsbury, 2010.

———. *Paul and the Dynamics of Power: Communication and Interaction in the Early Christ-Movement.* London: T&T Clark, 2009.

———. *Paul at the Crossroads of Cultures: Theologizing in the Space-Between.* London: Bloomsbury, 2013.

Ellemers, Naomi, Dick De Gilder, and S. Alexander Haslam. "Motivating Individuals and Groups at Work: A Social Identity Perspective on Leadership and Group Performance." *The Academy of Management Review* 29, no. 3 (2004): 459–78.

Ellington, Dustin W. "The Impulse towards the Disadvantaged in the Gospel Preached by Paul: An Analysis of 1 Corinthians 1:10–4:21 and 8:1–11:1." *Scriptura*, no. 115 (2016): 1–13.

Elliott, John H. "A Review of The First Urban Christians: The Social World of the Apostle Paul by Wayne A. Meeks" *RelSRev*, no. 11 (1985): 329–34.

Elliott, John H. "Social-Scientific Criticism: Perspective, Process and Payoff. Evil Eye Accusation at Galatia as Illustration of the Method." *HTS Theological Studies* 1, no. 67 (2011). Accessed on 5 May 2016. http://www.hts.org.za/index.php/HTS/article/view/858/1454#1.

———. *What Is Social-Scientific Criticism?* Minneapolis: Fortress, 1993.

Ellis, Earle E. *Paul's Use of the Old Testament*. Edinburgh: Oliver & Boyd, 1957.

Engels, Donald W. *Roman Corinth: An Alternative Model for the Classical City*. Chicago: University of Chicago Press, 1990.

Engstrom, Ted W. *The Making of a Christian Leader: How to Develop Management and Human Relations Skills*. Grand Rapids: Zondervan, 1976.

Eriksson, Anders. *Traditions as Rhetorical Proof: Pauline Argumentation in 1 Corinthians*. Stockholm: Almqvist & Wiksell International, 1998.

Esler, Philip Francis. *Community and Gospel in Luke-Acts: The Social and Political Motivations of Lucan Theology*. Cambridge: Cambridge University Press, 1987.

———. *Conflict and Identity in Romans: The Social Setting of Paul's Letter*. Minneapolis: Fortress, 2003.

———. *The First Christians in Their Social Worlds: Social-Scientific Approaches to New Testament Interpretation*. London: Routledge, 1994.

———. *Galatians*. New York: Routledge, 1998.

———. "Group Boundaries and Intergroup Conflict in Galatians: A New Reading of Gal. 5:13– 6:10." In *Ethnicity and the Bible*, edited by Mark G. Brett, 215–40. Boston: Brill, 1996.

———. "Jesus and the Reduction of Intergroup Conflict: The Parable of the Good Samaritan in the Light of Social Identity Theory." *Biblical Interpretation*, no. 8 (2000): 325–57.

———. "An Outline of Social Identity Theory." In *T&T Clark Handbook to Social Identity in the New Testament*, edited by J. Brian Tucker and Coleman A. Baker, 13–39. London: Bloomsbury, 2014.

———. "Prototypes, Antitypes and Social Identity in First Clement: Outlining a New Interpretative Model." *Annali di Storia Dell'esegesi* 24, no. 1 (2007): 125–46.

———. "The Socio-Redaction Criticism of Luke-Acts." In *Social-Scientific Approaches to New Testament Interpretation*, edited by David G. Horrell, 123–50. Edinburgh: T&T Clark, 1999/1987.

Esler, Philip F., and Ronald A. Piper. Lazarus, Mary and Martha: Social-Scientific Approaches to the Gospel of John. Minneapolis: Fortress, 2006.

Exler, Francis X. J. *The Form of the Ancient Greek Letter: A Study in Greek Epistolography*. Washington, DC: Catholic University of America Press, 2003.

Farr, Rob. "Theoretical Cohesion vs. Sophisticated Eclecticism." *British Journal of Social Psychology*, no. 25 (1986): 193–95.

Faulkner, Anne. "Jewish Identity and the Jerusalem Conference: Social Identity and Self-Categorization in the Early Church Communities." *Identity and Marginality* 6, no. 1 (2005): 1–19.

Fee, Gordon D. *The First Epistle to the Corinthians*. The New International Commentary on the New Testament. Grand Rapids: Eerdmans, 1987/ 2014.

———. *Jesus the Lord according to Paul the Apostle: A Concise Introduction*. Grand Rapids: Baker Academic, 2018.

———. *Pauline Christology: An Exegetical-Theological Study*. Peabody: Hendrickson, 2007.

Fielding, Kelly S., and Michael A. Hogg. "Social Identity, Self-Categorization, and Leadership: A Field Study of Small Interactive Groups." *Group Dynamics: Theory, Research, and Practice* 1, no. 1 (1997): 39–51.

Finney, Mark T. "Conflict in Corinth: The Appropriateness of Honour-Shame as the Primary Social Context." PhD diss., University of St Andrews, 2004.

———. "Christ Crucified and the Inversion of Roman Imperial Ideology in 1 Corinthians." *Biblical Theology Bulletin*, no. 35 (2005): 20–33.

———. *Honour and Conflict in the Ancient World: 1 Corinthians in Its Greco-Roman Social Setting*. London: Bloomsbury, 2012.

Fiore, Benjamin. "Covert Allusion in 1 Corinthians 1–4." *Catholic Biblical Quarterly*, no. 47 (1985): 85–102.

———. *The Function of Personal Example in the Socratic and Pastoral Epistles*. Rome: Gregorian University Press, 1986.

Fotopoulos, John. "1 Corinthians." In *The Blackwell Companion to the New Testament*, edited by David E. Aune, 413–33. Chichester: Blackwell Publishing, 2010.

Fraser, Colin, and George Gaskell, eds. *The Social Psychological Study of Widespread Beliefs*. Oxford: Oxford University Press, 1990.

Friesen, Steven J. "Poverty in Pauline Studies: Beyond the So-Called New Consensus." *Journal for the Study of the New Testament*, no. 26 (2004): 323–61.

———. "Prospects for a Demography of the Pauline Mission: Corinth among the Churches." In *Urban Religion and Roman Corinth: Interdisciplinary Approaches*, edited by Daniel N. Schowalter and Steven J. Friesen. Harvard Theological Studies 53, 351–70. Cambridge: Harvard University Press.

———. "The Wrong Erastus: Ideology, Archaeology, and Exegesis." In *Corinth in Context*, edited by Steven J. Friesen, Daniel N. Schowalter, and James C.

Walters, 224–49. Comparative Studies in Religion and Society. Supplements to Novum Testamentum 134. Koninklijke Brill NV: Netherlands, 2010.

Furnish, Victor P. "Corinth in Paul's Time: What Can Archaeology Tell Us?" *Biblical Archaeology Review*, no. 14 (1988): 14–27.

———. "The Jesus-Paul Debate: From Baur to Bultmann." In *Paul and Jesus*, edited by Alexander J. M. Wedderburn, 17–50. Sheffield: Sheffield Academic Press, 1989.

Gadamer, Hans-Georg. *Truth and Method*. 2nd English ed. Translated by Joel Weinsheimer and Donald G. Marshall. London: Sheed & Ward, 1989.

Gadenz, Pablo T. *Called from the Jews and from the Gentiles: Pauline Ecclesiology in Romans 9–11*. Tübingen: Mohr Siebeck, 2009.

Gager, John G. *Kingdom and Community: The Social World of Early Christianity*. Englewood Cliffs: Prentice-Hall, 1975.

Gallagher, Eugene V. "The Social World of Saint Paul." *Religion* 14, no. 1 (1984): 91–99.

Garland, David E. *1 Corinthians*. Grand Rapids: Baker Academic, 2003.

Garnsey, Peter, and Greg Woolf. "Patronage of the Rural Poor in the Roman World." In *Patronage in Ancient Society*, edited by Andrew Wallace-Hardrill, 153–70. London: Routledge, 1990.

Garret, Susan. "Sociology of Early Christianity." In *Anchor Bible Dictionary, Volume 6*, edited by David N. Freedman, 89–99. New York: Doubleday, 1992.

Gaventa, Beverly R. "The Maternity of Paul: An Exegetical Study of Galatians 4:19." In *The Conversation Continues: Studies in Paul and John in Honor of J. Louis Martyn*, edited by Robert T. Fortna and Beverly R. Gaventa, 189–201. Nashville: Abingdon, 1990.

Gehring, Roger W. *House Church and Mission: The Importance of Household Structures in Early Christianity*. Peabody: Hendrickson, 2004.

George, Timothy. *The New American Commentary Volume 30: Galatians, an Exegetical and Theological Exposition of Holy Scripture*. Nashville: Broadman & Holman, 1994.

Giddens, Anthony. *Central Problems in Social Theory: Action, Structure, and Contradiction in Social Analysis*. Berkeley: University of California Press, 1979.

Giessner, Steffen R., Daan van Knippenberg, Wendy van Ginkel, and Ed Sleebos. "Team-Oriented Leadership: The Interactive Effects of Leader Group Prototypicality, Accountability, and Team Identification." *Journal of Applied Psychology* 98, no. 4 (2013): 658–67.

Giessner, Steffen R., Daan van Knippenberg, and Ed Sleebos. "License to Fail? How Leader Group Prototypicality Moderates the Effects of Leader Performance on Perceptions of Leadership Effectiveness." *Leadership Quarterly* 20, no. 3 (2009): 434–51.

Giessner, Steffen R., and Daan van Knippenberg. "License to Fail: Goal Definition, Leader Group Prototypicality, and Perceptions of Leadership Effectiveness after Leader Failure." *Organizational Behavior and Human Decision Processes* 105, no. 1 (2008): 14–35.

Goodrich, John K. "Erastus of Corinth (Romans 16.23): Responding to Recent Proposals on His Rank, Status, and Faith." *New Testament Studies* 57, no. 4 (2011): 583–93.

———. *Paul as an Administrator of God in 1 Corinthians*. Cambridge: Cambridge University Press, 2012.

Gordon, J. Dorcas. *Sister or Wife?: 1 Corinthians and Cultural Anthropology*. Sheffield: Sheffield Academic Press, 1997.

Goulder, Michael D. *St. Paul versus St. Peter: A Tale of Two Missions*. London: SCM, 1994.

Haacker, Klaus. "Gallio." In *Anchor Bible Dictionary*, edited by David N. Freedman, 901–3. New York: Doubleday, 1992.

Hainz, Josef. *Ekklesia: Strukturen paulinischer gemeinde-theologie und gemeinde-ordnung*. Biblische untersuchungen 6. Regensburg: Pustet, 1972.

Hains, Sarah C., Michael A. Hogg, and Julie M. Duck. "Self-Categorization and Leadership: Effects of Group Prototypicality and Leader Stereotypicality." *Personality and Social Psychology Bulletin* 23, no. 10 (1997): 1087–99.

Hakola, Raimo. "The Burden of Ambiguity: Nicodemus and the Social Identity of the Johannine Christians." *New Testament Studies* 4, no. 55 (2009): 438–55.

———. "Friendly Pharisees and Social Identity in Acts." In *Contemporary Studies in Acts*, edited by Thomas E. Philips, 181–200. Macon: Mercer University Press, 2009.

———. "Social Identity and a Stereotype in the Making: The Pharisees as Hypocrites in Matthew 23." In *Identity Formation in the New Testament*, edited by Bengt Holmberg and Mikael Winninge, 123–40. Tübingen: Mohr Siebeck, 2008.

Halcomb, T. Michael. *Paul the Change Agent: The Context, Aims, and Implications of an Apostolic Innovator*. Wilmore: GlossaHouse, 2015.

Hall, Robert G. "Historical Inference and Rhetorical Effect: Another Look at Galatians 1 and 2." In *Persuasive Artistry: Studies in Honour of George A. Kennedy*, edited by Duane F. Watson, 308–20. Sheffield: Sheffield Academic Press, 1991.

Hamilton, Craig. *Wisdom in Leadership: The How and Why of Leading the People You Serve*. Kingsford: Matthias Media, 2015.

Hansen, Bruce. "All of You Are One: The Social Vision of Galatians 3.28, 1 Corinthians 12.13 and Colossians 3.11." PhD diss., St. Andrews University, 2007.

Harland, Philip A. *Associations, Synagogues and Congregations: Claiming a Place in Ancient Mediterranean Society*. Minneapolis: Fortress, 2003.

———. *Dynamics of Identity in the World of the Early Christians: Associations, Judeans and Cultural Minorities*. London: T&T Clark, 2009.

Harnack, Adolf von. *The Constitution and Law of the Church in the First Two Centuries*. Translated by F. L. Pogson. London: Williams & Norgate, 1910. Accessed in May 2015. https://archive.org/stream/theconstitutiona00harnuoft/.

Harris, Murray J. *Prepositions and Theology in the Greek New Testament: An Essential Reference Resource for Exegesis*. Grand Rapids: Zondervan, 2012.

Harvey, John D. *Listening to the Text: Oral Patterning in Paul's Letters*. Grand Rapids: Baker Academic, 1998.

Haslam, S. Alexander. *Psychology in Organizations: The Social Identity Approach*. London: Sage, 2004.

Haslam, S. Alexander, and Michael J. Platow. "The Link Between Leadership and Followership: How Affirming Social Identity Translates Vision into Action." *Personality and Social Psychology Bulletin* 27, no. 11 (2001): 1469–79.

Haslam, S. Alexander and Stephen D. Reicher. "Identity Entrepreneurship and the Consequences of Identity Failure: The Dynamics of Leadership in the BBC Prison Study". *Social Psychology Quarterly* 70, no. 2 (2007): 125–147.

Haslam, S. Alexander, Stephen D. Reicher, and Michael J. Platow. *The New Psychology of Leadership: Identity, Influence and Power*. New York: Psychology, 2011.

Haslam, S. Alexander, John C. Turner, Penelope J. Oakes, Craig McGarty, and Katherine J. Reynolds. "The Group as a Basis for Emergent Stereotype Consensus." *European Review of Social Psychology*, no. 8 (1998): 203–39.

Haslam, S. Aleaxander, Daan van Knippenberg, Michael J. Platow, and Naomi Ellemers, eds. *Social Identity at Work: Developing Theory for Organizational Practice*. New York: Psychology, 2003.

Hays, J. Daniel. *From Every People and Nation: A Biblical Theology of Race*. Downers Grove: IVP, 2003

———. "Paul and the Multi-Ethnic First-Century World: Ethnicity and Christian Identity." In *Paul as Missionary: Identity, Activity, Theology, and Practice*, edited by Trevor J. Burke and Brian S. Rosner, 76–87. London: T&T Clark, 2011.

Hays, Richard B. *Echoes of Scripture in the Letters of Paul*. New Haven: Yale University Press, 1989.

———. *First Corinthians*. Louisville: John Knox, 1997.

Harvey, Graham. *The True Israel: Uses of the Names Jew, Hebrew and Israel in Ancient Jewish and Early Christian Literature*. Boston: Brill, 2001.

Hemer, Colin J. "Observation on Pauline Chronology." In *Pauline Studies: Essays Presented to Professor F. F. Bruce on His 70th Birthday*, edited by Donald A. Hagner and Murray J. Harris, 3–18. Exeter: Paternoster, 1980.

Hengel, Martin. *The Zealots: Investigations into the Jewish Freedom Movement in the Period from Herod I until 70 A.D.* Translated by D. Smith. Edinburgh: T&T Clark, 1989.

Hester, J. D. "Placing the Blame: The Placing of Epideictic in Galatians 1 and 2." In *Persuasive Artistry: Studies in Honour of George A. Kennedy*, edited by Duane F. Watson, 281–307. Sheffield: Sheffield Academic Press, 1991.

Hickman, Gill R., ed. *Leading Organizations: Perspectives for a New Era.* Thousand Oaks: Sage Publications, 1998.

Hietanen, Mika. *Paul's Argumentation in Galatians: A Pragma-Dialectical Analysis.* London: T&T Clark, 2007.

Himes, Michael J. "Divinizing the Church: Strauss and Barth on Möhler's Ecclesiology." In *The Legacy of the Tübingen School: The Relevance of Nineteenth-Century Theology for the Twenty-First Century*, edited by Donald J. Dietrich and Michael J. Himes, 95–110. New York: Crossroad, 1997.

Hirst, Giles, Rolf van Dick, and Daan van Knippenberg. "A Social Identity Perspective on Leadership and Employee Creativity." *Journal of Organizational Behaviour* 30, no. 7 (2009): 963–82.

Ho, Sin P. D. "Cleanse Out the Old Leaven, That You May Be a New Lamp: A Rhetorical Analysis of 1 Cor 5.1–11.1 in Light of the Social Lives of the Corinthians." PhD diss., University of Sheffield, 2012.

———. *Paul and the Creation of a Counter-Cultural Community: A Rhetorical Analysis of 1 Cor 5.1–11.1 in Light of the Social Lives of the Corinthians.* New York: T&T Clark, 2015.

Hock, Ronald F. *The Social Context of Paul's Ministry: Tent Making and Apostleship.* Philadelphia: Fortress, 1980.

Hodge, Caroline J. *If Sons, Then Heirs: A Study of Kinship and Ethnicity in the Letters of Paul.* London: Oxford University Press, 2007.

Hoehner, Harold W. *Ephesians: An Exegetical Commentary.* Grand Rapids: Baker Academic, 2002.

Hogg, Michael A. "Social Categorization, Depersonalization, and Group Behaviour." In *Blackwell Handbook of Social Psychology: Group Processes*, edited by Michael A. Hogg and R. Scott Tindale, 56–85. Oxford: Blackwell Publishers, 2001.

———. "A Social Identity Theory of Leadership." *Personality and Social Psychology Review* 5, no. 3 (2001): 184–200.

Hogg, Michael A., and Paul Grieve. "Social Identity Theory and the Crisis of Confidence in Social Psychology: A Commentary, and Some Research on Uncertainty Reduction." *Asian Journal of Psychology*, no. 2 (1999): 79–93.

Hogg, Michael A., and Deborah J. Terry. *Social Identity Processes in Organizational Contexts*. Philadelphia: Psychology, 2001.

Hogg, Michael A., Deborah J. Terry, and Katherine M. White. "A Tale of Two Theories: A Critical Comparison of Identity Theory with Social Identity Theory." *Social Psychology Quarterly*, no. 58 (1995): 255–69.

Hogg, Michael A., and Daan van Knippenberg. "Social Identity and Leadership Processes in Groups." In *Advances in Experimental Social Psychology*, Volume 35, edited by Mark P. Zanna, 1—52. New York: Academic Press, 2003.

Hogg, Michael A., Daan van Knippenberg, and David E. Rast III. "The Social Identity Theory of Leadership: Theoretical Origins, Research Findings, and Conceptual Development." *European Review of Social Psychology* 23, no. 1 (2012): 258–304.

Holmberg, Bengt. "The Methods of Historical Reconstruction in the Scholarly Recovery of Corinthian Christianity." In *Christianity at Corinth: The Quest for the Pauline Church*, edited by Edward Adams and David G. Horrell, 255–71. Louisville: Westminster/John Knox Press, 2004.

———. *Paul and Power: The Structure of Authority in the Primitive Church as Reflected in the Pauline Epistles*. Philadelphia: Fortress, 1978.

———. *Sociology and the New Testament: An Appraisal*. Minneapolis: Fortress, 1990.

———. "Understanding the First Hundred Years of Christian Identity." In *Exploring Early Christian Identity*, edited by Bengt Holmberg, 1–32. Tübingen: Mohr Siebeck, 2008.

Holtzmann, Heinrich J. *Die pastoralbriefe: Kritisch und exegetisch behandelt*. Leipzig: Engelmann, 1880.

Hooker, Morna D. "A Partner in the Gospel: Paul's Understanding of His Ministry." In *Theology and Ethics in Paul and His Interpreters: Essays in Honor of Victor Paul Furnish*, edited by Eugene Lovering Jr., and Jerry L. Sumney, 83–100. Nashville: Abingdon, 1996.

Horrell, D. G. "Becoming Christian: Solidifying Christian identity and Content." In *Handbook of Early Christianity: Social Science Approaches*, edited by Anthony Blasi, Jean Duhaime, and Paul-Andre Turcotte, 309–35. Walnut Creek: Alta Mira Press, 2002.

———. "Ethnicisation, Marriage and Early Christian Identity: Critical Reflections on 1 Corinthians 7, 1 Peter 3 and Modern New Testament Scholarship." *New Testament Studies*, no. 62 (2016): 439–60.

———. "Introduction, Social-Scientific Interpretation of the New Testament: Retrospect and Prospect." In *Social-Scientific Approaches to New Testament Interpretation*, edited by David G. Horrell, 3–28. Edinburgh: T&T Clark, 1999.

———. "No Longer Jew or Greek: Paul's Corporate Christology and the Construction of Christian Community." In *Christology, Controversy and*

Community, edited by David G. Horrell and Christopher M. Tuckett, 321–44. Leiden: Brill, 2000.

———. *Pauline Churches or Early Christian Churches? Unity, Disagreement, and the Eucharist*. Exeter: University of Exeter Press, 2008.

———. "Paul." In *The Biblical World*. Vol. 2, edited by John Barton, 258–86. London: Routledge, 2002.

———. *The Social Ethos of the Corinthian Correspondence: Interests and Ideology from 1 Corinthians to 1 Clement*. Studies of the New Testament and Its World. Edinburgh: T&T Clark, 1996.

———. "Whither Social-Scientific Approaches to New Testament Interpretation? Reflections on Contested Methodologies and the Future." In *After the First Urban Christians: The Social-Scientific Study of Pauline Christianity Twenty-Five Years Later*, edited by Todd D. Still and David G. Horrell, 6–20. London: T&T Clark, 2009.

Horrell, David G., and Edward Adams. "The Scholarly Quest for Paul's Church at Corinth: A Critical Survey." In *Christianity at Corinth: The Quest for the Pauline Church*, edited by Edward Adams and David G. Horrell, 1–43. London: John Knox Press, 2004.

Horsley, Richard A. *1 Corinthians*. Nashville: Abingdon Press, 1998.

Hultgren, Arland J. *Paul's Letter to the Romans*. Grand Rapids: Eerdmans, 2011.

Hurd, John C., Jr. "Good News and the Integrity of 1 Corinthians." In *Gospel in Paul: Studies on Corinthians, Galatians and Romans for Richard N. Longenecker*, edited by L. Ann Jervis and Peter Richardson, 38–62. Sheffield: Sheffield Academic Press, 1994.

———. *The Origin of 1 Corinthians*. Macon: Mercer University Press, 1983.

Jackson, Linda A., Linda A. Sullivan, Richard Harnish, and Carole N. Hodge. "Achieving Positive Social Identity: Social Mobility, Social Creativity, and Permeability of Group Boundaries." *Journal of Personality and Social Psychology* 70, no. 2 (1996): 241–54.

Jaffee, Martin S. *Early Judaism*. Upper Saddle River: Prentice Hall, 1997.

Janson, Annick, Lester Levy, Sim B. Sitkin, and E. Allan Lind. "Fairness and Other Leadership Heuristics: A Four-Nation Study." *European Journal of Work and Organizational Psychology* 17, no. 2 (2008): 251–72.

Jeffers, James S. *Conflict at Rome: Social Order and Hierarchy in Early Christianity*. Minneapolis: Fortress, 1991.

Jervis, L. Ann. *The Purpose of Romans: A Comparative Letter Structure Investigation*. Sheffield: Sheffield Academic Press, 1991.

Jewett, Robert. *Dating Paul's Life*. London: SCM, 1979.

Johnson, M. P. "Review: Constantine R. Campbell, "Paul and Union with Christ: An Exegetical and Theological Study." *Journal of the Evangelical Theological Society* 56, no. 2 (2013): 431–34.

Judge, Edwin A. "The Early Christians as a Scholastic Community." *The Journal of Religious History* 1, no. 1 (1960): 4–15.

———. "Paul's Boasting in Relation to Contemporary Professional Practice." In *Social Distinctives of the Christians in the First Century: Pivotal Essays*, edited by David M. Scholer, 57–71. Peabody: Hendrickson, 2008.

———. "The Social Identity of the First Christians: A Question of Method in Religious History." *Journal of Religious History* 2, no. 11 (1980): 201–17.

———. *The Social Pattern of the Christian Groups in the First Century: Some Prolegomena to the Study of New Testament Ideas of Social Obligation*. Cambridge: Tyndale House, 1960.

———. "The Teacher as a Moral Exemplar in Paul and in the Inscriptions of Ephesus." In *In the Fullness of Time: Biblical Studies in Honour of Archbishop Donald Robinson*, edited by David Peterson and John Pryor, 185–202. Homebush West: Anzea, 1992.

Judge, Timothy A., and Ronald F. Piccolo. "Transformational and Transactional Leadership: A Meta-Analytic Test of Their Relative Validity." *Journal of Applied Psychology*, no. 5 (2004): 755–68.

Käsemann, Ernst. "Amt und gemeinde im Neuen Testament." In *Exegetische Versuche und Besinnungen*, edited by Ernst Käsemann, 109–34. Göttingen: Vandenhoeck & Ruprecht, 1960.

———. *Commentary on Romans*. Grand Rapids: Eerdmans, 1980.

———. "Die legitimät des apostels: Eine untersuchung zu II Korinther 10–13." *Zeitschrift fur die Neutestamentliche Wissenschaft und die Kunde des Urchristentums*, no. 41 (1942): 33–71.

———. *Essays on the New Testament Themes*. London: S.C.M. Press, 1964.

Katz, Daniel. *The Social Psychology of Organizations*. 2nd ed. New York: Wiley, 1978.

Keay, Robert D., Jr. "Paul the Spiritual Guide: A Social Identity Perspective on Paul's Apostolic Self-Identity." PhD diss., St. Andrews University, 2004.

Keener, Craig S. *Acts: An Exegetical Commentary, 15:1–23:35*. Grand Rapids: Baker Academic, 2014.

———. *Acts: An Exegetical Commentary, Introduction and 1:1–2:47*. Grand Rapids: Baker Academic, 2012.

Kennedy, George A. *New Testament Interpretation through Rhetorical Criticism*. Chapel Hill: University of North Carolina Press, 1984.

Kern, Philip H. "The Word of the Cross: The Language of the Cross in 1 Corinthians." In *The Wisdom of the Cross: Exploring 1 Corinthians*, edited by Brian S. Rosner, 78–99. Nottingham: Apollos, 2011.

Khoza, Reuel J. *Attuned Leadership: African Humanism as Compass*. South Africa: Penguin, 2011.

Kim, Yung S. *Christ's Body in Corinth: The Politics of a Metaphor*. Minneapolis: Fortress, 2008.

King, Pamela E. "Religion and Identity: The Role of Ideological, Social, and Spiritual Contexts." *Applied Developmental Science* 7, no. 3 (2003): 197–204.

Kittel, G., ed. *Theological Dictionary of the New Testament*. Volume I, A-Γ. Translated and edited by Geoffrey W. Bromiley. Grand Rapids: Eerdmans, 1964.

Kloppenborg, John S., and Stephen G. Wilson. *Voluntary Associations in the Graeco-Roman World*. London: Routledge, 1996.

Koelen, Maria A., and Anne W. van den Ban. *Health Education and Health Promotion*. Wageningen: Wageningen Academic Publisher, 2004.

Koester, H. *Ancient Christian Gospel*. London: SCM, 1990.

Kuck, David W. *Judgment and Community Conflict: Paul's Use of Apocalyptic Judgment Language in 1 Corinthians 3:5–4:5*. New York: Brill, 1992.

Küng, Hans. *The Church*. Translated by Ray and Rosaleen Ockenden. New York: Burns & Oates, 1967.

Kwon, Oh-Young. *1 Corinthians 1–4: Reconstructing Its Social and Rhetorical Situation and Re-Reading It Cross-Culturally for Korean-Confucian Christians Today*. Eugene: Wipf and Stock Publishers, 2010.

Lamont, Michele, and Virag Molnár. "The Study of Boundaries in Social Science." *Annual Review of Sociology*, no. 28 (2002): 167–95.

Lane, William L. "Social Perspectives on Roman Christianity during the Formative Years from Nero to Nerva: Romans, Hebrews, 1 Clement." In *Judaism and Christianity in the First- Century Rome*, edited by Karl P. Donfried and Peter Richardson, 196–244. Grand Rapids: Eerdmans, 1998.

Last, Richard. *The Pauline Church and the Corinthian Ekklēsia: Greco-Roman Associations in Comparative Context*. New York: Cambridge University Press, 2016.

Lawrence, Louise J. "Ritual and the First Urban Christians: Boundary and Crossing of Life." In *After the First Urban Christians: The Social-Scientific Study of Pauline Christianity Twenty-Five Years Later*, edited by Todd D. Still and David G. Horrell, 99–115. London: T&T Clark (Continuum), 2009.

Lieu, Judith. *Christian Identity in the Jewish and Greco-Roman World*. Oxford: Oxford University Press, 2004.

Lightfoot, Joseph B. *Saint Paul's Epistle to the Galatians*. London: MacMillan, 1892.

Lim, Kar Y. *Metaphors and Social Identity Formation in Paul's Letters to the Corinthians*. Eugene: Pickwick, 2017.

Longenecker, Bruce W. "Exposing the Economic Middle: A Revised Economy Scale for the Study of Early Urban Christianity." *Journal for the Study of the New Testament* 31, no. 3 (2009): 243–78.

———. *Remember the Poor: Paul, Poverty, and the Greco-Roman World*. Grand Rapids: Eerdmans, 2010.
Longenecker, Richard N. *The Epistle to the Romans*. Grand Rapids: Eerdmans, 2016.
———. *Galatians Vol. 41*. Word Biblical Commentary. Grand Rapids: Zondervan Academic, 2017.
———. "Taking Up the Cross Daily: Discipleship in Luke-Acts." In *Patterns of Discipleship in the New Testament*, edited by Richard N. Longenecker, 50–76. Grand Rapids: Eerdmans, 1996.
Lord, Robert G., Douglas J. Brown, Jennifer L. Harvey, and Rosalie J. Hall. "Contextual Constraints on Prototype Generation and Their Multilevel Consequences for Leadership Perceptions. " *The Leadership Quarterly* 12, no. 3 (2001): 311–38.
Lord, Robert G., Christy L. de Vader, and George M. Alliger. "A Meta-Analysis of the Relation between Personality Traits and Leadership Perceptions: An Application of Validity Generalization Procedures." *Journal of Applied Psychology* 71, no. 3 (1986):402–10.
Lowery, Stephanie. "Review: Jack Barentsen, Emerging Leadership in the Pauline Mission: A Social Identity Perspective on Local Leadership Development in Corinth and Ephesus." 2012. Accessed on 4 June 2015. https://wheatonblog.wordpress.com/2012/06/11/jack-barentsen-emerging- leadership-in-the-23pauline-mission-a-social-identity-perspective-on-local-leadership-development-in-corinth-and-ephesus/.
Lüdemann, Gerd. *Paul, Apostle to the Gentiles: Studies in Chronology*. Translated by F. S. Jones. Philadelphia: Fortress, 1980.
———. *Paul, the Founder of Christianity*. Amherst: Prometheus Books, 2002.
Lyons, George. *Pauline Autobiography: Towards a New Understanding*. Atlanta: Scholars, 1985.
Macrae, Rachel M. "Eating with Honor: The Corinthian Lord's Supper in Light of Voluntary Association Meal Practices." *Journal of Biblical Literature* 1, no. 130 (2011): 165–81.
Magezi, Vhumani. "God-image of Servant King as Powerful but Vulnerable and Serving: Towards Transforming African Church Leadership at an Intersection of African Kingship and Biblical Kingship to Servant Leadership." *HTS Teologiese Studies/Theological Studies* 71, no.2 (2015): 1–9. Art. #2907. http://dx.doi.org/10.4102/hts.v71i2.2907.
Malcolm, Matthew R. "Paul and the Rhetoric of Reversal." PhD diss., University of Nottingham, 2011.
———. "The Structure and Theme of First Corinthians in Recent Scholarship." *Currents in Biblical Research* 14, no. 2 (2016): 256–69.

———. "That God May Be All in All: The Glory of God in 1 Corinthians." In *The Wisdom of the Cross: Exploring 1 Corinthians*, edited by Brian S. Rosner, 201–18. Nottingham: Apollos, 2011.

Malherbe, Abraham J. *Social Aspects of Early Christianity*. Eugene: Wipf and Stock Publishers, 1983.

Malina, Bruce J. *Christian Origins and Cultural Anthropology: Practical Models for Biblical Interpretation*. Atlanta: John Knox Press, 1986.

———. "Early Christian Groups: Using Small Group Formation Theory to Explain Christian Organizations." In *Modeling Early Christianity: Social Scientific Studies of the New Testament in Its Context*, edited by Philip F. Esler, 96–113. London: Routledge, 1995.

———. *The New Testament World: Insights from Cultural Anthropology*. 3rd ed. Nashville: John Knox, 1981/2001.

———. "The Received View and What It Cannot Do: III John and Hospitality." *Semantics*, no. 36 (1986): 181—183.

———. "Review: The First Urban Christians: The Social World of the Apostle Paul." *Journal of Biblical Literature* 104, no. 2 (1985): 346–49.

———. *Timothy: Paul's Closest Associate*. Collegeville: Liturgical, 2008.

Mangu, André M. B. "State Reconstruction, Leadership Legitimacy and Democratic Governance in Africa." *Politeia* 27, no. 2 (2008): 1–24.

Marshall, I. Howard. *A Critical and Exegetical Commentary on the Pastoral Epistles*. The International Critical Commentary. London: T&T Clark, 2006.

———. *The Pastoral Epistles*. London: T&T Clark, 2004.

Martin, Dale B. *The Corinthian Body*. London: Yale University Press, 1995.

———. "Patterns of Belief and Patterns of Life: Correlations in the First Urban Christians and Since." In *After the First Urban Christians: The Social-Scientific Study of Pauline Christianity Twenty-Five Years Later*, edited by Todd D. Still and David G. Horrell, 116–33. London: T&T Clark (Continuum), 2009.

———. "Review: Justin J. Meggitt, Paul, Poverty, and Survival." *Journal for the Study of the New Testament*, no. 84 (2001): 51–64.

Masango, Maake. *Leadership in an African Context*. Pretoria: UNISA, 2002.

Mason, Steven. "Jews, Judaeans, Judaizing, Judaism: Problems of Categorization in Ancient History." *Journal for the Study of Judaism in the Persian, Hellenistic and Roman Periods*, no. 38 (2007): 457–512.

Maxwell, John C. *The 21 Irrefutable Laws of Leadership*. Nashville: Thomas Nelson, 1998.

May, Alistair S. *The Body for the Lord: Sex and Identity in 1 Corinthians 5–7*. New York: T&T Clark, 2004.

Mbevi, Misheck M. "Paul and Ethnicity: A Socio-Historical Study of Romans." MA Thesis, North West University, 2013.

McDougall, William. *The Group Mind*. Cambridge: Cambridge University Press, 1920.

———. *An Introduction to Social Psychology*. London: Methuen, 1908.

Meeks, Wayne A. *The First Urban Christians: The Social World of the Apostle Paul*. 1983. Reprint, New Haven: Yale University Press, 2003.

———. "The Man from Heaven in Johannine Sectarianism." *Journal of Biblical Literature*, no. 91 (1972): 44–72.

———. *The Moral World of the First Christians*. Philadelphia: Westminster, 1986.

———. "The Social Context of Pauline Theology." *Interpretation* 36, no. 3 (1982): 266–77.

Meggitt, J. J. *Paul, Poverty and Survival*. Edinburgh: T&T Clark, 1998.

———. "The Social Status of Erastus (Rom. 16:23)." *Novum Testamentum* 38, 3 (1996): 218–23.

Meritt, Benjamin D. *Greek Inscriptions, 1896–1927: Corinth; Results of Excavations Conducted by the American School of Classical Studies at Athens*. Vol. 8, Part 1. Cambridge: Harvard University Press, 1931.

Michaelis, W. "μιμέομαι, μιμητής, συμμιμητής." In *Theological Dictionary of the New Testament*, edited by Gerhard Kittel, 659–74. Translated by Geoffrey W. Bromiley. Grand Rapids: Eerdmans, 1967.

Middendorf, Michael P. *Romans 1–8*. Saint Louis: Concordia, 2013.

———. *Romans 9–16*. Saint Louis: Concordia, 2016.

Mihaila, Corin. *The Paul-Apollos Relationship and Paul's Stance toward Greco-Roman Rhetoric*. London: T&T Clark, 2009.

Miller, Anna C. *Corinthian Democracy: Democratic Discourse in 1 Corinthians*. Eugene: Pickwick, 2015.

Miller, David M. "The Meaning of Ioudaios and Its Relationship to Other Group Labels in Ancient "Judaism."" *Currents in Biblical Research* 9, no. 1 (2010): 98–126.

Miller, Marvin L. "The Performance of Ancient Jewish Letters: From Elephantine to MMT." PhD diss., University of Manchester, 2012.

Mitchell, Margaret M. "Concerning περὶ δὲ." *Novum Testamentum* 31, no. 3 (1989): 229–56.

———. *Paul and the Rhetoric of Reconciliation: An Exegetical Investigation of the Language and Composition of 1 Corinthians*. Louisville: John Knox, 1991.

———. "Rhetorical Shorthand in Pauline Argumentation: The Function of 'the Gospel' in the Corinthian Correspondence." In *Gospel in Paul: Studies on Corinthians, Galatians and Romans for Richard N. Longenecker*, edited by L. Ann Jervis and Peter Richardson, 63–88. Sheffield: Sheffield Academic Press, 1994.

Moo, Douglas J. *The Epistle to the Romans*. Grand Rapids: Eerdmans, 1996.

Morgan, Robert, and John Barton. *Biblical Interpretation*. Oxford: Oxford University Press, 1988/2003.
Morris, Leon. *The Epistle to the Romans*. Grand Rapids: Eerdmans, 1988.
Munck, Johannes. "'The Church without Factions: Studies in 1 Corinthians 1–4." In *Christianity at Corinth: The Quest for the Pauline Church*, edited by Edward Adams and David G. Horrell, 61–70. Louisville: John Knox, 2004.
———. *Paul and the Salvation of Mankind*. London: SCM Press, 1959/2004.
Murphy-O'Connor, Jerome. "The Corinth That Saint Paul Saw." *Biblical Archaeologist*, no. 47 (1984): 147–59.
———. *Paul: A Critical Life*. Oxford: Clarendon, 1996.
———. *Paul The Letter-Writer: His World, His Options, His Skills*. Collegeville: Liturgical, 1995.
———. *St. Paul's Corinth: Texts and Archaeology*. Collegeville: Liturgical, 1983/2002.
———. *The Theology of the Second Letter to the Corinthians*. Cambridge: Cambridge University Press, 1991.
Mzondi, Abraham M. M. "'Two Souls' Leadership: Dynamic Interplay of Ubuntu, Western and New Testament Leadership Values." PhD diss., University of Johannesburg, 2009.
Nanos, Mark D. "The Inter-and Intra-Jewish Political Context of Paul's Letter to the Galatians." In *The Galatians Debate*, edited by Mark D. Nanos, 396–407. Peabody: Hendrickson, 2002.
———. "Review: David Odell-Scott, Paul's Critique of Theocracy: A Theocracy in Corinth and Galatians." *Biblical Interpretation* 13, no. 4 (2005): 438–41.
———. "What Was at Stake in Peter's Letter 'Eating with Gentiles' at Antioch?" In *The Galatians Debate*, edited by Mark D. Nanos, 282–320. Peabody: Hendrickson, 2002.
Napier, Rodney W., and Matti K. Gershenfeld. *Groups: Theory and Experience*. Boston: Houghton Mifflin, 1981.
Neyrey, Jerome H. "God, Benefactor and Patron: The Major Cultural Model for Interpreting Deity in Greco-Roman Antiquity." *Journal for the Study of the New Testament* 27, no. 4 (2005): 465–92.
———. "Social-Scientific Criticism." In *The Blackwell Companion to the New Testament*, edited by David E. Aune, 177–91. Malden: Wiley-Blackwell, 2010.
Nguyen, V. Henry T. *Christian Identity in Corinth: A Comparative Study of 2 Corinthians, Epictetus and Valerius Maximus*. Tübingen: Mohr Siebeck, 2008.
Nicklas, Tobias, and Herbert Schlögel. "Mission to the Gentiles: The Construction of Christian Identity and Its Relationship with Ethics according to Paul." *HTS Theological Studies* 68, no. 1 (2012): 1–7.

Nkomo, Stella M. "In Search of African Leadership." *Management Today* 22, no. 5 (2006).

———. *Leading Organizational Change in the 'New' South Africa*. Pretoria: University of Pretoria, 2011.

———. "A Postcolonial and Anti-Colonial Reading of 'African' Leadership and Management in Organization Studies: Tensions, Contradictions and Possibilities." *Organization* 18, no. 3 (2011): 365–86.

Northhouse, Peter G. *Leadership Theory and Practice*. Thousand Oaks: Sage, 2004.

Oakes, Peter. "Constructing Poverty Scales for Graeco-Roman Society: A Response to Steven Friesen's 'Poverty in Pauline Studies.'" *Journal for the Study of the New Testament* 26, no. 3 (2004): 367–71.

O'Brien, Peter T. *Introductory Thanksgiving in the Letters of Paul*. Leiden: Brill, 1977.

———. *The Letter to the Ephesians*. Grand Rapids: Eerdmans, 1999.

———. "Paul's Missionary Calling within the Purpose of God." In *In the Fullness of Time: Biblical Studies in Honour of Archbishop Donald Robinson*, edited by David Peterson and John Pryor, 131–48. Homebush West: Anzea, 1992.

Odell-Scott, David W. *Paul's Critique of Theocracy: A Theocracy in Corinthians and Galatians*. London: T&T Clark, 2003/2009.

Oppong, S. H. "Religion and Identity." *American International Journal of Contemporary Research* 3, no. 6 (2013): 10–16.

Oropeza, B. J. *Jews, Gentiles, and the Opponents of Paul: The Pauline Letters*. Eugene: Cascade, 2012.

Orosius of Braga. "The Seven Books of History against the Pagans." In *The Fathers of the Church*, edited by H. Dressler. Translated by Roy J. Deferrari. Washington, DC: The Catholic University of America Press, 1964.

Paget, J. Carleton. "The Definition of the Terms Jewish Christian and Jewish Christianity in Historical Research." In *Jewish Believers in Jesus: The Early Centuries*, edited by Oskar Skarsaune and Reidar Hvalvik, 22–54. Peabody: Hendrickson, 2007.

Perkins, Pheme. *First Corinthians*. Grand Rapids: Baker Academic, 2012.

Peterson, David G. *Possessed by God: A New Testament Theology of Sanctification and Holiness*. Leicester: Apollos, 1995.

Phua, Richard L. *Idolatry and Authority: A Study of 1 Corinthians 8.1–11.1 in the Light of the Jewish Diaspora*. London: T&T Clark, 2005.

Pickett, Raymond. *The Cross in Corinth: The Social Significance of the Death of Jesus*. Sheffield: Sheffield Academic Press, 1997.

Pilch, John J. "The Honoree: Bruce John Malina." In *Social Scientific Models for Interpreting the Bible: Essays by the Context Group in Honor of Bruce J. Malina*, edited by John J. Pilch, 1–4. Boston: Brill, 2001.

———. "Rezension von: Meeks, Wayne A.: The First Urban Christians: The Social World of the Apostle Paul." *Catholic Biblical Quarterly* 47, no. 1 (1985): 169–70.

Plank, Karl A. *Paul and the Irony of Affliction*. Atlanta: Scholars Press, 1987.

Platow, Michael J., Scott Reid, and Sarah Andrew. "Leadership Endorsement: The Role of Distributive and Procedural Behavior in Interpersonal and Intergroup Contexts." *Group Processes & Intergroup Relations* 1, no. 1 (1998): 35–47.

Platow, Michael J., Stephanie Hoar, Scott Reid, Keryn Harley, and Dianne Morrison. "Endorsement of Distributively Fair and Unfair Leaders in Interpersonal and Intergroup Situations." *European Journal of Social Psychology* 27, no. 4 (1997): 465–94.

Platow, Michael J., Daan van Knippenberg, S. Alexander Haslam, Barbara van Knippenberg, and Russell Spears. "A Special Gift We Bestow on You for Being Representative of Us: Considering Leader Charisma from a Self-Categorization Perspective." *British Journal of Social Psychology* 45, 2 (2006): 303–20.

Polaski, Sandra H. *Paul and the Discourse of Power*. Sheffield: Sheffield Academic Press, 1999.

Polhill, John B. *Paul and His Letters*. Nashville: Broadman & Holman, 1999.

Porter, Stanley E. *The Apostle Paul: His Life, Thought, and Letters*. Grand Rapids: Eerdmans, 2016.

———. "How Do We Define Social Relations?" In *Paul and His Social Relations*, edited by Stanley E. Porter and Christopher D. Land, 7–34. Boston: Brill, 2013.

———. *Idioms of the Greek New Testament*. Sheffield: Sheffield Academic Press, 1994.

———. "Paul of Tarsus and His Letters." In *Handbook of Classical Rhetoric in the Hellenistic Period*, 330 B.C.–A.D. 400, edited by Stanley E. Porter, 533–86. Leiden: Brill, 1997.

———. "Understanding Pauline Studies. An Assessment of Recent Research: Part One." *Themelios* 22, no. 1 (1996): 14–25.

———. "When It Was Clear That We Could Not Persuade Him, We Gave Up and Said, 'The Lord's Will Be Done' (Acts 21:14): Good Reason to Stop Making Unproven Claims for Rhetorical Criticism." *Bulletin for Biblical Research* 26, no. 4 (2016): 533–45.

Porter, Stanley E., and Christopher D. Land. "Paul and His Social Relations: An Introduction." In *Paul and His Social Relations*, edited by Stanley E. Porter and Christopher D. Land, 1–6. Boston: Brill, 2013.

Punt, Jeremy. "1 Corinthians 7:17–24: Identity and Human Dignity amidst Power and Liminality." *Verbum et Ecclesia* 33, no. 1 (2012): 1–9.

———. "Foolish Rhetoric in 1 Cor 1–4 (1:18–31): Paul's Discourse of Power as Mimicry." Paper presented at the international meeting of the SBL in London, 4–8 July 2011.

———. "Identity Claims, Texts, Rome and Galatians." *Acta Theologica*, no. 19 (2014): 81–104.

———. "Review: Kathy Ehrensperger, Paul and the Dynamics of Power: Communication and Interaction in the Early Christ-Movement." *Neotestamentica* 45, no. 1 (2011): 150–51.

Reicher, Stephen, "Tajfel, Henri", *The Legacy of European Social Psychology*. Accessed on 25 August 2024). https://history.easp.eu/people/tajfel-henri.

Reicher, Stephen, Russell Spears, and S. Alexander Haslam. "The Social Identity Approach in Social Psychology." In *The SAGE Handbook of Identities*, edited by Margaret Wetherell and Chandra T. Mohanty, 20–60. London: SAGE, 2010. http://dx.doi.org/10.4135/9781446200889.

Rengstorf, Karl H. *Apostolate and Ministry: The New Testament Doctrine of the Office of the Ministry*. London: Concordia, 1969.

———. "ἀπόστολος". In *Theological Dictionary of the New Testament*. Vol. 1, A–Γ, edited by Gerhard Kittel and G. Friedrich, 398–447. Translated by G. W. Bromiley. Grand Rapids: Eerdmans, 1964.

Reumann, John. "Church Office in Paul, especially in Philippians." In *Origins and Method: Towards a New Understanding of Judaism and Christianity*, edited by Bradley H. McLean, 82–91. Sheffield: JSOT Press, 1993.

Rhodes, R. A. W., and Paul Hart. "Puzzles of Political Leadership." In *The Oxford Handbook of Political Leadership*, edited by R. A. W. Rhodes and Paul Hart, 1–21. Oxford: Oxford University Press, 2014.

Ricoeur, Paul. *Interpretation Theory: Discourse and the Surplus on Meaning*. Fort Worth: Texas Christian University Press, 1976.

Ridderbos, Herman. *Paul: An Outline of His Theology*. Translated by J. R. De Witt. Grand Rapids: Eerdmans, 1975.

Robertson, Archibald, and Alfred Plummer. *A Critical and Exegetical Commentary on the First Epistle of St. Paul to the Corinthians*. London: T&T Clark, 1961.

Roitto, Rikard. *Behaving as Christ-believers: A Cognitive Perspective on Identity and Behavior Norms in Ephesians*. Winona Lake: Eisenbrauns, 2011.

Romano, David G. "Post-146 B.C. Land Use in Corinth, and Planning of the Roman Colony of 44 B.C." In *The Corinthia in the Roman Period*, edited by T. E. Gregory, 9–30. Ann Arbor: Cushing-Malloy, 1994.

Rosner, Brian S. "The Logic and Arrangement of 1 Corinthians." In *The Wisdom of the Cross: Exploring 1 Corinthians*, edited by Brian S. Rosner, 16–31. Nottingham: Apollos, 2011.

Rotberg, Robert, I. "Strengthening African Leadership." *Foreign Affairs*, July/August 2004. Accessed on 9 June 2015. https://www.foreignaffairs.com/articles/africa/2004-07-01/strengthening-african-leadership.

Sampley, J. Paul. *Pauline Partnership in Christ: Christian Community and Commitment in Light of Roman Law*. Philadelphia: Fortress, 1980.

Samra, Jim G. *Being Conformed to Christ in Community: A Study of Maturity, Maturation and the Local Church in the Undisputed Pauline Epistles*. London: T&T Clark, 2006.

Sanders, J. Oswald. *Spiritual Leadership: Principles of Excellence for Every Believer*. 2nd ed. Chicago: Moody, 1994.

Sandnes, Karl O. *Paul – One of the Prophets?: A Contribution to the Apostle's Self-Understanding*. Tübingen: Mohr, 1991.

Sani, Fabio, and Steve Reicher. "Identity, Argument and Schism: Two Longitudinal Studies of the Split in the Church of England over the Ordination of Women to the Priesthood." *Group Processes & Intergroup Relations* 2, no. 3 (1999): 279–300.

Savage, Timothy B. *Power through Weakness: Paul's Understanding of the Christian Ministry in 2 Corinthians*. Cambridge: Cambridge University Press, 1996.

Scarborough, Thomas O. *A Deconstructionist Critique of Christian Transformational Leadership*. M.A. Thesis, South African Theological Seminary, 2009.

Schmithals, Walter. *Gnosticism in Corinth: An Investigation of the Letters to the Corinthians*. Nashville: Abingdon, 1971.

———. *The Office of Apostle in the Early Church*. Nashville: Abingdon, 1969.

Schnabel, Eckhard. *Acts: Exegetical Commentary on the New Testament*. Grand Rapids: Zondervan, 2012.

Schreiner, Thomas R. *Galatians. Zondervan Exegetical Commentary on the New Testament*. Grand Rapids: Zondervan, 2010.

Schüssler Fiorenza, Elisabeth. "Rhetorical Situation and Historical Reconstruction in 1 Corinthians." *New Testament Studies*, no. 33 (1987): 386–403.

Schütz, J. H. *Paul and the Anatomy of Apostolic Authority*. Louisville: John Knox Press, 1975/2007.

Schweizer, Eduard. *Church Order in the New Testament*. Translated by F. Clarke. Studies in Biblical Theology, 32. London: SCM, 1959.

Scroggs, Robin. "The Earliest Christian Communities as Sectarian Movement." In *Social-Scientific Approaches to New Testament Interpretation*, edited by David G. Horrell, 69–92. Edinburgh: T&T Clark, 1999/1975.

———. "The Sociological Interpretation of the New Testament: The Present State of Research." *New Testament Studies*, no. 26 (1980): 164–79.

Sechrest, Love L. *A Former Jew: Paul and the Dialectics of Race*. London: T&T Clark, 2009.

Seppälä, Tuija, Jukka Lipponen, and Anna-Maija Pirttilä-Backman. "Leader Fairness and Employees' Trust in Co-Workers: The Moderating Role of Leader Group Prototypicality." *Group Dynamics: Theory, Research, and Practice* 16, no. 1 (2012): 35–49.

Shaw, Graham. *The Cost of Authority: Manipulation and Freedom in the New Testament*. Philadelphia: Fortress, 1983.

Shkul, Minna. *Reading Ephesians: Exploring Social Entrepreneurship in the Text*. London: T&T Clark, 2009.

Shutte, Augustine. *Philosophy for Africa*. Rondebosch: University of Cape Town Press, 1993.

———. *Ubuntu: An Ethic for a New South Africa*. Pietermaritzburg: Cluster Publications, 2001.

Sindo, Vuyani S. "A Socio-Rhetorical Approach to the Pauline Theology of Reconciliation in 2 Corinthians." M.A. Thesis, North West University, 2014.

Sircar, S. S. "The Contribution of Sociological Research in the New Testament Studies: An Appraisal." *Indonesian Journal of Theology* 43, no. 1&2 (2001): 30–41.

———. "The Preaching of 'the Gospel of God': Paul's Mission to the Nations in Romans." PhD diss., Southern Baptist Theological Seminary, 2012.

Skarsaune, Oskar. "The History of Jewish Believers in the Early Centuries – Perspectives and Framework." In *Jewish Believers in Jesus: The Early Centuries*, edited by Oskar Skarsaune and Reidar Hvalvik, 745–81. Peabody: Hendrickson, 2007.

———. "Jewish Believers in Jesus in Antiquity – Problems of Definition, Method, and Sources." In *Jewish Believers in Jesus: The Early Centuries*, edited by Oskar Skarsaune and Reidar Hvalvik, 3–21. Peabody: Hendrickson, 2007.

Smit, Joop. "The Letter of Paul to the Galatians: A Deliberative Speech." *New Testament Studies*, no. 35 (1989): 1–26.

———. "What Is Apollos? What Is Paul? In Search for the Coherence of First Corinthians 1:10–4:21." *Novum Testamentum*, 44 (3): 231–51.

Snyder, G. F. "Review: Yung Suk Kim, Christ's Body in Corinth: The Politics of a Metaphor." *Brethren Life and Thought* 54, no. 1 (2009): 98–99.

Snyman, A. H. "Persuasion in 1 Corinthians 1:1–9." *Verbum Ecclesia* 30, no. 2 (2009): 1–6.

Spawforth, Antony J. S. "Roman Corinth: The Formation of a Colonial Elite." In *Roman Onomastics in the Greek East: Social and Political Aspects*, edited by Athanasios D. Rizakis, Sophia Zoumbaki, and Cl. E. Lepenioti, 167–82. Athens: Diffusion de Boccard, 1996.

Spence, Stephen. *The Parting of the Ways: The Romans Church as a Case Study*. Leuven: Peeters, 2004.

Stanley, David M. "'Become Imitators of Me': The Pauline Conception of Apostolic Tradition." *Biblica*, no. 40 (1959): 859–77.
Steffens, Niklas K. "Leaders' Personal Performance and Prototypicality as Interactive Determinants of Social Identity Advancement." PhD diss., University of Exeter, 2012.
Steffens, Niklas K., Sebastian C. Schuh, S. Alexander Haslam, Antonia Pérez, and Rolf van Dick. "Of the Group and for the Group: How Followership Is Shaped by Leaders' Prototypicality and Group Identification." *European Journal of Social Psychology* 45, no. 2 (2015): 180–90.
Steffens, Niklas K., S. Alexander Haslam, Stephen D. Reicher, Michael J. Platow, Katrien Fransen, Jie Yang, Michelle K. Ryan, Jolanda Jetten, Kim Peters, and Filip Boen. "Leadership as Social Identity Management: Introducing the Identity Leadership Inventory (ILI) to Assess and Validate a Four-Dimensional Model." *The Leadership Quarterly*, no. 25 (2014): 1001–24.
Steffens, Niklas K., S. Alexander Haslam, Michelle K. Ryan, and Thomas Kessler. "Leader Performance and Prototypicality: Their Inter-Relationship and Impact on Leaders' Identity Entrepreneurship." *European Journal of Social Psychology* 43, no. 7 (2013): 606–13.
Stepp, Perry L. *Leadership Succession in the World of the Pauline Circle*. Sheffield: Sheffield Phoenix Press, 2005.
Still, Todd D. "Organizational Structures and Relational Struggles among the Saints: The Establishment and Exercise of Authority within Pauline Assemblies. In *After the First Urban Christians: The Social-Scientific Study of Pauline Christianity Twenty-Five Years Later*, edited by Todd D. Still and David G. Horrell, 79–98. London: T&T Clark (Continuum), 2009.
Streeter, Burnett H. *The Primitive Church: Studies with Special Reference to the Origins of Christian Ministry*. London: Macmillan, 1929.
Sumney, Jerry L. "Christ Died for Us: Interpretation of Jesus' Death as a Central Element of the Identity of the Earliest Church." In *Reading Paul in Context: Explorations in Identity Formation: Essays in Honour of William S. Campbell*, edited by in J. Brian Tucker and Kathy Ehrensperger, 147–72. London: T&T Clark, 2010.
Sweatman, Carl S. "Review: Yung Suk Kim, Christ's Body in Corinthian: The Politics of the Metaphor." *Stone Campbell Journal* 12, no. 2 (2009): 311–12.
Swart, Gerrie. "Africa Leads the Way: The Trends and Triumphs of the Continent's Leadership Renaissance." *African Renaissance*, no. 5 (2008): 9–17.
Tajfel, Henri. "Cognitive Aspects of Prejudice." *Journal of Social Issues*, no. 25 (1969): 79–97.
———. "Criticism of a Social Science: The Context of Social Psychology." In *A Critical Assessment*, edited by Joachim Israel and Henri Tajfel. Published in

cooperation with the European Association of Experimental Psychology, New York: Academic Press, 1972.

———, ed. *Differentiation between Social Groups: Studies in the Social Psychology of Intergroup Relations.* London: Academic Press, 1978.

———. "Experiments in Intergroup Discrimination." *Scientific American*, no. 223 (1970): 96–102.

———. *Human Groups and Social Categories: Studies in Social Psychology.* Cambridge: Cambridge University Press, 1981.

———. "Quantitative Judgment in Social Perception." *British Journal of Psychology*, no. 50 (1959): 16–29.

———. "Social and Cultural Factors in Perception." In *Handbook of Social Psychology*, Volume 3, edited by Gardner Lindzey and Elliot Aronson, 315–94. Boston: Addison-Wesley, 1969.

———. "Stereotypes." *Race* 5, no. 2 (1963): 3–4.

Tajfel, Henri, M. G. Billig, R. P. Bundy, and Claude Flament. "Social Categorization and Intergroup Behaviour." *European Journal of Social Psychology* 1, no. 2 (1971): 149–78.

Tajfel, Henri, and John C. Turner. "An Integrative Theory of Intergroup Conflict." In *The Social Psychology of Intergroup Relations*, edited by Willam G. Austin and Stephen Worchel, 33–47. Monterey: Brooks-Cole, 1979.

———. "The Social Identity Theory of Inter-Group Behavior." In *Psychology of Intergroup Relations*, edited by Stephen Worchel and William G. Austin, 7–24. Chicago: Nelson-Hall, 1986.

Taylor, N. H. "Apostolic Identity and the Conflicts in Corinth and Galatia." In *Paul and His Opponents*, edited by Stanley E. Porter, 99–128. Leiden: Brill, 2005.

———. "The Composition and Chronology of Second Corinthians." *Journal for the Study of the New Testament* 14, no. 44 (1991): 67–87.

———. "Conflict as Context for Defining Identity: A Study of Apostleship in the Galatian and Corinthian Letters." *HTS Theological Studies* 59, no. 3 (2003): 915–45.

Tellbe, Mikael. *Christ-Believers in Ephesus: A Textual Analysis of Early Christian Identity Formation in a Local Perspective.* Tübingen: Mohr Siebeck, 2009.

Thate, M. J. "Paul, φρόνησις, and Participation: The Shape of Space and the Reconfiguration of Place in Paul's Letter to the Philippians." In *"In Christ" in Paul*, edited by M. J. Thate, Kevin J. Vanhoozer, and Constantine R. Campbell, 281–327. Tübingen: Mohr Siebeck, 2014.

Theissen, Gerd. *The First Followers of Jesus: A Sociological Analysis of the Earliest Christianity.* London: SCM, 1978.

———. *The Miracle Stories of the Early Christian Tradition.* Translated by John Kenneth Riches T. & T. Clark, 1983.

———. "Social Conflicts in the Corinthian Community: Further Remarks on J. J. Meggitt, Paul, Poverty and Survival." *Journal for the Study of the New Testament* 25, no. 3 (2003): 371–91.

———. *The Social Setting of Pauline Christianity: Essays on Corinth*. Translated by J. H. Schütz. Eugene: Wipf and Stock, 2004.

———. "The Social Structure of Pauline Communities." *Journal for the Study of the New Testament*, no. 84 (2001): 65–84.

Thiselton, Anthony C. "Book Review: Autobiographical Biblical Criticism: Between Text and Self." *Theology* 107, no. 840: 436–37.

———. *1 Corinthians: A Short Exegetical & Pastoral Commentary*. Grand Rapids: Eerdmans, 2006.

———. *The First Epistle to the Corinthians*. Grand Rapids: Eerdmans, 2000.

———. *Interpreting God and the Postmodern Self: On Meaning, Manipulation and Promise*. Endinburgh: T&T Clark, 1995.

———. "Realised Eschatology in Corinth." *New Testament Studies* 24, no. 4 (1978): 510–26.

———. "The Significance of Recent Research on 1 Corinthians for Hermeneutical Appropriation of this Epistle Today." *Neotestimentica* 40, no. 2 (2006): 320–52.

———. *The Two Horizons: New Testament Hermeneutics and Philosophical Description with Special Reference to Heidegger, Bultmann, Gadamer, and Wittgenstein*. Grand Rapids: Eerdmans Publishing, 1980.

Tidball, Derek. *An Introduction to the Sociology of the New Testament*. Exeter: The Paternoster Press, 1983.

Tite, Philip L. "How to Begin, and Why? Diverse Function of the Pauline Prescript within a Greco-Roman Context." In *Paul and the Ancient Letter Form*, edited by Stanley E. Porter and Sean A. Adams, 57–100. Boston: Brill, 2010.

Trebilco, Paul R. *Outsider Designation and Boundary Construction in the New Testament: Early Christian Communities and Formation of Group Identity*. Cambridge: Cambridge University Press, 2017.

———. *Self-Designation and Group Identity in the New Testament*. Cambridge: Cambridge University Press, 2012.

Tshiyoyo, M. M. "Leading through Servant-Hood: The African Context." *African Journal of Public Affairs* 5, no. 3 (2012): 199–209.

Tomlin, Graham. *A Theology of Leadership*, 2014. Accessed on 18 September 2015. https://lc17.alpha.org/node/84.

Tolmie, Francois D. *Persuading the Galatians*. Tübingen: Mohr Siebeck, 2005.

Tucker, J. Brian. "Baths, Baptism, and Patronage: The Continuing Role of Roman Social Identity in Corinth." In *Reading Paul in Context Explorations in Identity Formations: Essays in Honour of William S. Campbell*, edited by Kathy Ehrensperger and J. Brian Tucker, 173–88. London: Bloomsbury, 2010.

———. *Remain in Your Calling: Paul and the Continuation of Social Identity in 1 Corinthians*. Eugene: Pickwick, 2011.

———. *You Belong to Christ: Paul and the Formation of Social Identity in 1 Corinthians 1-4*. Eugene: Pickwick, 2010.

Tucker, J. Brian, and Coleman A. Baker. "Introduction." In *T&T Clark Handbook to Social Identity in the New Testament*, edited by J. Brian Tucker and Coleman A. Baker, 1-10. London: Bloomsbury, 2014.

Tucker, J. Brian, and Kathy Ehrensperger, eds. *Reading Paul in Context: Explorations in Identity Formation, Essays in Honour of William S. Campbell*. London: T&T Clark, 2010.

Turner, John C. "Henri Tajfel: An Introduction." In *Social Groups and Identities: Developing the Legacy of Henri Tajfel*, edited by W. Peter Robinson, 1-24. Oxford: Butterworth-Heinemann, 1996.

———. *Rediscovering the Social Group*. Oxford: Blackwell, 1987.

———. "Social Comparison and Social Identity: Some Prospects for Intergroup Behaviour." *European Journal of Social Psychology* 5, no. 1 (1975): 5-34. https://doi.org/10.1002/ejsp.2420050102

———. "Towards a Cognitive Redefinition of the Social Group." In *Social Identity and Intergroup Relations*, edited by Henri Tajfel, 15-40. Cambridge: Cambridge University Press, 1982.

Turner, John C., and S. Alexander Haslam. "Social Identity, Organizations, and Leadership." In *Groups at Work: Theory and Research*, edited by Marlene E. Turner, 25-65. Mahwah: Lawrence Erlbaum, 2001.

Turner, Nigel. *Grammatical Insights into the New Testament*. Edinburgh: T&T Clark, 1965.

Ullrich, Johannes, Oliver Christ, and Rolf van Dick. "Substitutes for Procedural Fairness: Prototypical Leaders Are Endorsed Whether They Are Fair or Not." *Journal of Applied Psychology* 94, no. 1 (2009): 235-44.

Van Dick, Rolf, and Rudolf Kerschreiter. "The Social Identity Approach to Effective Leadership; An Overview and Some Ideas on Cross-Cultural Generalization." *Frontiers of Business Research in China* 10, no. 3 (2016): 363-84.

Van Dijke, Marius, and David de Cremer. "How Leader Prototypicality Affects Followers' Status: The Role of Procedural Fairness." *European Journal of Work and Organizational Psychology* 17, no. 2 (2008): 226-50.

Vanhoozer, Kevin J. "From 'Blessed in Christ' to 'Being in Christ': The State of Union and Place of Participation in Paul's Discourse, New Testament Exegesis, and Systematic Theology Today." In *"In Christ" in Paul*, edited by M. J. Thate, Kevin J. Vanhoozer, and Constantine R. Campbell, 3-33. Tübingen: Mohr Siebeck, 2014.

Van Knippenberg, Barbara, and Daan van Knippenberg. "Leader Self-Sacrifice and Leadership Effectiveness: The Moderating Role of Leader Prototypicality." *Journal of Applied Psychology* 90, no. 1 (2005): 25–37.

Van Knippenberg, Daan. "Work Motivation and Performance: A Social Identity Perspective." *Applied Psychology* 49, no. 3 (2000): 357–71.

Van Knippenberg, Daan, and Michael A. Hogg. *Leadership and Power: Identity Processes in Groups and Organizations*. London: Sage, 2003.

———. "A Social Identity Model of Leadership Effectiveness in Organizations." *Research in Organizational Behaviour*, no. 25 (2003): 243–95.

Van Knippenberg, Daan, and Ed Sleebos. "Organizational Identification versus Organizational Commitment: Self-Definition, Social Exchange, and Job Attitudes." *Journal of Organizational Behaviour* 27, no. 5 (2006): 571–84.

Vermeulen, J. "Leiers wat dien en Bédien. 'n Pauliniese beskrywing van kerkleiers en hulle funksies in 1 & 2 Korintiërs." *Verbum Ecclesia*, no. 24 (2003): 232–48.

Viljoen, Francois P. "Matthew and the Torah in Jewish Society." *die Skriflig* 49, no. 2 (2015): 1–6.

Wallace, Daniel B. *Greek Grammar beyond the Basics: An Exegetical Syntax of the New Testament*. Grand Rapids: Zondervan, 1996.

Walters, James. "Civic Identity in Roman Corinth and Its Impact on Early Christians." In *Urban Religion in Roman Corinth: Interdisciplinary Approaches*, edited by Daniel N. Schowalter and Steven J. Friesen, 397–418. Cambridge: Harvard University Press, 2005.

Wan, Sze. "The Letter to the Galatians." In *A Postcolonial Commentary on the New Testament Writings*, edited by Fernado F. Segovia and Rasiah S. Sugirtharajah, 246–64. New York: T&T Clark, 2007.

Wanamaker, Charles A. "A Rhetoric of Power: Ideology and 1 Corinthians 1–4." In *Paul and the Corinthians: Studies on a Community in Conflict. Essays in Honour of Margaret Thrall*, edited by Trevor J. Burke and J. Keith Elliott, 115–37. Leiden: Brill, 2003.

Watson, Duane F. "A Rhetorical Analysis of Philippians and Its Implications for the Unity Question." *Novum Testamentum* 30, no. 1 (1988): 57–88.

Watson, Francis. "2 Cor. X–XIII and Paul's Painful Letter to the Corinthians." *The Journal of Theological Studies* 35, no. 2 (1984): 324–46.

Weber, Max, and Shmuel N. Eisenstadt. *Max Weber on Charisma and Institution Building*. Chicago: University of Chicago Press, 1968.

Welborn, Larry L. "The Corinthian Correspondence." In *All Things to All Cultures: Paul among Jews, Greeks, and Romans*, edited by Mark Harding and Alanna Nobbs, 205–42. Grand Rapids: Eerdmans, 2013.

———. "On the Discord in Corinth: 1 Corinthians and Ancient Politics." *Journal of Biblical Literature*, no. 106 (1987): 85–111.

———. *Paul, the Fool of Christ: A Study of 1 Corinthians 1–4 in the Comic-Philosophic Tradition*. New York: T&T Clark, 2005.

Wenham, David. "Review: Yung Suk Kim, Christ's Body in Corinth: The Politics of the Metaphor." *Journal for the Study of the New Testament* 32, no. 5 (2010): 94–97.

———. "Whatever Went Wrong in Corinth?" *The Expository Times* 108, no. 5 (1997): 137–41.

White, Adam G. *Where Is the Wise Man? Greco-Roman Education as a Background to the Division in 1 Corinthians 1–4*. New York: T&T Clark, 2015.

White, John L. *Light from Ancient Letters*. Philadelphia: Fortress, 1986.

White, Michael L. "Christianity: Early Social life and Organization." In *Anchor Bible Dictionary*: Vol. 1, edited by David N. Freedman, 927–35. New York: Doubleday, 1992.

Winter, Bruce W. *After Paul Left Corinth: The Influence of Secular Ethics and Social Change*. Cambridge: Eerdmans, 2001.

———. "Gallio's Ruling on the Legal Status of Early Christianity (Acts 18:14–15)." *Tyndale Bulletin* 50, no. 2 (1999): 213–24.

———. *Philo and Paul among the Sophists: Alexandrian and Corinthian Response to a Julio-Claudian Movement*. Grand Rapids: Eerdmans, 2002.

———. *Seek the Welfare of the City: Christians as Benefactors and Citizens*. Grand Rapids: Eerdmans, 1994.

———. "The 'Underlays' of Conflict and Compromise in 1 Corinthians." In *Paul and the Corinthians: Studies on a Community in Conflict; Essays in Honor of Margaret Thrall*, edited by Trevor J. Burke and J. Keith Elliott, 139–56. Boston: Brill, 2003.

Winter, S. "Review: David Odell-Scott, Paul's Critique of Theocracy: A/Theocracy in Corinth and Galatians." *Journal for the Study of the New Testament* 27, no. 5 (2005): 105–6.

Witherington III, Ben. *The Acts of the Apostles: A Socio-Rhetorical Commentary*. Grand Rapids: Eerdmans, 1997.

———. *Conflict and Community in Corinth: A Socio-Rhetorical Commentary on 1 and 2 Corinthians*. Grand Rapids: Eerdmans, 1995.

———. *Grace in Galatia: A Commentary on St. Paul's Letter to the Galatians*. London: T&T Clark, 2004.

Witmer, Stephen E. *Divine Instruction in Early Christianity*. Tübingen: Mohr Siebeck, 2008.

Wright, Archie T. "Jewish Identity, Beliefs, and Practices." In *The World of the New Testament: Cultural, Social, and Historical Context*, edited by Joel B. Green and Lee M. Mcdonald, 310–24. Grand Rapids: Baker, 2013.

Wright, Nicholas T. *The Climax of the Covenant Christ and the Law in Pauline Theology*. Edinburgh: T&T Clark, 1991.

———. *What Saint Paul Really Said: Was Paul of Tarsus the Real Founder of Christianity?* Oxford: Lion Publishing, 1997.

Wright, Walter C. *Relational Leadership: A Biblical Model for Leadership Service.* Buckinghamshire: Paternoster, 2000.

Yeo, Khio-K. *Rhetorical Interaction in 1 Corinthians 8 and 10: A Formal Analysis with Preliminary Suggestions for a Chinese, Cross-Cultural Hermeneutic.* Leiden: Brill, 1995.

Yukl, Gary A. *Leadership in Organizations.* 5th ed. Upper Saddle River: Prentice Hall, 2002.

Langham
PARTNERSHIP

Langham Literature, with its publishing work, is a ministry of Langham Partnership.

Langham Partnership is a global fellowship working in pursuit of the vision God entrusted to its founder John Stott –

to facilitate the growth of the church in maturity and Christ-likeness through raising the standards of biblical preaching and teaching.

Our vision is to see churches in the Majority World equipped for mission and growing to maturity in Christ through the ministry of pastors and leaders who believe, teach and live by the word of God.

Our mission is to strengthen the ministry of the word of God through:
- nurturing national movements for biblical preaching
- fostering the creation and distribution of evangelical literature
- enhancing evangelical theological education

especially in countries where churches are under-resourced.

Our ministry

Langham Preaching partners with national leaders to nurture indigenous biblical preaching movements for pastors and lay preachers all around the world. With the support of a team of trainers from many countries, a multi-level programme of seminars provides practical training, and is followed by a programme for training local facilitators. Local preachers' groups and national and regional networks ensure continuity and ongoing development, seeking to build vigorous movements committed to Bible exposition.

Langham Literature provides Majority World preachers, scholars and seminary libraries with evangelical books and electronic resources through publishing and distribution, grants and discounts. The programme also fosters the creation of indigenous evangelical books in many languages, through writer's grants, strengthening local evangelical publishing houses, and investment in major regional literature projects, such as one volume Bible commentaries like the Africa Bible Commentary and the South Asia Bible Commentary.

Langham Scholars provides financial support for evangelical doctoral students from the Majority World so that, when they return home, they may train pastors and other Christian leaders with sound, biblical and theological teaching. This programme equips those who equip others. Langham Scholars also works in partnership with Majority World seminaries in strengthening evangelical theological education. A growing number of Langham Scholars study in high quality doctoral programmes in the Majority World itself. As well as teaching the next generation of pastors, graduated Langham Scholars exercise significant influence through their writing and leadership.

To learn more about Langham Partnership and the work we do visit langham.org

Milton Keynes UK
Ingram Content Group UK Ltd.
UKHW022040131124
451149UK00015B/1556

9 781839 739699